GOD IN MAN'S WORLD

by

Walter W. Davis

Biblical Standards Publications
287 Caldwell Drive
Maggie Valley, NC 28751

ISBN 0-9678798-0-9

Cover design by Carol Loper.

TABLE OF CONTENTS
GOD IN MAN'S WORLD

DEDICATION

In grateful remembrance of my parents – Rev. James Daryl Davis and Mary Ellen (Wilson) Davis – who lovingly disciplined and nurtured me in the fear of God, teaching me by precept and example; insured my education; and engendered in me an enduring faith in God and respect for His Word.

PREFACE

At a convention of Christian historians several years ago, there was a well-attended panel discussion on the subject of the Christian professor's role in the classroom. Arriving somewhat late, I took a seat in the audience, expecting to hear the three panelists – each from a different college or university – tell how they brought their faith to bear in their teaching. How disappointed I was to hear nothing that was distinctively Christian. One member of the panel did opine that Christian professors should be fair in their treatment of students and professionally objective in their lectures and assignments. As an example, he stated that he had several Muslim students enrolled in a course on Middle Eastern history; therefore he was careful not to cast aspersions on their faith and was using the *Koran* as a supplementary textbook. "Are you also using the Bible in the course?" he was later asked. "No," he replied. It was presumably unfair to give equal treatment to the Bible lest that be construed as an attempt to propagandize a captive audience. I wondered how any student subjected to alleged "objectivity" of this sort would ever have an opportunity to investigate the truth.

After the presentation, a short time was allowed for members of the audience to respond to what had been said and to pose questions. My comment was that objectivity was a noble, if unattainable goal that was not restricted to Christian historians. Every historian concerned with uncovering and presenting truth must strive for objectivity, but should not a Christian historian go further? Was it not possible that principles taken from the Bible – whether attributed to the Bible or not – could be presented as foundational to historical study? (Here I gave two examples – one of them being "the principle of sowing and reaping," which I hoped everyone could readily grasp during the approximately 40 seconds I had to speak.)

Response came not from the panel but from an agitated young man in the audience who blurted out: "I don't understand what that man [meaning me] is talking about! The Bible has nothing to do with the historical discipline, and we should not peruse it for principles pertaining to history. As Christian historians all we need to do is to show love and follow the dialectic." The audience seemed to assent to the statement, perhaps deeming it profound because it was abstruse.

My inclination to respond was strong. I wanted to ask, "To what dialectic are you referring: to the Hegelian dialectic, to the dialectic of Karl Marx, or to another dialectic – perhaps one conceived in your own mind?" However, I knew I must remain silent, and within a few moments the meeting closed. Perplexed and grieved by what had occurred, I turned to leave when a professor whose work I respected greeted me with, "Walt, thank you for your remarks! What you said was very pertinent and well-stated, but they didn't even understand what you were saying."

The kind words encouraged me and soothed my soul, and subsequently the convention's key-note speaker helped restore my belief that Christian historians are aware of their responsibility to make an impact on our society and to uphold lasting values in these postmodern times.

As I recalled the incident several months later, my thoughts went back to 1964 when as a new Ph.D. I was asked to offer a course on historical thought and historiography. At the time, I had no desire to do so; but as an assistant professor with no seniority, I had no choice in the matter. The fact was that I had never developed a philosophy of history and preferred simply to do research and teach about the events of the past rather than to grapple with anything concerning their purpose and meaning. Certainly I believed that God was the Creator of everything including history, but I had never made an effort to think through the implications of this belief. My faith was one thing and my chosen vocation quite another. It is little wonder that some years later when I was prayerfully seeking answers to some personal problems I was awakened in the middle of the night by the arresting question: "What are you doing?" "Oh, Lord," I replied, I'm teaching history at the University of Arizona and writing a book." Without upbraiding me for that prideful response, the Lord gently implanted the thought, "Yes, and of what eternal value is that?" The question devastated me, for I recognized that even if every one of my students learned everything I was teaching – and even more – it was of little *eternal* consequence. Obviously something was sadly lacking.

For the next week, I went about the campus like a dead man, depressed by the sense of being a parasite, giving to society nothing of eternal value. Should I give up my chosen profession? I did not know, but I no longer had the enthusiasm for sharing my knowledge with others or for stimulating students to engage in independent research. Although I continued to go through the motions of teaching, I had no relish for making a living by doing something having no lasting merit or purpose.

Mercifully, God speedily rescued me with "a second touch" of His grace. Into the despondency of my self-doubt and brokenness; into the soul of a Christian disillusioned with "churchianity" – observance of religious rituals, rules of conduct, staid forms of worship, and godly aphorisms that were true but often unsatisfying; into the heart of a man who knew the Bible and was striving to live a godly life while powerless to control his own temper came rejuvenating Reality as I gave myself unreservedly and fully to Jesus Christ and received the "fullness of His Spirit." Almost immediately, new revelations seemed to spring forth into my consciousness from God's Word, overwhelming love encompassed my being, and the power to overcome personal weaknesses, to witness for my Savior, and to speak forth His words of healing and power that His works might be effected engendered within me an unaccustomed sense of well-being and peace. Much more than mere euphoria, however, was my bedrock knowledge that God was the Supreme Reality, the Maker and Master of everything, who was in ultimate control of all world events. By God's enabling, I was able to ask my wife and children to forgive me for wrongs I had inflicted on them, and now I was able to cope with problems that in the past had "sent me into orbit."

My wife and I soon began hosting a weekly praise-and-prayer meeting in our home attended by believers of every denomination as well as an occasional non-believer. The love that we experienced and the spiritual truths that we learned from Spirit-filled brothers and sisters in Christ was incredible; yet it was God Himself who graciously and lovingly led us and arranged every circumstance. Not only did He answer our prayers – some quite miraculously – but He revealed Himself to us in new ways. Finally, He tested us in the "furnace of affliction," uprooted us from the home and locale that we loved, and planted us time and again in new places or situations, blessing us always with further spiritual and intellectual growth. It was while ministering in these new and unforeseen circumstances (except by God who had informed us by several of His prophets had we only taken their words to heart) that history began to take on an eternal importance. It became clear that God's truth encompasses all partial truths studied in history and the humanities and that everything has its proper purpose and function, being part of an integral whole created and sustained by God. Man might go his own willful way (the Creator permits him to do so), but God remains in ultimate control – a fact inexplicable to the natural mind. Moreover, the Almighty rules through principles set forth in His word – unchanging principles that are universally applicable to persons, peoples, and nations in every era of history.

However, God's superintending providence is not understood today. Certainly it is not taught in the graduate schools preparing young men and women to be professional historians. Why then should I have wondered at the callous response to my recommendation that a Christian historian's philosophy and presentation of history should be grounded in biblical principles? Doubtless I would likewise have considered such a proposition absurd had it not been for the Lord's gracious intervention in my life. That realization was very humbling, and I contemplated preparing a treatise for Christian historians dealing with historiography – the collection and evaluation of historical evidence and the recording of what seemed to have happened in a plausible, well-written narrative. Over the years, I have yearned for a historiography textbook based on God's Word that would recognize God as the Author and Sustainer of history, and by this time I was acutely aware of the need for such a work. Although historical methodology was easy enough to teach, it was much more difficult to instill in students a desire to write history from a biblical perspective. Indeed, most of them, like me in my years as a graduate student and young professor, were unable to get beyond what they were taught (or not taught) in graduate school concerning methodology and a working philosophy of the human saga, and how it should be applied in their teaching.

To fail to recognize the hand of God in history is to falsify and misconstrue the record and render it meaningless; yet most historians – even those who are Christians – teach subject matter to their students without reference to God because that is the way they were trained. Of course, Christian historians may "baptize" their lectures with prayer and perhaps make occasional allusions to Scripture, but more is required if students are to be rescued from the God-denying, existential currents of our day. Biblical principles must be elucidated and incorporated in the teaching of history if the discipline is to present a whole, purposeful, undistorted view of reality. Without such instruction, Western Civilization is doomed.

That someone should write a Bible-based interpretation of history that could be used in historiography courses being offered at Christian colleges and universities was beyond question; yet after considering the undertaking, I tried to dismiss it from mind. I had a more interesting, if not more important project to do. Specifically, I wanted to write the sequel to my *Eastern & Western History, Thought & Culture, 1600-1815* which would present a similar, comprehensive, synthetic view of world culture for the years 1815 to the present. Like Jonah, I tried to ignore God's call to perform the task that former colleagues and my wife were urging me to do – to write a book explicating the biblical principles of history. Only after a fruitless four years of obstinacy, was I finally moved by my beloved mate's tears to set pen to paper.

As I began to write, I realized that what I was saying was not only for professors and students of history but for the entire Christian family. It was to be a book expounding biblical principles that could be used in classroom lectures but also a book of instruction for interested readers, of reference for others, and of encouragement for all of God's people who would take the time to read it. Chapters I through XIV (and to a lesser degree XXXII and XXXIII) deal principally with historiography by portraying (along with the time-line in Appendix I) a concise summary of Western history that demonstrates the constant tension and recurring cycles of man's quest for knowing God on the one hand and his obstinate deification of self on the other. Chapters XV through XXXI are not unrelated: they are also historiographical in nature but from a different vantage point. Chapter XV provides synopses of the most common interpretations of history as a backdrop for comparison with the God-given, eternal principles that comprise the real dynamics shaping all human history (Chapters XVI through XXXI). In the last two chapters (XXXII and XXXIII), the penalty for violating biblical principles as man moves away from his Maker and toward global governance in contemporary Western culture is explicated and the eventual outcome projected.

Many historians will object to my interjection of biblical truths that are seldom if ever considered in the training of professional historians. Nevertheless, I stand on their veracity and on the Apostle Paul's affirmation that "what is seen is temporary [and I would say often illusory] but what is not seen is eternal" (II Corinthians 4:18). Others may protest that contemporary and future events do not lie within the province of the historian, and technically that is true: future events are not history. Yet in the light of the historical record and the Word of God, it is possible to postulate what is to come, and I believe it is incumbent upon Christians capable of discerning the times to do so. Should a historian be prohibited from presenting perceptions gained in part from knowledge of the past but not pertaining to it? Why should anyone be silenced in this manner?

Not all believers will see end-time events as I do, but it may be hoped that we can examine these matters afresh and share with one another new biblical insights as God reveals them. No one will see the entire picture, and some will perceive things differently, but prayerful and honest, rigorous investigation by various members of the body of Christ will not only alert us but enable us to prepare for what, in my opinion, is the soon-coming "end of the age."

This matter concerns all of us, not just professional historians. Still, it is hoped that historians, especially Christian historians, will profit from considering anew a providential view of history that is as old as the early church and an interpretive survey of the Western experience (from the creation to Christ's second advent) and that Christians of every walk of life may find guidance for daily living and procure a Bible-based understanding of contemporary society. Those who may have little interest in history and do not wish "to become bogged down" in reading an interpretation of history attempting to show the "God-honoring" vs. "man-worshiping" cycles of the Western experience, may desire to skip the opening chapters of this work and commence with chapter XI, which introduces some of the roots of modern humanism. Even the philosophical currents developed here may seem too onerous for persons nurtured on the instantaneous "bites" of information presented on television. It is hoped, however, that thoughtful readers will take time to consider chapters XIII and XIV (skipping at their discretion chapter XV dealing with historiography) and read the chapters concerned with biblical principles (chapters XVI through XXXI) and those depicting the contemporary scene and the end of the age (chapters XXXII and XXXIII). All readers should be challenged by the Scriptural principles presented in the middle of the book – principles that pertain both to individuals and nations.

An eminent law professor and my former Dean, Herbert Titus, has said that "law is too important to be entrusted exclusively to lawyers." The same may be said of history. Persons from diverse backgrounds need to have an appreciation and understanding of history; therefore, it is hoped that *God in Man's World* will be read and pondered not only by historians and would-be historians but by people from every walk of life. If some of the philosophies and historical expositions remain a bit hazy to the layman, the biblical principles presented should be quite clear and, if digested, will provide practical and useful guidelines for personal living and positive, edifying correctives for our society, culture, and government. God's Word is practical in every realm of human experience if we will only apply it.

The explanations of biblical principles in this book are largely the outgrowth of a course entitled "Principles of History" that I offered for eleven years at Regent University in Virginia Beach, Virginia. To the best of my knowledge, most of these principles are not presented in other historical or historiographical treatises. Many of them overlap, because God's truth is both multi-faceted and an integrated whole. If certain portions of this work seem somewhat repetitious, remember that the Bible itself develops certain truths and precepts from a variety of vantage points and repeats them so that the wise will assimilate them. In discussing each biblical principle, I have earnestly and prayerfully endeavored to "rightly divide the Word of truth," basing my interpretations on the clear and contextual meaning of the passages being cited. Undoubtedly there are readers who will differ with some of my expositions, though I trust that no preconceived theological or philosophical framework will prevent them from accepting God's own Word on the various issues. In certain instances I have been quite emphatic, because our society with its relativistic, postmodern culture has led many people astray, necessitating a strong emphasis on biblical truth that is seldom given. We desperately need a "wake-up call"; for the end of the age – the culmination of human history as we know it – is at hand.

It is imperative in these last days that God's Word be attended. For this reason, I make no apologies for attacking unbiblical "isms" or even God-denying academic disciplines, though there are genuine Christians involved in even those disciplines and some have discerned their unbiblical fallacies. I thank God for that and trust that more and more Christians will not mindlessly accept everything they are taught in graduate school or absorb the falsehoods so prevalent in contemporary culture but will apply the Bible perceptively and courageously in their disciplines and vocations. If something does not accord with God's truth, it should be discarded. "Let God be true, and every man a liar" (Romans 3:4).

Although readers may not agree with all of my expositions, each and every person should benefit from considering the biblical references. Only God's Word is inerrant; I am not. For this reason and also because all of my interpretations must be checked alongside of Scripture, the references are copious.

The Bible in any honest translation – Catholic or Protestant – is true, though there may be somewhat differing nuances. Although my favorite is the New King James Version (especially as published in the *Spirit-filled Life Bible* (ed. by doctors Jack Hayford, Sam Middlebrook, & Jerry Horner; Thomas Nelson Publishers of Nashville, TN, 1991), the quotations cited in this volume are taken from the New International Version (NIV) unless otherwise indicated.

My parents (now deceased) to whom this book is dedicated inculcated in me a healthy fear of the Lord and taught me to rely upon His Word. Other saints of God have rescued me from foolish actions, lent assistance at critical times, and nourished my faith in countless ways. I have been privileged also to sit under the instruction of truly great teachers – both in my formal education and in Christian circles – and to have worked with and under the direction of godly academicians who have made a permanent impression on my life and beliefs. I thank God for each one of them!

I am deeply thankful also for other Christian co-workers – in whatever capacity – and for the myriad students, especially those at Oral Roberts University and Regent University, who have sharpened my thoughts, sometimes through disagreement and challenge, have shared their insights and knowledge as well as some of their problems, dreams and aspirations, and have encouraged and helped me in many inexplicable ways.

Additionally and more specifically, I owe a tremendous debt of gratitude to Mr. David Ringer, esteemed former colleague and friend whose learned views in the humanities are always valuable and pertinent, who read the entire manuscript, giving me the benefit of his sage advice; to my wife Dorothy who has prayerfully supported me in every endeavor, virtually commanded me in the name of the Lord to write this book, and provided its title; to our daughter, teacher *par excellence* Patricia Beth Felder, who painstakingly read a sizable portion of the manuscript and saved me from numerous grammatical errors – an onerous task at any time but especially when doing it for one's father; to our son, attorney Douglas Wayne Davis, who set up my computer, programed the codes controlling the margins, and kindly and patiently spent hours of his time unscrambling problems, putting the text in proper format, and overseeing preparation of the Index; and to Mrs. Carol Loper, gifted artist and creative illustrator, who without reading the manuscript, prepared the cover design depicting God's superintending hand in history. Each of these dear ones has given inestimable assistance; yet those who have read the manuscript in whole or in part have views differing from mine concerning the eschatological propositions presented in the last chapter. For this reason, I consider their labor of love especially precious. I thank them from the bottom of my heart. They have blessed me immeasurably.

A final tribute is due the family of God – beset in every generation with trials and problems but persevering and keeping the faith through them all. How precious are the people of God whose love for our Lord and Savior Jesus Christ helps keep us constant in the faith as we work together in expectation of His imminent return. Let us persevere together until the end, helping and encouraging one another through our words, deeds, and exercise of the special gifts entrusted to each of us, preferring one another in love, and thanking our God – Father, Son, and Holy Spirit – for our great salvation!

GOD IN MAN'S WORLD:
A CHRISTIAN DIALECTIC IN HISTORY

What is history? Who creates history? Is history determined by a Creator-God, natural forces, or man? Can history be defined in a manner acceptable to most thinking people and the bulk of historians? Does history consist of what actually happened or what is said to have happened? Is our record of the past essentially accurate? Does history have any meaning or purpose? Does it have any utility? Can a knowledge of history and involvement in historical studies and scholarship have any practical value? What is the cultural scope of history? Does it have a personal application? Can it improve my personal life? Does it have a salutary affect on society? On morals? On laws? On culture? Is history confined to mundane events in this world? Is the practice or writing of history a science or an art? What are the historian's sources? Is it possible to have history relate exactly what happened? Does history help to determine events? Should it? Should history influence or help guide current decision-making? Can the study of history be beneficial to me personally, regardless of my vocation? Does a person's view of history reveal as much about himself as it does about the nature of history?

Chapter I

HISTORY: ITS NATURE, CAUSES, AND PURPOSES

History has been defined or characterized by numerous persons and from many vantage points. Dionysius of Halicarnasses (d.8 B.C.) defined it as "philosophy teaching by example," while one modern writer looks to historical examples of "the trustier human ways" as the basis for "an amplitude of noble life." Roman orator and statesman Marcus Tullius Cicero (106-43 B.C.) extolled history as "the witness of the ages, the light of truth, the life of memory, the mistress of life, the messenger of antiquity." Miguel de Cervantes (1547-1616) said: "History is in a manner a sacred thing, so far as it contains truth; for where truth is, the supreme Father of it may also be said to be, at least inasmuch as concerns truth.... [The mother of truth is history], the rival of time, the depository of great actions, the witness of what is past, the example and instruction of the present, the monitor of the future."

Others, however, have been less laudatory and more skeptical. One has characterized history as "the process whereby a complicated truth becomes a simplified falsehood." Equally sardonic is English politician and essayist Augustine Birrell's (d.1933) allusion to "that great dust-heap called history," Oscar Wilde's (d.1900) dismissal of history as "merely gossip," and Henry Ford's (d.1947) disdainful assertion that history is "bunk." Even noteworthy historians have expressed skepticism or perplexity over the nature of history. Edward Gibbon (d.1794), renowned author of *The Decline and Fall of the Roman Empire* averred that history was "little more than the register of crimes, follies, and misfortunes of mankind," and Thomas Carlyle (d.1881) cynically observed: "Happy is the people whose annals are blank in history books."

Could it be that cynicism toward history is indicative of a nullifidian mind-set that rejects a Creator God? After all, the Bible acknowledges the benefits to be derived from history and commands the people of God to inform their children of "what we have heard and known, what our fathers have told us" and to tell "the next generation the praiseworthy deeds of the Lord, His power, and the wonders He has done." (God's hand in the history of the nation is to be recognized – Psalm 78:2-4. Cf. Deuteronomy 32:7, Psalm 71:18 & Psalm 145:4, 10-12). Moreover, Scripture teaches that the Lord God is the Creator of the universe and everything in it – including mankind, animals, and plant life. As sovereign Creator of man, the entire natural order, time, and history, He is the Supreme Lawgiver and ultimate Ordainer of events – a fact that prideful, willful man would like to forget or refute. Indeed, Charles Darwin (d.1882) and his intellectual successors have proposed their own substitute for Divine creation by purporting that man and history have resulted from impersonal biological forces.

The Darwinian theory provides the basis for existential attitudes that would deny any significance or rational pattern to historical occurrences. According to the evolutionary view, history is simply the story of the long struggle of man, by exercise of his reason, to understand his environment, to adapt to it in an advantageous manner, and to pursue his own ends. Past, present, and future are all joined together in the value-neutral, endless, and ever-changing process of history. As the highest evolved creature, man is obliged by his activities to give history whatever meaning it is capable of bearing – that is, to create his own history. How easy it is for modern man to accept such a view – to believe that there is no purpose to events beyond what he makes of them. By exalting himself as master of history, however, man actually diminishes himself; for in failing to recognize God in whose image he was created, man cuts himself off from the very Ground of his being, becoming like a leaf fallen from the tree that has given it life. No wonder that to many learned agnostics history has no meaning or purpose and teaches nothing.

It is man, of course, who – aside from Holy Writ and perhaps a few accounts written from a spiritual perspective – determines what events are worthy of record and, therefore, is the arbiter of what becomes recognized as history. For antiquity, reliable sources are frequently sparse. This is especially true of what is generally called "pre-history" or "pre-literary history." Geological discoveries of changes in the earth and archeological findings of graves, human bones, artifacts, pictures or pictographs, primitive tools, household implements, pottery, figurines, coins, and ruins have provided evidence of human habitation; and paleontologists have assisted archeologists in assigning dates on the basis of pottery designs, the strata in the earth where the objects were discovered, types of metal (if any) used, and the carbon 14 test. Still, source material is fragmentary, necessitating much detective work and a number of bridging hypotheses in an attempt to reconstruct the story of these early humans, a story that continues to resist the best efforts of science.

Even written evidence uncovered by archeologists fails to dispel the mystery of these early societies – either because inscriptions have not been deciphered (as in the case of Cretan Linear A), or because their scarcity or narrowness of scope continues to require much educated guesswork. Inscriptions on seal stones, obelisks, buildings, and papyrii or clay tablets bearing tax or price lists, commercial records, grocery lists, law codes, genealogies, chronicles of kings, military or diplomatic records, funeral memorials, or religious myths or legends based on oral traditions have shed tremendous light on ancient communities and civilizations; yet there remain countless gaps, leaving ample room for conjectural interpretations by historians seeking to recreate what happened from a paucity of clues.

Research on modern events presents the opposite problem. The investigator is faced with looking at a nimiety of pertinent evidence (most of it indirect evidence) that can never be adequately examined, evaluated, and presented. However diligent, disciplined, industrious, and competent he may be, the researcher must ignore masses of evidence – be it official government documents; personal letters, dairies, memoirs, and autobiographies; records of social agencies; tax receipts; scientific data; business statistics; newspaper accounts; court records; genealogies; military orders; executive orders or requests; confidential reports; legal papers; notebooks or memoranda kept by principals involved; firsthand oral accounts or tapes of conversations; interviews; speeches; public or private statements; sociological surveys; compiled questionnaires; medical or physical evidence; laws and regulations; opinions of eye-witnesses; "the spirit of the times" as revealed in culture; or any other source of information germane to the topic being addressed. From the masses of relevant information, he is obliged to select only a manageable body of material – if possible, on a rational, systematic, dispassionate basis – while disregarding the rest. Italian philosopher, historian, and literary critic Benedetto Croce (d. 1952) has observed that the historian's main work is not to record but to evaluate, for if he does not evaluate, he can not know what is worth recording; but even the task of evaluating the sources and choosing "the best" exceeds human capacity. This fact, aside from the possibility of bias on the part of the historian – who, after all, is a part of the historical process, operating within the cultural milieu of his time (as well as his personal circumstances, beliefs, and predispositions or prejudices) – rules out any possibility that a perfect, definitive account of what actually happened can be written. Even the most honest, knowledgeable, unbiased, and enterprising scholar can not reconstruct events exactly as they occurred. Finite man can operate only in the realm of relative, not absolute accuracy and completeness; yet he can strive toward the goal of presenting what actually happened (what German scholars have termed *Historie*) while transforming it into *Geschichte* by demonstrating its essential meaning.

The historian should approach his task with a healthy humility; recognizing his inability to render a flawless account. Nevertheless, in an honest quest for truth, he may be able to represent the events of the past and their significance with an acceptable, even a high degree of accuracy. While history as it actually happened can never be perfectly known in this world, history defined as the written record of what occurred, despite its inadequacies and limits, can be generally reliable and of inestimable value. Regardless of his personal predispositions, therefore, the Christian historian should always approach his subject with integrity. He should evaluate his sources critically and honestly and interpret them judiciously and with veracity: opinions should not be advanced as "history." Not all historians have adhered to this high standard, and none have attained plenary and unimpeachable verity. Thomas Jefferson recognized this fact when he said: "A morsel of genuine history is a thing so rare as to be always valuable."

In the minds of most serious thinkers, history has a double denotation: (1) events as they actually occurred and are related to the deeds, thoughts, and cultural achievements of mankind, and (2) the narrative account or record of these occurrences. Some would even extend the definition to include investigative examination of the past and writing about it, but, more precisely, these functions comprise what is known as historiography. We shall focus, therefore, on the second concept: that history is, as Jacob Burckhardt (1897) has stated, the "record of what one age finds noteworthy in another." History can not be avoided or escaped. We are all a part of the ongoing saga and would do well to acquaint ourselves with it; because, as James Harvey Robinson has proclaimed: "History is all we know about everything man has ever done, or thought, or hoped, or felt."

One further dimension should be added, for man is not the only actor or even the chief actor in history. Though unperceived by natural man, God's superintending hand has not been withdrawn from the affairs of this world, and it is His control that ultimately gives meaning to everything. In recognition of this reality, Christian historians may wish to subscribe to a definition similar to the following:

> "History is the record of people and events, of occurrences and influences affecting mankind and human society, composed principally of the deeds, thoughts, and aspirations of man – God's highest creation, made in the Divine image; it is the record of man's hopes, dreams, plans, creativity, efforts, achievements, and failures as he has sought to effect his will in a universe created, sustained, and controlled by a sovereign Deity."

5

God has revealed Himself in history and, if properly attended, it may promote wisdom and understanding, but it is not the Word of God. History, as man can apprehend it, is not capable of substituting for Holy Writ in guiding human ethics and actions. Among secular thinkers, this fact is not always comprehended; for we hear writers, speakers, and would-be shapers of public opinion insisting that history teaches all sorts of lessons commensurate with their own opinions or points of view. In doing so, they are presumptuous or at least responsible for placing undue faith in the validity of the thoughts and deeds of finite men. Furthermore, if they are using history as their sole guide for action, they have a very limited perspective – like a person driving down the highway with both eyes fixed on the rear-view mirror. To do so is to risk accident.

On the other hand, a driver should not only keep his eyes on the road ahead and have a constant awareness of where he is, but glance occasionally in the rear-view mirror. Certainly, no prudent person would consciously seek amnesia – would not consciously refuse to refer to the collective experience of mankind. In one way or another, every activity has a historical base or is fundamentally historical. Musicians not only perform music composed at a particular time and reflecting a particular culture, but they wisely acquaint themselves with significant information about the composer: the milieu in which he lived, the circumstances under which he worked, the influences to which he was exposed, and the defining characteristics of his pieces. A person contemplating taking over a particular business wants to know how it fared under his predecessor, a physician elicits a medical history from first-time patients, and so it goes.

Be this as it may, prospective students will frequently question whether they can earn a living with a bachelor's degree in history. For these inquirers and for history buffs willing to probe beneath the surface, here is a compilation of personal benefits to be derived from studying history. A person's study of history can:

> 1) Provide a basis for understanding how God's master plan has been unfolding and is being revealed in the affairs of this world, and for recognizing the individual's place in it.

2) Demonstrate the interrelationship of God and man throughout the generations of human experience that may prove a source of wisdom.

3) Give him a sense of God-given historical purpose and mission that will be manifested in his life and actions.

4) Reveal to him something of the causes and meaning of human events so that he may understand his own society and culture. "He who knows only his own generation remains forever a child."

5) Enable him to acquire a knowledgeable sensitivity for man's aspirations and actions -- his virtues and weaknesses, his successes and failures – which reveal his God-given potential and his limitations, in order that he may praise God for what He has done and is doing in human lives and view his estate and that of his neighbors with appreciation, understanding, and realistic humility.

6) Sharpen his critical faculties and help him to organize and present his thoughts in an orderly, logical manner, so that he may be intellectually equipped to deal with the pressing problems of this generation.

7) Assist him in making useful and dispassionate value judgments consonant with God's Word.

8) Foster tolerant attitudes and an appreciation for people of backgrounds differing from his own, for whom Jesus Christ died.

9) Provide a background for evaluating philosophy and religious thought and for understanding and enjoying the fine arts, music, and other forms of cultural or intellectual expression.

l0) Prepare him for study in other disciplines or for careers in such varied areas as theology, Christian ministry, government, law, teaching, librarianship or archival work, and international affairs.

ll) Integrate all human knowledge and activity into a comprehensive whole that glorifies the Creator.

In view of the benefits to be derived from the study of history, let us faithfully heed the Scriptural admonition to pass on "what we have heard and known" to the next generation and to celebrate the praiseworthy deeds of the Lord, His power, and wonders (cf. Psalm 78:4).

Chapter II

GOD AND MAN IN WESTERN HISTORY: FROM THE BEGINNING TO THE "FULLNESS OF TIME"

The vast majority of contemporary historians write as if the affairs of this world are attributable entirely to the interplay of mundane forces and human activities without regard to any alleged Transcendent Being or supernatural powers. To the biblically-minded person, however, history has no meaning or purpose apart from God. The Bible-believer rests in the assurance that the Creator God is in ultimate control of all things. He is confident that every event, either directly or indirectly, serves God's predestined purpose and is not merely the consequence of impersonal forces – biological, economic, psychological, environmental, or any other – that would render the human experience largely accidental. Natural forces may appear to be determinant in certain instances, but they are under Divine control. Science, civil governments, social forces, and human agents or agencies may have their effect – individually or collectively – on a particular course of events, but they are subject to the eternal design and will of the Creator. Nevertheless, man has an important role to play. Created in God's image and designated ruler and regent over the earth, man is responsible to his Maker but also free to accept, reject, or ignore Divine direction and to act according to his own desires. How God can effect His foreordained purposes while allowing man to exercise the God-like property of free will, can not be comprehended intellectually, but the Bible declares this truth and human experience verifies it. We shall provide evidence of this in a later chapter.

Throughout history, the tension and interplay between the Eternal One and humanity is evident. Its general character may be described, with the aid of the accompanying diagram (see Appendix I), somewhat as follows.

Above the median line is the sector where God is worshiped and honored, while below the line is the sector where man follows his own volition and worships himself and his own achievements. All life and the laws that govern the universe emanate from the Eternal One, whose revelation is made available to mankind through Holy Writ. He is the Creator of everything (except Himself), including mankind and Lucifer – a guardian cherub whose prideful rebellion caused him to be evicted from his position (see Isaiah 14:12; Ezekiel 28:12-19; Luke 10;18; I Timothy 3:6; I Peter 2:4; and Jude 6). Subsequently, this fallen angel, Satan, led our human progenitors astray. According to the Book of Genesis, our first forefathers, as created by the Lord God, enjoyed direct fellowship with Him until their disobedience brought separation from Him and sin and death to the entire human race. Consequently, every person born into the world possesses a sinful nature, is spiritually dead (separated from God), and inevitably experiences physical death. Cut off from his Creator, man is compelled to rely on his impaired mind (synonymous with soul, comprised of the intellect, emotions, and the will) and the physical resources around him. Try as he might by his own abilities, he is unable to resume his previous relationship with the Infinite Being, a relationship on which his very life depends. His own natural faculties, no matter how diligently and fervently employed, are all inadequate to the task, though exercise of reason and use of empirical methodology may bring a degree of success in the temporal world. It is upon earthly pursuits, therefore, that he concentrates his efforts, priding himself on his attainments, seeking a form of immortality through deeds and achievements that may be remembered after his demise, and humanistically considering himself free, the master of his own destiny.

Man's self-reliant hubris keeps him from recognizing his Creator: just as in the ancient world men rejected Him, followed their own designs, and became so incredibly evil that the Lord decided to destroy them by a flood. Only Noah, who had an inclination toward God, and his family were spared. He and some of his descendants had an awareness of an Almighty, All-Holy Being (witness Abraham, Isaac, Jacob, and Joseph) and inclined their hearts toward Him. Moses was even called and empowered by the great "I Am" to deliver from bondage the descendants of the patriarchs, who had become enslaved in Egypt. He led them forth through the Sinai Desert and, after 40 years of wandering, to the borders of the land that was to be their heritage. After Moses's death, his understudy Joshua commanded the Israelite armies as they conquered the land of promise. However, they never eradicated all of the demonized people of the land (Leviticus 17:7 and 18:27-28; Deuteronomy 13:5-10; 18:9-14; and 32:17) as Yahweh had directed, and, despite their covenant with Him – elicited by the aged Joshua – whereby the Lord God would bless them as long as they served Him and Him only, Israel soon fell into syncretic religious practices.

Their apostasy incurred punishment in the form of oppression by various pagan tribes. Time and again, Israel would repent and be delivered by a judge raised up by Yahweh, only to relapse into idolatry. Their final judge, Samuel, anointed Saul king, and his immediate successors, David and Solomon, established a strong monarchy before it split (about 930 B.C.) into two kingdoms: Israel, the larger, northern kingdom, and Judah, the southern kingdom with its capital at Jerusalem. While Israel quickly fell into apostasy and idolatry, Judah, ruled by kings from the linage of David, retained its spiritual moorings longer. Prophets of the Lord God delivered stern warnings of impending judgment as both kingdoms became involved in syncretic religious practices. Israel fell to Assyria in 721 B.C. and exited from the pages of history while Judah hung on – surrounded by hostile nations on all sides – until 586 B.C. when Jerusalem was burned and the temple built by Solomon was destroyed by the army of Babylonian King Nebuchadnezzar. All but a remnant of Judah's citizens were taken captive to Babylon. At last they began to recall the prophetic messages of Isaiah and Jeremiah and to return to the faith of their fathers (note the move toward God on the time line pictured in Appendix I). In their synagogues (where they assembled for prayer and instruction after the destruction of the temple), the exiled Jews were heartened by Isaiah's prophecy that they would be restored to the land of promise (see, for example, Isaiah 44:24-26). How electrified they must have been when Persian King Cyrus, who conquered Babylon in 539 B.C. and extended his hegemony over all the territory from the Indus River to the Mediterranean and from the Caucasus Mountains to the Indian Ocean allowed them to return to Jerusalem to rebuild the temple. (More than 150 years previously, Isaiah had foretold this and had mentioned Cyrus by name. See Isaiah 44:26 through chapter 45:13. See also the prophecy of Jeremiah alluded to in II Chronicles 36:22-23 and its fulfillment in Ezra 1:1-8.) Not all availed themselves of this opportunity, but a remnant returned in 538 B.C. under Zerubbabel, a descendent of King David. When the people ceased working on the temple, the prophets Haggai and Zechariah alternately scolded and exhorted them to put Yahweh first in their lives and to look for a Messiah who would restore righteous rule. Work on the temple was resumed thanks to the good will of the Persian monarchs, and the structure was completed and dedicated in 516 B.C. Nevertheless, the post-exilic remnant was surrounded by unsympathetic, sometimes hostile neighbors, and worship languished. It was under these circumstances that Ezra the scribe headed a second group of returnees, courageously put an end to mixed marriages between the followers of Yahweh and their idolatrous neighbors, and reinstituted Mosaic Law as the core of religious life. A contemporary, Nehemiah, arrived a few years later (about 445 B.C.) as civil governor and superintended reconstruction of the wall around the capital city, fortifying it against possible enemy attack.

If the Jews enjoyed a religious and political restoration, however, animism, nature worship, superstition, magic, fertility cults, and man-made religions of every sort held most of the world in thrall, and humanism reigned supreme in the Greek city-states. To be sure, the Greeks had a plethora of gods. The ancient gods of Homeric legend were still ostensibly respected, one or another of them being officially accepted as the patron of a particular city; and Zeus was represented as king of gods and men in most of the city-states, albeit in humanized form. Allegedly, he was the guardian of justice, but his own amorous escapades with goddesses and mortal women provided a degenerate example, while homosexuality was not only tolerated but romanticized. Indeed, the Greeks were largely amoral and their gods anthropomorphic. They created gods on their own terms, sometimes made fun of them, and endowed them with human attributes: strength and virility, treachery and cruelty; subtlety and deceit, sophistry and duplicity; high-mindedness and magnanimity, vengefulness and rapacity.

Man was the focal point of Greek culture. By the 5th century B.C., historians such as Thucydides were attributing occurrences to the actions of men rather than the gods; religious festivals emphasized practical matters in this life – preparing young men to be valiant warriors and girls to be mothers, maintaining political unity or order, celebrating the fruitfulness of the earth and the gods putatively influencing it. Sculptors were depicting the nude human figure (in isolation from the environment) idealistically, as the epitome of physical power, vitality, potency, vigor, beauty, and grace. Drawings on vases and frieze inscriptions depicted the exploits of legendary heroes; young athletes competed in the nude in the Olympic games honoring Zeus; the Athenian writer of tragedies Euripides created characters whose destiny was determined by their own thoughts, emotions and actions; philosophers scorned the suppression of one's natural impulses, stressing rather the perfection of one's nature, a reflection of divinity. The "Funeral Oration" of Pericles (as related by Thucydides) lauds human self-sufficiency: "each single one of our citizens, in all the manifold aspects of life, is able to show himself the rightful lord and owner of his own person..."; and some exceptional mortals such as Hercules became "super-heroes" hardly to be distinguished from the gods.

Alexander the Great (r.336-323 B.C.) benefited from this mystique, which predisposed the Greeks to accept his "deification." In Egypt, he was received as son of Amon-Re (whom the Greeks equated with Zeus), and the Persians also offered obeisance. After Alexander's unexpected death in 323 B.C., many of the Hellenistic kings (including Antiochus Epiphanes) capitalized on his example for political reasons and ruled as "god-kings." Their conquerors, the Romans, also adopted the concept of divine-kingship. Julius Caesar was posthumously proclaimed to be "Jupiter Julius," a temple was dedicated to him and a priest designated for his worship. Caesar's nephew and successor, Octavius (d.14 A.D.), although somewhat cautious in claiming divinity, accepted the sacred appellation Augustus and was worshiped by his subjects as a "present and corporeal god."

The descending line on the chart (appendix I) indicates this era of paganism, humanism, and idolatry – a period of extreme spiritual darkness; yet, as the Apostle Paul observed, "where sin abounded, grace did much more abound" (Romans 5:20b, KJV). Into this sinful and reprobate cultural milieu, the Lord God, from a heart of infinite love, sent His "only-begotten Son, that whosoever believes in Him shall not perish but have everlasting life" (John 3:16, NKJV).

According to Galatians 4:4, this Divine intervention, the turning point of history, took place "in the fullness of time." What is the meaning of this term? The answer is doubtless fully known only to God, but some thoughts based on Scripture and history are worth considering. In the first place, this was a time – similar to that of Noah – when the hearts of very few people were disposed to follow the Creator-God. Mankind as a whole was oblivious of Him, and even His chosen people, the Jews, had repeatedly demonstrated their inability to observe His Law. From a human perspective, there was no hope: man deserved only to be destroyed, but Yahweh had promised Noah never again "to destroy all living creatures" (Genesis 8:21; cf.Genesis 8:22-23 and 9:8-11).

If this era was the "fullness of time" because the wickedness of mankind had reached its plenitude, it may also be considered the most opportune moment for the Savior of the world to appear in human flesh. For one thing, Alexander the Great and his successors had spread Hellenism and with it the Greek language, which became the *lingua franca* – a common language suitable for spreading the teachings of Jesus Christ throughout much of the ancient world. Moreover, Rome had brought the major portion of this area under its hegemony. From Britain and the Atlantic Seaboard to the Caspian Sea, from North Africa and Egypt to the Euphrates River, the Roman standards were triumphantly displayed. In the first century B.C. a corrupt, strife-filled, savage Roman Republic was superseded by the Roman Empire (27 B.C.), which re-established internal tranquility and just and orderly rule. Under the Empire, the differences between various peoples and ethnic groups were beginning to break down to a greater extent than in the past. Though an Imperial unity was not attained easily or immediately, it was being vigorously fostered and increasingly accepted. The *Pax Romana*, together with Roman law, brought a certain sense of security to people weary of injustice and warfare and forced adaption to changing regulations and modes of government. Under these circumstances, people were less occupied than in the past with preserving life and limb or receiving justice, and perhaps more open to receiving the "good news" of God's love. Moreover, the message of Jesus Christ could be disseminated more quickly than ever before thanks to a vast network of roads built for military purposes by the Emperor Augustus (27 B.C.-14 A.D.).

The first to receive the message, however, were the Jews, a people not sanguine about Roman rule but ready to welcome the advent of a Messiah predicted by the Old Testament prophets, whose writings had been carefully recorded on scrolls and read to everyone attending the synagogues. Over the centuries, the Jews had suffered greatly from dispersion and subjection to foreign rulers, many of whom were harsh or capricious. Even their own Hasmonean kingdom (143-63 B.C.) was rent with factionalism between those wishing to adapt to a Hellenized culture and those opposed to it. Particularly involved were two rival parties – the Pharisees, who vehemently opposed Hellenization, and the Sadducees, who were moderately receptive to it. Tragically, bitter civil wars characterized most of the period, and fraternal strife ultimately led to Roman intervention under General Pompey, who put an end to Jewish independence. Tetrarchs (most notably "Herod the Great") appointed by Rome as chief administrators in Judea (as the Romans called Judah) were often ambitious, arbitrary, despotic, and cruel; and the procurators, who replaced them during the reign of Caesar Augustus, were even worse. Jewish patriots, especially the Zealots, did everything they could to discredit and weaken Roman rule, while the Jewish populace developed a sharper awareness of their heritage and eagerly looked for the promised Messiah who, they believed, would vindicate them, overthrow the Romans, and establish a righteous, peaceful, and prosperous Jewish kingdom in Judea. Surely it was "the fullness of time" for the advent of God's incarnate Son.

Jesus of Nazareth was born under unpropitious circumstances to poor parents descended from King David, and we know little about Him until after He was baptized by His cousin John and began to speak in an authoritative way about how man should relate to God. Jesus's teaching was appealing, going beyond Jewish rituals or practices that had burdened God-fearing Jews – teachings such as the "Sabbath was made for man, not man for the Sabbath," which engendered a new liberty regarding Talmudic interpretations of the Law. Even His teaching that God required a higher standard than external observance of the Law ("...I tell you that anyone who looks on a woman lustfully has already committed adultery with her in his heart," Matthew 5:28) put all, as sinners, on the same footing and struck at the hypocrisy of legalists whose dogmas tended to place insurmountable impediments in the way of persons seeking to live godly lives. At the same time, it implied a better solution for the problem of guilt than methodical (and universally imperfect) conformity to religious rules. His emphasis on "the first and greatest commandment": "Love the Lord your God with all your heart and with all your soul and with all your mind" and the second greatest commandment :"Love your neighbor as yourself" (Matthew 22:37-38) and the loving compassion characterizing His ministry apparently touched the hearts of some listeners, while arousing curiosity in others. Much of His instruction was presented in stories (parables) that required listeners to plumb deeper to understand the message. Even His twelve closest followers were sometimes bewildered by what He was saying and requested further explanation. However, they came to believe His claim that He was "the Way, the Truth, and the Life" (John 14:6) – the only One through whom anyone could receive eternal life. His statements that He would be sacrificed for the sins of all mankind (for example, John 12:23-36) were not explicit, and apparently were imperfectly understood during His earthly life; but the prospect of a future life that would never end was very attractive, especially to the Hellenized Jews of the diaspora (who outnumbered Palestinian Jews by more than 4 to 1) and eventually also to

Romans, some of whom had already heard devotees of the mystery cults speak of a life to come. Multitudes came to hear Jesus, to witness His miracles, and to receive healing or provision, though the majority seem never to have understood His non-political message of love and reconciliation through simple faith between God and man. Most Jews were looking for a different type of Messiah than the "suffering Servant" of Isaiah 53, and their religious leaders accused Jesus of blasphemy for claiming to be one with Yahweh. Therefore, they turned Him over to the Roman authorities to be executed by crucifixion. Miraculous signs attended His death, and His resurrection three days later was attested to by His disciples and a throng of other witnesses. After the outpouring of the Holy Spirit on the day of Pentecost, Christ's followers boldly proclaimed the good news of a Messiah-Redeemer, who had come as the "Lamb of God" to suffer and die for the sins of all humanity, had arisen from the dead and ascended into heaven, and was making eternal life available to everyone trusting in His sacrifice and acknowledging Him as Savior and Lord.

Chapter III

THE TRIUMPH OF CHRISTIANITY

Christianity grew rapidly for a number of reasons. First of all, the fervor and conviction of common men and women who were eye-witnesses to Jesus's ministry and all that followed was astounding, as were also the miracles, particularly miracles of healing, that accompanied their testimony. Then too, the egalitarian concept that all men are equal in the eyes of God could hardly fail to attract non-Jews and persons from the lower classes, as did also the doctrine of the imminent return of the Messiah to earth and a life hereafter. (Those engaged in dangerous occupations – gladiators, for example – would appreciate this.) Likewise, Jesus's talk about peace, though imperfectly comprehended, could appeal to merchants, clerks, and other middling groups; and His moral teaching was astonishing, going beyond the Law while liberating believers from its bondage. Moreover, Christians carried on a custom already begun by the Jews of the diaspora – ministering to the needs of the indigent, prisoners, the hungry, the fatherless, and widows – giving to them in the name of Jesus; and their love for one another (despite strong differences of opinion among some ecclesiastical leaders) was manifested in acts of kindness, their desire to be together, and sharing of their goods (Acts 2:42-47). The very fact that they were a minuscule minority caused them to cherish one another and to act in a spirit of unity. As time went by, disagreements did come to the surface, of course; but adversity and persecutions usually helped to solidify their amity and concern for one another and confirmed suffering believers in their faith. Indeed, their steadfastness in the face of persecution was occasionally noted by Roman officials and solders, who could not but wonder at the severity of punishments being meted out to a compliant and morally upright people, whose only crime was a refusal to participate in official cults involving Emperor worship. This "living witness" won more and more converts over time.

In the first century, however, one of the primary reasons for the expansion of Christianity was the work of the Apostle Paul, who not only was an indefatigable missionary, but explicated the teachings of Jesus Christ, forging them into a lucid and cohesive theology applicable to people of every gender, race, and station in life. In fact, Paul (with the concurrence of Peter) liberated believers from observing certain Jewish practices, such as circumcision and strict dietary laws, that would have limited Christianity's appeal to Gentiles. Henceforth, Christianity was a faith of universal dimensions and attractiveness, open to anyone confessing his faith in Jesus Christ and submitting to His lordship.

In his early ministry, Paul made a practice of entering the synagogue on the Sabbath and, when invited, to speak to those assembled, explaining how Jesus was the Messiah, the fulfillment of Old Testament prophecy. Invariably present were a number of God-fearing exiles who had been exposed to the Greek Septuagint version of the Old Testament. They were often open to Paul's message, receiving it with joy. However, within a short time – either persuaded that certain Old Testament ceremonial practices, especially circumcision, were still binding, or wishing to mollify Jewish Zealots denouncing them as "Hellenizers" – they began to urge Gentile converts to Christianity to be circumcised. To Paul, this was a denial of the full efficacy of the grace of God available through Jesus Christ, and he strongly protested at the Council of Jerusalem (50 A.D.) and in his epistle to the Galatians against falling back into a legalism that would nullify the Gospel. Although he and Peter were able to persuade the Council not to require Gentiles to observe Old Testament rites, the church in Jerusalem gradually accommodated the Judaizers and even became identified with the revolt against Roman rule that broke out in 66 A.D.

Several Roman generals, including the redoubtable Vespasian, tried to quash the rebellion, but it was his son Titus who, after horrendous losses on both sides and a siege that weakened the defenders, sacked the city and torched the temple in 70 A.D. For the Jews this was not the end, for subsequent revolts burst forth in the next century; but their suppression caused widespread dispersion of the sons of Israel and led to the Talmud's ascendency in the formation of their religious beliefs.

Significant changes likewise took place in the church. The destruction of Jerusalem and decimation of its church caused Rome to assume stronger ecclesiastical leadership. Perhaps this was inevitable in any case, owing to Rome's prestige as capital of the Empire and crossroads for peoples of many ethnic groups. It was also the city where, according to tradition, both Paul and

Peter were martyred, and the Petrine theory was effectively taught to sanction the primacy of the bishops of Rome over those of other episcopal sees. As time went on, its bishops were to demonstrate their competence and equanimity in rendering decisions on cases submitted to them. Therefore, the Bishop of Rome eventually would be recognized as the "Papa" (Pope) for the church.

The early church was blessed with stalwart leaders who contributed to its survival and growth, but the apostle Paul recognized from the very outset that Christianity's success would not depend on human efforts or eloquence. The Gospel, he wrote, "came to you not simply with words, but also with power, with the Holy Spirit and deep conviction" (I Thessalonians 1:5). Similarly, in Romans 15:18-19a, he stated: "I will not venture to speak anything except what Christ has accomplished through me in leading the Gentiles to obey God by what I have said and done – by the power of signs and miracles, through the power of the Spirit." In the final analysis, therefore, it was the Spirit of God who assured Christianity's success in spite of internal squabbles, heresies, and the sporadic but incredibly cruel efforts of the state to compel believers to sacrifice to the Imperial deities. When faced with confiscation of property and martyrdom, many Christians did recant; but the majority stood firm. By the 4th century, persecution of Christians was becoming more and more unpopular with the general populace; yet Diocletian and Maximian tried once more to eradicate Christianity by torture and executions. Surcease came only after Constantine, marching under the sign of the cross, defeated a rival for the Imperial throne. In the following year, 313, he and his co-ruler issued the so-called Edict of Milan, according toleration to all religions.

Almost immediately, divisions began to arise within the church, principally between the followers of an Alexandrian priest named Arius (d.336) – who said that Jesus Christ was a created being and, therefore, not co-equal and co-eternal with the Father – and those of Athanasius (d.373), whose Trinitarian doctrine was declared orthodox by the Council of Nicaea in 325. Despite this decision and Emperor Constantine"s exhortation for his subjects to accept Christianity in its orthodox form, Arianism continued to spread, especially among the German tribes that ultimately overran the Western Empire. Rifts persisted, therefore, within the church, which moved from a tolerated faith to a favored one over the next half century. However, it was not until 380 under the

Emperor Theodosius, that Christianity became the state religion and all others were proscribed.

Pagans were now second-class citizens and began to be exiled as disloyal subjects, with the unfortunate result that considerable numbers of them sought admission into the church. As a consequence, the urgency for the church to evangelize the pagans diminished. Acceptance of professing but unregenerate members, not cleansed of pagan beliefs and practices, diluted the spiritual life of the church, which began to settle into the world, willing now to compromise on particular issues and to assimilate certain extraneous ceremonies in exchange for state sponsorship, protection, and assistance. As time went on, the civil government exercised increasing influence over ecclesiastical matters – to the point that the eastern branch of the church became virtually subservient to the Eastern Emperors, and miracles and the exercise of the "gifts of the Spirit" began to subside. Thus, Imperial favor and preference accomplished what persecution could not.

Throughout history, when Christians have lost their "saltiness" (Matthew 5:23), the civilizations, kingdoms, or national structures of which they were a part have declined. II Chronicles 7:13-14 plainly states: "If...My people who are called by My name humble themselves and pray, and seek My face and turn from their wicked ways, then I will hear from heaven, will forgive their sin, and will heal their land." Note that God is speaking here of *His* people, not of unbelievers. *God's people* must turn from *their* wicked ways, must humble themselves before God and prayerfully seek to do His will. Only then, will God save their land.

In ancient Rome, just as in our nation today, Christians were apparently not entirely true to the commission of Jesus Christ (Matthew 28:19-20). They relaxed and began to lose their zeal after receiving the recognition of the state, but Roman morals were deplorable long before Christians ceased to be persecuted in 313. Indeed, many of the causes for Rome's eventual fall were present as early as the 2nd century. By then taxation was steadily mounting to pay for maintenance of temples, public baths, pagan religious processions, feasts, and spectacles for the amusement of the lower classes. Already the bureaucracy and state welfare services were being rapidly expanded, and a balance-of-payments problem resulted from the Roman populace's materialistic demand for luxuries not produced in the Italian peninsula but imported from the Orient. Constantly rising taxes, inflation, and a decline in personal freedom and sense of responsibility were the results, and eventually the class structure became more rigid as the middle class was virtually squeezed out of existence and the free farmers were reduced to servitude. Corruption increased, municipal liberty was curtailed, the currency was devalued, government welfare continued to increase, taxes became more onerous; licentiousness, gluttony, immorality, and the pursuit of pleasure prevailed among the wealthy classes; and food doles, sports spectacles, and violent games kept the masses pacified.

All the while, of course, the sturdy independence of the Roman citizenry was being eroded, and the armies could no longer be filled with native recruits. More and more, Rome granted special privileges and land to foreigners, many of them German "barbarians," who would promise to settle down within the Empire and defend its frontiers. However, their patriotism was often suspect. Huge sums were expended by emperors to insure the loyalty of the army, but even so, by the 3rd century, army factions were deposing and installing emperors. Civil wars exacerbated Roman weakness, so that ultimately the warlike barbarians were able to breach her military frontiers. Long before the final collapse (usually denoted as taking place in 476), there had been a breakdown of integrity, independence, morals, and the economic and social systems. Rome had sowed the wind and reaped the whirlwind (cf. Hosea 8:7).

Chapter IV

EMERGENCE OF CHURCH DOMINION FROM ROME

As represented on the diagram (Appendix I), the foregoing synopsis of the Jewish and early Christian experience portrays the quest of a small but significant segment of mankind for a relationship with God. The quest became more organized and methodical in the 4th century as the gap between East and West in both secular and ecclesiastical affairs widened. Knowledge of Greek language and thought was declining in the West, and the Latin church fathers – most notably Ambrose (340-397), Jerome (c.340-419), and Augustine (354-430) – helped to consolidate the theology, organization, and liturgy of the western church.

As Bishop of Milan from 374 until his death, Ambrose upheld orthodoxy against the Arians (who denied the Trinity) and counseled emperors on matters affecting the church. "The Emperor," he insisted, "is in the church, not above it"; therefore, in matters of faith or morals, bishops could judge emperors. Suiting actions to words, he humbled Theodosius for ordering a massacre of rebellious Thessalonians. Well-schooled in the classics, Ambrose was an accomplished writer, eloquent speaker, and hymn-writer.

Equally conversant in pagan letters but inclined toward asceticism, Jerome translated the monastic rule of Pachomius into Latin and promoted monasticism in Rome, while inveighing against heresies and the luxury, corruption, and worldliness he saw there. More importantly, he translated the Scriptures into the Latin Vulgate, which eventually became the authorized Catholic Bible.

Augustine's influence was even more pervasive. Trained in classical literature and philosophy, he delved into Manichaeism in his youth and, according to his *Confessions*, lived as a wastrel and fornicator prior to his conversion. For the last 35 years of his life, however, he served as Bishop of Hippo and wrote on almost every aspect of the Christian faith, denouncing heresies of every sort and emphasizing the need to believe in order to understand. Though steeped in Platonic thought, he employed it effectively in the service of orthodoxy and, in his *City of God*, defended Christianity against pagan critics. The Divine plan, he believed, was being worked out in human history – a predestinarian premise observable also in his theology, which shaped historical writing throughout the middle ages and beyond.

The weakness and breakdown of Imperial authority in the West in the course of the 5th century allowed the church to develop autonomy within the state and ultimately to exercise many temporal functions. It was a stabilizing force during the barbarian invasions when Germanic and Roman cultures were being fused and became, to a significant degree, the preceptor of emerging kings and their subjects. Still, headstrong rulers such as Frankish King Clovis (r.481-511) and his Merovingian successors were difficult to curb, even when allied with Rome. Clovis's conversion, in fact, was probably more a matter of policy than religious persuasion; for by upholding orthodox Christianity against the Arians, he received the support of the Catholic clergy as he carried his conquests to a successful conclusion, thereby uniting Gaul in the year of his death. More than this, the Merovingian monarchs employed churchmen as some of their chief administrators.

Under Pope Gregory the Great (r.590-604), the papacy grew in strength toward the end of a chaotic 6th century that saw the Lombards conquer most of the Italian peninsula. Not only did Gregory organize the defense of Rome and relieve the plight of the poor, but he attempted to expand the spiritual hegemony of Rome by dispatching Italian missionary Augustine of Canterbury (d.c.605) to Britain. Earlier Britain had been converted by Roman and Celtic Christians, but since the withdrawal of Roman troops and the Anglo-Saxon invasions (late 5th century), it had relapsed into paganism. Success attended Augustine's mission although rivalry and friction between Celtic and Roman Catholic Christians continued until well into the 7th century.

After the Synod of Whitby (664), Roman and Celtic traditions tended to intermingle under the authority of Rome, and Anglo-Saxon missionaries set forth for the continent, where Celtic missionary Columbanus (d.615) had founded monasteries extending from Gaul through the Alps and into the Italian peninsula. Cloisters became centers from which Christianity was disseminated.

Most non-Celtic monasteries operated under Benedictine rule, which had been endorsed by Gregory the Great. Its moderate, common-sense balance of divine services, manual labor, reading and scholarship caused it to be adopted far and wide; and its self-contained communities became centers of civilization – reclaiming wastelands, preserving manuscripts, and fostering learning. Therefore, when English missionaries such as Winfrith of Nursling (better known as St. Boniface, c.675-754) moved into the trans-Rhenish German territories that were under nominal Frankish rule, their efforts were complemented by existing monastic communities.

Not surprisingly, Boniface's missionary efforts also enjoyed the support and protection of Frankish ruler Charles Martel, who was eager for the wild pagans within his realm to accept the Christian faith and become more tractable. With the advantages of monastic and royal support and imbued with religious fervor, Boniface succeeded in bringing much of western Germany into the Roman Catholic fold and founded several monasteries – most notably Fulda, which became a great center of learning and missionary activity.

On several occasions Roman pontiffs needed the assistance of Frankish rulers to rescue them from threats posed by the Arian Lombards and to deal with militant Moslem expansion. After the death of their founder Mohammed in 632 and a period of internecine strife, Islamic armies had taken the offensive, moving eastward to vanquish Persia before wheeling westward to conquer most of the Middle East, Egypt, North Africa, and by 711 Visigothic Spain. Subsequent Islamic incursions into southern Gaul appeared to pose a threat to Christendom, a fact that the church could hardly ignore. Although Charles Martel disregarded Rome's plea for assistance against the Lombards, he met the Moslem onslaught – probably out of self-interest, for he did not hesitate to confiscate church lands and distribute them to his fighting men. In any event, Charles defeated the Moslems at Tours in 732, and his successors were able to compel their withdrawal to the Iberian Peninsula.

Charles Martel's grandson, Charlemagne (r.768-814), did collaborate with Rome. On two occasions, he swept into the Italian peninsula to rescue the pope from the Lombards and in return was crowned "Emperor of the Romans" in 800 by Leo III – thus perpetuating the rift between the Eastern and Western empires. Four years later, Charlemagne's thirty-two-year campaign against the heathen

Saxons terminated after the vanquished remnant were baptized into the Catholic faith. Almost invariably, the Emperor's administrators were literate churchmen, and learned clerics abounded at his court in Aachen (Aix la Chapelle). Here Charlemagne established a palace school whose luminaries included his biographer Einhard (d.840), Paul the Deacon (author of *The History of the Lombards*), and Alcuin of York (d.804), who served as the Emperor's advisor on educational and religious matters. Under Charlemagne's aegis, scholars of the court school developed a legible style of handwriting and, in collaboration with Rome, standardized the liturgy and revised the *Apostles' Creed*.

In all of this activity, Charlemagne considered himself God's agent to spread Christianity and succor the church. He did not, however, seek to dominate the church in the manner of the Byzantine Emperor. His death in 814 left a great void; for his successors proved unequal to the challenge of maintaining the Empire. Fragmented by rebellions and civil wars and assailed by devastating Viking raids, the once-extensive Empire collapsed, thereby encouraging emergence of feudal government and a more-or- less self-sufficient manorial economy that was already taking shape in response to Moslem disruption of commerce in the Mediterranean. A desire for security and survival prompted people to look to local nobles for protection and the means of subsistence. These fighting men, in turn, commended themselves to more powerful nobles or lords in a relationship requiring mutual obligations – not only for the purpose of waging war, but for government, administration of justice, and the cultivation of land holdings to support themselves and their dependents.

Theoretically, every nobleman except the sovereign – the Emperor or King – was to swear fealty to a higher lord; and the church, with its vast land holdings and hierarchical administrative structure, came to enjoy great prominence and power, exercising temporal rule as well as spiritual authority. Church courts reserved to themselves all cases involving clergymen, clerics, and university communities. In its monasteries and schools, the church promoted learning. It provided assistance to the poor and sponsored hospitals, orphanages, and numerous social services. The church also helped to build roads and bridges, introduced new crops and farming methods, and strove to curb greed in the economic sphere through prohibitions against usury and regulations such as the "just price." Moreover, it endeavored to limit bloodshed by pressing nobles (in the 10th and 11th centuries) to uphold the Peace of God, prohibiting attacks on non-combatants, and the Truce of God, which proscribed private wars on holy days and during specified seasons of the year. Though church regulations were sometimes disregarded, the pervasiveness of ecclesiastical influence can hardly be overstated.

Chapter V

CHURCH AND STATE IN THE MIDDLE AGES

The church was involved in every aspect of medieval life, and inevitably its pervasive influence brought it into confrontation with powerful temporal rulers, though problems were rather minor (owing to the weakness of Charlemagne's successors) until the 10th century after the Imperial dignity had passed from the Franks to the Saxons. As a matter of fact, Otto I (Emperor from 962 to 973) was crowned Holy Roman Emperor in recognition of his pacification of the marauding Magyars and his rescue of Rome from the resurgent Lombards. In the long run, however, the attempts of Otto and successive emperors to rule both Germany and Italy failed, principally because of the determined resistance of the papacy. For a time, Emperor Henry III (r.1039-1056), scion of the Franconian ruling house, was able to depose scandal-ridden, contentious popes and to secure the election of reform-minded prelates to the Holy See, but no pontiff could tolerate a dominant Imperial presence in the Italian Peninsula. A struggle between crown and altar was bound to occur, and, win or lose, the church would find itself resorting to power politics with both spiritual and worldly weapons that would distract it from its spiritual mission and eventually corrupt it.

To a large extent, the church had little choice but to resist Imperial influences and encroachments upon its authority that could render it almost an arm of the state. For example, emperors typically determined what prelates would accede to the papacy until 1059 when a Roman Council ended this abuse by conferring the right of election upon the Cardinals. Needless to say, the emperors were not pleased, but matters came to a head when Pope Gregory VII (r.1073-1085) prescribed several reforms proposed by the Cluniacs – most significantly, enforced celibacy of the clergy, elimination of simony (the purchase of church offices), and termination of lay investiture of bishops. An acrimonious struggle ensued in which the Pope excommunicated Emperor Henry IV (r.1056-1106), freeing his vassals from their oaths of fealty to him. The Emperor found it propitious to pose as a penitent, beseeching absolution, but the issue was not resolved until 1122. In that year, a compromise known as the

Concordat of Worms was worked out, whereby the Emperor gave up his right to invest bishops with a ring and staff – symbolic of their spiritual office – but retained the right to be present (or have a representative present) at their election and to invest them with their temporalities – their Imperial fiefs and secular powers.

Unfortunately for the peace of the Empire and the spiritual welfare of the church, the stupendous struggle between the Holy Roman Emperors and the papacy continued, complicated by conflicts between rival claimants to the Imperial throne. Successive emperors rebutted papal claims to supremacy and repeatedly conducted military campaigns into the Italian peninsula to put down rebellions encouraged by the papacy. By clever diplomacy, Hohenstaufen Emperor Henry VI (r.1190-1197) managed to gain possession of most of northern and southern Italy, effectively isolating the papal states, only to die suddenly at the height of his power. Again, the Empire was torn asunder as rival candidates fought for the Imperial crown, enabling the strongest medieval pope, Innocent III (r.1198-1216), to recover central and southern Italy. Innocent embroiled himself in Imperial politics, making and ruining several emperors in his attempts to ensure coronation of one willing to renounce ambitions in Italy inimical to the church's patrimony.

Innocent emphatically insisted that when the spiritual and secular authorities were in conflict, the latter must yield to the former and that all matters involving justice, morality, or religion came under the paramount authority of the church. He laid England under interdict (compelling King John to hold the kingdom under papal lordship), made several lesser countries fiefs of Rome, commanded the king of France to take back his lawful wife, exploited the misguided sack of Constantinople by Christian crusaders to bring the Byzantine church under Roman authority (quite temporarily as it proved), disallowed secular rulers to tax the clergy without papal consent, undertook regular visitation and superintendence of monasteries and convents, and convened the Fourth Lateran Council (1215), which, among other things, defined transubstantiation (thereby conferring unique power on priests), declared all seven sacraments essential for salvation, confirmed many previous disciplinary canons, and eliminated trial by ordeal. He also declared the Waldensians (an evangelical sect adhering to the simple teaching of Christ, denouncing worldliness, and considering the sacraments non-essential) to be heretics, created the machinery of the Holy Office, and even launched a crusade against the non-Christian Cathari of southern France, who were effectively liquidated by northern knights motivated by a desire for plunder more than by godly fervor.

Innocent III's pontificate marked the high tide of the church's power, though there was no dearth of successors who sought to emulate him. The Inquisition was made official in 1233 and placed under the direction of the Dominicans. In areas under investigation, inquiries concerning the presence of heretics were made, and informers were encouraged to come forward, being assured that their names would not be divulged. Not only were suspects never told the names of their accusers (who may have been scoundrels or enemies bent on vengeance), but they were considered guilty until proven innocent and not accorded the right to counsel. Practically nobody came through unscathed. Many suspects were tortured to force them to name accomplices, and even those confessing erroneous beliefs and repenting would usually be given a heavy penance and would suffer confiscation of land and property. Most pitiable, of course, were the "guilty," who were turned over to the secular arm for execution. The possibilities for abuse are quite evident; for secret investigations left the accused no recourse: they were completely at the mercy of their judges, be they weak, incompetent, emotionally unstable, or even demented.

The papacy's attempts to undermine Imperial power also continued, becoming very determined during the reign of Frederick II (r.1220-1250). Known as "Stupor Mundi," wonder of the world, Frederick was a man in advance of his age. He wrote a book on hunting with falcons, engaged in all sorts of empirical investigations (some of them extremely cruel), founded a university at Naples to train bright young men for Imperial service, reorganized the medical school at Salerno, encouraged the literary arts and vernacular poetry, accelerated the assimilation of classical and Arabic learning in the West – often through Arabic translations of ancient Greek manuscripts on philosophy and science (frequently inimical to Christian orthodoxy), and headed a brilliant court where irreverence, skepticism, and heretical opinions were in vogue. He patronized learned Jewish translators (and probably Moslems as well), and was never quick to heed papal admonitions or directives. He delayed a promised crusade against the Moslems and, when he did go, negotiated with the infidel instead of fighting – winning Jerusalem but not satisfying the Pope. Little wonder that the papacy (surrounded by territories governed by the heretical prince) distrusted and feared him. Although Frederick focused his attention upon Sicily and southern Italy, he was also nominal sovereign of the northern segment of the peninsula as well as the German territories. Since he gave little attention to the latter, his German barons attained autonomy, while the unruly Lombard states, never amenable to feudal control, set an independent course in cooperation with Rome. In his latter years, Frederick was worn down by rebellion after rebellion, all of them encouraged by Rome (during his reign, he was excommunicated three times), which left the German portion of his empire in dissolution.

One should not minimize the effectiveness of the church's diplomacy or the spiritual weapons used to implement it. In an era when the church and civilization were closely identified, the prestige of "Christ's vicar on earth" was enormous. People were taught that there was no salvation outside the church and that partaking of the sacraments was essential to a right relationship with God. Excommunication, therefore, was a fearful thing to the average person, for it would bar him from making confession of his sins and participating in the mass. Sacraments of any kind, in fact, were not to be permitted to an excommunicated person – commoner or prince; and if subjects perceived their prince to be excluded from the good graces of the church, the obligation of obedience to him was nullified. Barons who had sworn fealty to a king or emperor were freed from their feudal oaths if their suzerain was excommunicate; thus vassals wishing to aggrandize themselves at the expense of their lord, ignore certain demands upon them, or free themselves entirely from his authority were able to do so with impunity so long as his armed retainers were not strong enough to overcome them. For that matter, the loyalty of retainers might also waver if they were convinced of the untenability of their prince's spiritual and political position, or that their own salvation was jeopardized by service to him. Even serfs and commoners during this age of faith and credulity regretted any squabble between their prince and the pope, though they may not have understood the reason for it or the issues at stake. This was especially true when excommunication of the lord was accompanied by interdict upon the land; for then, whether they supported him or had nothing to do with him, subjects could not partake of the Eucharist or receive any of the sacraments, including extreme unction, until their lord did penance and the ban was lifted.

For their part, irreligious sovereigns or pious rulers at odds with Rome were aware that in the final analysis their political strength depended on the faithfulness and obedience of their vassals and, to a lesser degree, the good will and loyalty of their common subjects; therefore, they dreaded excommunication and interdict, and the very threat of them was sometimes enough to forestall challenges to church policy.

On the other hand, as 13th-century popes decreed excommunication and interdict more and more frequently, their effectiveness began to subside. Moreover, the church was already beset by new modes of thought and economic changes that were undermining its spiritual authority (and would eventually erode its political influence), though these trends would not be fully recognized until the beginning of the 14th century.

Chapter VI

THE UNREMITTING SPIRITUAL STRUGGLE:
FAITH VS. REASON

A number of factors contributed to the decline of papal influence. For one thing, the crusades and the defeat of Moslem naval contingents in the Mediterranean by Italian and Norman seamen in the early 11th century had re-established commercial intercourse with the Levant and, concomitantly, had brought about a new awareness of other cultures.

We have already seen how Hohenstaufen Emperor Frederick II stimulated cultural interchange and translation of ancient writings at his court – a natural development in view of the long-standing mingling of Hellenistic, Saracen, and Christian cultures in southern Italy under the Normans. In a less amicable manner, Moslems and Jews in the Iberian peninsula had a profound affect upon the culture emerging during the *Reconquista*. So it was that Moslem and Jewish thought influenced Christian philosophy – either by stimulating new ideas, by making translations of and commentaries on the pagan philosophers, or by precipitating reaction to tenets considered heretical. As the thoughts of Arab philosopher Ibn Sina (known in the West as Avicenna, 980-1037); Moses ben Maimon (Maimonides, 1135-1204), Jewish rabbi, physician, and philosopher; and Ibn Rushd (Averroës, 1126-1198) – Spanish-Arabian barrister, physician, astronomer, and philosopher – began to circulate in the West and Latin translations of ancient Greek manuscripts became more available, an intellectual revolution began to take place that challenged Christian theology. Averroës's interpretations of Aristotelian thought were particularly troublesome to the church, because they implied that philosophy based on human reason was superior to theology based on revealed truth. They also implicitly denied personal immortality and freedom of the human will: a person at birth possessed only a "potential intellect" that must be activated by Universal, Active Intelligence into which, at physical death, his "acquired intellect" would be absorbed. Averroëism became fashionable in sophisticated Italian society as well as in portions of southern France and Spain, despite papal attempts to censor Aristotle's works and to denounce academics propagating Averoëistic doctrines in the universities, which were intended to be champions of orthodoxy. One "thorn in the flesh" was University of Paris philosophy professor Siger of Brabant (c.1235-1281), who was conversant with the works of Aristotle and those of many Jewish and Moslem thinkers. He taught that the universe was eternal and renounced the doctrines of personal immortality and a bodily resurrection.

If the faith were to survive, it appeared, theologians would have to come to grips with pagan philosophy and explain it within a Christian framework, while rationally dispensing with those tenets that could not be brought into conformity with orthodox beliefs. Several, including the great German scholar Albertus Magnus (1193-1280) made the attempt; but it was his famous student, Thomas Aquinas (1225-1274), who managed to harmonize Aristotelian and Christian thought. Not only did he write commentaries on Aristotelian philosophy, but he refuted the Averroëists and reconciled revealed truth with that acquired through reason in his *Summa contra Gentiles*. In that work and in his *Summa Theologica*, Aquinas worked out a synthesis of faith and reason, asserting that theology and philosophy were equally valid – each in its own sphere – and that they did not contradict one another. On the contrary, revelation and "right reason" (natural reason guided by faith or revelation) were complementary means of arriving at truth: revealed spiritual wisdom could illumine the intellect, leading men to an intellectual comprehension of God, and, by the same token, rational inquiry could enhance one's understanding of revealed truths. In the event of an apparent incompatibility between revealed truth and that rationally apprehended, human reason had erred; therefore, it must back off and make another attempt to reach accord with Divine revelation.

Thomas Aquinas's synthesis of faith and reason did not immediately settle the debate attending the issue, nor did it lay to rest philosophical disputes between Platonic realists espousing universals ("archetypes" in the mind of God) and the more Aristotelian nominalists who maintained that only particulars were real (universals were merely names by which individual things were defined or categorized) and that universals could be understood and explained in the light of them. Nevertheless, Aquinas probably saved Christianity from heresies grounded in Aristotelian philosophy.

The Tuscan poet Dante Alighieri (1265-1321) echoed his assumptions in his *Divine Comedy*; for while the Roman poet Virgil (70-19 B.C.), epitomizing human reason, is able to guide Dante through hell and to the very summit of Mount Purgatory, it is Beatrice – symbolizing Divine love, Divine revelation, Divine grace – who must lead him into paradise and the presence of God. A keen observer of his times, Dante was all too aware of the spiritual decadence into which the church was slipping; for he described meeting maleficent churchmen and a total of seven popes in hell.

Other God-fearing believers refrained from direct criticism of the church, while tacitly renouncing its impiety, worldliness, venality, and excessive emphasis on form and ritual. One such was Francis of Assisi (c.1181-1226) who donned a hermit's gray-brown robe, foreswore all wealth and luxury, took a vow of poverty, and went about begging his food when necessary and ministering to lepers, the ill, the poor, and "all God's creatures." He and his followers, who became known as the "Friars Minor," were willing to perform menial tasks and perambulated the countryside and into villages and towns preaching and joyfully singing to the glory of God and in appreciation of His handiwork – the whole realm of nature. Pope Innocent III granted them permission to live as mendicants and also approved a female auxiliary, the Poor Clares, who emulated the brothers in reaching out to the sick and needy. Surprisingly, the Franciscans' humble manner of living appealed not only to the poorer classes, but also to devout men of wealth, who bestowed gifts upon the Order. As the Franciscans began to acquire considerable corporate wealth after Francis's death, a rift developed between the "spirituals," who insisted on maintaining absolute poverty, and the "conventuals," who believed property-holding was not amiss, since the property really belonged to the church. Over time, they also came to value education in a way not foreseen by their founder. Gradually their simplicity and ardor diminished as their mission was carried out in more regulated and conventional ways; yet their immediate affect on the church was salubrious.

Such was also the case with the group of devout churchmen known as the Friends of God – including Meister Eckhart (d.1327), Johann Tauler (d.1361), Heinrich Suso (d.1366), Jan van Ruysbroeck (d. 1381), and Gerard Groote (d.1384) – who spawned an upsurge of mystical piety in the Rhineland and the Netherlands as they sought to commune directly with the risen Savior through the inner way of prayerful meditation and complete renunciation of self. The Christian mystics generally tried to divest themselves of all thoughts, all images, and all sensations in order to enable God's presence to fill the void. Though some of the mystics did call into question certain church practices, their attempts at spiritual union with the Creator and Savior of mankind were not aimed against the church. Nevertheless, if man could achieve direct union with God without recourse to the priesthood, perhaps, thought some, the sacramental system need not be considered all-important as the church was teaching.

Probably the most remarkable of this group was Groote, a learned layman who condemned the immorality and sloth of the clergy, especially of the Franciscans who were already departing from the standards established by their founder. Groote's most influential work was accomplished shortly before his death: the founding of the Brethren of the Common Life, a semi-monastic organization of lay folk who worked to support themselves while devoting as much time as possible to copying manuscripts and conducting schools that eventually came to emphasize the humanities, taught from a Christian perspective. The Brethren schools, which became justly famous in the Lowlands and the German Rhineland, sought to instill purity of doctrine, clean living, diligent study, useful work habits, humility of spirit, and communion with God and submission to His will. One noted graduate of a Brethren school was Thomas à Kempis (d.1471), whose *Imitation of Christ* has inspired myriads of Christians to lives of prayer, contemplation, devotion, and service. As for the schools of the Brethren of the Common Life, they would continue for several centuries to produce graduates steeped in Christian humanism, strong in faith and intellect.

Chapter VII

SPIRITUAL AND POLITICAL DECLINE OF THE CHURCH

As noted earlier, the church appeared to be at the peak of its power and prestige during the pontificate of Innocent III, and its image was enhanced by the arts, particularly by the awe-inspiring Gothic Cathedrals constructed during the 12th and 13th centuries. However, spiritual decline (shown on the diagram in Appendix I) was already incipient. In part, this decline was due to the papacy's efforts to maintain its temporal powers in the tumult of pressures and threats from secular sovereigns, and also to Christianity's exposure to pagan and heretical ideas. Actually, however, the causes for decline went much deeper.

As trade with the Near East and Africa resumed and increased in the wake of Christian recovery of the Mediterranean from Moslem naval forces in the early 11th century, the feudal-manorial system started to deteriorate. Large-scale international trade required a standard medium of exchange and products for export not easily supplied on the relatively self-sufficient medieval manors. Advantageously located for exploiting commerce in the Mediterranean, the Italian city-states took the lead in producing or acquiring goods acceptable for export; developed stable monetary systems, letters of exchange and credit, trading corporations, and banking houses that accepted deposits; lent money to princes, kings, tradesmen, churchmen, and men of affairs; and assisted in various types of financial transactions.

As a money economy developed, princes began to hire mercenary soldiers rather than to rely exclusively upon their vassals, while their estates lost their self-sufficiency. No longer did each manor try to produce most of the articles it used. Instead, it would purchase certain necessities and luxuries from city artisans or tradesmen, while selling its own food products, flax, wool, and raw materials in urban markets. Consequently, the rural populace and townspeople generally became interdependent.

Nobles and peasants alike were affected by the money economy and endeavored to obtain ready cash to pay for their needs. Gradually, some serfs were able to have the personal services they owed to their lord commuted in exchange for cash payments, while the nobility's real income declined because of inflation, obliging them to go into debt – to mortgage their lands in order to live in a manner they felt befitted their estate. Failure to repay their debts brought loss of their estates or portions thereof, and these lands were purchased by new owners, some of them of non-noble origin. In other instances, a lord might find it more convenient to allow his former serfs to farm his estate on a share-crop basis rather than to try, with minimal success, to impose ancient obligations. This was especially true after the populace of Europe was decimated in mid-14th century by the Black Plague, which created a severe shortage of farm labor in various areas. Increasingly, too, serfs who were beginning to see the possibility for a better life would run away into a town. In some areas, particularly in the German lands, if a runaway could remain free for a year and a day, he was no longer legally under the jurisdiction of his former lord. So it was by many means – by remission of obligations in exchange for monetary payments, by new tenant farming arrangements, by escape from the manor, by some fortuitous circumstance, or because of the pressing financial or labor needs of the lords – that one-time serfs gradually were becoming sharecroppers or free farmers with land of their own while the one-time feudal lords were becoming noble landlords.

Indeed, the nobles even began to lose their monopoly on waging war. This was in large part due to the employment, during the 14th and 15th centuries, of new weapons – the longbow, the Swiss pike, and the Bohemian handgun – which made the trained, mounted knight vulnerable to a foot soldier or, in some cases, to the simple, untrained peasant recruit. Once the prince or king realized that battles could be won without relying completely upon mounted knights whose allegiance was sometimes dubious, he could use a relatively small cavalry force and hire or recruit peasant non-noble archers and footmen. This made him less dependent upon his feudal levies than in the past; therefore, as time went on, his vassals became less important to him.

For centuries the nobles had been very influential, and stronger ones had frequently done just about as they pleased, regardless of their prince's wishes. Now, however, with the coming of a new money economy and the advent of new weaponry, including artillery, a king could force his restless and rebellious vassals into line by hiring armies to fight against them and employing artillery, when necessary, to batter down walls of their castles. The nobles could no longer consistently and effectively obstruct the king's authority although they continued to try for many years.

Not only had the nobles lost their monopoly on fighting the king's battles, but they were beginning to lose their positions in the royal administration. The king often preferred to use non-noble townsmen in his service – men who would be completely dependent upon him and amenable to carrying out his orders without question. They were frequently men trained in business or practical affairs, literate men of ability, men seeking to please the king in order to enhance their social position, prestige, or opportunity for obtaining wealth. Moreover, these men, whom we might refer to as members of a barely emerging middle class, were often quite eager to cooperate with the king for reasons over and above their own personal preferment. Even townsmen who were not involved in the royal service might willingly lend their prince money and in return receive certain rights – perhaps the privilege of exercising a degree of local self-rule, the protection of the king's justice (which was usually more equitably and fairly applied than the arbitrary justice of the old feudal courts), or freedom from hated customs restrictions. So it was that townsmen found it advantageous to serve the king or further his interests while he, on his part, found their assistance very beneficial in subordinating the nobility to his will and in helping him to acquire or maintain preeminent authority within his realm.

We see, then, the rise of a new class of townsmen – a nascent middle class – and the concomitant rise of strong monarchies in England, France, and, somewhat later, in Spain. At the same time, we see the declining power of the old feudal nobility and the church.

This decline in the medieval church is not at all surprising if one remembers that its political and economic interests were, to a great extent, interrelated with those of the old feudal and manorial systems that were being steadily undermined. The leadership of the church came almost exclusively from the noble class and shared its views. The church owned much land all over Europe (just as did the secular lords) and cultivated large tracts of this land by means of serfs; therefore, the factors that weakened the medieval order were bound to have the same effect on the church. For one thing, it was more difficult for the church to hold its own in the political melee with territorial rulers who could no longer be easily cowed by threats of excommunication or interdict. These rulers, sometimes enjoying the support of an incipient middle class and possessing funds to hire armies, were no longer so dependent upon their feudal levies or troops as once had been the case. As a consequence, it was more difficult than in the past for popes to use the vassals of a secular prince against him or to compel him to do the bidding of the Holy See. Furthermore, the territorial rulers were no longer willing to recognize the complete immunity of the church and clergy from the state's jurisdiction or taxation; and this fact frequently prompted struggles with the church that greatly damaged it. Then too, patriotism to the crowned head of a territorial state was gradually weakening both the local feudal loyalties and the concept of Christian unity under a universal church. Tradesmen and moneylenders did not like the church's prohibition on usury or the doctrine of the "just price." Therefore, they were sometimes disposed to collaborate with the king in helping to put down the nobility or to resist the church.

The changing political realities took the papacy by surprise. When Edward I (r. 1272-1307) of England and Philip IV ("The Fair," r. 1285-1314) of France – at war with each other and in need of money – levied taxes on church properties, Pope Boniface VIII (r.1294-1303) contended (as had Innocent III almost a century earlier) that secular rulers could not require payment without papal consent. The French king was particularly intransigent, assuming not only the right to tax the clergy but also to try a French prelate – a papal legate – in a civil court. When Boniface rebuked him, threatening excommunication, Philip sought public support by convening representatives of the French clergy, nobility, and the rest of the populace in the first Estates General, which protested the papal pronouncements. Boniface replied with the bull *Unam Sanctum*, stating that the Roman pontiff was the sole head of Christendom – superior to all temporal rulers – and warning Philip that there was no salvation outside the church; therefore, he needed to submit to the Holy See for the sake of the eternal well-being of his soul. Nothing daunted, the French King had an assembly of nobles and the higher clergy charge the Pope with illegal election, sorcery, idolatry, simony, unchastity, murder, heresy, and irreligion and dispatched his henchman, Guillaume de Nogaret, to arrest the pontiff and bring him back to be tried before a general church council. Nogaret apprehended the aged pontiff at Anagni and held him for several days before the town's citizens rescued him. The humiliated pope died within the month.

It was clear to the rulers of Europe that the papacy was no longer the dominant force it had been under Innocent III, but most of them were dismayed when, two years later, Clement V (r.1305-1314) moved the papal court from Rome to Avignon, a city surrounded by French territory. Clement, former Archbishop of Bordeaux and counselor to the king, was hard-pressed to maintain the church's freedom of action in the face of several demands by the French monarch, among them that Boniface VIII's prohibition against taxation of the clergy and his proclamations against the French crown be rescinded, that he be tried as a heretic, and that the Order of Templars be examined. Philip had borrowed heavily from the order and now wanted to liquidate his debt and seize what assets he could; consequently, he charged the Templars with heresy, idolatry, and immorality and pressed the pope to condemn them. Clement temporized as long as he could, but finally, at the church Council of Vienne (1312), in order to avoid condemning Boniface VIII (who was exonerated), he dissolved the Templars and allowed about five dozen of them who had confessed under merciless torture to be burned at the stake. In a dramatic climax to this sordid affair, Templar Grand Master Jacques de Molay called from his death pyre for the pope and king to join him before the judgment seat of God within the year. Both died within a matter of months.

The years from 1309-1377, when the popes resided at Avignon, were sad ones for the church. Abandoned by the papacy, the city of Rome was thrown into a state of turmoil, lawlessness, and neglect; and respect for the church plummeted as its vices, venality, and corruption became increasingly evident. Papal revenues were not as certain as in the past – not merely because of a loss of support, but because of the changing economy. Until nearly the end of the 13th century, the church's wealth, like that of the nobility, had been largely in the form of land. With the rise of the new money economy, however, there came a need for liquid assets – for cash – in order to support the growing costs of church administration and a luxurious papal court. Annates, amounting to the first year's revenue from a benefice, were demanded, and revenues from vacant sees were reserved for the papacy. Little wonder that popes were generally in no hurry to make new appointments! Little wonder also that when a new bishop was designated, he might be one transferred from another see, leaving a vacancy that could be exploited for further funds. Papal pardons, dispensations, and audiences were granted for monetary payments, indulgences began to be sold during the crusades and created a scandal, and benefices were reserved for the highest bidder and sold to favorites and those who could afford them. Consequently, wealthy men would sometimes acquire several benefices or spiritual offices. Unable to be present everywhere, they became absentee bishops and, therefore, could not look after the spiritual needs of their dioceses. Monks were sometimes indolent and ignorant, concubinage of the clergy was not at all uncommon, papal judgments were rendered in exchange for fees that were difficult for the common clergy to pay, and avarice was evident on every hand: every sin seemed to have its price either for dispensation or absolution.

That there should be mistrust in European capitals of a church administration so ostentatious, led by a succession of French popes, and situated almost within French territory is not surprising, and the church's policies did little to allay these apprehensions. Pope John XXII (r.1316-1334) did everything he could to enrich the papal fisc and vigorously intervened in German and Italian affairs. Ultimately, however, he found himself unable to impose his will by use of excommunication and other tactics that had proved successful in the past.

Allied with one of the emperors against John were the Spiritual Franciscans and several theologians who asserted that the papacy had betrayed its trust and should be brought under the authority of a general church council, while John's heavy-handed attempts to control Imperial politics prompted a reaction from the German princes. In 1338, they emphatically declared that they would not tolerate papal intervention in Imperial elections. Pope John even suffered the humiliation before his death of having the University of Paris repudiate as heretical a doctrine he had supported.

English opposition to the Avignonese popes was particularly obdurate since the crown did not want to pay taxes to a pope seemingly dominated by its enemy, the king of France. On the whole, Englishmen supported Edward III (r.1327-1377) who withstood papal demands for payment of the "Peter's pence," declaring: "The Vicar of Christ is supposed to lead God's people to pasture, not to fleece them."

The crown also tried to outlaw papal appointments, without royal assent, of officials from the curia or other foreigners (some of whom remained absentee bishops) to English sees, and endeavored to restrict appeals from ecclesiastical courts to Avignon without the king's consent. The royal statutes promulgating these restraints did not always end the stipulated abuses, but they did enable the monarchy to confiscate part of the spoils.

Although papal interference in the internal affairs of the church in England was markedly less than in the Holy Roman Empire, there had long been complaints against the luxury and moral laxity of the clergy. The literature of 14th-century England reflects this disillusionment – Geoffrey Chaucer's *Canterbury Tales* being a good example. The avarice, worldliness, and immorality of the clergy brought for them a widespread lack of respect. The wealth of the church also attracted unfavorable attention, as did its exercise of the "benefit of clergy," whereby churchmen and affiliates of the university communities apprehended in crimes were tried in episcopal tribunals whose sentences were usually lighter than those imposed by royal courts. Denouncing these perceived abuses and also representing the royal position against payment of the "Peter's pence" was an Oxford don named John Wyclyf (d.1384). Thus, nationalism and calls for church reform went hand in hand, enabling Wyclyf – protected by John of Gaunt, who was acting as regent for the aged monarch – to speak his mind without undue fear of retribution from the church.

Wyclyf called for a return to a simple Christianity, for an end to episcopal pretensions to temporal power and to the concept of papal supremacy, and for disendowment of church wealth not used for spiritual purposes. He even denied the efficacy of pilgrimages and the veneration of the saints. He questioned the clergy's power to grant absolution for sins, attacked the doctrine of transubstantiation, and questioned the sacraments as a means of grace, especially when administered by sinful priests. His appeal was to the authority of the Scriptures, and he aided and encouraged the translation of the Bible into English. Moreover, he founded the Lollards – lay preachers (most of them trained at Oxford University) who carried their message into the countryside and towns, continuing this mission even after Wyclyf's death. Wyclyf's ideas and his work *De Ecclesia* (On the Church) were appropriated later by a young Bohemian preacher named John Hus (c.1369-1415) and, therefore, continued to reverberate.

In the meanwhile, the lamentable worldliness of the church and its crumbling prestige caused moral pressure to mount for the return of the papacy to Rome. Recognizing that the Holy See could not command the broad respect it desired so long as it seemed tied to France, and heeding the urgings of Catherine of Siena (1343-1380), Pope Gregory XI (r.1370-1378) did relocate to Rome in 1377. Unfortunately, his death in the following year, precipitated a further scandal. The newly-elected pope, Urban VI (r.1378-1389), quickly antagonized the French cardinals, causing them to defect and to elect a rival, Clement VII (1378-1394), who established his administrative residence at Avignon.

Now there were two popes (and after 1409, three), each claiming to be the sole Vicar of Christ on earth. During this great papal schism that continued until 1417, successors to deceased pontiffs were quickly elected by their respective adherents, while the nations lined up with one "pope" or another as suited their national interests or dispositions. Countries believing the popes at Avignon were tools of the French monarchy – England, most of the German states, Bohemia, and Flanders – sided with Rome, while France, Scotland (which was at war with England), and the Kingdom of Naples (frequently at odds with Rome) acknowledged the Avignon popes, as did Spain after some hesitation. However, within the various countries, rival bishops arose, while monetary levies by each claimant to the see of St. Peter increased because of the narrower tax base, bearing down heavily on supporters of either.

The schism promoted skepticism in all circles concerning the oneness and purity of Christ's body. Consiliarism – the concept that the entire body of Christ was best represented in a general church council that should determine major church policies and assign their administration to a pope – was reconsidered. However, the first attempt to implement such a solution (1409) failed, eventuating in three popes rather than two.

Schism and scandal within the church lent credibility to the calls for reform issuing from numerous quarters, not the least Bohemia. Here John Hus preached passionately against clerical abuses, earning for his honesty the enmity of the Archbishop of Prague. Alienation from the Archbishop became final when Hus, along with Czech nationalists at the University of Prague, prevailed on their king to revise the charter, so that Czech rather than German professors would control the University. The king, resentful of attempted church interference, stood by Hus when the Archbishop excommunicated him. Thus, Hus, like Wyclyf before him, enjoyed the support of his king. As a matter of fact, Hus agreed with much of what Wyclyf had written, though not *in totum*. He was a popular preacher at the Bethlehem Chapel, where he presented his messages in the Czech vernacular. He believed that the civil authority needed to supervise the church, denounced indulgences, denied the infallibility of immoral popes, asserted the primacy of Scripture, and gave the Eucharist cup, as well as the bread, to the laity. Hus agreed to appear before a church council at Constance to answer charges of heresy after being guaranteed a safe conduct to and from the council by the Emperor Sigismund (r.1411-1437). Once there, however, Hus was imprisoned (much of the time in a dank, unlighted cell), subjected to repeated interrogations, deprived of any opportunity to answer his accusers from Scripture at the public hearings, accused of rejecting transubstantiation (which he did not), and sentenced, with the perfidious concurrence of the Emperor, to be burned at the stake as a heretic.

Shortly after Hus's execution, the pope who had summoned him to appear before the Council of Constance (1414-1418) was himself deposed; and by 1417 the fiasco of schism ended with the deposition or resignation of all claimants and the election of Martin V (r.1417-1431). The Council also provided for convocation of regular church councils, but by mid-century the consiliar movement expired, and unrestrained papal monarchy was revived.

In the meantime, successive crusades led by the Emperor Sigismund against the followers of John Hus were hurled back time and again until a rift among the Czechs caused them to accede to a compromise that allowed the cup to the laity. Czech nationalism continued to burn, however; and Hussitism, though suppressed, was not dead. Its influence would be manifested in reform movements to come.

Chapter VIII

HUMANISM REVIVED: THE "RENAISSANCE"

The medieval church – already weakened by internal squabbles, corruption, economic shifts to which it was struggling to adapt, new political realities that undermined its influence, and doctrinal challenges – was also confronted by an unprecedented cultural and intellectual ferment arising in the Italian city-states. The papacy, whose patrimony was centered in the peninsula, could not ignore this "Renaissance" as it was called – essentially a rebirth of ancient humanistic modes of thought and expression – and, indeed, soon found itself, to a significant extent, affected by its assumptions and infiltrated with its devotees.

Why, one may ask, did the Italian peninsula become the cradle of the Renaissance and the locus of contention between a God-oriented world-view and a man-centered philosophy? No certain and definitive answer can be made, of course, but a few observations appear to be pertinent. It should be remembered, for example, that Greek, Jewish, Arab, and Christian cultures had long intermingled in the southern portion of the peninsula, even receiving considerable encouragement during the reigns of the Emperor Frederick II (d.1250) and Angevin King Robert of Naples (1309-1343) – onetime host of Bocaccio (d.1375), admirer of Petrarch (d.1374), and patron of learning and translators of Greek manuscripts. Upon Robert's death, however, the cultural eminence of Naples ended (leaving a slight residual influence in the rest of the peninsula) as incessant strife between claimants to the throne supported by rival popes turned the kingdom into a feudal backwater.

On the other hand, northern Italy, where the Renaissance blossomed forth, had never been brought under the sway of feudal monarchs. The Holy Roman Emperors had endeavored to impose their rule, but the north-Italian city-states did not want any feudal monarch telling them what to do. Their trade had never been stifled to the extent that it was north of the Alps. Their economy was absolutely incompatible with the self-sufficient manorial economy characterizing the feudal regimes, and they wanted no part of it. Geographically, the Italian city-states were located advantageously to carry on trade in the Mediterranean, so that, once Moslem dominance was broken, their economies began to thrive. The resulting prosperity enabled cities, rulers, or wealthy individuals with a surplus of money to patronize or subsidize literature and the visual arts and provided men of means with sufficient time to enjoy the new forms of cultural expression.

Successful management of commercial enterprises necessitated some knowledge of practical affairs, the ability to read and write, and some skill at bookkeeping and accounting; therefore Italian merchants were generally literate, keen-minded, forward-looking men. Moreover, a considerable degree of individual freedom was required by anyone engaging in commerce, cloth production for the export trade, or banking, as was also a degree of judicial or administrative autonomy. It might almost be said that the very conditions of the times created a particular type of person – men interested in acquiring wealth and enjoying the fruits of it, hard-headed, individualistic men who were deeply involved in the day-to-day affairs of their businesses or city government. Many were civic-minded, with their loyalties being focused on their own city or locale, so that a great spirit of individualism, independence, and self-reliance may be observed.

Rivalry between the various city-states ran high, and wars were frequent. The most important political entities were the republics of Venice and Florence, Milan (which was ruled by a despot), the feudal kingdom of Naples, and the clerio-feudal papal monarchy; but city-states abounded in northern Italy under diverse forms of government.

Urban civilization had long been a hallmark of this sector of Italy. Even the nobles had lived in towns from the 13th century onward, so that the aristocracy influenced and was influenced by the cultural milieu of the cities rather than by the atmosphere of isolated feudal castles. City life was more conducive to cultural pursuits than were the courts of noble barons north of the Alps. While the latter were not devoid of pageantry and chivalrous amusements, their outlook was essentially traditional, not subject to the challenges of new thoughts and patterns of life spawned by the urban environment of northern Italy, whose cities were not only centers for commercial intercourse but for the exchange of ideas. Well-to-do merchants and entrepreneurs, eager to add luster to the names of their houses, would commission artists, sculptors, metal workers, and skilled artisans to produce commemorative monuments or works of art; and popes, city bosses, and despots wishing to enhance their positions and strengthen their political hegemony patronized humanist scholars to grace their courts, defend official policies with their pens, or serve as diplomats or administrative secretaries.

Most of the early humanists were products of a physical and intellectual environment that differed in certain respects from that prevailing outside the Italian peninsula. A number of universities had sprung up north of the Alps during the 12th, 13th, and 14th centuries, but they stressed religious thought, theology, and scholastic philosophy concerned with things of the spirit and the life to come. In Italy, on the other hand, universities such as Bologna and Naples emphasized legal studies, public administration, rhetoric, and practical politics in this present life. The very climate of sunny Italy seemed to favor a love of pleasure (though this was certainly not lacking in courtly circles elsewhere), and the ubiquitous ruins of ancient Rome were poignant reminders of the grandeur and glory of a great civilization whose presence was still felt by every imaginative and curious-minded Italian.

The early humanists (those of the 14th century such as Petrarch and Bocaccio) helped to revive an interest in antiquity and strove to recover manuscripts. As time went on, humanists (persons interested in the humanities) did not merely preserve classical writings but studied Greek and Latin authors and sought to emulate them. Indeed, the later humanists tried to pattern their own writing style after that of Cicero, so that flowery written expression and colorful oratory became more important than content during the 15th century.

Since the humanists imbibed ancient pagan thought, their own thought patterns were generally secular in tone; and before long, the "here and now" became more important to them than the world to come. The history of mankind was important, and the dignity and individuality of man were stressed. Man was master of his own destiny, according to a number of humanists, including Niccolò Machiavelli (1469-1527), Florentine statesman and political observer. Success or failure was not determined by Divine intervention but by man's own capacities, and nobility was not a matter of one's birth but a product of his character. The ideal person would be versatile – a true "Renaissance Man," skilled in writing and the social graces, in conversation, in the arts, as well as in athletics. He would be the universal man, the man who could do all things well. While some humanists were Christian, the majority of Italian humanists did not let their religion bother them too much. To many of them, meditation upon man's ultimate end was no longer of major importance; for man had not only the next world to contemplate but this present life to enjoy.

Most humanists were not at the universities; they were writers – literary men, diplomats, civil servants, advisers to rulers, and secretaries or abbreviators for popes. By the 15th century, however, there were also humanist professors teaching the Greek and Latin classics in most of the Italian universities. Coincidentally, a number of notable humanist educators established themselves outside the universities, taking students into their homes to be taught under the tutorial system. Promising young men who could not afford to pay for their education would sometimes be permitted to do odd jobs in exchange for their board and room; thus, the boarding school concept of education was inaugurated. The advent of humanist educators brought an end to the church's monopoly on education. To be sure, this fact should not be overemphasized, because students continued to flock to universities offering clerical training; but now there was an alternative. In the humanist schools, the humanities, anatomy, physical education, the arts, and moral training were included in a curriculum that stressed the "whole man." Man's knowledge need no longer to be limited chiefly to theology and law; man's mind and body were important as well as his spirit. Henceforth, the classical writers and pagan philosophers of antiquity would be studied and appreciated for their own sake, not just to lend credibility to church doctrines. Moreover, practical studies in mathematics became more important than in the past, for men of affairs could benefit from them.

Late in the 15th century, the vernacular tongue began to be employed afresh in writing, after a hundred-year interval of stilted Latin. Translations of literary and religious works into the common tongue and the invention of movable type in mid-century helped to popularize the new thought patterns, encouraged literacy, and made a steadily increasing volume of printed material available to the non-scholarly reading public.

A great change also was evident in art themes and styles. Humanistic themes had crept into this means of cultural expression, which had once been virtually controlled by the medieval church; and even religious themes were, more often than not, handled in a humanistic fashion in paintings or sculpted marble that revealed man as he was, without any apologies. The nude form, proper perspective, naturalism, dramatic use of light and shade, and application of principles of unified composition began to be stressed. Art was no longer exclusively didactic – it need not be employed for the sole purpose of teaching some doctrinal truth, engendering piety in the faithful, or pointing men to God: it was now appreciated as a pleasurable aesthetic expression that could be appreciated for its own sake. Artists now were respected as men possessing special talents or artistic genius; no longer were they looked upon as mere craftsmen, nor was the church their only patron.

The scope of man's interests vastly broadened during the age of the Renaissance, and his aspirations and thoughts began to undergo a tremendous change. Still, many of the old patterns and ways remained, though they were now leavened by the yeast of Renaissance culture and weakened thereby. Sad to say, the papacy, a great patron of humanist learning, was not immune to these worldly attitudes and manifestations; and the church continued to concern itself with temporal affairs that sometimes brought it into conflict with the secular rulers, who viewed the pope as a foreign prince. Even some of the humanists in papal service scoffed at church practices, ridiculed scholasticism, called into question church doctrines, and expressed skepticism about its mission. For example, Poggio Bracciolini (1380-1459), a longtime employee of the curia who publicly defended the policies of Rome, made no attempt to conceal his contempt for the clergy and made cynical remarks about church beliefs and practices. Although barbs of this sort were injurious, bringing opprobrium upon the church and fostering mockery that discredited and weakened it, popes continued to hire *literati* and to overlook their indiscretions. The church even sponsored humanist writing projects and cultural undertakings that diverted it from its spiritual mission and diluted traditional doctrines.

Much of the syncretism of religious thought was the product of organized scholarly undertakings. At the Medici court in Florence, Marsilio Ficino (d.1499) was honored, given a villa, and paid to head a Platonic Academy. He translated numerous Greek classics into Latin – among them Plato's *Dialogues* and the works of Plotinus – and presided at regular meetings of the Academy, to which interested discussers were welcomed. One ardent participant was the precocious young humanist philosopher Pico della Mirandola (1463-1494) who, after exposure to Averroëistic philosophy, the mystical theosophy of the Jewish *Cabala*, and Platonic philosophy, determined to compose a synthesis of all religions, based on the premise that all reflected a single truth. In support of his thesis, he set forth 900 *Conclusions* on which he invited debate. In his introductory "Oration on the Dignity of Man," Pico exalted human potentiality far beyond biblical teaching. To the credit of the Holy See, thirteen of his propositions were declared heretical, but humanists had already introduced so much from the *Cabala*, the Zoroastrian oracles, and Hermetic Gnosticism that the syncretism infecting the church could not be reversed.

The church's departure from the exclusive "narrow way," prescribed by its Founder and Head, by accommodating to pagan philosophies and trying to effect change through political involvement – relying on the "arm of flesh" rather than proclaiming clearly and unequivocally the salvation message entrusted to it – plunged it to new depths of degradation, mirroring in its humanistic trough (see the diagram in Appendix I) the abominations of ancient Greece and Rome.

Worldly rather than spiritual interests became increasingly apparent in the lives and policies of pontiffs such as Sixtus IV (r.1471-1484), Innocent VII (r.1484-1492), Alexander VI (r.1492-1503), Julius II (r.1503-1513), and Leo X (r.1513-1521). Sixtus was an able scholar and patron of the arts to whose initiative can be credited restoration of many bridges and buildings in Rome and construction of the Sistine Chapel. However, he engaged in unconscionable nepotism, conferring lucrative benefices upon numerous relatives and appointing religiously unqualified, impious men to the College of Cardinals in an attempt to consolidate papal control over the central portion of the peninsula. To this same end, he conspired to overthrow the unofficial ruling house of Florence – the Medici – in a nefarious and bungled plot resulting in the murder of one Medici cub, injury to Lorenzo the Magnificent (1449-1492), and a temporary unsettling of the peninsular balance of power.

Sixtus's successor, Innocent VII, encouraged a rebellion against the king of Naples but pursued a more sensible and pacific foreign policy after his son married a daughter of Lorenzo de' Medici. He kept a pretender to the throne of the Turkish Empire in custody, receiving money for his upkeep from the Sultan, who also agreed to leave Europe in peace so long as the pope did not back the claims of his rival. Innocent continued the restoration and beautification of

Rome, advanced his children as best he could, created new offices whose sale would enrich papal coffers, and established a bank of pardons and dispensations for the same purpose.

The need to obtain money to pursue an ambitious foreign policy led Alexander VI not only to sell church offices at exorbitant prices, but to seize properties of deceased prelates with unseemly haste. Reasonably successful in protecting church properties in Italy from the incursions of the French and a munificent patron of painters, sculptors, and builders, Alexander VI, nevertheless, was a fornicator and adulterer whose most notorious children – Cesare and Lucretia Borgia – epitomized the amoral and immoral atmosphere prevalent in Rome. With his father's backing, Cesare headed an army and employed murder, deceit, and treachery of all sorts to bring as much territory as possible under papal hegemony. Machiavelli, sent by Florence to negotiate with Cesare, could not but admire the ruthless, unscrupulous means by which Cesare conquered and ruled. Machiavelli's book *The Prince*, setting forth how rulers should conduct themselves to gain and retain political power, reflects, in chilling detail, Cesare's brand of power politics.

In point of fact, Machiavelli had a more than adequate number of political exemplars of "the end justifies the means" in addition to Cesare – other Italian despots and Ferdinand the Catholic of Spain among them. Even stern, resolute Pope Julius II, who led troops against papal foes in person, could have provided Machiavelli a military model of success. Julius continued the support of artistic projects characteristic of humanist popes, prevailing upon aesthetic geniuses such as Raphael (d.1520), Bramante (d.1514), and, most notably, Michelangelo (d.1564) – often against his will – to fulfill papal commissions.

Julius's successor, Leo X, son of Lorenzo de' Medici, did likewise. Generous, epicurean, and a lover of art and literature, Leo was less concerned with spiritual matters than with cultural pursuits and diplomacy – at which he was cunningly adept. His military and diplomatic forays as well as his luxurious court and his determination to rebuild Saint Peter's in Rome necessitated extraordinary revenues that he attempted to raise by every means at his disposal, including simony and the sale of indulgences.

Protests against corruption, greed, and irreligion within the church were not entirely absent in the Italian peninsula, where the excesses tended to be viewed cynically but with passive resignation; but they were rare. To be sure, humanist scholars like Lorenzo Valla (1407-1457) exposed as forgeries documents such as the "Donation of Constantine," which upheld church claims to temporalities in the Italian peninsula; but few *literati* were sufficiently concerned (though they may be skeptical of corruption and venality within the church) to mount an attack. Most were content to devote themselves to literary pursuits while enjoying papal or ecclesiastical largess.

Nevertheless, there were several disenchanted churchmen who deplored the flood of secularism swamping the church. Best known, perhaps, is Girolamo Savonarola (1452-1498), an ascetic and passionate Dominican friar who fearlessly preached against vice and pagan practices, denouncing in the process both Lorenzo de' Medici and Pope Alexander VI. Bolstered by Florentine supporters appreciating his courage and the manner in which he secured the withdrawal of a French army in 1494, Savonarola became *de facto* ruler of the city for several years. He called for reform within the church, established a theocracy, declaring that Jesus Christ was the rightful sovereign of Florence, and instigated a collection of "vanities" – costly garments, false hair, cosmetics, jewelry, games of chance, popular literature, objects of art considered to be immoral, and the like – to be burned in the public square. Excommunicated by Alexander VI for his temerity and insubordination, Savonarola zealously continued to preach against idolatry, harlotry, vice, avarice, and worldliness within the church until a loss of public support brought him down. Accused by the citizens of overthrowing their constitution and by the church of collusion with foreign powers, heresy, and conspiracy to depose the pope, Savonarola was tortured and finally led to the *piazza signoria*, where he and two followers were hanged from a gibbet and roasted to death as boys pelted them with stones. His austere insistence on holy living, simple and confident faith in revealed truth, and belief in supernatural occurrences and blessedness in the life hereafter had proved unfashionable and incapable of satisfying the yearnings and aspirations of men and women exposed to the intellectual stimulus and titillation of the pagan classics and the sensual pleasures of a thriving society increasingly oriented toward man's enjoyment of the present world.

Chapter IX

REFORMATION CURRENTS

North of the Alps, humanism came later than in the Italian peninsula, not making much of an impact before the latter decades of the 15th century. Moreover, it was shaped by traditional German piety, and many German humanists received training in institutions founded by the Brethren of the Common Life, which propagated the "new learning" within a distinctly Christian framework. For these reasons, therefore, German humanists, on the whole, were not as inclined to assimilate the pagan attitudes from antiquity as were their Italian counterparts. Like them, they saw much that was wrong within the medieval church, but they wanted to do something about these problems and used their knowledge of classical languages to study, not so much the pagan classics as works of the church fathers and ancient scriptural manuscripts. Scholarship in Hebrew was not without its risks, as Johann Reuchlin (d.1522) discovered. In upholding the benefits to be derived from Hebrew studies, he brought upon himself a lawsuit and difficulties with the church – a fact that prompted negative reactions from linguistic scholars and attacks upon ecclesiastical narrow-mindedness.

When humanists castigated the church of their day for its abuses and obstructionism, they usually did so by trying to demonstrate how contemporary beliefs and practices differed from those of the early church or from biblical norms. The church, they contended, had become wealthy and powerful and out of tune with the simple teachings of Jesus Christ. Therefore, many church tenets, traditions, ceremonies, teachings, and conventions began to be viewed as non-essential, unscriptural accretions by humanists dedicated to the study of the biblical languages and church history. It was their contention that contemporary practices were far removed from those of the early church and should be purged. The abuses that were all too evident within the church lent credence to these charges.

Some German humanists – John Wessel of Gansfort (d.1488) is a good example – went so far as to disparage the authority of priests to assign penances.

Unless the heart was truly repentant, he asserted, even the Mass would be received in vain; on the other hand, if there were true contrition, the external ritual was superfluous. The church, according to Wessel, was composed of saints known to God alone; therefore, the pope and the visible church were unnecessary. Indeed, neither the pontiff in Rome nor the ecclesiastical hierarchy were infallible. It was the Bible, not the church, which provided the rule of faith.

Numbered among the northern Christian humanists were Frenchmen like Jacques Lefèvre d'Étaples (d.1536), Englishman John Colet (d.1519), and, most importantly, Desiderius Erasmus of Rotterdam (d.1536). Erasmus was educated at Deventer in a school of the Brethren of the Common Life. As he delved into God's Word, he concluded that the original text was sometimes obscure in the Vulgate edition; consequently, he produced a Greek New Testament based on the Greek manuscripts available to him, accompanied by a Latin translation. This momentous work, improved by corrections within a few years, was almost immediately consulted by scholars who carried the translation a step further, preparing vernacular editions of the entire Bible that made it comprehensible to the literate man in the street. Erasmus also heaped criticism upon clerical pride and immorality, excoriated "spitters" of syllogisms," satirized in his *Praise of Folly* all manner of abuses and observance of external forms, and called for a return to the inner piety and elementary practices of the primitive church. Erasmus's works were widely read and respected, and a number of reformers – including Juan de Valdes (d.1541), Juan Luis Vives (d.1540), John Oecolampadius (d.1531), John à Lasco (d.1560), and Ulrich Zwingli (d.1531) – were deeply influenced by him; yet the learned Dutchman stopped short of breaking with the Roman church, remaining within it, though aware of its weaknesses and errors, in the hope that exposure of ecclesiastical malfeasance and the proper education of churchmen would bring about reform.

Erasmus's expectations were not entirely without foundation. Church scandals were relatively few in the Iberian peninsula, where Ferdinand of Aragon and Isabella of Castile had completed the *Reconquista* by conquering the last Moorish stronghold of Granada in 1492. In what they considered to be the interests of national unity, they instituted the Spanish Inquisition – not only to stamp out any heretical currents, but as an instrument to subordinate recalcitrant nobles to the royal will. Employed against Jews and any Christians considered unorthodox, the Inquisition made religious dissent extremely dangerous and therefore rare. Under the Catholic monarchs, an intense nationalism arising from the *Reconquista* marched hand in hand with religious orthodoxy as propagated and enforced by the reform-minded Franciscan scholar-primate Francisco Ximénes de Cisneros (d.1517). As confessor to the queen, Archbishop of Toledo, sometime regent of Castile, and later Inquisitor-General and Cardinal of Rome, Ximénes exercised tremendous influence. He instituted the University of Alcalá where the *devotio moderna* or new learning was taught and the so-called *Complutensian Polyglot* was prepared – the first complete Bible presented in its original languages along with translations that could be compared. Because of the Cardinal's herculean efforts, the blatant forms of ecclesiastical abuses evident elsewhere were largely avoided.

Reform currents could even be observed in small groups established in sophisticated and skeptical northern Italy, where a Genoan layman named Hector Vernazza had founded the "Oratory of Divine Love" as early as 1497. Members of this society promoted private devotions and charitable work among orphans, the poor, and sick. Reform-minded men were attracted to the Oratory, and similar societies were established in several key cities, including Rome and Venice. The latter Oratory gave rise to the Theatines – an order founded by Gaetano da Thiene, that dedicated itself to devout living under a vow of poverty that permitted no begging, engaged in preaching and teaching to check the spread of heresy, and provided loving care for orphaned children, the sick, and the needy.

While the salutary example and work of these and other small religious organizations helped to retard the church's decline, it would take much more – in fact, a revolution – to bring significant reform, so corrupt had the church become and so implacably determined to defend the established system to which most high churchmen were attached by reason of their careers, reputations, or monetary considerations. At the crucial moment, however, in the German states, where resentment concerning the replacement of traditional legal customs with Roman law and princely disenchantment with both Imperial and papal authority were generating a spirit of nationalism, an uncompromising man of God appeared – an Augustinian Eremite monk named Martin Luther (1483-1546).

Luther was a professor of biblical studies at Wittenberg University, founded by Saxon Elector Frederick the Wise (d.1525). From the days of his youth, Luther had been painfully aware of his own sinful inability to meet the requirements of a holy and awesome God. This realization caused him much spiritual torment until his study of the book of Romans brought the liberating realization that Jesus Christ had manifested the Father's eternal love by submissively taking the punishment for everyone's sins in His death on the cross. Christ's sacrifice and subsequent resurrection, Luther suddenly perceived, guaranteed eternal salvation to all who would receive their Savior by faith; for "the just shall live by faith" (Habakkuk 2:4 and Romans 1:17). Although it took some time for Luther to think through and work out all the logical consequences of this doctrine, he eventually became convinced that good works, fasts, pilgrimages, and even the sacraments were unnecessary for salvation – that justification before Almighty God came only through man's acceptance by faith of Jesus Christ and what He had already accomplished. From his further studies, involving Scripture and the writings of Paul and Augustine, Luther was strengthened in the conviction that faith frees the repentant sinner from the bondage of sin and that free and unmerited Divine grace makes him righteous and wholly acceptable in the eyes of God.

Luther's concepts almost inevitably led him to criticize some of the church's practices arising from the doctrine of good works. But the issue that led to his open protest and eventual break with the church was the matter of indulgences. In church doctrine, indulgences were tied up with the system of obtaining absolution by which a penitent sinner could obtain forgiveness of sins. There were four steps through which the sinner must go: (1) contrition, (2) confession, (3) penance, and (4) absolution. Once forgiven, the penitent sinner was free from the guilt of his sin and the fear of eternal damnation. However, he still might suffer the consequences of his sin in this world and also might suffer punishment for it in purgatory.

Plenary indulgences that would remit the need for further penance, even for sins not yet committed, so that the soul could pass on to its final beatitude, could be granted by the church, it was taught, out of a "Treasury of Merits" earned by Christ and the saints. Plenary indulgences had been bestowed upon knights going on crusade in order to attract men to join in these hazardous undertakings, and gradually partial indulgences came to be offered to those who contributed to the crusades. Later, indulgences were dispensed to those making pilgrimages or performing other good works until, in the 14th century, Boniface

VIII and the Avignonese popes began to accept monetary payments as constituting the major part of the necessary good works. In the 15th century, this practice was made applicable even to the souls of the departed, requiring only a monetary payment. The common people believed that purchasing indulgences would free departed loved ones or themselves from the punishment and guilt of sins, aside from any penance; and all too often the professional hawkers of indulgences did nothing to disabuse them of this erroneous opinion. A popular saying summarizes their view fairly well:

> "As soon as the coin in the coffer rings,
> The soul from purgatory springs."

The matter of indulgences came to a head when Albert of Brandenburg, already head of two episcopal sees, became Archbishop of Mainz, making him the primate for the Holy Roman Empire and one of the seven electors. To purchase the Archbishopric, Albert had paid an enormous sum – much of it borrowed from the Fugger banking house of Augsburg; and he needed some means of raising sufficient funds to repay the debt. At the same time, Pope Leo X was looking for a means of securing money to rebuild St. Peter's basilica in Rome. An arrangement was made, therefore, whereby indulgences would be preached in northern Germany by the Dominican John Tetzel, with the proceeds being split between the Pope and the Archbishop-Elector of Mainz, whose portion was to be kept by the Fuggers in repayment of his debt.

Although Frederick the Wise had prohibited the sale of indulgences in Saxony, a number of Luther's parishioners were going across the border into Thuringia to purchase them; and, subsequently, many would not bother to show up in church. By this time, Luther had begun to make a distinction between *penance*, the satisfaction for a sin committed, and *repentance*, a change of mind and heart. It was the latter, he felt, that was necessary for salvation.

Luther determined, therefore, to call attention to what he considered to be an abuse by inviting public academic disputation on the subject of penance and indulgences. Accordingly, about noon of All Saints' Eve (October 31, 1517), he nailed his "Ninety-Five Theses" to the doors of the University Church of Wittenberg.

These posted propositions, which were quickly prepared in printed form and disseminated throughout the German states, contended that the church could remit penance only for what it had imposed on earth, that the pope had "no jurisdiction over purgatory," that the dogma of the "Treasury of Merits" was questionable and too obscure to be presented to the people, that indulgences were "pernicious" in that they induced complacency ("a false sense of security") and thereby imperiled salvation, and that it was not right for a pontiff, who could afford to expend his own vast wealth for rebuilding St. Peter's, to suck money away from "all Christendom" (and from poor Germans who could never hope to attend the basilica) for this purpose. "Better that it should never be built than that our parochial churches should be despoiled."

Leo X did not immediately recognize the gravity of the situation, calling the theses the fantasies of a drunken monk. A papal warning was conveyed to Luther, of course, but the Emperor Maximilian's death in 1519 necessitated careful handling of the German electors, one of whom was Luther's prince. Luther was, therefore, left alone for the time being, while his ideas – thanks to the printing press – were gaining increasing popularity in Germany and were being circulated in most of the capitals of Europe. A debate at the University of Leipzig between Luther and Professor Johann Eck (d.1543) of the University of Ingolstadt simply added fuel to the controversy. It was not until after the election of the King of Spain to the Imperial dignity as Charles V (r.1519-1556) that the pope belatedly issued the bull *Exsurge, Domine*, warning the Wittenberg professor to abjure his heretical concepts within 60 days or be excommunicated.

In the meantime, Luther had published an appeal to the German princes to take a hand in reforming the church and now wrote other treatises that effectively explicated his views: the priesthood of all believers (no intermediary between God and man was necessary), the preeminent authority of Scripture rather than the pope or church traditions, justification by faith alone, and limitation of the sacraments to the two – baptism and the Eucharist – specifically prescribed in the Bible. Luther denied that Christ was sacrificed anew in the Mass: His sacrifice on Calvary, he said, was efficacious once and for all time. Transubstantiation of the Eucharistic elements was also rejected, though Christ was really present in and under the bread and wine; doctrines concerning indulgences and a "treasury of merits" were dismissed; the cup should be given to the laity; and laymen, as well as clergymen, were called by God and should serve faithfully in the vocations in which they were involved.

If the pope thought that condemnation of Luther's dissident views and the threat of excommunication would silence him, he was mistaken. Luther received the minacious bull in October of 1520, purported that it had been forged by Johann Eck, and ceremoniously burned it at the city dump, along with a copy of canon law. The die was now cast. A papal bull of excommunication was quickly issued only to be returned to Rome by the papal legate because it condemned, not only Luther but Ulrich Von Hutten, a German nationalist whom at that moment it would be imprudent to offend; consequently, the bull was not published until about 10 months later. In the meantime, newly-elected Emperor Charles V – shocked that a monk should openly challenge the authority of the papacy, thereby jeopardizing unity within both church and Empire, yet conscious of the support Luther enjoyed from the German populace and some powerful nobles – summoned him to appear before the upcoming meeting of the German Diet at Worms. The order was couched in careful language and included the Emperor's guarantee of safe conduct to and from the convocation because Charles, beset with unrest in the Empire and faced with a Turkish threat on his eastern frontier, did not wish to affront the Saxon Elector or to aggravate Luther's other supporters. Still, Luther recalled that a similar guarantee of safe conduct had been given, slightly more than 100 years previously, to Czech reformer John Hus with whose reform sentiments he was closely identified. He knew that he, like Hus, might be burned at the stake; yet he bravely informed his prince:

> "If Caesar calls me, God calls me. If violence is used, as very well it may be, I commend my cause to God. He lives and reigns who saved the three youths from the fiery furnace of the king of Babylon, and if he will not save me, my head is worth nothing compared with Christ. This is no time to think of safety. I must take care that the gospel is not brought into contempt by our fear to confess and seal our teaching with our blood."

Presenting himself before the Diet in April of 1521, Luther acknowledged authorship of the pile of books placed before him – not disavowing any; and, when pressed to repudiate the "errors" within them, he boldly replied:

"I will answer without horns and without teeth. Unless I am convicted by Scripture and plain reason – I do not accept the authority of popes or councils, for they have contradicted each other – my conscience is captive to the Word of God. I cannot and I will not recant anything, for to go against conscience is neither right nor safe. God help me. Amen."

When further attempts to elicit concessions from Luther failed, he was permitted to leave for Wittenberg as the Emperor had promised. Within a fortnight, Charles had the Diet place him under the Imperial ban as an excommunicated heretic (actually excommunication had not yet been published by the church) not to be harbored by anyone. His followers were likewise condemned, and his books were to be burned. Already, however, Luther had been spirited away to the Wartburg castle, belonging to Frederick the Wise, where he was kept in protective custody for almost ten months. While there, Luther kept in touch with events, directing his Wittenberg followers as best he could (even paying them a secret visit on one occasion), and devoted himself to writing and prayer. His paramount accomplishment during this period was his translation of the New Testament into the common tongue, making it comprehensible to every literate German and incidentally contributing to the development of a standard German language. Translation of the entire Bible had to await his return to Wittenberg.

Henceforth, Luther's life's work was to consolidate the new church that he had founded. To that end, he tempered the iconoclastic proclivities of some of his followers; reformed the liturgy and order of worship in the Wittenberg parish church; composed hymns; helped produce a creed – the Augsburg Confession – and two catechisms; and, with the aid of his chief lieutenant, Philip Melancthon (1497-1560), established a strong educational system. He died in 1546, shortly before the eruption of the religious wars that would rend the German states for almost two decades.

There can be little doubt that Martin Luther – through his well-publicized challenges to the Roman church, his eventual break with it (though reform was all he originally intended), his new doctrines, his emphasis on preaching and liturgical reforms, his making the Bible available in vigorous, intelligible German, and his establishment of Lutheran schools – unleashed a religious revolution that provided Protestant alternatives to Roman Catholicism, effected reforms, and turned peoples' eyes once more toward God (see the diagram in Appendix I).

What accounts for Luther's success, and why did the religious revolution begin in the German territories rather than elsewhere? No definitive answers to these questions can be made, but a few observations may be in order. As we have seen (p.55), Spain – with its burgeoning nationalism tending to coincide with religious orthodoxy, its crown-sponsored Inquisition determined to eliminate religious or political dissent, and its relative freedom (owing to the work of Cardinal Ximénes) from egregious forms of clerical decadence and misconduct – was not as susceptible to reform currents as were other countries.

France also was somewhat inured to such currents – though certainly they were not absent – until after religious revolt was fairly far advanced in the German states. In part, this insensitivity was due to a Gallicanism expressed in documents such as the Pragmatic Sanction of Bourges (1438) and the Concordat of Bologna (1516) that enhanced royal control over the French Church and distanced it from unwanted papal domination. Furthermore, the French peasantry was relatively prosperous and satisfied – less susceptible to social unrest than the German peasantry and therefore less apt to affiliate themselves with movements, religious or otherwise, against the established order. Toward the end of the 15th century, the Cluniacs, other monastic orders, and reform-minded bishops sought to clean up abuses, while John Standonck, head of the Collège de Montaigu in Paris, and Cardinal Georges d' Amboise pressed for reforms. The Cardinal's reform of the mendicant orders was carried out under the aegis of the king. The crown normally upheld "Gallican liberties" and, because of its growing centralized authority, was able to exercise considerable influence in religious matters that enabled reform-Catholicism to flourish under the impetus of Christian humanists Guillaume Budé (d.1540), Lefèvre d'Étaples, Guillaume Briconnet (d.1533), and others. Under the circumstances, there was no great hue and cry against the church in France before the time of Luther.

Much the same was true of England, which since the time of Wyclyf had tried to conduct its affairs without interference from Rome. An anti-French, anti-papal nationalistic bias prevailed during most of the 14th century when the popes resided at Avignon, and the Tudor monarchs did not take kindly to outside influence from Rome or, for that matter, from any quarter. Henry VII (r.1485-1509) actually oversaw many of the affairs of the English church and was a generous benefactor of the universities of Oxford and Cambridge while effectively promoting English trade and industry, so that the people's concern about religious matters was rather minimal. This would change, of course, under Henry VIII (r.1509-1547), who sparked a religious revolution of his own for personal and political reasons; but by that time the Lutheran Reformation in the German territories was well under way.

As for the Italian peninsula, several powers – including the Holy Roman Empire, Spain, and France – were contending there, but papal influence remained dominant in religion and culture. Dissidents such as Savonarola could be dealt with rather summarily in most cases, while intellectuals, calloused to ecclesiastical corruption, which was seen so closely as to become almost commonplace, usually chose to remain silent or at least prudent in expressing their opinions. To a large extent, the prosperous, secular society of northern Italy kept much of the populace content, while the cultural Renaissance tended to divert attention from spiritual matters and provided a sort of safety valve that relieved pressure harmlessly.

Conditions were quite different in the Holy Roman Empire. While the old feudal baronies were rapidly becoming weaker or even disappearing in England, France, and Spain as powerful kings centralized their control over their respective realms, political fragmentation remained the norm in the German territories and central Europe. In the Holy Roman Empire – largely confined to the German states and Bohemia by the end of the 15th century – more than 300 sovereignties existed. These included the German principalities (among them a number of episcopal sees) and Imperial free cities. To be sure, all of them rendered a nominal allegiance to the Holy Roman Emperor, but in actuality conducted themselves as autonomous sovereignties according to what they conceived to be their individual interests.

In prior centuries, every time an Emperor died, rival claimants would vie for the Imperial title by trying to line up support from fellow rulers. Thus, competing factions arose and warfare was almost inevitable until 1356 when Emperor Charles IV (r.1346-1378) regularized Imperial elections by issuing a "Golden Bull." According to this document, the most powerful princes of the

Empire – the King of Bohemia, the Duke of Saxony, the Margrave of Brandenburg, the Count Palatine of the Rhine, and the Archbishops of Mainz, Trier, and Cologne – were accorded the right to choose a new Emperor.

The fact that the Imperial title was attained by election rather than through hereditary right caused each aspirant to make concessions to the electoral princes in the hope of securing their support. Under these circumstances, the princes gained more and more rights and liberties while Imperial authority continued to decline. After 1437, Habsburg princes were almost invariably elected as Holy Roman Emperors, chiefly because the bulk of their hereditary possessions lay toward eastern Europe, thus compelling them to defend the eastern frontier against the Turks or other enemies. Still, their election was not merely a foregone conclusion; for the Imperial office must be purchased with promises, concessions, and monetary bribes that not only debilitated it, but often stretched Habsburg financial resources to the limit.

Even after his election, the Emperor was not able to implement policies on his own initiative. His authority was limited by a *Reichstag* or Diet composed of the electors, the lay and ecclesiastical princes, and representatives of the free cities. The Diet jealously guarded princely prerogatives and would not even grant funds for defense of Imperial territories except in time of dire and imminent peril. Consequently, the Emperor was obliged to curry the favor of all the great princes, while sustaining his administration and foreign policy with taxes exacted from his own hereditary holdings or with large sums of money borrowed from the Fuggers or other banking houses.

The fact that the Holy Roman Emperor reigned over a loose amalgamation of largely independent territories rather than heading a strong, centralized monarchy helps to explain why Charles V was unable to quash the Lutheran "heresy." By enjoying the support of many of the princes – especially those in the north German territories – Luther was able to consolidate his reform movement despite papal appeals to the Emperor to crush it.

Intellectually, the way had been prepared for Luther's revolt by German humanists who had debunked Thomist scholasticism, denounced church corruption, and criticized the papacy for exacting exorbitant revenues from the German states. An inchoate nationalism was arising to which German humanists such as Conrad Celtis (d.1508) and Jakob Wimpheling (d.1528) contributed. In the case of Celtis, there was apparently only a desire to inculcate or stimulate a sense of national pride and loyalty within his countrymen, but the anti-foreign tirades of Wimpheling did not spare the papacy. The German humanists also appealed for a return to what they imagined to be the "pristine purity" of the early church. Moreover, it may be recalled that Erasmus's Latin translation of the New Testament based on Greek manuscripts renewed the intelligentsia's interest in scriptural studies.

Luther himself consulted Erasmus's work while preparing his own German translation of the New Testament. The influence of Luther's German Bible, rendered in the everyday language of the people, can hardly be overstated nor, for that matter, can the impact of the printing press, which made Luther's pamphlets, broadsides, leaflets, and writings of all types quickly available to the literate masses. Although Luther was not the first to urge church reforms – Wyclyf, Hus, and Savonarola (to mention only three) had preceded him – he was the first to be able to disseminate his challenge widely through the printed word. As we have seen, he also founded a school system that helped perpetuate his reforms, thanks to his scholarly friend and ally Melancthon; and Luther's hymns, composed to folk music and dance tunes to encourage congregational singing, doubtless popularized his movement.

One should not overlook, of course, the personal leadership of Luther – a courageous, determined, hardworking professor who knew how to appeal to incipient German nationalism in the pungent and even coarse language of the common man. Scholars had made cerebral appeals for reform before his time, and the 14th-and-15th-century Rhenish mystics had espoused a direct spiritual union with the risen Savior that served to undercut the priest-dominated sacramental system of the Roman church. However, none had taken their case to the people as did Luther, nor did any predecessor go as far as he. It is very difficult to believe that a less gifted, less fervent, and less courageous person could have succeeded in carrying out such a far-reaching religious revolution.

From the very first, Luther's writings appealed to the energetic German burghers and to the princes, whose military support ultimately assured the success of his movement. For a short time, even downtrodden farmers favored Luther's works, because they mistakenly interpreted his treatise entitled *On the*

Liberty of the Christian Man as an appeal for social freedom and justice. Although Luther lost much of the peasants' support after he insisted that the German princes suppress the peasant revolt of 1525, he still retained the support of a broad segment of German society.

Not all the princes accepted Lutheranism purely out of religious conviction. The fact is that some of them sought to obtain political and economic advantages by declaring themselves to be Lutherans. By doing so, they could not only halt the outflow of tithes and other monies to Rome but also confiscate and secularize church lands and properties. Moreover, by eliminating ecclesiastical courts, they could increase the scope of their judicial jurisdiction.

Therefore, for practical as well as pious reasons, German princes found Luther's cause attractive, making it almost impossible for the Emperor to halt the movement. As a matter of fact, Charles V, though a devout Catholic, did not always see eye-to-eye with the papacy. Because of this, the tenuous nature of his position, and the fact that he was kept busy for almost twenty years fighting on two fronts against France and the Ottoman Turks, he adopted a conciliatory policy toward his Lutheran vassals, needing their assistance as well as that of his Catholic nobles against his enemies. Only in 1546 was he free to take military action against Lutheran forces, and by that time it was too late: Lutheranism was already solidly established. The Lutheran princes allied with France and fought Charles's armies to a standstill. By the Peace of Augsburg signed in 1555, Lutheran and Catholic princes were to have the right to determine the faith of their subjects, who could make the choice of adhering to the state religion or migrating elsewhere. Henceforth, most of the north German states became Lutheran, while the Danubian territories ultimately remained Catholic.

Outside Germany Lutheranism had its greatest impact on the Scandinavian counties where religious reform marched hand in hand with nationalism, but Lutheran ideas permeated all of Europe, contributing to religious ferment that frequently resulted in resistance to Rome and institution of new creeds, practices, and forms of Christian worship.

Were all of these intricate influences and circumstances the product of mere chance? Were they determined by the activities of men alone? To the

Christian historian believing in the sovereignty of God as the Creator and Sustainer of mankind, the entire natural order, and the universe, the answers to both propositions is a resounding "No!" Although historians customarily explain causes and effects (much as we have done) in terms of the "facts" of which they are aware and consider worthy of note, arranging them in a logical, interpretative pattern, the Christian historian – if he thinks biblically – must realize that the explanations just presented deal only with secondary causes that are subordinate to the eternal decree of God, though in some manner (not always apparent to man) instruments of it. History has meaning because of the divine decree, a decree effecting an eternal purpose that confers significance on every event and human action. Not all human actions are in accord with the Creator's perfect ways or His desire for man's well-being, but He is so loving and wise as to allow man to make his own decisions and to act as he wills, and is great enough to orchestrate everything to effect His eternal purpose. Thus, all human actions and events are brought together, shaped, and coordinated by Providence in such a way that the Divine will is ultimately realized. Renaissance man and the church had departed from God to an alarming degree; yet even in their selfish and prideful waywardness, they could not escape His superintendence. If men chose to damn themselves by rejecting Him, they could do so and suffer the consequences (which He desired that they be spared); but they could not alter or subvert His eternal decree. Had religious and cultural developments of the Renaissance been different or had men not given so much latitude to their humanistic proclivities, esurience, ambitions, and self-serving actions, perhaps God would have permitted matters to occur and develop in a different way. But this is to beg the point; for His "ways are past finding out" (Romans 11:33), though His Word does say that "where sin abounded, there grace did much more abound" (Romans 5:20). The omnipotent, longsuffering, patient Creator may allow matters to run their course up to a point but never beyond His power to restore. At any rate, the true believer in Divine Providence can rest in the assurance that He took what measures were necessary – in the milieu of the time – to restore the balance, without infringing man's free will, to keep everything under control. In this case, drastic measures were required – to the point of fracturing the body of Christ; and God raised up a Luther to bring it about. From the degraded man-centeredness of the Renaissance, there was, if only for a relatively brief period of time, a return to an upward view and a concern for godliness (see the diagram in Appendix I) and a purified faith in the eternal God portrayed in the Bible.

In the wake of Luther's break with the Roman Church, other Protestant movements arose. Ulrich Zwingli instituted reform doctrines in Zurich that spread to various urban cantons in Switzerland and to Strasbourg and other cities in the German Rhineland. For a time, it appeared that a religio-political alliance might be forged with the German Lutherans, but disagreement on one matter – the real presence versus the symbolic presence of Jesus Christ in the Lord's Supper – prevented it. Left on their own, the reformed Swiss cantons were unable to prevail against a coalition of the Catholic forest cantons and Austria in a civil war that took Zwingli's life. By the Peace of Kappel (1531), each canton was permitted to choose its own religion, so that religious division in Switzerland was sealed.

The reformed faith was finally consolidated there by the work of Jean Calvin (1509-1564), a French humanist scholar converted to the reformed faith. His *Institutes of the Christian Religion*, at first published in 1536 (final edition, 1559), propounded a systematic and logical theology emphasizing the total depravity of man because of original sin; man's inability to keep God's law and thereby to attain salvation through good works; salvation by faith in the redeeming sacrifice of the incarnate, divine Christ, who had been slain for the sins of all mankind; and the awesome majesty and power of God – the omnipotent, omniscient, omnipresent Creator of the universe who knew whom would be saved or damned according to His predestination. Calvin joined Guillaume Farel (d.1565) in trying to institute reform in Geneva. At first their stringent mandates were not well received, and they were compelled to leave; but Calvin returned in 1541 and, after years of arduous work and opposition from "libertines," he succeeded in establishing Geneva as a "holy city" under a "theocracy" that, nevertheless, recognized the benefits of commercial activity and fostered growth of representative government. Because it was simple and easy to install, Calvin's polity was adopted in other parts of Europe, and his constitutional principles were eventually applied in the New World.

Calvinism was introduced into Scotland by John Knox (d.1572), who managed to oust the Catholic queen and establish a Presbyterian Scottish Kirk. It also took root in France, where its persecuted adherents – the Huguenots – fought a series of religious wars against the crown and ecclesiastical authorities until accorded toleration and specified rights under the Edict of Nantes, issued by Henry IV (r.1589-1610) in 1598.

Calvin's influence was felt in England, though the Anglican Church, established by Henry VIII and confirmed by Elizabeth I (r.1558-1603), proved more congenial to the English temperament and preferable to a monarchy forced to cope with a strong Catholic minority, dissident Protestants, and the possibility of foreign invasion.

In the Lowlands, Calvinists vied with Catholicism, Erasmian influences, and Anabaptism, and led an insurrection against Catholic Spain. Their co-belligerents from the southern (Belgian) provinces gave up the struggle in 1579, but the Dutch fought on to achieve virtual independence by 1609. The faith that sustained the Dutch in their fight for freedom was rent for a time, but after the Synod of Dordrecht (1609), orthodox Calvinism prevailed in the Dutch Reformed Church.

It should not be supposed that religious turnabout was limited to Protestantism. As we have seen (pp. 54-55), there were scattered initiatives for reform from within the Roman Church prior to (or almost coincidental with) the Lutheran revolution. However, the papal curia was loathe to end abuses whose abrogation might bring a sizable decrease in monies flowing into Rome; and, in view of the material benefits accrued from having the church administration in Rome, most sophisticated Italian leaders and rulers – though aware of ecclesiastical malfeasance – were adverse to disturbing the *status quo*. However, shock waves emanating from the rupture within the church in Germany alarmed bishops Gasparo Contarini (d.1542) and Giovanni Pietro Caraffa (d.1559). Contarini hoped to restore church unity by implementing practical reforms and seeking doctrinal reconciliation with Lutheran dissenters, while Caraffa, who eventually became Pope Paul IV (r.1555-1559), wished to squelch all dissidents, as was being done in Spain, make an end to abuses, and reform the priesthood. Reform was also the object of the Observant Franciscans, who founded the Capuchin Order in 1526 to preach and minister to the masses and to conduct missions even beyond the Italian peninsula.

One of the major thrusts for reform was started by a former Spanish soldier, Ignatius of Loyola (d.1556), who was converted while recuperating from a severe wound. He dedicated himself wholeheartedly to the service of Christ and the church, frequently mortifying the flesh through fasting and prayer and, at the age of 33, commencing a resolute quest for an education. After completing his elementary studies, he attended the universities of Alcalá and Salamanca for brief periods of time, running afoul of the Inquisition while at both institutions because of his zeal. After being cleared of suspicion, he completed his education at the Collège de Montaigu in Paris. While there, he attracted a band of disciples who joined in practicing his "Spiritual Exercises" of purging the flesh and soul, contemplating the life of Christ and His mission as Savior of the world, identifying with His sufferings, uniting spiritually with the resurrected and ascended Lord, and submitting to His direction to win men from Satan to Christ. The "Exercises" were aimed at inspiring, after meditation, a sort of mystical exaltation by which men might be constrained to dedicate their lives.

In 1534, Ignatius and six followers vowed to observe perpetual celibacy and poverty in God's service. Among these men was Francis Xavier (d.1552), who later died in Asia after carrying the Gospel to India, the East Indies, and Japan. Their dedication included a promise to accept no fees after becoming priests, and to go to the Holy Land to convert Moslems. If this should prove impossible, the men promised to place themselves at the pope's disposal. In order to prepare himself for service, Ignatius, after ordination, spent an entire year in solitude, consecrating his life to God.

When he and nine companions met to carry out their vows, Venice was at war with Turkey, rendering it impossible to go to the Holy Land. Therefore, Ignatius and two members of the group journeyed to Rome where Ignatius's order – the Society of Jesus – received official sanction from Pope Paul III (r.1534-1549).

The aim of the Jesuit Order was to carry salvation to others, instruct youth, strengthen the faith, and defend it against heretics. Young men wishing to join the Order must spend two years studying and practicing the "Spiritual Exercises." At the end of this period, the more worthy novices took the vows of celibacy, poverty, and obedience and became *scholastici*. These *scholastici*, after twelve years of rigorous education in theology, science, and the humanities in Jesuit colleges, were ordained as priests. If they succeeded in measuring up to all tests and took the fourth vow of absolute obedience to the pope, they were admitted to the central element of the Order.

An overall leader or general of the Order was chosen by the general congregation to hold office for life. Also chosen were heads of provinces and rectors. These officials, although having absolute jurisdiction within their particular fields, were watched closely by agents of the general congregation. The organization and discipline of the Society of Jesus emulated military patterns.

In 1550, Ignatius, the first general of the Order, set up the *Collegium Romanum* to train priests by his methods. Two years later, the *Collegium Germanum* was also established in Rome for the same purpose. Other colleges were soon opened; and, owing to its fervent missionary activity, the Society of Jesus composed, by Ignatius's death in 1556, twelve provinces – spread throughout the world from Europe and Latin America to Asia. The Jesuits tended to purify the teachings of the church and institute internal reform. To effect their program, they established a uniform system of education in all Catholic countries, concentrating their efforts on secondary education as well as on training exceptional young men for the priesthood in their colleges. Besides this and their widespread missionary activities, the Jesuits preached and heard confessions, directing the consciences of the penitent and instilling orthodox beliefs and devotion to the church in the minds of the young. They became particularly influential as confessors to princes and kings, who not infrequently sought their advice on much more than religious matters. Jesuit influence was also strongly in evidence at the Council of Trent, which finally proscribed a number of church malpractices and raised a doctrinal standard to which adherents could rally.

Convocation of a general church council had been delayed for years, because the curia feared such a gathering might usurp papal authority. On the other hand, Emperor Charles V – painfully cognizant of the religio-political rifts within the Empire – had repeatedly urged Clement VII to convene a council in the hope it would adopt reforms that would mollify his Lutheran vassals. Even the German Catholic estates had pressed for a church council, but the pontiff had remained obdurate until the sack of Rome by Imperial forces in 1527 weakened his position. Reluctantly, he admitted that a council should be called. Nevertheless, he entertained not the slightest desire for a church council that he believed might limit his power or infringe on his prerogatives. He, therefore, continued to vacillate and procrastinate.

The fact that he had allied the Holy See with Francis I (r.1515-1547) made him even more disinclined to call a council; for the French king – at war with Charles – had never wanted a council for the very reason that the Emperor desired one. Besides, Francis reasoned, why should he assent to a council that might bring about reconciliation between German Lutherans and Catholics? This was certainly not in his interests. Although peace was concluded between the King of France and the Emperor in 1529, the political realities remained the same. Faced by a serious threat from the Turks on his eastern frontier, Charles needed the support of all his nobles – Catholic and Lutheran – and again appealed for the pope to convene a general church council, while Francis I cleverly weakened the Emperor's position by allying with some of the German Lutheran princes. Thus, Charles was in no position to force the issue of a church council. For these very involved reasons (note that human machinations do have an affect on history), it was not until after the death of obstructionist Clement VII that any progress toward convocation of a church council was made.

With the election of Alexander Farnese as Pope Paul III (r.1534-1549), hope arose that something might be done; for the new pope appeared sincerely interested in reform. In fact, in January of 1535, he expressed a desire for a council and sent legates to the principal courts of Europe to obtain their consent in regard to time and place before calling for a council to meet at Mantua in the spring of 1537. In the meanwhile, Pope Paul had appointed a commission to study needs for reform whose membership included cardinals Contarini and Caraffa, Englishman Reginald Pole (d.1558), and Jacobo Sadoleto (d.1547) – all advocates of reform. The results of the study were presented to the pontiff in March of 1537. The *Plan for Reforming the Church*, as the report was called, said that papal laxity and greed were responsible for the vices of simony and nepotism, that the popes had looked upon church properties as their personal possessions, and that they appointed inferior men to bishoprics and important posts. It was recommended that appointments should be made on the basis of merit and suitability, that there should be no reservations, that remote bishoprics or benefices should not be granted to prelates who could not possibly serve them, and that priests should be adequately prepared before being ordained.

The Pope had the document discussed in his presence but deferred any action upon its recommendations pending a church council. By the following year, it became a source of some embarrassment, to the extent that the curia forbade its publication. Copies continued to circulate, however; and Protestants occasionally cited the report as vindicating their contentions.

As for the scheduled church council, it was delayed for various reasons and finally suspended indefinitely. Similarly, a council called for Trent, an Imperial city located just north of the Italian frontier, had to be postponed for almost three years because of renewed hostilities between France and the Emperor. However, an attempt at religious reconciliation, favored by the Emperor, did take place at Regensburg in 1541. Here Catholic and Protestant spokesmen met to try to resolve their differences, but the colloquy foundered on the issue of the sacraments.

It was, therefore, only after numerous failures and delays that a general church council began to deliberate at Trent late in 1545. Even so, the first assembly proved to be only one of three taking place in different periods of time – 1545-1547, 1551-1552, and 1562-1563 – and under three different popes. The council was strictly a Roman Catholic affair and dominated by the papacy since only bishops and heads of religious orders in attendance – mostly Italians – were permitted to vote. For the most part, traditional doctrines and practices of the church were defined and confirmed. Scripture and tradition were to be considered equally valid in determining matters of faith and practice; the Lutheran doctrine of justification by faith alone was renounced: works were also important for salvation; the legitimacy of all seven sacraments was affirmed and their efficacy upheld regardless of the character of the ministrant; the doctrines of transubstantiation and the sacrifice of the Mass were reaffirmed, as was also that of indulgences, though abuses connected with their sale were to be eliminated; the Vulgate translation of the Bible was declared to be the only authentic and authorized version; bishops were advised to institute reforms in their dioceses, to establish and supervise seminaries for training the clergy, to supervise the lower clergy, to preach in their dioceses every Sunday or provide for a substitute, and to see to it that no one preached without their permission; provision was made for revision of the *Index of Prohibited Books* introduced in 1559 by Paul IV; and the Inquisition was to be strengthened.

The imprint of Cardinal Caraffa (from 1555-1559, Pope Paul IV) is clearly visible in the spirit and decrees of the Council of Trent, which made no compromises with Lutheran or Reformed doctrines, enunciated traditional dogmas clearly and emphatically, demanded stringent extirpation of clerical abuses, and mandated rigorous standards of conduct and belief. Paul IV did not shrink from employing the Roman Inquisition (reinstituted at his instance more than two decades before his pontificate) in the most relentless fashion against any persons suspected of the slightest religious deviation. A number of prelates suspected of liberal views were accused, subjected to torture in an attempt to elicit confessions, tried in secret by non-juridical procedures, and incarcerated or burned at the stake. Onetime papal secretary Pietro Carnesecchi was incinerated in 1567, and reform-minded Cardinal Giovanni Morone (d.1580) who, as a delegate to the Colloquy of Regensburg, had hoped for reconciliation with Protestants and reunification of the church, was immured until freed by the Pope's death. Suspects in both Italy and Spain (where *autos de fé* – ceremonious burning of groups of "heretics" – were zealously employed) were given short shrift. "Trials" tenaciously sought to validate charges rather than to ascertain guilt or innocence, and sentences were carried out with a matter-of-fact, ruthless efficiency that could not fail to intimidate anyone differing in any degree with Tridentine dogma. Lands and goods of executed heretics were sequestered, and if deceased persons were posthumously judged heretical, the legacies of their descendants would be confiscated. Needless to say, the writings of convicted heretics were burned as a matter of course, but so were any books placed on the *Index* that could be seized. Quite understandable, if not excusable, was the prohibition of books written by Protestants, satires on church practices, and tomes containing salacious material; but censorship of scholarly works allegedly tainted with views inconsistent with what was deemed proper could, in the long run, prove counterproductive. Censorship in the next century of Galileo's *Dialogue on the Two Great World Systems* (1661) is but one case in point. By these severe means – especially Employment of the "Holy Office" – "heresy" was virtually stamped out in Spain and Italy.

If anything, the Spanish Inquisition was more abhorrent than that of Rome. Since the time of Inquisitor-General Tomas de Torquemada (r.1483-1498), the Spanish Inquisition had been used, often at the behest of the monarchy, to attack not only Moors, Jews, and heretics but any noncompliant person on the grounds that his bloodlines were impure. Almost anyone could be hailed before the Inquisition on these grounds, and the very intimation that an investigation might be undertaken was enough to strike terror into the stoutest heart. King Philip II (r.1556-1598) made no pretense of his hatred of Jews, blaming them for the "heresies" that had torn the German states asunder. Shortly after ascending the throne, he used the Inquisition to eliminate Jews and Christians whose beliefs were suspect, burning thousands of Jews and Protestants (who were often said to have impure, that is Jewish or Moorish blood in their veins) between 1559 and 1565, most of them in *autos de fé*. He also introduced the Inquisition into the Lowland provinces, sparking a rebellion against Spanish rule by his Flemish and Dutch subjects.

In the German states, the endeavor of rewinning territories infected by Protestantism was more formidable than in Spain and Italy, but a succession of able popes wisely entrusted the task to the Society of Jesus. Within a short time, many schools and colleges were founded by Dutch Jesuit Peter Canisius (d.1597) and others, which played a significant role, along with Canisius's catechism and energetic preaching, in bringing wavering South German states back into the Catholic fold. Owing largely to the work of the Jesuits, the Roman Church was able to consolidate its position in most of the region and ultimately to re-win Poland and Bohemia; but northern Germany, the Scandinavian countries, the Dutch Netherlands, England, and Scotland remained Protestant. Catholicism continued to predominate in Ireland, while France suffered a series of devastating civil wars before Catholicism reestablished its supremacy.

Chapter X

RELIGIOUS DISUNITY AND POLITICAL REPERCUSSIONS

By the end of the 16th century, the religious fervor that had marked the early stages of the Protestant revolution had begun to subside. In part, this was to be expected as the freedom to follow their beliefs without interference from Rome became accepted as a matter of course, causing formerly militant members of the Lutheran or Reformed faiths to be less alert or more concerned with earning a livelihood than in the contentious earlier years. Spiritual decline was manifested in the tendency of most Protestant groups to turn inward – to look primarily to promoting their own religious agenda without being properly concerned about evangelism. In contrast with the zealous missionary efforts of the Franciscans, Dominions, and Jesuits, the Protestants – with a few exceptions – were rather slow, if not apathetic, about actively carrying out Christ's great commission. Indeed, it sometimes appeared that Protestants devoted more time and energy to contending with one another than to propagating the Gospel. Squabbles between Lutherans and Calvinists, the major rivals, were particularly disagreeable. In fact, their antipathy for each other sometimes seems to have equaled their contempt and hatred for the "Romanists," making it easier for the Jesuits' determined and well-organized efforts to succeed.

Animosity extended beyond the larger denominations. Catholics and Protestants of almost every stripe generally favored toleration in areas where they were weak, but did not practice it where they were in control or in the majority. Especially vulnerable were Anabaptists – owing to their pacifism, refusal to participate in civil government, and ardent pursuit of radical religious and social reforms – and Antitrinitarians. Both groups were persecuted unmercifully by Catholic and Protestant rulers as injurious and potentially destructive of political and religious order.

A few voices for toleration were heard, but not many until the savagery and senselessness of the devastating religious conflicts – culminating in the Thirty Years' War (1618-1648) – engendered revulsion against religious intolerance. Not surprisingly, disillusionment set in among believers while non-believers and freethinkers attempted to discredit Christianity with charges of hypocritical and barbarous conduct. Worst of all, the incessant warfare, with its incredible brutality and carnage, desensitized soldiers and non-combatants alike, particularly in Germany, and brought moral and spiritual decay.

It was in this climate of spiritual malaise when Protestants were hardened by warfare, lax in proclaiming the gospel, and vulnerable to the attacks of intellectuals, that many began to develop a sort of "fortress mentality." Sometimes this attitude was understandable, if not altogether warranted. In France, for example, the Huguenots constituted a tiny minority, residing for the most part, in territories protected by walled towns. These sanctuaries had been allowed under the Edict of Nantes to guarantee that Huguenots would not suffer persecution. Over the years, however, and especially after the assassination of Henry IV in 1610 when central administration was weak, these fortified cities had become almost autonomous. Louis XIII (r. 1610-1643) had not been able to cope with the Huguenots or other disruptive nobles during his minority, but when Cardinal Richelieu (r.1624-1642) became his chief minister in 1624, matters began to change. Richelieu was determined to centralize authority in the hands of the crown. He suppressed the recalcitrant Huguenots by force of arms, depriving them of their fortifications while continuing to allow them freedom of conscience.

Sad to say, the crown's guarantees proved meaningless in the next generation under King Louis XIV (r.1643-1715), a determined absolutist. Despite the fact that Huguenots loyally supported the crown, the king began to undermine the Edict of Nantes by the narrowest legalistic interpretations that, in effect, discriminated against his Protestant citizens' civil rights. After 1682, Huguenots were excluded from public offices, economically ostracized, and compelled to billet soldiers in their homes whose flagrant excesses went unpunished.

In the meanwhile, Louis had also taken steps to minimize papal influence in France. He declared his right to collect revenues from vacant sees and to dispense benefices within them and had the Bishop of Meaux, his court preacher and advocate of royal absolutism – Jacques Bénigne Bossuet (d.1704) – draw up the *Four Gallican Articles*, which were proclaimed by a Council of the French clergy in 1682. These articles declared that the pope had no jurisdiction in temporal matters, that a general church council was superior to the Roman pontiff, that the liberties of the French Church could not be infringed, and that papal decisions regarding the Gallican Church could not be promulgated without its approval.

Bossuet assiduously supported his king on all religious issues and, as tutor to the Dauphin, wrote a *Discourse on Universal History* (1681) that recognized the sovereignty of God in human affairs. Imbued with Gallican propensities, he generally sympathized with the Jansenists, austere followers of the predestinarian tenets of Augustine (as enunciated in the *Augustinius* written by Cornelius Jansen [d.1639] of the University of Louvain), who lived lives of sobriety and piety and accused the Jesuits of laxity. Ultimately, however, despite his admiration for Jansenist writers, Bossuet joined with the Jesuits and Francois de Salignac de La Mothe-Fénelon (d.1715), Archbishop of Cambrai and tutor of the king's grandson, to expose what he considered to be heretical ideas in Jansenism. He also opposed the Quietists, whose emphasis on contemplation and inner devotion appealed to such notables as Mme. Guyon (d.1717) and Fénelon. Certain Jansenists also wrote against the Quietists whose mystical practices appeared to threaten the sacerdotal system of the church; and their chief proponents were finally silenced.

The king's vendetta against the Huguenots did not let up. He pressed them so vigorously that thousands of conversions were reported by 1685; therefore, Louis alleged that there were no longer any Huguenots and revoked the Edict of Nantes. More than 200,000 Huguenots fled from France – among them many skilled artisans, businessmen, and soldiers – to take up residence in Prussia, the Swiss cantons, England, the Dutch Netherlands, her colonies in South Africa, and the English colonies in America. From an economic vantage point, their departure was costly, though religiously and legally France officially became once again a country of one faith.

Nevertheless, a rift remained within the French Church between Jansenists and Jesuits. The Jansenists – under the leadership of Mother Angélique, Abbess of Port Royale in Paris and patroness of a group of laymen and clerics who took up residence in the old Port Royale nunnery outside Paris and founded schools for boys – fostered morality, truthfulness and following one's conscience with conviction and dignity. Mother Angélique's brother, Antoine Arnauld (d.1694), wrote a treatise entitled *Concerning Frequent Communion* in which he upheld the sanctity of the Eucharest but criticized confessors who allowed worldly persons to receive it without proper preparation. The Jesuits, ensconced as confessors at the royal court, forced Arnauld into retirement by falsely charging that his treatise denigrated the Eucharist.

In mid-century, a new Jansenist champion arose – the brilliant mathematician Blaise Pascal (d.1662) – whose *Provincial Letters* (1656-1657) accused the Jesuits of casuistry, allowing people to be absolved from their sins on the basis of subtle and evasive excuses rather than requiring sincere repentance and heartfelt contrition. In making his point, Pascal quoted selections from Jesuit writings verbatim, much to their discomfort; consequently, the "letters" were placed on the *Index* to minimize their influence. Unfortunately for the Jansenists, certain clergymen and aristocrats, who had been connected with the Frondes (rebellions) against the monarchy, espoused their cause, thereby discrediting it in the eyes of the court. After Mother Angélique's death in 1661, increasing pressure was brought to bear on the nuns at Port Royale, who were compelled to sign a *Formulary* renouncing five propositions emphasizing irresistible Divine grace on pain of having their convents closed. However, pressure from Rome moderated for a time after prominent Jansenist bishops favored the Vatican's position on certain church vs. state issues.

The controversy resumed toward the end of the century, owing to the publication of Pasquier Quesnel's (d.1719) *Moral Reflections on the New Testament*, which accentuated the irresistible power of God's grace, the fruitlessness of human effort, the identification of sin with self-love, strict observance of the Sabbath, the sublimity of suffering persecution for righteousness' sake, the futility of abstaining from sin merely to avert punishment, and the necessity for every Christian to have direct access to the Bible. Alarmed by the growing popularity of Jansenism, the pope issued a bull in 1705, insisting that the *Formulary* be strictly enforced. Opposition to the bull arose from the Archbishop of Paris, Louis Antoine Noailles (d.1729), and other clergymen on the basis of Gallican principles, but this Gallican-Jansenist coalition of expedience was thwarted by the collaboration of pope and king. Earlier a defender of Gallican liberties, Louis XIV, in his latter years, had come more and more under the influence of his morganatic wife – Francoise d'Aubigne, Mme. de Maintenon (d.1719) – who wished to eliminate any religious currents she considered out of line with mainstream Catholicism.

Accordingly, Louis urged the French church to approve Clement XI's (r.1700-1721) bull *Unigenitus* (1713), which denounced Quesnel's *Moral Reflections* with the intent of laying the Jansenist movement to rest. In the end, the king had his way – overriding all opposition by accepting the bull shortly before his death in 1715. It was registered by the *Parlement* of Paris in 1720.

Still, though officially condemned, Jansenism continued to exert a powerful influence on French thought. This was not only felt within certain segments of the clergy, but also within the economically powerful middle class. The *parlements* likewise tended to be both Jansenist and Gallican in their sympathies. Jansenism, therefore, continued to exercise a significant impact even after its official demise and helped to educate a political opposition to absolute monarchy in the course of the 18th century. Furthermore, the Jansenists had aroused opposition to the Jesuits that was not to subside until after the expulsion of the Society of Jesus from the realm in 1764.

No kingdom was immune to sharp religious differences or strife – England perhaps least of all. Although Elizabeth I had managed to consolidate the Church of England, there remained many dissenters – Catholics, Presbyterians, Baptists, Puritans, and others. The impolitic policies of James I (r.1603-1625) and Charles I (r.1625-1649) brought religio-political opposition to a head in 1639, resulting in two civil wars (1642-1648) that forever changed the constitutional character of the realm. Independents and Puritans under Oliver Cromwell's (d.1658) leadership beheaded Charles I and established a Commonwealth, and later a Protectorate, that accorded unprecedented religious toleration (even to Jews but not to Catholics whose loyalty was suspect), suppressed insurrections in Scotland and Ireland (where determined opposition was met with ruthless force), and improved England's political and economic position abroad. However, the Protectorate failed to allow political freedom and the moral latitude desired by the majority of citizens.

Reaction set in after Cromwell's death, and the executed king's son was invited to take the throne under stipulations set forth by Parliament in 1660. For a short time after the "restoration" that installed Charles II (r.1660-1685) as king, many people – especially Anglicans and the gentry – favored him and welcomed relaxation of former restrictions on theater-going, public drunkenness, dueling, swearing, gambling, cock-fighting, and immoral practices. It presently became apparent, however, that the king and his supporters were simply repressing a different segment of the citizenry, because they did not hesitate to enforce religious uniformity and punish non-conformers such as John Bunyan (d.1688) with imprisonment. These measures, the licentious nature of Charles's court, and his secret treaty with France calculated to reinstitute royal absolutism and the Roman Catholic faith, began to alarm members of Parliament. They and other influential Englishmen were wary, therefore, when his successor, James II (r.1685-1688), openly acknowledged his Catholicism and undertook, not only to extend religious rights to Catholics but to place them in high positions in the Anglican Church, the government, the army, and the universities.

By 1688, Parliament had enough; and when it was announced that James had sired a son to be his successor, Parliament invited James's daughter and her husband – Dutch Stadtholder William of Orange – to assume the throne under stipulated terms. The so-called "Glorious Revolution" of 1688 was effected without armed conflict. James fled to France, while William III (r.1688-1702) and Mary (r.1688-1694) acceded to the throne as constitutional monarchs, subject to restrictions on their authority specified in a "Bill of Rights." In the following year, freedom of worship was accorded to all religious denominations except Catholics and Unitarians.

The settlement came too late to prevent the emigration of a number of Separatists and Puritans to the New World, where they settled along the eastern seaboard of North America. Freed from the religious strife and inhibiting social structure of Europe, they stated in their charters (as did the leaders of all subsequent English colonies) their intention to spread the Gospel, and they founded colleges and seminaries to educate young men to be ministers and missionaries. Their evangelical fervor and initiative contrasted with the general inertia of European Protestants, though their zeal began to flag by the next century. The pietist movement arising in the German states for a time reinvigorated Protestant groups, and the Moravian Brethren and Methodists contributed to the First Great Awakening (at its height between 1740 and 1745 but continuing after that) in the American colonies – a movement sparked by Jonathan Edwards (d.1758) and fueled by the preaching of Englishman George Whitefield (d.1770) and fiery evangelists from several denominations. People thronged to hear them – often at open-air meetings – and thousands wept, humbly bowed, fell to their knees, or prostrated themselves as they repented and received Jesus Christ as their personal Savior. So far-reaching and profound was this religious awakening that all of society felt its salutary affects. Americans were being prepared for the crucible of their war for independence.

England experienced a similar phenomenon under the anointed preaching and educational and social involvement of English revivalist John Wesley (d.1791). Barred from speaking in most Anglican Churches, he and his followers carried the message of redemption through faith in Jesus Christ into the highways and byways, preaching anywhere they could attract a crowd. Methodist schools, orphanages, and other agencies designed to meet the needs of a society just beginning to experience the onset of the Industrial Revolution were established, and oversight of converts was entrusted to competent spiritual leaders from all classes. Other Christian denominations were moved to join the Methodists' efforts to eradicate debauchery, prostitution, gambling, dueling, excessive working hours for children, and the slave trade. Morality improved, governmental corruption declined, some abuses within the established church began to be restrained, and respect for legal authorities increased. Indeed, the grosser excesses of English society portrayed so graphically in the paintings of William Hogarth (d.1764) were curbed to a significant degree, so that it is not unreasonable to postulate that the Wesleyan revival helped forestall a revolution such as convulsed France in the latter 18th century.

Chapter XI

DEISM, RATIONALISM, AND THE HUMANISTIC "ENLIGHTENMENT"

Even though revivalism in America and Great Britain countered the general religious turbulence and decline (see diagram in Appendix I), in both England and on the Continent a surrogate religion already was vying with orthodox Christianity. In the minds of numerous intellectuals, Christianity had shown itself to be hypocritical and bigoted, even violently oppressive, obstructive of scientific inquiry (the church's opposition to the heliocentric theory of Copernicus [d.1543], its disposition of Giordano Bruno [d.1600], and its restriction of Galileo [d.1542] were cited as evidence), and laden with outmoded superstitions.

Deism had its inception in 17th-century England, arising in part from a desire to lay aside some of the religious animosities of the past. Lord Herbert of Cherbury (d.1648) had enunciated a minimal number of beliefs that he said were common to all religions: that there was a Supreme Being to be worshiped, that worship and morality constituted virtue, and that everyone should abandon wrongdoing and expect rewards in this world and the next for righteous deeds.

A desire to seek religious harmony motivated John Tillotson, Archbishop of Canterbury from 1691 to 1694, and other latitudinarian clergymen in the Church of England to seek reconciliation between Puritans, Presbyterians, Anglicans, and all true Christians by minimizing religious differences in an effort to agree on essentials. Theology, they maintained, should be based on logic and strive toward enlightened moderation. Religion should be non-dogmatic, socially oriented, and acceptable to all persons of good will: forms of church government were matters of indifference. The latter premise sounded plausible and was biblically sound if not carried to the point of sacrificing or attenuating cardinal doctrines in a sentimental pursuit of ecumenical unity.

To thinkers disillusioned with theological distinctions upheld by various sects and the strife engendered by all transcendently-sanctioned religions, or to those outraged by what they dubbed "ecclesiastical obscurantism" of recent scientific discoveries, a new basis for religion and ethics was needed – one not dependent upon revealed truth. Scientific discoveries – especially Sir Isaac Newton's (d.1727) demonstration (*Philosophiae Naturalis Principia Mathematica*) that the physical universe was held in equilibrium by laws of motion that could be verified by mathematics – stirred intellectuals to look for natural laws that would pertain to every realm of human endeavor. In that of morals and ethics, an alternative to revealed biblical precepts was proposed by Anthony Ashley Cooper, Third Earl of Shaftesbury (d.1713). He looked to nature as a sure guide, believing that basic harmony existed in this God-pervaded universe, providing a paradigm for human ethics: "what is beautiful is harmonious and proportionable; what is harmonious and proportionable is true; and what is ... both beautiful and true, is ... agreeable and good." Alexander Pope's (d.1734) dictum that "whatever is, is right" reflected this viewpoint, so that the natural order was considered capable of providing moral guidance to individuals that, if followed, would redound to the good of society as a whole.

Deism was becoming increasingly popular in Great Britain and on the Continent. Most Deists were willing to accept Jesus Christ's moral and ethical teachings without acknowledging His divinity or other fundamental Christian doctrines. They were willing to recognize, on the basis of reason, a universal deity that was *Alpha* but not *Omega* – to postulate a "Prime Mover" or "First Cause" that had created the universe in such a way that "natural laws" would govern it without any supernatural intervention. As a moral and intelligent being free to do whatever he willed, man was capable of following his natural instincts in accord with perceived natural laws.

Inevitably, of course, natural religion based on a created order flawed by the fall of man could not provide inerrant guidance. Because of this inadequacy, the very concept of natural religion was bound to deteriorate. While the more conservative Deists believed in a "Prime Mover" and were willing to have the "unenlightened" populace worship a conventional God as a deterrent to vice and crime, devotees of the Roman poet Titus Lucretius Carus (c.99-55 B.C.), whose *De rerum natura* (On the Nature Of Things) was avidly read in the 18th century, saw no need "to hypothesize" a Prime Mover, contending that matter had always existed and that the universe had generated itself and was self-sustaining. Man himself, according to Julien Offray La Mettrie (1709-1751), author of *L'Homme machine* (The Human Machine, 1747), was merely a biological product that might be regarded either as an animal, a plant, or a machine whose mental processes were attributable purely to physical factors. In like manner, Claude Adrien Helvétius (1715-1771) insisted: "Man is purely physical.... Moral man is merely physical man considered from certain points of view.... The soul is only the body itself envisaged relative to a particular one of its functions."

Materialistic assumptions of this sort required some explanation of how man could possess an ethical awareness. Helvétius denied any *a priori* or transcendentally-inculcated moral values (such as those spoken of in Romans 1:18-19 and 2:14), attributing the ethical sense primarily to experiences; for, according to him, man's actions were motivated largely by self-love, moderated by a concern for the well-being of others. Thus, like sensationalist philosopher Étienne Bonnot de Condillac (d.1790), he wished to base human knowledge and actions, not upon what he alleged were non-existent abstract principles, but upon ones arising from sensations and experiences in life. Human beings, Helvétius believed, were molded by environmental influences; therefore, the environment should be manipulated in order to compel men, through a desire to attain pleasure and avert pain or distress, to act virtuously and promote the public interest.

There was no necessity in these materialist philosophies to recognize deity or even any metaphysical principles. Even belief in a depersonalized, beneficent "First Cause" postulated by most Deists, was distasteful to Paul Henri Thiry d' Holbach (1723-1789). According to him, man's nature alone, operating according to mechanistic principles, would bring him enlightenment and happiness; "myths" of a God and a divinely-ordered universe were not only unnecessary but harmful – the main source of human degradation.

Denis Diderot (1713-1784) concurred, although his views on the subject evolved over the years. In his early writings, he seemed to hold to the deistic concept that man could perceive the moral principles found in nature, but by mid-century he was denying any need for moral absolutes – whether Divinely-imparted or observed in nature: instead, morality could be learned experientially through the senses. In some of his latter works – *Le Neveu de Rameau* (Rameau's Nephew), *Le Rêve de d'Alembert* (D'Alembert's Dream), and *Jacques le fataliste* (Jacques the Fatalist) – Diderot assumed a relativistic attitude toward ethics while boldly and cleverly presenting naturalistic views in an apparent attempt to accommodate freedom of the will with scientific determinism. In essence, he believed in a morality grounded in principles of nature that could be discovered scientifically and sociologically and expressed in positive terms. In the last analysis, Diderot believed, one's natural inclinations and instincts would provide a stronger behavioral motivation and sense of duty than any alleged divinely-instilled sense of moral obligation. Therefore, man should be free to discover moral principles empirically, without reference to religious criteria, but should follow his instincts with due concern for the "general will" and the common interest. In effect, then, it was man, not God, who was the measure of all things and who prescribed law and established moral bounds for the benefit of society. It is evident, therefore, that the 18th-century "enlighteners" – whether Deists rationally presupposing laws implanted in nature by a Prime Mover; materialists positing a self-generating universe without transcendent purpose whose inexorable laws controlled everything, including mankind; or empiricists whose ethics were determined by experience – left God out of the equation by disclaiming revealed truth.

From the outset, the humanistic French *philosophes* discarded church doctrines concerning a Creator God whose laws, revealed through Holy Scripture, must be obeyed; but, by the end of the 18th century, few would even defer to supposed universal laws of nature. Man was fully capable, they asserted, of creating his own moral standards, through reason or empirical sensationalism, and they would brook no restraints save those imposed by society or their own judgment. Even society's restraints must not be arbitrary; for its nature, demands, and mores were in a constant state of flux. So it was that the "enlighteners" fell prey to idolatry, confidently and arrogantly following their own relativistic and utilitarian "natural laws" that they interpreted as encompassing all forms of behavior – even aberrant ones – said to result from human nature or instincts.

Thus, we see that the *philosophes*, like the intellectuals of classical times and the Renaissance, propagated a man-centered view of the universe, depicted on the diagram (Appendix I) as a declivity from God. The cultural troughs displayed to represent antiquity, the Renaissance, and the so-called "Enlightenment" reflect a recurring humanistic pattern, though the humanism of each period is somewhat different. For example, Renaissance humanism was not entirely secular in its characteristics and thrust and, in any case, was halted, moderated, or altered (depending on the locale) by the Reformation. Still, Renaissance humanism had derived much of its inspiration from classical antiquity and exuded the same spirit, though in a different milieu that helped shape it and propel it in new directions.

Eighteenth-century humanism followed a more independent course – continuing to manifest the self-confident, man-glorifying, eudaemonistic attitudes of previous humanist movements, but in an accentuated, more extensive fashion claiming a rational and empirical base and leaving nothing outside the scope of legitimate investigation. Though relatively few in number, the *philosophes* exercised a tremendous influence on society, partly because of the changing nature of the times and partly because of their tireless efforts. Diderot's *Encyclopédie*, for instance, was welcomed by a society on the brink of technological breakthroughs and industrialization, and its practicality and popularization of scientific advances and ideas made it particularly appealing to the upper middle class. As the *Encyclopédie* attained wider readership, its scientific emphasis, indirect attacks on Christianity, and subtle propagation of the "gospel of reason" were eagerly received, not only in France but throughout Europe.

For a time, there was opposition from within the French Church to the humanistic, anti-religious currents being disseminated. (As the diagram in Appendix I is supposed to indicate, there is, throughout history, a continuous tension between forces trying to draw man upward to God and those pulling him down, away from his Creator.) However, there was a lack of deep spirituality in much of the French Church and no unity of purpose and action. Internal disputes, especially those between Jansenist sympathizers and the Jesuits, prevented church solidarity and tended to discredit its message of forgiveness, love, and peace. Ironically, after the Jesuits were expelled from France in 1764, their opponents – who had tried for more than fifty years to rid the land of the Society of Jesus – found the task of standing alone in defense of the faith against the *philosophes* impossible. Coincidentally, rifts were widening between Gallican and ultramontane elements within the Church, so that its will and ability to carry out its evangelical mission to win converts and teach them (Matthew 28:19-20) was attenuated, allowing libertines and freethinkers to prevail.

In reality, therefore, the triumph of secular humanism in 18th-century France and the results stemming from it, may be ascribed to the failure of the church to be "salt and light" in society, a lesson that all Christians should take to heart. Our contemporary problems and the current cultural malaise are primarily due to the failure of the church – to its self-centeredness, self-satisfaction, and lack of commitment to its spiritual Head; to its departure from biblical standards; to the jealousy between various Christian bodies and depreciation of Christians who, though orthodox in their beliefs, are of a different denomination; and to its apathy (having "left their first Love") and resistance to the urging of the Holy Spirit to carry out Christ's great commission.

Historians differ concerning what role the "Enlightenment" played in incubating or causing the French Revolution. Most agree that it was not the primary causative factor; yet there is no doubt that its influence was significant. Not only did the *philosophes* wish to unshackle men's minds from "outmoded" Christian doctrines which they termed irrelevant superstitions occlusive of free inquiry; not only did they ridicule all formal religious creeds; they also undermined traditional morals, recklessly excoriated political and social inequalities, and, in short, weakened the bulwarks supporting the French monarchy and society. In doing so, they cited examples from England, where institutions and political reforms predicated on Christian principles were developing.

They also expressed admiration for the American colonies during their war for independence and gave them aid, while only imperfectly understanding the principles that motivated them. The American revolt against Great Britain was based on principles stated in the Bible, often in a form handed down through English common law. The Old Testament book of Deuteronomy was cited more frequently by American political thinkers of that era than any other book, and Samuel Rutherford's (d.1661) *Lex Rex* provided them with a Scriptural basis for equality before the law and for limiting royal authority through a covenant between monarch and citizenry. John Locke was familiar with Rutherford's work and adopted many of its ideas in his *Two Treatises on Civil Government* (1690). In it, he proposed a "social compact" that would guarantee unalienable rights, government by the consent of the governed, separation of powers, and the right to overthrow a despotic ruler. From Charles Louis Secondat, Baron de Montesquieu's (d.1755) *De l' Esprit des Lois* (Concerning the Spirit of Laws), the American colonists gleaned further ideas concerning restraint of government through separation of powers and checks and balances. Montesquieu's ideas, of course, were familiar enough to the French *philosophes*, but whereas Thomas Jefferson (d.1824) and other American leaders based their resistance to British rule on biblically-inspired principles, the *philosophes* – convinced of man's essential goodness, perfectibility, and autonomy – scorned all transcendent constitutional sanctions.

As a matter of fact, the spiritual void evident in French intellectual circles left the country wide open to radical Freemasonry and all manner of occult influences. Indeed, the king's brother – Louis Philippe, Duke of Orléans (d.1785) – who had been connected with the Illuminati and was head of Parisian Freemasons, harbored in the *Palais royale* fanatical agitators and *provocateurs*, many of them from the dregs of society. It was this riffraff that promoted sedition, engaged in hooliganism, and finally led forth the mob to overthrow the Old Regime. Little wonder that the Revolution was decidedly different from the American Revolution!

France's revolutionary leaders, uninhibited by constraints other than a putative regard for the "general welfare," employed intimidation and violence to achieve their ends. It is instructive to note that Jean Jacques Rousseau's (d.1778) ambiguous definition of "the general will" did not connote majority opinion, but a subjective ideal – *what ought to be*. This opinion, together with his dictum that to flaunt the "general will" was to remain a slave, provided the rationale for Maximilien Robespierre's (d.1794) "Reign of Terror": persons opposed to the "general will," as determined by the Committee of Public Safety (controlled by Robespierre) were "liberated" by the guillotine. The same rationale has been used by godless dictators ever since to force compliance to their totalitarian rule through mass executions carried out "in behalf of the people" – in Mao Tse-tung's China, for example, in the name of the Chinese people.

Without God, there is no liberty, a fact that the revolutionary drafters of the "Declaration of the Rights of Man and the Citizen" – a document resting, not on God-given rights and duties, but only on the hoped for indulgence of civil government – did not recognize. Within a relatively short time, the inadequacy of such "guarantees" became evident as a number of church functions were assumed by the civil authorities, church properties were seized, ecclesiastical ceremonies and processions restricted, and a 10-day week mandated, effectively eliminating the Lord's Day. *Fêtes* celebrating Nature were instituted, then a Republic of Virtue; but Christianity was suppressed whenever possible. After Napoleon's rise to power (r.1799-1814, 1815), a Concordat with the papacy (1801) restored freedom of worship in France, the Christian calendar was to be reinstituted in 1806, and Catholicism was recognized as the faith of the majority of French citizens. Church properties that had been confiscated by the government and sold for profit were to remain in the hands of purchasers, while the French Church was brought under the oversight of the civil government.

True Christianity can not be "tamed," however, by governmental regulation or rational arguments; for the Spirit of God can not be controlled, and every man possesses an inner awareness of the existence of a Supreme Authority, a Power anterior and superior to himself (Romans 1:18-20 and 2:13-15). Although this Supreme Authority had been denied, or at least considered irrelevant by the 18th-century "enlighteners," man's deepest yearnings could not satisfied by their rational inferences and empirical validations.

Chapter XII

THE 19TH-CENTURY CHALLENGE TO CHRISTIANITY: ROMANTICISM, POSITIVISM, AND EVOLUTIONARY THEORIES

Reaction to rationalism came quickly in the wake of Napoleon's defeat. As a matter of fact, the limitations of a purely rational approach to knowledge already had been recognized by German philosopher Immanuel Kant (d. 1804). In his *Critique of Pure Reason*, he said that man could apprehend the material or physical realm (which he called the phenomenal realm) through the senses, assisted by reason and scientific investigation. However, there was also a noumenal realm, knowledge of which remained impervious to man's natural faculties. Noumenal knowledge could be known only intuitively though reason could reveal the fact of its existence and ethical and esthetic experiences some of its aspects. Kant's recognition that reason and scientific inquiry could go only so far coincided with the late-18th-century reaction against a rationalism that many intellectuals (especially in the German states that had suffered from Napoleonic armies purportedly spreading the benefits of the French "enlightenment") denounced as sterile and incomplete.

Reaction against rationalism was fostered by romanticism, which stressed intuition, feelings, individuality in concert with persons of like background, and cultural sensitivity as avenues to wisdom and knowledge. Manifestations of romanticism were far-reaching and sometimes extreme. Reason was inferior to fervently-held experiential impressions and inner awareness; liberty of spirit and the inherent virtue of the common folk were extolled; the simple life, primitivism, and medieval attributes were idealized; the beauty, grandeur, and tranquility of nature, the mysteries of the night, and the romance of exotic places were celebrated; the bizarre, the melancholy, eerie, and weird were appreciatively recognized; nature (naturalism), deity within nature (pantheism), and the elemental forces of the cosmos were adulated; and the concord of man with all living things was declared – quite in contrast to the cerebral tenets of the "Age of Enlightenment."

Romanticism did have some very positive aspects. It promoted variety, beauty, literary imagination, stirring artistic expression, grandeur and emotion in music, and other pleasing effects. On the other hand, romantics, on the whole, worshiped the creature or the creation rather than the Creator. Inherent in the romantic breast was a strong pantheistic strain that approached idolatry of nature and natural forces to the denigration, if not the exclusion, of a personal Savior-God. Search for the vital energy within – the creative life forces in the inner man – could lead to a sort of self-adulation or deification. Indeed, ego-centrism has become one of the hallmarks of this form of mystical, sentimental humanism that can be just as unbalanced in its own way as was the rationalistic humanism of the 18th-century "Enlightenment." In a sense, romanticism provided a soulish counterfeit for a true spiritual corrective to arid rationalism, just as today's New Age religion and occultism are providing soulish responses to sterile scientism or empiricism when only a genuine religious experience – acceptance of Jesus Christ as personal Savior – can fill the spiritual vacuum in man.

Divergent cultural currents are frequently in tension; therefore, it is not surprising that, in its 19th-century heyday, romanticism vied with scientism or "positivism" for the allegiance of cultural elites and intellectuals. Scientific discoveries were causing certain forward-looking thinkers to hail scientific method as the pre-eminent gateway to truth. One such person was Auguste Comte (d.1857). He idolized scientific method and brazenly dismissed, on the basis of no reliable evidence, what he termed the religious and metaphysical stages through which, he said, earlier generations of mankind had passed. According to Comte, man finally had reached the positivist stage of development; consequently, he could safely reject the gullible beliefs of the past and subject every alleged fact to the test of scientific methodology. Anything that could not be examined and proven empirically, including religious beliefs, was of no consequence. Scientific methodology had proven its validity to expand man's knowledge of the universe, and the same methodology should be applied to man's actions through a new science – sociology – so that these actions could accurately and realistically be evaluated, understood, and explained without reference to metaphysics or "revelation." Indeed, scientific methodology was virtually apotheosized and applied, not only to sociology, but also to theology ("Higher Criticism" of the Bible), history (historicism), anthropology, literature, and eventually the study of the human psyche (psychology). Every claim or supposition not provable by scientific method must be considered suspect and probably false – certainly of no significance. Thus, the spiritual realm was deprecated under the onslaught of materialistic reductionism.

Time-honored beliefs also were undermined by the philosophical speculations of Ludwig Feuerbach (d.1872), who postulated that God was merely the ideal construct of man's imagination: no deity had created man; rather, man had created God. This premise prompted Friedrich Wilhelm Nietzsche (1844-1900), late in the 19th century, to proclaim the death of God, since man's actions, according to Nietzsche, did not bear witness to any supernatural being.

In the meantime, evolutionary theories that were generally inimical and detrimental to Christianity were being propagated by various thinkers. Georg Friedrich Hegel (d.1831) postulated that every thesis in the realm of ideas gave birth to an opposite viewpoint or antithesis and that thesis and antithesis would continue to clash until resolution was achieved in synthesis. Equilibrium, however, was only temporary; for the synthesis became the new thesis, which begat a new antithesis, and so on. Hegel's dialectic explained, to the satisfaction of many thinkers, the dynamic changes that were constantly occurring. Nothing was stagnant; nothing remained the same. Change was progressive and should be welcomed. "Truth" was not absolute because it was constantly evolving; and at each stage in the dialectical process, correct opinions probably lay about midway between the two extremes of thesis and antithesis. Furthermore, once an early thesis and antithesis had been subsumed into the dialectical process, their repetition was highly unlikely. They had made their contribution to the evolving higher "truth" and need not be reconsidered. Thus, Christianity, which had doubtless made a contribution to human thought in earlier stages of the dialectic, was not directly relevant in the higher stages. On this matter, Comte and Hegel would have agreed.

In Hegel's dialectic, man's mind was able to call reality into being through the dialectical process, but ultimate reality or truth could never be realized until the final synthesis was reached – a merger of all partial truths into one rational whole. Only that which was rational was real; therefore, nothing existed unless evoked by the mind of man. In other words, everything was ideational; for neither things nor ideas actually existed until man conceived them; therefore, man's reason evoked reality, and from the human spirit arose the world spirit capable of pronouncing judgment on morals, conduct, and world affairs. Hegel equated this world spirit with history, which he called the "world's court of justice." History was not merely the record of man's past, it was the motivator of his present thoughts and actions, the mover of nations, the determiner of values – a universal rational spirit, the practical realization of cosmic reason that expressed itself in the state. Therefore, although Hegel started with the creative mind of man, he believed that man's highest aspirations and yearning for freedom were realized only in collective man, represented in the state. Consequently, man's true liberty consisted in submitting to the superior rationality of the state – the mouthpiece of the "world spirit," the "Divine idea as it exists on earth," the source of man's dignity and of all spiritual reality.

Like Hegel, Karl Marx (1818-1883) believed in the power of collectivism, and he adopted Hegel's dialectic – applying it, however, not in the ideational realm, but in the political-economic realm. He borrowed also from Feuerbach, echoing his view that man is the creator of religion for his own ends: "Religion is the sigh of the creature overwhelmed by unhappiness...," said Marx. "It is the opiate of the people."

Unlike Feuerbach, however, Marx could not view mankind in an abstract manner. Instead, he sought to restore divinity to real men through transformation of society (the positivistic doctrines of Auguste Comte may be observed here). To him, the mystical yearning for religious assurance was caused by a bad social system. To liberate man from his religious superstitions, a frontal attack must be made on existing society, which was dominated by the capitalist, entrepreneurial, managerial class that owned and controlled the means of production and exploited downtrodden workers in pursuit of its own selfish ends.

Marx's "realism" was in and of itself a rejection of God in favor of what he conceived to be the inexorable economic determinism of dialectical forces. The dialectic was not moved by progressive ideational conflict and resolutions, as with Hegel, but by a class struggle between "haves" and "have nots." According to Marx, the old unproductive nobles who had dominated Europe until the French Revolution had been supplanted, after a struggle, by the bourgeois capitalist class that had established and taken control of the new industrial order whose profits were being made at the expense of the workers ("the proletariat") – the true productive class. A just society would emerge only when the workers rose up and seized the means of production, thereby ushering in a utopian, classless society in which owners, managers, and workers would be one and the same. Once this was achieved, the necessity for civil government would be no more, and the state would simply wither away. However, pending this final utopian synthesis, the class struggle must proceed inexorably, and those who would oppose it would be ground up in the dialectic. It would be best, therefore, to join this great historical force that eventually would succeed in establishing a universal classless society. The cause was a noble one, greater than any individual considerations. Workers of the world were encouraged to arise and strike off the chains that bound them. They should abet class struggle by any means at their disposal: by propaganda and disinformation, by indoctrination and teaching, by conspiracy and espionage, by terrorism and revolution, and by stirring up animosities or taking advantage of them whenever possible. The "soaking-the-rich" philosophy of the political left in present-day America and the portrayal of certain elements of society as "victims" are but two evidences of a Marxist bent of mind.

While Marxism has influenced opinion in this country more than is generally recognized (especially since World War II), it has had its greatest impact in the former Soviet Union, Eastern Europe, East Asia, Africa, the Carribean, and Central America. In recent years, advocates of liberation theology have depreciated the spiritual mission of the gospel, while calling for the church to effect political and social salvation by Marxist ideology and methods. In the name of Christ, they denounce as "exploiters" and "oppressors" anyone or any nation that is better off than the "suffering masses" on whose behalf they claim to speak. Engendering a spirit of envy against alleged oppressors, they speak of an existential need for action, not words alone. Any means may be used – dissemination of disinformation and propaganda, preaching violent revolution for the sake of winning the great class struggle, and undermining the established order through theft, sabotage, terrorism, and even mass murder. The necessity for a change of heart and a new life in Christ Jesus is minimized, social theory takes precedence over Holy Writ, and demonic methods are employed in a supposedly God-ordained cause. (That Christians are to engage in spiritual, physical, and material ministry to the poor, downtrodden, and oppressed is beyond question, but promoting violent revolution is contrary to the teaching and example of our Lord.)

Just as dangerous and antithetical to God as Marxism and presented in subtler terms, is another evolutionary theory espoused by Marx's contemporary Charles Darwin (d.1882). Indeed, Darwinian thought pervades our society, our attitudes, our institutions, and all contemporary culture. No intellectual movement of modern times has had a greater influence than the theory of biological evolution through natural selection enunciated by Darwin and explicated by a host of humanist-materialists.

Chapter XIII

THE DENIAL OF GOD IN THE 20ᵀᴴ CENTURY: THE UBIQUITOUS LEGACY OF DARWIN

Evolutionary thought cuts in two directions in our culture. On the one hand, we can see the influence of the concept of the "survival of the fittest" as popularized by Herbert Spencer (d.1903), which may be construed as a rationale for racism and exploitation of the weak by the strong; cut-throat competition such as that commonly attributed to the industrial moguls and banking magnates (the so-called "robber barons"); territorial expansion, colonization, and imperialism; and a postivistic concept of human progress that can be empirically ascertained and measured and promoted by the "science" of sociology. On the other hand, Darwinistic macro-evolutionary theory denies a Creator and absolute standards, morals, and law. Things occur by chance or in an impersonal fashion; for there is no Creator-God. Therefore, values are derived purely from societal norms, while man's conduct is determined either by his unconscious mind – as Sigmund Freud (d.1939) would have us believe; by the individual unconscious and that of the human race – as Carl Jung (d.1961) proposes; or by his environment – as John B. Watson (d.1958), B.F. Skinner, and other behaviorists insist. In any case, man can not be held responsible for his actions since they are allegedly prompted or caused by powers not entirely under his control.

Human law, therefore, need not be based on eternal verities (constituting the law of nature and nature's God) but rather should evolve to suit the changing ethical attitudes of society. In this century, in fact, reference to a transcendently-sanctioned law has become *passé* at best; for the only law that matters consists of human enactments that can be studied empirically by the case method without regard for any putative *a priori* precepts. For several decades, American jurists who were legal Darwinists were more or less content to render decisions considered to be in accord with the evolving needs of society and, in so doing, reflected mainly the "change by chance" aspect of evolutionary thought. More recently, however, and particularly since World War II, they, like many behaviorist psychologists and sociologists, have striven to assist the evolutionary process by rendering decisions calculated to improve society by molding its institutions in such a way as to make it likely to survive. In either case, survival is an important goal, perhaps the preeminent one – at least, philosophically – for the judicial activists.

The same dichotomy may be observed between pragmatic "educators," film makers, persons controlling the media, and government officials and bureaucrats determined to play God by creating society in their own image, and their equally humanistic, existential counterparts who view everything as the absurd product of pure chance. Life to the latter has no meaning or purpose; for there is no Creator, and man himself is simply the highest form of animal to have evolved to this point in time. This mind-set, endemic in evolutionary thinking, was manifested in the paintings of the Dadaists and other artists disillusioned by the senselessness and horrors of World War I. Others, like painter Jackson Pollock, have splashed or squirted or blown or dripped paint on canvases purely at random in a frenzied refutation that man is a creator made in the image of God; and musicians, such as John Cage, have engaged in chaotic and meaningless chance compositions that essentially deny a creator. A similar nihilism is seen in the works of surrealist painters, who have dredged up grotesque, nightmarish fantasies from the subconscious mind – to which Freud, not recognizing a Creator-God, had repaired to try to explain the human psyche and devise therapy for the emotionally disturbed.

In the absence of a Creator-God as the Originator of moral law, how can truth be determined? How can one judge what is right or wrong? Utilitarian philosophers had attempted in the early 19th century to present alternatives to biblical standards. They maintained that what was useful was good; therefore, one's actions could be gauged by what would bring "the greatest good to the greatest number" of people, or what would promote the greatest balance of pleasure over pain. In the post-Darwinian era, the utilitarian principle of determining one's practices on the basis of their putative results was dusted off and stated in somewhat different terms by the philosophical pragmatists. According to William James (d.1910), Charles Peirce (d. 1914), and other pragmatists, a theory or action was true and good if it was effective. Of course, what is effective for one person may not be effective for another, and the effectiveness of a particular idea or action may change from one time to another; therefore, pragmatism was and is a relativistic guide for proper thought and deeds, depending upon what each individual makes of it. According to pragmatists, moral beliefs are determined, not by intellect alone, but by the will. If a person does not want a world of moral reality, his thoughts will never make him believe in one. Truth is what one makes it to be: a decision is true if commitment to it renders one's life richer and "more meaningful."

Obviously, pragmatism is a philosophy based on nothing but "shifting sands": there are no absolutes in this philosophy – indeed, how can there be without recognition of a God to establish eternal and universal laws? The individual is reduced to believing or doing what, at any given time, he decides will bring a desired result. But how can finite man accurately predict the result? Only the rejected infinite God can know that. He alone knows the end from the beginning – the consequences of every human thought and deed; and He has provided a manual that will guide men inerrantly through every perplexity and difficulty to their best end.

How pitiful that men, in their prideful independence, accepted the evolutionary lie that there is no God, or, if there is one, *he, she,* or *it* is superfluous. No wonder the existentialist feels trapped in a meaningless universe devoid of purpose and truth. To him, man is "an empty bubble floating on a sea of nothingness" who, Jean Paul Sartre insisted, is "condemned to be free." All man can do is to create his own values to suit the existential moment (an onerous burden) by taking some sort of action – not to be judged "good" or "bad" by any imaginary standard – to "authenticate" himself and, perhaps, demonstrate a certain self-imposed responsibility for his fellow men. Ernest Hemingway's (d.1961) novels and short stories are replete with existentialist correlations and illations. So-called Christian existentialists such as Alfred North Whitehead (d.1947), Pierre Teilhard de Chardin (d.1955), Ernst Block, and Dutch Catholic theologian E. Schillebeeckx generally honor Jesus Christ for exemplifying how a person can infuse a senseless life or pointless universe with meaning. In their view, however, God, as creative purpose and destiny of the world, has not yet been fully actualized. He is, in Block's language, "the God who is not yet," whose fulfillment depends upon "inventing" himself or being "actualized" in man's growing love and creativity.

The affect of Darwinism on theology is too extensive for cursory presentation, but is easily discerned in the postulate of Julius Wellhausen (d.1918) that the religion of the ancient Hebrews gradually evolved from primitive animism in patriarchal times, through henotheism in their tribal experience, to monotheism during and after the time of the prophets. Wellhausen's anti-supernatural premises were no doubt attributable to a fixation upon the scientific assumptions of his day, particularly the Darwinian theory.

Much the same can be said of another German theologian, Rudolf Bultmann (d.1976), who spent most of his professorial career at the University of Marburg. In keeping with the scientistic, Darwinistic, existential currents circulating in intellectual circles, Bultmann subjected Holy Writ to rigorous criticism, debunking accounts of miracles as myths that should be discarded as cultural husks that were concealing the *kerygma*, the essential kernel of the New Testament message. Using what he called "form criticism," he set out to purge scriptural texts of anything deemed incongruent with literary forms said to characterize the era in which they were written. But he went far beyond this. In his determination to "demythologize" the Gospels, Bultmann called into question anything not explicable by modern science or even modern philosophy and psychology. On these bases, he denied the existence of demons and repudiated Christ's incarnation and virgin birth, His sacrificial atonement for the sins of mankind, His resurrection from the dead and bodily ascension, and the belief that He will return to earth to claim His own. These denials and his conviction that God could not intervene in the affairs of this world were tantamount to disclaiming God's sovereignty and the divinity of Jesus Christ. What was important, Bultmann contended, was not the accuracy of the biblical account, but whether people believed it had some positive experiential import for their lives. In reality, then, the Bible's influence on the existential experience of the believer was all that mattered.

"Modernist" theologians throughout the Western world took their cue from Bultmann, questioning the inerrancy of Scripture and disavowing its authority, or at least subordinating it to their scientific icons. There was a receptivity to the reductionist tenet of scientism that no truth or reality exists beyond what can be confirmed empirically. As a consequence, modernists – whether Catholic or Protestant – were prone to compromise Christian doctrines to make them conform to supposed scientific, philosophical, or psychological "facts." In so doing, they were following an evolutionary paradigm that predisposed them to accommodate or capitulate to almost every novel concept presenting itself. (The existentialist bent is readily apparent here.) In the guise of remaining relevant to contemporary society and its needs, they were willing to downplay or reinterpret doctrines and doctrinal terminology while deferring to modern thought patterns and emphasizing interior sentiment manifesting itself in social activism.

Within the Roman Catholic Church, modernism was effectively laid to rest by 1910, owing to the decisive denunciations of Pope Pius X (r.1903-1914), but it continued to percolate within Protestant circles until challenged by Swiss theologian Karl Barth (d.1968). Barth initiated a theology known as neo-orthodoxy that reaffirmed God's transcendence and grace and the necessity of salvation through faith. He averred an intention to return to the theological tenets of the Reformation (though, in fact, he did not) and denigrated the modernists' beliefs in Divine immanence, their uncritical acceptance of modern science, somewhat paradoxical stress on feelings, disregard for biblical truth or the revelation of God in Jesus Christ, and confidence in man's natural, inherent goodness and capacity for gradual improvement. In this and in his courageous opposition to Adolf Hitler (r.1933-1945), Barth is to be admired; yet, his own existential roots prompted him to equivocate on the authority of Scripture, referring to it as God's Word imperfectly communicated to mankind through fallible writers. The story of creation and other "fantasies," though not literally true, conveyed truth about God and His creation that men could appropriate to their benefit. So it was that the veracity and significance of the Bible was deemed contingent upon man's understanding of it – whether in a rational or non-rational way: men made the final assessment on the basis of their existential experiences.

Moral relativism was the outgrowth of a nimiety of "isms" circulating in the Western world from the late 19th century onward. American intellectuals assimilated a strange assortment of anti-biblical ideas, including positivism and the various evolutionary ideologies of Hegel, Marx, and Darwin, not to mention Nietzsche's nihilism, utilitarian-pragmatism, Freud's psychoanalytical methodology, and the environmental determinism of the behaviorists – all of the latter based in one way or another on Darwinian premises. Moreover, these ideologies tended to amalgamate as they spread into every realm of thought or professional endeavor – be it theology, history, law, politics, foreign affairs, economics, psychology, literature and the fine arts, sociology, or education.

In pedagogy, for example, psychologist Edward Lee Thorndike (d.1949) frankly stated in his published dissertation entitled *Animal Intelligence*:

"Nowhere more truly than in his mental capacities is man a part of nature. His instincts... his inborn tendencies to feel and act in certain ways, show throughout kinship with the lower animals, especially with our nearest relatives physically, the monkeys."

Acting on his words, Thorndike experimented with small animals, which he placed in a box equipped with an escape lever. When an animal discovered that pressing the lever led to freedom and a bit of food, it quickly learned to trip the lever. On the basis of his findings, Thorndike began to apply his "stimulus-response" (S-R) method to train children to "want the right values" without resorting to "religious superstition," which "must be eradicated."

Likewise, psychologist-educationist G. Stanley Hall (d.1924) adopted a Darwinian motif in his recapitulation theory – the idea that every child evolves from the most primitive stage of the human race. As he put it: "the child repeats the race. This is a great biological law." Therefore, children were closer to their "totemic ancestors" (animals) than were adults, and should be studied and emulated. One should take care not to use coercive methods to train them. They must be allowed to unfold more or less naturally once their curiosity and interest were aroused. Permissiveness was better than strict discipline, and encouraging spontaneity and freedom of choice was better than placing a student in a structured curriculum, because "the school including its buildings, all its matter and method, revolve about the child, whose nature and needs supply the norm for everything." Teachers must be trained to "respect the rights of childhood" so that the schools will be the new agencies for the evolutionary progress of mankind. As such, the schools possess a holier "consecration than the church." They will usher in a justice, service of mankind, happiness, and virtue for the "greater glory of man." According to Hall, the "school is the training ship for the ship of state," and civics must be the "new religion of the secular schools."

Consonant with these sentiments were the "instrumentalist" concepts of John Dewey – that ideas were to serve as tools to cope with situations and shape or reorganize a "given environment." The teacher, as "the prophet of the true God and the usherer in of the true kingdom of God," should involve students in collectivistic activities. According to Dewey, traditional education with its emphasis on abstract thought, memorization, and individual development fostered "selfishness." Therefore, the focus of education should be shifted: school subjects should center "not on science, nor literature, nor history, nor geography, but on the child's social activities." Learning should not be for personal edification or aggrandizement: it should serve a social purpose. Therefore, individual achievement and competition should be played down in favor of "democratic" group dynamics relevant to the problems of mankind. Socialism and collectivism were fostered, and Dewey leaned toward behavioristic means of furthering one-world views. Thus, Dewey sacrificed personal intellectual growth and well-being to presumed social needs, and promoted love of society instead of love of God and eternal verities.

Deweyite "progressives" of the 1950's spoke much of including students in decision-making regarding classroom rules, what should be studied, and other matters affecting them. Individuality should not be promoted. In fact, it was discouraged through use of the "look-say" method of reading instruction that fosters semi-literacy and, therefore, inhibits independent thinking. Individuality was also discouraged by instilling a sense of peer dependency – so that a pupil would doubt his own ideas unless they were approved by the group. Although some "progressive" educationalists (disciples of Dewey) might speak of personal attainment, individuality was considered relatively unimportant, even potentially detrimental to society. Of far greater moment was social adjustment to the peer group and to society at large. This, to Dewey, was true democracy. As he cleverly expressed it, "The foundation of democracy is faith in the capacities of human nature; faith in human intelligence and in the power of pooled and cooperative experience."

To realize his potential, therefore, everyone should engage in integration downward, by surrendering his individualistic proclivities and exclusive or elitist concepts and identifying with the masses. By this means, a "socialization of the intelligence and the spirit" would take place in unity with the community, and the state schools would promote reformation (socialization) of values. Today, even some college and university administrations have swallowed these egalitarian absurdities so contrary to the principles of individual responsibility, the full exercise of one's talents, and the reality of Divinely-established jurisdictions and ministries within society and the body of Christ.

Evolutionary theories of the Hegelian, Marxist, or Darwinian type or a combination thereof have also had an impact on public affairs to a far greater degree than can be briefly explicated here. It is noteworthy, however, that Marxist-Leninists have long recognized that new directions in history frequently come in the wake of dramatic crises, unrest, upheaval, trauma, or destruction of time-honored values. Indeed, they have often tried to promote estrangement or enmity between classes or ethnic groups and to exploit periods of rapid change or turmoil to win converts to their ideological propositions, to undermine the established order, and to precipitate radical social, political, economic, and cultural revolutions. The United States has undergone several tumultuous crises in this century that could easily invite ideological intrusion – World War I, the Great Depression, World War II, and the civil rights movement among them. Each of these has left a distinct imprint on American society and our national life.

World War I – together with the quantum theory of mass-energy, Werner Heisenberg's uncertainty principle, Albert Einstein's (d.1955) theory of relativity, the anti-Christian view of man presented in Freud's psychological postulates, and the intellectual upheaval accompanying them – caused a loss of faith in traditional verities and settled values. Old absolutes wilted, and a sexual revolt took place against "worn-out" 19th-century mores, later greatly accentuated by the dishonest, unscientific "research" of Alfred Kinsey (d.1956), whose unwarranted conclusions have promoted free sex, perversion, and child-abuse. Pessimism, a sense of hopelessness, cynicism, depersonalization, and a feeling that there was nothing to hold on to began to permeate society. There was an existential quest to establish some sort of meaning for oneself, a relativistic, nihilistic sense of values, and a hedonistic, materialistic drive for personal gratification.

Although World War I did much to shatter traditional beliefs, it was the stock market crash of 1929 and the economic depression that followed that called into question the viability of the free enterprise system. Capitalism had failed, it was said. New models were needed. The Bolshevik experiment in the Soviet Union was lauded by uncritical (and sometimes untruthful) journalists and academicians, and students at elite colleges and universities were indoctrinated in Marxism-Leninism. Although proposed communistic solutions were unheeded by the common man, who was largely oblivious to them, intellectuals

– soon to become our leaders and opinion-makers – were affected. Labor unions became more adversarial and confrontational as men such as Walter Reuther (who had lived in the Soviet Union as a boy), Harry Bridges, and other leaders of the labor movement spoke in class-struggle terms. Education was viewed more and more as an agency for promoting socialism and changes in society as educationists such as John Dewey and George Counts praised the Soviet system and propagated "progressive education" by networking with administrators across the country who had been turned out at the Teachers' College of Columbia University (or at satellite institutions). Margaret Sanger's "birth control" concepts and her proposals for sterilizing parents potentially unfit to bear children found an audience among liberals who lamented the predicament of poor families with "too many mouths to feed." Keynesian economics – the idea of stimulating the economy through increased government spending in times of economic depression – was introduced by Franklin Delano 's administration (1933-1945); and public welfare, at first resisted by poor but proud and self-reliant citizens, gradually became acceptable as the Federal government initiated one make-work or relief program after another. In the process, the Federal government began to be viewed as the guarantor of livelihood, the solver of social problems, and the fount of all blessings.

World War II, in its turn, contributed to the destabilizing social forces. The poignant pleas of soldiers going overseas, perhaps never to return, touched the heartstrings of young women willing to sacrifice their virtue under the banner of patriotism. Joseph Fletcher was soon to justify relativistic morals so long as a person was motivated by "love" in a given situation. Close-knit families found it increasingly difficult to maintain intimate bonds as various members left for war or departed to other locales to seek work in defense industries. Family ties were subjected to additional strain as mothers and young women began to enter the work force in large numbers. "Rosie the Riviter" was an actuality, not merely a song, and many "Rosies" continued to work in industry or business after the war.

By that time also, the United States had become a mobile society: large families might be separated as the children reached adulthood and traveled to different cities and even other states to pursue careers or search for lucrative jobs. Numerous blacks began to move from agrarian jobs in the South into the cities, often to northern urban centers. Alarmed whites began to leave the inner-city for the suburbs, causing declining urban populations, an erosion of the tax base, and rising welfare costs.

White flight also brought instability and a loss of identity to inner-city communities. Neighborhoods where families had lived and worked and drawn close to one another now were filling up with "strangers," and community leaders often departed or resigned because of changes with which they felt unable to cope. Consequently, close-knit communities began to break down, as the influx of "outsiders" to leadership posts and local school boards brought changes in old patterns of education.

Much the same was occurring in rural areas, where one-room schools and small high schools started to disappear, local school boards began to merge with those of neighboring hamlets or townships, and school districts were redrawn into larger administrative units to oversee new "consolidated schools." As a result of this process of centralization, parents no longer were able to exert the influence they could when they were able to express their opinions personally and on a day-to-day basis to members of their local school boards. Administrative control of schools shifted to "specialists" no longer subject to as much direction from the elected boards as in the past. Bureaucracy grew and education became increasingly depersonalized. Professional educationists introduced a variety of new courses and innovative methods while placing less emphasis on teaching the "basics" that parents understood. Communication between parents and teachers became less frequent and sometimes strained.

At the same time, the National Education Association (NEA) began to push its "progressive" agenda and to centralize its planning in the hands of elite ideologues. Capitalizing on the teacher shortage brought on by the departure of 350,000 teachers for higher-paying jobs during the war and noting the disparity in financial support from district to district, the NEA began agitating for Federal aid to education. To further its political activism, however, the NEA needed large sums of money; therefore, in 1944 it increased its annual dues and urged teachers to join not only their local and state affiliates but the national organization as well. Nevertheless, few states opted for unified membership until the late 1950's when the Soviet Union's launching of Sputnik in the fall of 1957 provided the NEA with an unprecedented rationale to lobby for Federal funds for education, allegedly to enable the nation to "catch up" and stay ahead of the Russians. By 1972, teachers belonging to local or state affiliates were compelled to join the national organization. This mandate assured NEA administrators a vast new source of money that has enabled it to become the most powerful labor union in the nation – one that promotes educational mediocrity (or, more accurately, disaster) and a radical agenda detrimental not only to education but to society as a whole.

While the NEA speaks of educational reform and lobbies state legislatures and the Federal government for more and more funds, it ignores statistics demonstrating that increased funding for public education has not improved student performance but rather, by contributing to a totally rotten system, has actually contributed to educational decline. For years NEA spokesmen have proclaimed their desire to determine who will or will not teach, and as early as 1981 its executive secretary stated: "The main purpose of our organization is not education of children, it is or ought to be the extension and/or preservation of our members' rights."

Sad to say, this union posing as a professional organization has used the enormous sums of money collected from its members and its political clout at the Federal, state, and local levels virtually to sanctify a monopolistic system of statist education that, judged by any objective criterion for measuring educational competence of students, is not only an abysmal failure but an agency for brainwashing young minds with left-wing ideologies. The NEA opposes private and parochial education as well as home schooling and any government initiative to allow tuition tax credits or vouchers that would enable parents to choose where their children are to be schooled. Indeed, the NEA would like to have children enrolled in pre-kindergarten day-care centers to enable the state, rather than parents, to mold young minds. And what is to be taught in the government schools? Not basic academic courses – those providing the intellectual tools necessary to learn and understand any subject matter – so much as their own "basics" (termed that to delude uninformed parents): courses such as "values clarification," social adjustment, cross-cultural understanding and empathy, human relations, "intellectual rapport," the "arts of compromise and reconciliation," "consensus building," and "planning for global interdependence."

The NEA's hidden and radical agenda includes opposition to any form of prayers (even student-initiated prayers or a "moment of silence") in the schools, but toleration of every form of "free expression" (except for Christian statements): "transcendental meditation" under numerous rubrics; New Age religion; occultism (as expressed, for example, in "Dungeons and Dragons" and other ungodly games often allowed and sometimes authorized for students of exceptional ability); opposition to English as our official language; condemnation of attempts to delete salacious or undesirable reading material from school libraries (conversely, the NEA wants to censor literature depicting parents in positive terms, warning young people against sexually transmitted diseases and the dangers of promiscuity, favorable treatment of the free enterprise system, references to God in a Judaic-Christian sense, and other subjects deemed politically objectionable or socially incorrect); opposition to the teaching of creationist alternatives to evolutionary dogmas; hostility to using the genuine phonics method for teaching reading (while misleading parents to believe "phonics" are a part of reading instruction); promotion of courses on the horrors of nuclear warfare to indoctrinate students to espouse a "nuclear freeze" and disarmament; support for giving additional funds to the United Nations; promotion of multicultural, global, and environmental courses that are vehicles for leftist propaganda; advocacy of sending women into combat; drastic reduction of the Constitutional right to bear arms; support for legalization of marijuana, forced busing to achieve racial integration, socialized medicine, shift of monies from the Federal Defense budget to social and education programs, government-funded abortions, homosexual rights and acceptance, unisex insurance, sex education (including instruction on deviant sexual practices that are illegal in many states and AIDS education at every level without parental consent), affirmative action initiatives and quotas to insure that minorities or disadvantaged persons will be admitted to universities or positions regardless of their achievements or competency qualifications, remuneration for various vocations based on "comparable worth" arbitrarily determined by bureaucrats rather than by natural market forces, global citizenship, "values clarification" courses (offered under numerous titles) that deny moral absolutes and advance self-determination of values, and redistribution of wealth throughout the world; and opposition to tax cuts, freedom of choice in education, competency tests for teachers or salaries based on merit, and installation of a defensive shield against potential missile attacks by enemies.

In view of the dominance of the NEA and professional educationists, the United States has few public schools in the true sense of the term, for the public has almost no control over them. They are state schools pure and simple – capable of indoctrinating students in ungodly, radical ideologies at taxpayers' expense just as did the onetime Nazi regime in Germany, the Stalinist dictatorship in the former Soviet Union, Mao Tse-tung's tyrannical communist government in China, and every other self-exalting totalitarian despotism. Their educational monopoly in this nation must be broken. Otherwise, there can be no genuine education except in the relatively few hard-pressed private schools and in homes where dedicated parents are willing to sacrifice to insure that their children will not be subjected to the Darwinian mind-set, iniquitous peer pressure, violence, and anti-Christ world views present in most so-called public schools. Without God as the Author and Center of knowledge, wisdom, and morality, there can be no true education.

The decline of post-secondary education was not so rapid, but as Federal funds began pouring into the colleges and universities in the wake of Sputnik under the provisions of the National Defense Education Act of 1958 and other legislation, rapid changes took place, some of them probably unforeseen. At first, the results were mixed. On the one hand, an immediate boost was given to science programs serving the national security, to the study of certain languages not commonly known in the United States, and to other programs considered important to the nation. On the other hand, the nature of the academy was drastically altered by the influx of Federal monies. With the funds have come a multitude of government regulations, restrictions, directives, questions, and forms to be filled out, necessitating the hiring of numerous bureaucrats and secretaries to file documents, keep records, and administer expenditures. In fact, it would not be amiss to say that overhead costs accompanying Federal grants have largely defeated the purpose for which they were issued. Waste and corruption in management and dispersal of funds have frequently occurred, and soaring costs of a college education have far outpaced the inflation index – rising twice as fast as the economy in general. The "remedy" often employed has been to spend more, raise tuition to ever higher levels, and apply for more Federal funds. To obtain them, new programs were invented and instituted. During the late 1960's and 1970's, even some minor state colleges and universities were adding ill-advised Ph.D. programs and hiring large faculties to staff them. To justify these programs and in some cases to help pay for them, colleges needed to attract more and more students. However, tempting fellowship stipends calculated to recruit able students brought further expenditures; therefore, academic requirements and admissions standards have often been lowered to attract students able to pay the tab.

In undergraduate education, conditions are just as bad and in most cases worse. Almost anyone who can sign a check is admitted to some schools, contributing to an inevitable erosion of standards despite the institution of all manner of remedial courses to bring the under-prepared up to minimal competency. Moreover, with the proliferation of trendy courses on the occult, tapping one's inner resources, gay and lesbian studies, Marxist and feminist courses of every description, copious offerings concerning human sexuality, and similar abominations that seem almost endless, and with the concomitant jettisoning of a general education core required of all students, almost anyone with money to spend and time to dabble can acquire a college degree. In all too many colleges, there are few if any common courses; therefore, a student may "earn" 130 semester hours (or whatever is required for graduation) by enrolling in and attending almost any classes he chooses outside his major.

Grade inflation, spawned during the period of the Vietnam War and the campus protests, has been continued by professors who themselves are products of that era and sympathetic to its social and political aims. It was also, for the most part, radical professors of the 60's and 70's who handed out inflated grades as a protest against the war, enabling students subject to the draft if they lost their educational deferments to remain *bona fide* college students. Of course, politicization of grading rendered college attendance almost meaningless, and the academy has never recovered from grade inflation and erosion of requirements.

Not all of the malaise in academia can be attributed to Federal funding, of course; but it has been a major factor. For one thing, when Federal money began flowing into colleges and universities during the 1960's, the chief emphasis was on research, especially in the natural sciences, which generally encourage an atmosphere of value neutrality. This attitude was translated into ethical relativism in the so-called social sciences, and demands were made for cohabitation of unmarried men and women in university dormitories and for the equal acceptance by the administration of any view, however bizarre or wrongheaded. Many old-time faculty members were at first shocked, but they were frequently outnumbered by new faculty, hired because of Federal largess, who did not always know the reasons for university policies. University presidents were also unequipped to stand up to the onslaught of protesters, flag-burners, and social activists. Hired not so much for their moral and intellectual leadership as for their ability to raise money and oversee processing of Federal grants, they were often taken by surprise and bewildered by what was happening, undecided as to what response should be made, and anxious to avoid or terminate confrontation through compromise or accommodation. The results were woeful.

The emphasis on hiring research scientists and scholars to be eligible for Federal monies altered academic priorities. Now research was lauded and required of any professor seeking advancement. This in itself was salutary provided professors were able to engage in fruitful research without letting their teaching suffer. In all too many cases, however, eminent professors were allowed to devote almost all their time and energies to research projects that brought prestige to the university while students were taught by adjuncts and graduate students. In recent years, numerous complaints have arisen regarding graduate assistants from Third-World nations who can not speak English well enough to convey their thoughts to students. And so the problems unleashed during the 60's go on and on.

Still another result of government funding – whether by the Federal government or the states – has been the diminution of religious training, even in church-affiliated colleges and universities. To attract government funds, many Christian institutions reconstituted their boards, purging them of clergymen lest they be viewed unfavorably by government bureaucrats charged with dispensing grant monies. Core courses on the Bible, chapel services, and other Christian exercises or means of education were eliminated or minimized – all in pursuit of the almighty dollar. The same quest has led to increasing politicization of education, as few university or college administrators wish to be too adamant about refusing to hire professors of radical views for fear of losing government gold or inviting a costly law suit.

Similar fears cause many universities surreptitiously to enforce quotas in admitting students. "Disadvantaged minorities" are accorded preferential treatment to an inordinate degree, often being admitted despite marginal or unsatisfactory SAT scores. The results have been high attrition rates, discrimination against meritorious persons who are refused admission to maintain "ethnic balance," lowered academic standards, and unfairness to minority students of two categories: (1) those who are handed a degree without receiving a legitimate education, who are often not able to hold a good position once their inadequacies are discovered, and (2) thoroughly competent men and women who have applied themselves to learning and have earned a degree honestly only to have it tarnished because of increasing public awareness that rigorous academic standards are not insisted upon for many minority students. Still another unfortunate result of affirmative action is that it creates an adversarial relationship, not only between whites and favored minority students, but between blacks and Spanish-Americans, each striving to convince authorities that they are more disadvantaged and thus more "deserving" of preferential treatment than members of the other group. What a shame it is when civil government exacerbates such rivalries or animosities because it refuses to follow biblical principles! Had it adhered to the clear teaching of Scripture, there would be no question regarding special treatment for one ethnic group or another; for, according to the Bible, impartial treatment is to be accorded to everyone – white, black, Hispanic, Indian, Asian, male or female, rich or poor. Several biblical verses could be cited, but one – Leviticus 19:15 – should suffice: "Do not pervert justice; do not show partiality to the poor or favoritism to the great, but judge your neighbor fairly."

Although segregation was once considered racist, today campus minority groups are demanding their own ethnic or cultural clubs, dorms, or dining arrangements that tend to divide ethnic groups and isolate them from the mainstream of the student body. Indeed, provisions for voluntary segregation is breeding less tolerance than in the past and fostering opinionated attitudes rather than informed ones. Ironically, it is in the name of tolerance and multiculturalism that "appropriate," "sensitive" attitudes are prescribed. A ban on inappropriate laughter was put into effect at the University of Connecticut several years ago, codes adopted at the University of Michigan restricted students' First Amendment rights, and politically correct euphemisms and "non-pejorative speech" are insisted upon on campuses where free speech is given lip service but not permitted. In the guise of social sensitivity, the right to voice opinions, however innocent or correct, is quashed unless those opinions accord with admissible suppositions. Thus, indoctrination and disingenuous, euphemistic speech is valued over a search for truth.

Professors who dissent from the correct speech line are likely to be subjected to organized vilification and denied promotion or tenure. Faculty members who wish to secure university grants-in-aid for research projects must also be careful to adhere to the party line or at least not "make waves." Nor are applicants for grants from liberal private foundations – the Rockefeller, Ford, and Carnegie foundations, for example – likely to receive assistance unless their proposals are politically correct, that is, in harmony with a humanistic, globalist world view. Any attempt to uncover the machinations of national or international power brokers is anathema to these foundations. They prefer to patronize safe research, focused on secondary, or at least non-threatening issues, conducted by academicians content to remain in their subsidized playpens and to enjoy the plaudits of liberal peers and pundits.

Subordinating truth to a social concern through arbitrarily established canons of "correct and sensitive speech" is unbiblical and, in the long run, self-defeating and destructive of the very society it is intended to improve. When will we cease the folly of ignoring proven, scripturally-based principles in favor of "panaceas' concocted by "liberal" humanists? Certainly not until the Darwinian mind-set, with its myriad connotations, is broken and God is elevated to His proper place in the hearts and minds of our people.

Chapter XIV

THE DARWINIAN LEGACY CONTINUES:
THE ONGOING CULTURAL MALAISE

The decadence of education and the incidence of immorality, crime, and violence within the United States has increased exponentially since 1962 when the United States Supreme Court began eliminating Christian influence from the public schools under the guise of "separation of church and state" (turning the Constitution on its head), while allowing almost every other form of religious expression or practice. During the same period, while the majority of churches were sleeping, satisfied with maintaining the *status quo*, the "civil rights" movement – which had its inception in Christian activism stemming from the social ministry of the black churches and their appeal to the Christian conscience – was gradually co-opted by humanistic liberals who pressed, not only for racial equality, but for women's rights, rights for the physically and mentally disadvantaged, and "homosexual rights" that exceeded both biblical and traditional norms. It is to the church's shame that it did not press more aggressively for basic human rights guaranteed by the Creator (not just by civil government as the term "civil rights" incorrectly connotes) for ethnic minorities, women, and any who may have suffered discrimination through no act or fault of their own.

Although the progress made in "civil rights" over the last 50 years is not likely to be undone by the present separatist attitudes of some vociferous minority students, their demands could prove to be counter-productive by arousing aversion to their methods and mistrust of their motives and aims, thereby retarding further gains. This, of course, would be nothing new; for minority rights were realized slowly and painfully in the aftermath of World War II. Although significant gains were made, they were attained far too slowly for black citizens who had suffered generations of discrimination and mistreatment. The armed forces were desegregated in 1948 by Presidential executive order; and, in 1954, the Supreme Court ruled the old "separate but equal" doctrine unconstitutional, mandating that public schools and universities be integrated. One by one, discriminatory practices were outlawed. Enforcement did not come easily, however, even after Congress, prodded by President Lyndon Johnson (r.1963-1969), passed a strong Civil Rights Act in 1964 and the Voting Rights Act the following year. Peaceful protests continued; but also riots, looting, burning, and senseless destruction occurred in many cities across the country as militant blacks took to the streets.

Adding to the turmoil were the writers of the "New Left," who lashed out against the free enterprise system, "rotten government," moral repression, and America's war in Vietnam. Many of the protesters were from affluent, privileged families, but they were thoroughly disillusioned with life and existentially trying to fill a spiritual void (that they did not even recognize) through drugs, religious cults, sexual promiscuity, and communal living while vehemently denouncing "the establishment" and everything connected with it.

On college and university campuses throughout the country, long-haired, often unkempt and bizarrely-dressed students used sit-ins, occupation of college buildings, threats to burn down ROTC buildings, boycotts or disruption of classes, kidnaping of administration officials, and the like to demand co-ed dorms; trendy courses (from Black Studies, Chicano Studies, and Women's Studies to those dealing with homosexuality and witchcraft); a voice in choosing faculty members; peace in Vietnam; and all manner of political and social demands having little, if anything, to do with academic concerns. In a sense, the mindless violence, obscene acts, foul language, and despicable initiatives calculated to shock the populace and destroy the established order were evidence of a frustration and inner rage that radical civil-rights activists and truculent, nihilistic students felt deeply but could not logically and reasonably and coherently express. Their revolt manifested a deep-seated hatred of American institutions and any restrictions or restraints, a malevolence spawned in a spiritual vacuum for which a complacent church unresponsive to its God-given mission to preach the gospel (whether in pleasant places or in disagreeable and dangerous ones) and to make disciples of the nations — was partly responsible.

The civil rights struggle should have been unnecessary; for equal rights for everyone had been declared in our founding documents, though, unfortunately, the Constitution had allowed slavery. It was our national sin to enslave persons from Africa, treat them as chattel, and then, for more than 100 years after their legal emancipation, continue to treat them as second-class citizens – politically, economically, and socially. The heart of the natural man is disparately wicked; therefore legislation alone can not efface racism whether engaged in by whites, blacks, Hispanics, or any other group. Nevertheless, legislation to right wrongs is a step in the right direction that Christians should support. Beyond this, however, Christians should take the lead in teaching and exemplifying Christ-like love that may break down barriers, minister healing to souls of afflicted or embittered people, and promote understanding and reconciliation.

Though inexcusable, the strident and violent student rebellions are understandable; for a society that glorifies attainment by any means of prominent positions, honors, and material gains, regardless of family obligations or responsibilities to society, has given disillusioned young people little, if anything, to cling to – no moral foundation, awareness of purpose, work ethic, challenge to fulfill some worthy objective beyond themselves, faith in God, or sense of duty to family, God, and country. Nations and societies, as well as persons, always reap what they have sown.

If ever the church of Jesus Christ needed to tap into spiritual resources through fasting and prayer and communion with the Almighty God through Jesus Christ, if ever it needed the empowering of the Holy Spirit for demolishing "strongholds" of the Enemy and "arguments" and "pretensions" raised against God's Word (see II Corinthians 10:4-5), if ever His people needed to be "salt and light" in society, it is now. We are living in a time that may be compared to the days of Noah – a time when "evil men and seducers" are becoming worse and worse (II Timothy 3:13); a time of deceit, moral depravity, drug abuse, crime, lawlessness, and rebellion; a time of idolatry of all sorts – modern Molech worship in the form of abortion, and worship of self, nature, money, technology, pleasure, power, human achievement, civil government, celebrities, witchcraft, demonic forces and entities, the goddesses of feminism, Satan himself, sexual prowess and gratification, and myriads of other false gods; a time when truth, integrity, righteousness, justice, and mercy are becoming rare, because we have rejected the One who is Truth and Righteousness. We are living in a cut-flower culture – cut off from the Creator-God, the very Source of life – that may possess a transient glitter or beauty, but is rapidly decaying and giving off the stench of death. Our culture is but a lifeless caricature of what God means it to be. Like a cut flower, it may appear lovely and alluring for a short season, but it is only Satan's counterfeit of a vital, growing, and productive flowering plant. As a moth lured to a flame, we are being drawn ineluctably to our destruction – desensitized by prevailing attitudes, lurid television and movie presentations, sensual fantasies, pornography, comforting pop psychology, empty and purposeless, God-denying art and literature, and other manifestations of a hedonistic, insouciant, pococurante, cynical, and unsatisfying existence.

Truly, we are immersed in a cultural cesspool, sometimes referred to as a post-Christian or postmodern culture. Verities of earlier times are gone or at least not recognized as in the past. Everything seems to be in a constant state of flux that no one or anything can halt. Right is called wrong, and wrong is called right; but, after all, who can say what is right if there is no God, or rather no recognition of God? Man is simply a part of nature, having no objective meaning apart from the natural order. Even humanism is limited; for human beings can not create meaning individually – only collectively. According to postmodernists, individuality is an illusion. Man's very thoughts, they contend, are shaped by his language, his experiences, and his interaction with others; therefore, he is formed by society and his cultural environment. Postmodernists insist that no reality exists aside from that constructed by society; consequently, "moral law" is nothing more than what society accepts. "Reality" and fiction, they allege, are not dichotomous: they can be virtually the same, since men determine both. Despite the nonsense spouted by the postmodernists, there is little doubt that television blurs the distinction between the actual and the fanciful, and many of today's artists and musicians concentrate on the process – the performance – rather than on the finished production.

Postmodernists believe that there are no objective frameworks or guides, nor any world views: the writer or artistic agent is free to improvise as his inclinations and the circumstances seem to dictate. For example, literary deconstructionists insist that many meanings can be derived from historical accounts, a poem, a novel, or any other type of narrative; and readers may put whatever construction they wish upon the works of an author, even those of a Shakespeare. Viewing language as a cultural tool for wielding power, deconstructionists try to disrupt its authority by assigning various alternative interpretations that will dethrone the works of white European authors – traditionally studied – in favor of those by native Americans, blacks, women, homosexuals, and other "victimized" peoples.

Admittedly, no cannon of literary works should remain sacrosanct to the point of excluding meritorious writings of minorities or women, but to accord uncritically equal weight to all literature is absurd. To devotees of pluralism and multiculturalism, all cultural values are relative and all groups and beliefs should be tolerated and given consideration. Their facile acceptance of almost all concepts and modes of expression depreciates anything of quality. According to postmodernists, rhetoric or style is superior to substance, and truth may be apprehended in a multiplicity of ways – all of relatively equal validity. Andy Warhol's "pop art" – consisting of mundane objects from everyday life mingled together in a more-or-less random fashion – tends to trivialize art of the great masters or any art infused with meaning or a message.

The same is true in the religious realm where monistic, Hindu-inspired New Age religion eclectically borrows bits and pieces from many sects, sees positive aspects in all of them, and thereby demeans the Christian faith. As a matter of fact, Christianity has been marginalized in our society to the point that it is considered by many people to constitute simply another subculture. This false impression is enhanced when cults like that headed by the late Jim Jones or the Branch Davidians try to lay claim to Christian roots.

Never before in the history of our nation has ignorance of the Scriptures, unbelief, apostasy, idolatry, rebellion against God, and acceptance of myths and man-contrived "solutions" to spiritual needs been so prevalent. The theory of evolution is taught as scientific fact in our "public schools" while teaching of creationism is banned. No wonder our educational system has failed; the family is breaking down; crime is rampant; alcohol and drug abuse is out of hand; wife-beating and child abuse are common; sexual immorality and sexually-transmitted diseases are epidemic; profanity, indecent language and acts, pornography, and filthy television programs are becoming accepted; innocent blood is shed without compunction in abortion mills; demonically-inspired games are popular; occult practices and Satan-worship are increasing; materialism and the pursuit of wealth is a national disease; patriots are discouraged; "animal rights" and environmentalism exceed biblical and even rational bounds; strident demands of all manner of "minorities" and feminists are mounting; political and social correctness take precedence over appropriate free speech; distrust of one another, divisiveness, and racism engender anger and frustration; corruption reigns in our political system and the body politic; God is ignored and ridiculed;

persons and institutions standing for godliness are misunderstood, disparaged, and persecuted; and our civil leaders seem overwhelmed, bewildered, disinclined to act on principle in behalf of the public interest, and unable to institute needed reforms or effect positive changes.

Many people of God have left their "First Love" (cf. Revelation 2:4). Even Christian colleges and seminaries are all too often in the hands of administrators and faculties willing to compromise with the world for the sake of money, prestige, and worldly recognition. As a consequence, abominable humanistic doctrines having their inception in ancient Greek thought and heresies of the early church have been dusted off, refined, and given a modern dress by philosophers and theologians to deceive, if possible, "even the elect" (cf. Mark 13:22). Chief among these is probably what is generically referred to as "process theology," ostensibly based on positivistic and evolutionary theories, which is taught in many seminaries, even evangelical ones. Intellectuals such as Clark Pinnock, Charles Hartshorne, David Griffen, H.P. Owen, Schubert Ogden, Norman Pittinger, Nelson Pike, Lewis Ford, Stephen Davis, and John Cobb, Jr. advocate this false theology. Inspired by the conjectural proclamations of English Unitarian mathematician, philosopher, and longtime Harvard professor Alfred North Whitehead (d.1947) and former Boston College professor John Brightman (d.1953), "process theology" assumes that God is not infinite, as the Bible teaches. Rather, it is proposed, God and man are both interdependent with nature and its evolutionary processes and, therefore, subject to progressive changes. God is not absolute, it is asserted, but simply a part of the cosmic system. However, God is not necessarily in everything and everything is not in God as *pantheism* teaches, but rather is operating in the world in cooperation with the creative process that will continue throughout time. To Whitehead, God was the soul of the world, but the world was his body. "Neither God, nor the world, reaches static completion," he wrote. "Both are in the grip of the ultimate metaphysical ground..., both are lesser beings who are being molded by the ultimate ground, the impersonal force called 'Creativity'."

Theologically, this attempt to bring God down to man's level and to elevate man to His level by subjecting them both to an impersonal, unpredictable, evolutionary, creative force is termed *panentheism*, but Henri Bergson (1859-1941) postulated much the same thing. He reduced God to a "life force" (*élan vital*) resident in every man (thus making man Divine – one with God), which pressed him on to "unceasing life, action, and freedom" in harmony with the evolving universe. In effect, Bergson demoted God, refusing to acknowledge Him as Creator and providential Overseer of everything. No longer is He considered infinite, omniscient, and omnipotent (though He apparently remains omnipresent in nature); He is reduced to what man defines Him to be: God must be comprehensible to man through reason, intuition, and experience; for natural man rejects the reality of anything he can not understand. In other words, man wants to create God in his own finite image – to create a deity with human attributes, nothing more – reducing Him to an intellectual construct, a mentally manageable divinity incapable of making moral demands. So it is that intellectuals would bring God down to their level (cf. Romans 10:6), while elevating themselves into beings of infinite potential. There is a definite affinity between many of these hypotheses and New Age religion, whose monistic assimilation of elements from all religions, even Christianity, can delude lukewarm believers not well-grounded in God's Word.

In point of fact, however, the living God is not limited in any way by man's foolish speculations. His Truth knows no barriers, and His rule will ultimately prevail. In the final analysis, God may be mocked, denigrated, spurned, denied, and marginalized by a society sliding down the slippery slope to the abyss, but He is still there – the great I Am – in the center of everything. The United States of America was founded on Judaic-Christian principles, and Christianity was the very fountainhead of our culture, not an appendage to it. Contrary to what the world would have us believe, religion is not merely a component of culture; rather, culture is an outgrowth or expression of religion. Religion – some form of religion: Christianity, Buddhism, communism, humanism, or whatever – constitutes the wellspring of any given culture. Therefore, if we as Christians supinely accommodate ourselves to a secular culture emanating from a false religion, we are attenuating our witness and perhaps even endangering our souls. Christ has no concord with Belial, and "what does a believer have in common with an unbeliever?" (II Corinthians 6:15).

In our national life, we have in effect rejected godly culture founded on the revealed Truth – Jesus Christ – or, at best, we have worked out a comfortable compromise with the philosophic, psychological, sociological, scientistic, evolutionary, existential intellectual currents of this world and perhaps even have dabbled in mystical cults, false eastern religions, or the occult. Even Christians have fallen prey to a spirit of cultural syncretism. This must be renounced; for if we truly aspire to spiritual oneness with our risen Lord, we must commune with Him and feed on His Word until, inundated with His fullness, our hearts beat with His. Only then, will our thoughts be His thoughts and our deeds His – performed without hesitation under the impulsion and power of His Spirit.

Let us not be deluded. The problems and wickedness of this nation and of the world will not be resolved by human effort, but only by Divine intervention; yet men continue to pursue every option except turning to their Maker. Indeed, though they are perishing without God, they refuse to accept His authority or even to recognize Him, continuing instead to flow along heedlessly, often arrogantly, in the humanistic trough (see the diagram in Appendix I) that commenced in the 18th century and has expanded and deepened ever since. When will it bottom out? Only God knows, but many Christians believe that judgment on this land and the nations of the earth is long overdue. Thanks be to God for his great mercy, which infinitely exceeds ours! He does not desire that anyone should perish. We may rest in the assurance that our Lord is fully in control of the affairs of this world, and will someday return to earth to judge all mankind.

In the meantime, it is the duty of Christians to carry out His great commission to convert and teach mankind and, in so doing, bring about reformation of society so that His life-giving Word will be honored and more readily accepted and observed. At present, despite some encouraging signs of religious revival, most people remain obdurate – much as in the time of Noah. It may very well be that God's judgment will fall heavily upon our nation. Indeed, it is inevitable, we believe, in the light of the sinful seeds that have been sown. What is sown will be reaped. That truth can be affirmed by a study of King David's life and the tragedy that his sins brought for himself and the nation of Israel, notwithstanding his repentance and reception of God's forgiveness.

Judgment is coming upon the United States and the nations of the world just as surely as it came upon Noah's world. Nothing less than such Divine judgment will effect God's purpose. When a crisis – such as the 1992 war in the Middle East – confronts us, pious-sounding appeals for prayer may be issued by government leaders and the news media, but they are immediately forgotten once the critical period is over. Just as in the days of Noah, mankind is not concerned about God or what He wants; therefore, it will take a cataclysmic event or series of events to jar people from their preoccupations and self-satisfied preconceptions. Furthermore, even if the majority of people desired to bring about, in the fullest sense, the realization of God's kingdom on earth, they could not do so without His intervention. Only when everything is tottering, when everything is shaken loose that can be shaken loose, will Christ's church be purified and multitudes of unregenerate people receive Him into their hearts.

At present, man is going in his own way. In his quest for meaning, in his spiritual yearning, he remains unfulfilled and hopeless, because he continues to reject the very source of his being – the One in whose image he is created, Jesus Christ, the Way, the Truth, and the Life. Without Him, life on earth is, indeed, an existential nightmare, without any meaning or purpose aside from what can mythologically be concocted or hedonistically experienced. Little wonder that contemporary man is groping for answers. He is striving, on the one hand, to usher in some form of utopia based on the alleged "brotherhood of all mankind" and a false confidence in his ability to construct a humanistic, one-world government coupled with a uniform and universal medium of economic exchange. On the other hand, he is seeking to fill a spiritual void (often unconsciously) through hedonistic sexual gratification, the anesthetic of TV; a euphoric, "mind-expanding trip" or escape from reality through the use of alcohol or drugs; "self-actualization" through meditation, recitation of mantras, "imaging," "centering," "channeling," reliance on spirit guides, and other New Age techniques; or the attainment and exercise of occult powers through spiritualism, witchcraft, or Satan-worship. All are equally doomed to failure. A perfect society can only be constituted by the Creator: no man-made schemes for world governance can work, for man's nature is flawed and sinful (though "doctrines of demons" that prey on human hubris would lead us to believe otherwise); and personal rejection of the One in whom we "live and move and have our being" (Acts 17:28) tragically and inevitably must end in death – not merely of the body, but of the eternal soul. The death-dealing attitudes of contemporary society can only be reversed by personal and national repentance and acceptance of the God of our forefathers. If we receive Him into our lives and apply His principles in our society, disaster may be averted.

Chapter XV

INTERPRETING HISTORY: CULTURAL CURRENTS AND HISTORIOGRAPHY IN THE WEST

Our thesis that God is great enough to allow man the liberty to render his own decisions without losing control of what is occurring and, in fact, seeing to it that His eternal plan is effected posits a type of dialectical process between the Divine forces and the forces of evil. Warfare is being waged in heavenly places (Ephesians 6:12) but also on earth. Short of His sovereign intervention in human affairs whenever He ordains it, God conducts the battle in the temporal sphere through His Holy Word, the ongoing activities of the Holy Spirit in the spirits of His people (and even in the consciences and minds of the ungodly to bring them to repentance and conversion), and the worship and cultural involvement of believers. Opposing these powerful forces for righteousness are the forces of evil, arising in part from the sinful nature of man but also prompted in many cases by Satan, the arch-deceiver of the ages, leader of demonic entities, and sponsor of false religions and occult beliefs and practices. This conflict is basically a spiritual one – a contest for the allegiance of mankind; but it has intellectual, emotional, voluntaristic, and physical manifestations in both individuals and national entities. Chapters I through XIV have endeavored to demonstrate how this dialectic has operated in the Western world through the centuries – from the creation until the present time; and we believe the tension and struggle will continue, in ever-increasing intensity and ferocity, until Jesus Christ directly intervenes again by returning to earth to succor His people and rule the nations.

Western man's historical philosophies and interpretations of the meaning (or meaninglessness) of history have fluctuated greatly from antiquity to the present time in a manner fairly similar to the oscillation of God-honoring and man-centered cycles already described. It would be fruitless to reiterate the nature and meaning of these cycles in an exhaustive fashion, for this has been done many times (from divergent vantage points to be sure) in numerous tomes dealing with historiography. Therefore, only generalizations will be given here to provide a contrasting backdrop for the scriptural principles applicable to human history and God's role in it to be explicated in succeeding chapters.

At the very outset, let it be said that the ancient Hebrews, not the Greeks as usually asserted, were the first to transcend mere chronology and to present a full-blown historical narrative infused with meaning and purpose. According to the Old Testament, they were a people specially chosen by God to proclaim His truth, follow His ways, and bring salvation to the peoples of the earth. Though they did not always seem to understand the full import of their God-given mission, they knew that they were chosen to carry out His will, and they looked forward to the coming of a Messiah who would restore the nation of Israel and rule with righteousness and justice. With this hope in mind, the Hebrews tenaciously maintained their identity (though occasionally lapsing into intermarriage with pagans and apostasy or syncretic religious practices) through centuries of bondage, oppression, and dispersion throughout the nations of the world. Cognizant of their chosenness and Divine calling, their writers related the story of Yahweh's dealings with His people, without embellishment or any attempt to justify their misdeeds. They portrayed persons and events with equal honesty, not flinching to relate unsavory details as well as those of a more creditable nature, and explaining historical occurrences in the light of Israel's obedience to the Lord God. Following the Divine Law was the pathway to blessing; but disobedience and unfaithfulness incurred censure and punishment. Eschewing the cyclical views of time with its blind recurrence to which the Greeks, Orientals, and other ancient peoples subscribed, the Hebrews saw their past, present, and future in the light of God's plan and superintendence, and their response to His prescribed way.

Although Herodotus (484-425 B.C.), the first noteworthy Greek historian, wrote many centuries after the early Hebrews and does not manifest their unbiased honesty, he is generally referred to as the "Father of History." The appellation is quite possibly indicative of an anti-religious animus on the part of modern humanistic or postmodern historians who would like to denigrate the historicity of the Bible despite the fact that evidence for the veracity of the events it records exceeds that presented by non-Jewish writers of antiquity.

Greek historians, by the time of Herodotus and Thucydides (c. 456-396 B.C.) were renouncing earlier Homeric myths that the gods precipitated events affecting man, though they generally continued, as did their Roman counterparts, to believe that patterns in history were repeated in rhythmic cycles. Both the humanistic Greeks and the practical, worldly-minded Romans saw man as the determiner of events through application of his will, thoughts, and deeds. Man, not some transcendent Deity, was the maker of history. Institutional development, however, was generally overlooked by Roman historians such as Livy (59 B.C. to 17 A.D.), who makes no attempt to explain why Rome was as it was but simply accepts the existence of things as he knew them – as if everything was fixed or had just sprung into being in the form known to him.

Early Christian historians had much in common with their Jewish predecessors. Both looked to history for evidence of God's dealings with man, perceived a continuous conflict between good and evil, and adhered to a linear view of time. According to Christian historians, time, as it applied to humanity, commenced with God's creation of the earth and mankind, was divided between B.C. and A.D. by the first advent of Jesus Christ – Deity incarnate in human flesh – and would be brought to a climactic conclusion by Christ's second coming as omnipotent Ruler and Judge. Inexact systems of dating were now superseded – the Greek method of dating by Olympiads and the Roman scheme of dating by the administrations of consuls. Thereafter, for centuries the unfolding years were designated by a system that commemorated the birth of the Savior, until modern humanists, in an effort to obliterate His memory, retained the numeration intact while changing the designations from "Before Christ" to "Before the Common Era" and "In the Year of our Lord" to "The Common Era." What a change from the practice of the early Christian historians who endeavored to glorify their Lord in every way possible, rejected the Greek notion of the primacy of man and much of pagan culture, and emphasized the priority of faith over reason! Christian historians were conscious intellectuals who looked to the future with hope at a time when Roman writers – caught up in the uncertainty of the times, even if not fully aware of their decadence – tended to seek consolation from the past. Christians were not only appreciative of their Judaic roots and God's past involvement in human affairs and provision of salvation through the substitutionary death and resurrection of Jesus Christ, they also were conscious of their on-going purpose as God's agents, and confident of their future eternal state. Moreover, their historical sense was doubtless strengthened as they contended for the faith against various heresies, refuting the

Gnostics and defending orthodoxy, for example, by appealing to Scripture and history.

The same was true of the theological disputes between Arius and Athanasius, in which Bishop Eusebius of Caesarea (C.263-339) played a moderating role. As a major participant in ecclesiastical affairs and confidant of the Emperor Constantine, Eusebius had first-hand information concerning both secular and religious matters. His *Ecclesiastical History*, tracing church development from Apostolic times until the reign of Constantine, is a major source of information on that topic; and his biography of the Emperor, in which he acclaimed his Imperial patron as the Divinely-ordained custodian of Christ's church, may have contributed to the rise of Caesaropapism in the Byzantine Empire.

In the West, the shape of historical writing for almost a millennium was heavily influenced by church father, theologian, and Bishop of Hippo Aurelius Augustine (354-430). In response to pagan citizens of Rome who blamed Christianity for weakening the body politic resulting in Alaric's (c.370-410) sack of the "Eternal City" in 4l0, Augustine penned his monumental *The City of God,* in which he envisioned a cosmic conflict between good and evil. He insisted that kingdoms and rulers rose and fell according to a Divine master plan that was beyond man's comprehension. The people of God need not be concerned about causality, for everything was in His hands. Why Imperial success or prosperity may occur under undeserving emperors could never be explained; but the Almighty was long-suffering, and no one merited His grace and mercy. Punishment for certain sins or wrongdoing might be "reserved for the last judgment," while at other times it was inflicted in this world. Although God's workings and ways were inscrutable, everything was under His providential superintendence and care; therefore, Christians should harbor no misgivings. They should play their proper roles in human affairs while recognizing that the Divine will would eventually prevail. All worldly states were transient: only the city of God, comprised of those trusting in Jesus Christ, was eternal. Christ's church would ultimately triumph, and the Divine plan would be fulfilled.

This view of history was accepted and propagated by the overwhelming majority of historians throughout the Middle Ages, though usually in a somewhat altered form presented by Paulus Orosius (c. 385-420), a pupil of Augustine, who drew attention to blessings attributed to godly rule that his mentor never expressed. The very title of Bishop Otto of Freising's (d.1158) *Chronicle of the History of the Two Cities* reflects Augustine's thesis. Just as Augustine conceived of the interaction of God and man in time – from the creation through the crucifixion and resurrection of Jesus Christ to the final judgment – so medieval chroniclers were generally universal in outlook, commencing their narratives in Eden and surveying events down to their own day, emphasizing, in the process, Divine intervention and rendering spiritualized interpretations not necessarily consonant with the clear import of events. There were exceptions to this pattern, of course. For example, a Benedictine monk known as "the Venerable Bede" (d.735) wrote a remarkable *Ecclesiastical History of the English People* – based on broad acquaintance with and careful evaluation of written and oral sources – that is itself an indispensable source for historians delving into the growth of Christianity in England and Anglo-Saxon culture. The work, intended to instruct "posterity" in righteous beliefs and conduct, deserves high praise. On the whole however, medieval chroniclers – monks and clergymen for the most part – tended to view events from the perspective of the church, and related "miraculous occurrences" difficult to verify. Also, in many instances, they were working for a patron or writing for a restricted audience whose approbation was desired. Since they seldom had collections of source materials at their disposal and frequently lacked the opportunity to exchange views with men of other localities, they could write with relative accuracy and assurance only on contemporary events that they had observed or knew about through reliable witnesses. Under these circumstances, it is hardly surprising that medieval chroniclers ordinarily made no attempt to analyze the social, intellectual, or economic forces underlying historical developments. In a sense, it is astonishing that, lacking formal techniques of scholarship and adequate sources, they did as well as they did. Without them, we would know little of the period known as the Middle Ages.

The Augustinian view of God's control of history began to crumble in the 15th century, though Bishop Bossuet remained an adherent as late as 1681. In the Italian peninsula, where skepticism concerning church practices and teachings was endemic during the high Renaissance, it was man, not God, who was glorified by the *literati*. The great Italian humanists were all historically-minded but were seldom good historians though they were very interested in the historians of antiquity and antique culture. They assiduously uncovered ancient manuscripts but were too prone to accept Livy and other classical writers at face value and to subordinate accuracy to a brilliant literary style. Leonardo Bruni (1374-1444) – sometime papal secretary and longtime chancellor of Florence – successfully combined history and rhetoric in his *History of Florence*, which was widely acclaimed. Owing in part to this work, but also to lesser works penned by humanists concerned more with didactic ends and a flowing, eloquent style than with factual veracity, historical writing became an independent literary genre. Whether decrying theological bias or simply ignoring ecclesiastical viewpoints, the humanists focused on secular affairs and saw no need for Divine causation: man was the mover of events. Machiavelli, for example, in his *History of Florence*, described the interaction between foreign and domestic affairs and emphasized that political developments determined history. Man, he believed, was the master of his own destiny. Machiavelli and those emulating him wrested politics from any religious or ethical framework and honored contemporary "heroes" – however cruel, irreligious, and immoral they might be. Most humanists did not hesitate to eulogize despots or wealthy men of affairs in exchange for their patronage, and they concentrated on histories of individual city-states instead of looking for universal patterns or stressing the history of mankind. In keeping with their adulation of classical authors, and perhaps in reaction against Christian historians, the Italian humanists discarded the linear view of chronology and revived the concept of recurring cycles. Past events, according to Francesco Guicciardini (1483-1540), could illuminate the future. Furthermore, past and current occurrences remained essentially the same, repeating themselves "under changed names and colors," so that only the most discerning observers would recognize them.

The anticlericalism of the *literati* did have some positive effects. Inconsistencies in church dogma and practices and clerical abuses were exposed, providing impetus for reform, as has been noted previously. It also prompted investigations such as that undertaken by Lorenzo Valla (d.1457), who proved that the so-called "Donation of Constantine," purportedly granting lands and temporal powers to the church, was an 8th-century forgery. The church had long suspected that the "document" was spurious and for many years had refrained from pressing any claims based on it; nevertheless, the caustic tone of Valla's critique aroused its ire. However Valla's methodology was sound. He is generally considered to be the father of textual criticism, an invaluable tool for determining the authenticity of documents.

During the course of the 16th century and for a half century thereafter, humanist historical writing was largely curtailed by the polemical "histories" written by partisan Protestants and Catholics. Each side marshaled whatever evidence it could to excoriate the other. Among the chief antagonists were Matthias Vlacich (1520-1575) – a contentious Lutheran who, with the help of other scholars, published a voluminous work, popularly known as *The Magdeburg Centuries*, that sought to disprove and derogate Catholic dogmas and rituals – and Cardinal Caesar Baronius (1538-1607) – confessor to Pope Clement VIII, papal diplomat, and head of the Vatican Library – whose penchant for suppressing evidence and obfuscating issues made his *Ecclesiastical Annals* even less credible than *The Magdeburg Centuries*. More heat than light was generated during this controversy, which, at a later date, was exploited by rationalists to discredit Christianity; yet many important documents on the early history of the church were uncovered, and a linear conception of chronology was restored.

With the coming of the 17th century, a new concern for technique and method was manifested in historical writing. Attempts were made to assign chronology where dating was obscure or unknown and to systematize the story of mankind into periodical categories like "ancient," "medieval," and "new." Moreover, manuscripts and other source materials began to be collected in a systematic manner, and critical methods for authenticating them were devised.

After the publication of Sir Isaac Newton's *Principia* late in the century, thinkers became enamored with science and motivated to discover natural laws that would govern all human activities. These laws could be ascertained through the power of human reason and empirical investigation, they insisted, and would be applied by "enlightened men" for the benefit of society at large. One need not adhere to outmoded religious beliefs or look for supernatural explanations for anything pertaining to man's life and work. Explanations were at hand for anyone willing to employ scientific methodology and reason. Ignorance must be overcome and credulity laid aside: man must free himself from religious superstitions of the past, follow the laws of nature, and promote liberty, humanity, and virtue. By doing so, man would experience unprecedented progress. Indeed, he could eventually perfect himself and his civilization; for through enlightened effort progressive improvement was inevitable and a man-made utopia attainable.

This ideology, shared by most of the French *philosophes* and a smattering of other continental and British thinkers, was expressed in Diderot's *Encyclopédie*, in French salons, in coffee houses and cafes, in many European courts, in secret societies, and in every venue where intellectuals gathered. Although most of the men and women of the "Enlightenment" gave less attention to history than to scientific experimentation and philosophical speculation, they came to recognize its importance for propagating their views. This attitude is evident in the statement of Henry Saint John, Viscount Bolingbroke (d.1751) that "history is philosophy teaching by example" and in Marie Antoine Nicholas de Caritat, Marquis de Condorcet's (d.1794) conviction that historical accounts not only could confirm human progress but suggest in what directions it should go and how it could be expedited.

Francoise Marie Arouet de Voltaire (d.1778), the most influential historian of the 18th century, was also the "Enlightenment's" most representative figure – scientific dabbler, philosopher, dramatist, satirist, poet, essayist, and historian. In 1751, he published *The Age of Louis XIV*, a composite picture of the era of the "Sun King." Institutions, politics, commerce, wars, art, music, letters, and society were all treated in this work, which sought to portray the spirit of the times. By encompassing the full range of human culture, Voltaire moved beyond the narrower themes of the past and provided a model to be emulated. In other works, including his *History of Charles XII* (Sweden) and *Essay on the Manners and Spirit of the Nation*s, he displayed both brilliance and bias. Thinking his own age to be the apex of human achievement and enlightenment to that point, he disparaged the Middle Ages, deeming them unworthy of consideration. The church, he believed, had stood in the way of human progress and prohibited free thought. The only periods of history worthy of note were the classical age of Greece and Rome, particularly as it pertained to Greek humanism, and the Renaissance. In all of his historical works, Voltaire cultivated the humanist credenda of natural religion and morality, toleration, humanitarianism, anti-Christian bias, and continuing cultural progress: application of "enlightened ideals," it was believed, would lead mankind to ever greater achievements.

Voltaire's limpid, polished, and ingratiating style and breadth of scope are laudable; yet he and like-minded rationalists were limited by their dogmatic preconceptions. Their contempt for the Middle Ages and their virtual apotheosis of reason left little disposition to try to feel the pulse of a past civilization that they believed had nothing to recommend it. Worshiping reason, they *irrationally* did not endeavor to place themselves in a position to understand intuitively or vicariously a culture they deemed despicable. In fact, they manifested an almost exclusive affinity for their own culture, acclaiming its superiority to those of all previous eras and seeking to advance their "enlightened" agenda while making little attempt to understand the differences in the milieu and outlook of other ages. By the same token, they were prone to render exaggerated commendations of "the noble savage" and Chinese civilization on the basis of superficial research. Still, their facile generalizations had their intended effect, predisposing historians who followed them toward a secular perspective and instilling in the minds of the intelligentsia skepticism about the relevance of Christianity for the well-being of mankind.

There can be no doubt, however, that man does not live "by bread alone" or, for that matter, by reason alone. The French Revolution and the Age of Napoleon brought great disillusionment concerning the rationalistic propaganda of the *philosophes*, particularly in the German territories, which, after all, had borne the brunt of French occupation. German intellectuals reacted against the philosophic postulates that appeared to have spawned Gallic attempts to disseminate the presumed blessings of "liberty, equality, and fraternity" throughout Europe, even by the sword. Immanuel Kant's premise that unaided reason and empirical investigation could go only so far, not being able to plumb the noumenal realm of knowledge, helped prompt German thinkers to expand their conception of noetic activity. Admittedly, reason constituted an important part of this activity, but far from all of it. In fact, an unbalanced dependence on reason could, they believed, lead one astray. Intuitive percipience, emotional apprehension, and even spiritual comprehension were also necessary.

Pietist-romantic clergyman Friedrich Schleiermacher (1768-1834) stirred the souls of Prussian youth fighting against Napoleon with his eloquent, emotion-packed, patriotic appeals, and pressed for a national educational system to serve as an instrument for moral regeneration and the rejuvenator of national strength; and other leaders in the war for liberation similarly employed romanticism as an ideological weapon. Rational appeals alone would not arouse the German masses to determined resistance. Not all would understand them. It was, therefore, no torpid intellectual hostility that was directed against France: it was a passionate, often unreasoning hatred that gripped the German soul and permeated every fiber of his being.

However, German romanticism was more than an expression of patriotism or a nationalistic weapon: it was, as we have seen (p.90), a protest against the shallowness and sterility of the thought processes of the "Enlightenment" and, as in England, an antidote to the social adjustments caused by the incipient industrial revolution and the materialism accompanying it. German romantics welcomed flight from cities into a natural environment and practiced *Sehnsucht* – turning inward and yearning for what might be – in trying to escape the unpleasant realities of the times. Also, like other continental romantics, they harked back to the Middle Ages – an imagined "golden age." A Gothic revival took place in architecture and literature, which stimulated in turn medieval historical studies, resulting in an impetus to record and relate past events as well as to compile a monumental collection of documentary sources. Romanticism aroused an interest in the particularism and individuality that characterized various peoples or nations in counterdistinction to the generalizations of the 18th-century *philosophes*; and it promoted investigations of the cultural aspects of history, since the *Volksgeist* and *Weltanschuung* of a people must be *felt*: they could not be understood through reason alone. The folk spirit could be observed best in the medieval epoch – the repository of the ideals constituting the heart and soul of the German community. This sentiment was in basic accord with the views of pre-romantic Johann Gottfried Herder (1748-1803), who extolled the uniqueness of every age and every organic community – German or non-German – because each, he maintained, possessed distinctive folkways, customs, literature, music, and religion that should be fostered for the enrichment of all mankind. Consequently, peoples should be studied within their own social, intellectual, and cultural milieus. This attitude contrasted with the air of superiority assumed by 18th-century historians toward past generations, which they tended to judge by the standards of their own era. On the other hand, romantics shared the "Enlighteners" confidence that human progress was cumulative and continuous.

In their own day, German romantics idealized the good, solid qualities of the German character evinced by commoners, especially peasants, who allegedly were closest to the natural state of human innocence. In spite of being poor and sometimes downtrodden, even victimized in some respects (Russian romantics picked up this theme), the common people possessed admirable virtues worthy of emulation. Their humble condition and not infrequent mistreatment doubtless served to shape their character and accentuate their sterling qualities, which in times of adversity or defeat were all the more apparent. From this romantic truism, there has emerged in our own day a phony celebration of real or imaginary victims. Certain artificially-posited groups of people – minorities of all sorts, women, the physically or mentally handicapped, homosexuals, and any other group that may emerge (excepting white males and Christians) – are said to deserve society's special empathy and are to be accorded compensatory assistance or privileges. To be disadvantaged or "victimized" is *prima facie* evidence of virtue, based on the supposition that the world is too coarse and evil to treat a pure soul fairly; therefore, degradation or failure vindicates a person, attesting to his nobility and purity. On that account, society should go out of its way to accommodate and acclaim not so much actual victims, but sociologically-designated ones.

In 19th-century Germany, romantics venerated the *Volksgeist* – the spirit arising from the people or national spirit – which provided the state with its corporate individuality. The state was more than its composite parts, more than simply a multitude of individuals bound together by some rational contract: it was a people related by blood, descent, traditions, culture, history, common interest, and a similar *Weltanschauung*. Germany was a corporate body that, like any living organism, needed to grow if it were not to deteriorate and die. Obviously, a strong, nationalistic government could exploit such ideas to inaugurate and carry out an aggressive foreign policy, while also citing the Darwinian dictum "the survival of the fittest" to excuse expanionist initiatives; for did not the very dominance of an energetic and forceful nation validate its superiority and concomitant right to extend its hegemony? Indeed, was a powerful and highly civilized nation not obliged to pursue its highest destiny in the interest of human progress?

Such ideas were not confined to Germany: in fact, in Great Britain they were exceptionally strong, not just in the Foreign Office, but in popular attitudes and culture. Similar concepts fueled the colonial-imperialistic efforts of most Western powers, and the competition to establish or take over colonies or spheres of influence led to bitter rivalries, "saber rattling," and clashes between these nations, which contributed, most historians agree, to the outbreak of World War I.

Ironically, the nations drawn into this conflict appear not to have wanted matters to develop to the point of armed conflict, but their heedless optimism, careless actions, belligerent posturing, exaggerated sense of national honor, opportunistic striving to obtain some advantage at the expense of other nations, systems of alliances, and heightened preparedness for conflict eventuated in a war that took more than ten million lives; cost defeated countries their colonial empires; weakened the traditional ruling classes; brought financial distress, increased taxes, and inflation in most European nations, and economic collapse in Germany; displaced millions of people; together with the scientific discoveries of Einstein and the "uncertainty principle" of Heisenberg, called into question traditional beliefs and long-accepted absolutes; contributed to decaying values and morals; gave rise to cynicism and God-denying existentialism; devastated the human psyche; removed many of the customary restraints of civilized life and gave impetus to all sorts of radical movements, including anarchism, communism, syndicalism, racism, and ultra-nationalism; and planted seeds of mistrust, resentment, and hatred that would lead to an even greater cataclysm two decades later.

The theory of inevitable progress had received a crippling if not a mortal blow; yet intellectuals did not re-examine their humanistic premises or look to God's Word for consolation or direction. On the contrary, they oppugned Christianity, professing disbelief in its relevance and verity, looking instead for scientific answers to social and ethical problems.

This reverential attitude toward science and its proposed application, not just to investigation of the physical universe, but to providing answers to all manner of human problems, was not new: it went back to Comte (pp.91-92), perhaps even to Diderot. As applied to history, the scientific method demanded that investigators concentrate on original source materials, testing them or having them tested to ascertain their authenticity and reliability and subjecting them to rigorous internal criticism; ferreting out inconsistencies and possible reasons for biases; considering whether the primary witnesses were able and willing to tell the truth; taking account of how close they were to the matters recorded and how much time had elapsed before they wrote their observations; evaluating what they may have to gain, if anything, in saying what they did; and seeking for corroboration or contradiction from other primary witnesses. Ascertaining the causes of historical phenomena and their results was of the utmost importance. The scientific investigator might start with certain hypotheses concerning the causes of specific developments or occurrences (multiple causes were and are usually postulated) and subject them to "scientific" scrutiny based on an analysis of "reliable data" from original sources. Always, however, there was an unspoken presupposition that the explanations of "causes" must be rational and natural (supernatural explanations were rejected out of hand), for causation must be explicable in terms of the general experience of the human race.

Probably the greatest practitioner of the scientific approach was the great German historian Leopold von Ranke (1795-1886). In his concern to avoid over-romanticizing history to glorify or substantiate certain presuppositions or opinions (as 18th-century historians were inclined to do), Ranke advocated presentation of facts as they actually occurred. Unfortunately, his intent to relate everything *wie es eigentlich gewesen* was misinterpreted by admirers ready to divest history of everything but the "facts" and to allow the truth to emerge somehow in the reader's mind. Ranke himself did not engage in such sterile presentations of events. He did seek to base his works on primary evidence and to be dispassionate and objective in handling his materials, but he never refrained from rendering interpretations based on his findings. In his seminars, he taught his students to seek out and use "the purest, most immediate" documents – analyzing their authors according to their affiliations, temperaments, and opportunities for access to first-hand information – and to propound conclusions, not on the basis of presumptions or preferred interpretations, but commensurate with the evidence uncovered.

Ranke himself worked within a theistic framework, duly recognizing that God was the Author and Controller of history, while confining himself to empirical means of investigation and, to a preponderant degree, interpretation. He wrote a justly famous *History of the Popes,* a history of the world, and histories of every major country of Europe, seeing in each a corporate personality. In this perspective and in his emphasis on the personalities of people he considered to be causal agents of history – through their actions, thoughts, efforts, and sufferings – Ranke displayed a romantic bent; yet, to him, scientific methodology appeared to offer the best, though not a perfect, means of reconstructing the human experience of the past essentially as it happened, without imposing upon it the attitudes and spirit of his own day. In a number of respects, Ranke was a transitional figure incorporating both romantic and positivist qualities in his research and writing, and he manifested a propinquity for historicism, but without rejecting the supernatural.

Ranke's disciples, however, generally sought to pursue total objectivity by scientific means, but no human attempt to relate only the facts is possible. The "facts" must be interpreted in some fashion to make them intelligible. Furthermore, how can a writer know what facts to select unless he has a world view by which he judges what is essential or important? Objectivity is a noble goal, but every historian should recognize his incapacity to arrive at complete truth, try as he may. Only God knows all the facts, and only He is capable of rendering appraisals that are totally fair and accurate.

Such was the faith in a scientific method, however, that it continued to be applauded and applied according to historiographical canons that rarely acknowledged God or the necessity to undertake the quest for historical accuracy with appropriate humility. For those conversant with Hegel's conception of history as the progress of human freedom and the expression of the world spirit (see pp.92-93), history assumed a paramountcy practically tantamount to deity. It molded man's thought patterns and values and controlled his development, for man existed in a closed system: there could be nothing beyond the human experience in the here and now as manifested in "the interior spirit of the age" – no transcendental causes. Past events helped determine the present, but there was no room for Divine purpose or involvement. Not all devotees of historicism, as this ideology is termed, were Hegelian, but those who were believed that the course of history was ineluctable and that whatever evolved was acceptable. Everything was in a constant state of flux; therefore, it was incumbent upon historians to place themselves vicariously within the period being studied, identifying themselves, as much as possible, with the cultures, thought patterns, and feelings of the people in order to understand them experientially.

One 20th-century devotee of historicism, Robin G. Collingwood (1889-1943), maintained that historical truth may be discovered and historical occurrences explained through a reflective re-enactment of the thoughts of persons whose activities have determined the course of events. While this methodology might yield some insights, Collingwood's premise denies God's hand in history or that anything can happen outside the causal influence of men. For example, how can one adhere to this premise and explain the sudden death of Czarina Elizabeth (r.1741-1762) of Russia, an event that saved Prussia from almost certain defeat in the Seven Years` War (1756-1763)? Her demise was neither planned nor predicted. For that matter, other historical events or movements can not be explained merely by identifying with the persons involved in them and re-enacting their thoughts. Who, for example, would be so foolish to say that the Industrial Revolution was planned? If historical evolution determines man's beliefs as well as the manner in which everything unfolds, there are no absolutes: anything whatsoever becomes admissible, even acceptable. Removing God from history is, therefore, unthinkable.

Although American historians did not adopt historicism, some were influenced by Marxist concepts of economic determinism (pp.93-94), according to which the dialectic moving the wheels of history was energized and pressed forward by a class struggle between those exploiting the economic system for their own profit and the exploited lower classes. Charles Beard (1874-1948), in his *An Economic Interpretation of the Constitution* (1913), spoke of class conflict between the lower classes – the small farmers and the Eastern workingmen – and the merchants, financiers, manufacturers, and big landholders who finally succeeded in creating a Constitution capable of protecting the monied interests and property owners.

Similarly, proponents of the conflict theory of sociological thought view society as being managed to protect the interests of a dominant class or classes. Therefore, social phenomena are analyzed through statistical surveys and opinion samplings to uncover how they serve the interest of particular groups. Unlike the structural school of sociology popularized by Émile Durkheim (1858-1917) and, more recently, Robert Merton and Talcott Parsons, that tend to see various societal structures such as family, government, education, and religion as working together to reach a consensus of values, rules, and norms for the sake of maintaining a stable, functional society, the conflict theorists dismiss absolutes, legislated restrictions, and authority of any type because they are viewed as serving controlling interest groups. No evidence to the contrary will assuage this skepticism. For instance, progressive legislation passed early in this century in response to popular outcry to improve conditions for laborers is debunked as the veiled efforts of big government and the business community to appease and delude the working class. Characteristically, sociologists play down the importance of individuals or particulars while analyzing problems affecting collective units. From their vantage point, a divorce is not so much a personal tragedy as a manifestation of a broader problem with the institution of marriage. By the same token, particulars in history are relatively unimportant. History is determined by "social forces," not by individuals: in fact, individual attitudes, conduct, and perceptions are shaped by these social forces, leaving no room for any transcendental influence.

The modern fixation on social forces was not that of Thomas Carlyle (1795-1881), who looked on history as the cumulative biographies of the great personages – those who had overturned decadent institutions and initiated changes or opened up new pathways, in his estimation, of ethical truths. Heedless of scientific methodology and slothful in research, Carlyle, nevertheless, brought life to his characters and, like a romantic painter, splashed vivid color here and there, ignoring details such as diplomatic relations and constitutional and economic developments to portray a stirring, captivating pageant that seemed to convey reality to his readers. His *French Revolution* (1838), *Oliver Cromwell's Letters and Speeches* (1845), and biography of Frederick II of Prussia present his primary thesis – that history is essentially determined by strong, heroic leaders.

The romantic spirit was also strongly evident in the histories of Frenchman Jules Michelet (d.1874), whose multi-volume *The History of France* (1833-1867), *The People* (1846), and *The French Revolution* are veritable historical dramas, honoring the contribution of common people to the cause of human liberty. Using tableaux rather than adhering to a strictly narrative approach, Michelet focused on persons and scenes illustrating his thesis and reflecting glory on his beloved country.

Likewise, the romantic penchant for writing patriotic history is seen in the works of 19th-century American authors. George Bancroft's (1800-1891) *The History of the United States from the Discovery of America* (10 volumes, 1834-1887) is a patriotic history that recognizes Providence in America's epic and extolls the struggles of her people to attain and perpetuate liberty, without, paradoxically enough, dealing with the issue of slavery. In so doing, he buttressed the righteous self-image of the young nation. Sometimes criticized for its "didacticism," Bancroft's great work was nonetheless founded on solid research while suiting the temperament of the times.

As the romantic impulse gradually began to wane in the latter half of the 19th century, American historians – often imbued with a semi-Hegelian view of the state – concentrated on the nation's politics, government, diplomacy, and wars. This focus began to change as a new group of writers – trained in applying the methodology of the natural sciences to historical research – started to replace the patrician, amateur historians who (with few exceptions, including Bancroft who had been trained in Germany) had tended to view history as a literary genre. As we have seen above (p.136), regard for the Darwinian theory prompted historians like Charles Beard to try to apply it in their research and interpretations. Similarly, Frederick Jackson Turner (1861-1932) stressed the evolution of the American character and institutions as a result of the advancing frontier.

Early in the 20th century, historians of the so-called "Progressive School" took a broader look at society than had their predecessors, trying to demonstrate that it was the product, not merely of political forces, but of the interplay of economic, technological, social, and psychological influences. More than this, they endeavored to use history to motivate reforms for the furtherance of democracy and egalitarian ideals that presumably would benefit future generations. Intellectual history, the history of science and technology, economic history, and social history became new specialities to redress the balance *vis à vis* political history, as this "New History" became more acclaimed. Possible influences from any quarter were given consideration. Geographer Ellsworth Huntington (1876-1947) gave historians some grist to grind with his theory, expressed in *Civilization and Climate* (1915) and other monographs, that climate, availability of water, type of terrain, and scarcity or abundance of natural resources contributed to the nature and distinctiveness of various civilizations, as Montesquieu had postulated early in the 18th century.

Surprisingly, cultural history – despite the initial boost given it by Voltaire – was slower to emerge, though Swiss historian Jacob Burckhardt's (d.1897) *The Civilization of the Renaissance in Italy* (1860) and John Addington Symonds's

(1840-1893) *The Renaissance in Italy* (7 volumes, 1875-1886) provided some impetus. Recently, however, a more systematic attempt at a composite, holistic humanities approach to history has emerged – one calculated to take into account the many cultural factors that characterize and explain divers civilizations.

Numerous illustrations of the relevance of cultural studies for providing insights into historical personalities and understanding of the movements, developments, and occurrences affecting particular civilizations could be given, but a sketch of one must suffice: the influence of romanticism on the fiendish leader of Germany's Third Reich – Adolf Hitler (1889-1945). Hitler's involvement in the occult, well-documented by several authors, undoubtedly inculcated a dominant idiosyncrasy in his personality; and the influence of Friedrich Nietzsche (d.1900) is frequently cited. The parallels in the thought of Nietzsche and Hitler are undeniably striking. Nietzsche despised Christianity for propounding an ethic suitable only for slaves and visualized an *Übermensch* (superman) who would subordinate inferior humans and establish a type of morality and creativity far superior to conventional, rational norms by penetrating into the irrational quintessence of humanity. Spurning the rational and delving into the recesses of the human psyche smacks of romanticism, and Nietzsche's proposition that the superman should ruthlessly exercise "the will to power" to establish his own myths or values to animate culture partakes of both romanticism and Darwinian thought.

Curiously, in view of his adulation of the will to power, Nietzsche criticized Hegel's apotheosis of the state, which through perseverence and conflict, would eliminate corruption and decadence, emerging victorious as the world spirit to usher in new progressive stages of humanity. Hitler, however, eclectically borrowed from Hegel, Nietzsche, and all manner of "isms," among them Darwinism and romanticism. His favorite operas were the florid, bombastic extravaganzas of romantic composer Richard Wagner (1813-1883), with their celebration of heathen Teutonic myths and occult rituals, which he drank in with "intoxicated ecstasy."

The dark side of romanticism appealed to the *Führer* and, in some respects, was commensurate with his ends. For instance, it promoted anti-Semitism where previously there had been toleration. It extolled the passionately loyal Teutonic youth of yore who was ready to give his life on the field of battle for the imagined glory of being conducted to Valhalla. The resultant militarism, narrow nationalism, and arrogant attitudes of superiority could be exploited by the Nazi leader. Cleverly presented, romanticism could be employed to help achieve the thousand-year Reich managed and controlled by supermen imbued with Nietzsche's will to power; for the German people were thoroughly disillusioned by the economic hardship they had endured after the cessation of hostilities in 1918, angry because their troops allegedly had been forced to lay down their arms by a civilian clique that had "stabbed them in the back," and disgusted with the apparent inability of the Weimar Republic – foisted upon them by the victorious Allied powers – to provide stable government. This was a people who, in the course of the 19th century, had seen liberal spokesmen calling for representative government either leave the country after the revolutions of 1848 or make peace with the political leadership in return for orderly, honest and stable, if authoritarian, government; a people accorded little input in choosing its rulers, but who gloried in scientific progress, the unification of Germany under Chancellor Otto von Bismarck, and Germany's reputation for scholarship enjoyed throughout Europe and the world; a people mesmerized by the success of Bismarck's heavy-handed policies; a people seeking for its place in the sun; a people imbued with a romantic trust in the strong leader in touch with the world spirit whose actions may not be immediately apprehended; a people whose churches had for a long time submitted to governmental guardianship and whose humanistic philosophy, experience, and psyche welcomed energetic, effective state leadership; a people proud of their culture and outraged, after the humiliating defeat of World War I, by the treaty imposed upon them. Such a people was receptive to the demonic genius that was Adolf Hitler.

Indeed, for all the great intellectual accomplishments of the German people, they were vulnerable to the neo-romantic distrust of intellectual ratiocination evident among Nazi elites. Non-rational avenues to knowledge were encouraged: intuition, feelings, magic, and all sorts of occult practices. Subordinates were to obey the *Führer* instinctively, moved by primitive natural forces or heroic legends to emulate the martial discipline of the Middle Ages rather than to covet the luxuries and economic security that were snares to less disciplined nations.

The Nazi slogan "Blood and Soil" epitomized this neo-romantic quest for glory and conquest in the manner of a pagan Wagnerian opera. The German people, already conditioned to unquestioning obedience to civil authority and steeped in the romantic notion that the leader (like a great poet or artist or other creative genius) grasped truth intuitively which may be hidden from others, were prone not to interfere with their *Führer* until his masterpiece was completed. Unswerving dedication could be given to a hero leader prescient enough to divine the will and aspirations of the Volk and strong enough to smash any nation or group that tried to prevent or restrain their expression.

Hitler played the role of the romantic leader to the hilt and took every conceivable measure to mold the collective Volk mentality to his will. Hitler understood well the psychological impact of mass meetings and played, as a master musician, upon the collective consciousness fostered during the romantic epoch. On one occasion, he stated to a henchman:

> "At a mass meeting, thought is eliminated. And because this is the state of mind I require, because, it secures to me the best sounding-board for my speeches, I order everyone to attend the meetings, where they become a part of the mass whether they like it or not, 'intellectuals' and bourgeois as well as the workers. I mingle the people. I speak to them only as the mass.... The masses are like an animal that obeys its instincts. They do not reach conclusions by reasoning."[1]

Children were to be taught to despise their minds. The process of cognition was depreciated in favor of developing proper instincts and "character." "We don't intend to educate our children into becoming miniature scholars," said a leading Nazi educator. "The real values resting in the German child are not awakened by stuffing a great mass of knowledge into him.... Therefore,... let us have ten pounds less knowledge and ten calories more character!" Hitler himself insisted: "I will have no intellectual training. Knowledge is the ruin of my young men...."[2] He wanted youth whose

---

[1]Quoted in Leonard Peikoff, *The Ominous Parallels* (NY: Stein & Day,1982), p.41.

[2]Quoted in *ibid.*, p 42.

"character" reflected Nazi ideals. "A violently active, dominating, intrepid, brutal youth – that is what I'm after." Thus the dark and mystical aspects of romanticism not only helped prepare the way for Hitler, but were appropriated by him to further his own diabolical ends.

The Holocaust unleashed by the Nazi regime, in which at least six million Jews and perhaps an equal number of other so-called "sub-humans" were exterminated, can never be forgotten by those living through the horror, or, for that matter, by any fair-minded person with an ounce of human kindness. Memories of these atrocities and the awesome carnage of World War II (17,000,000 military men and 18,000,000 civilians lost their lives) are permanently etched in the minds of those experiencing them firsthand, and virtually everyone who lived through the era will never forget it.

The bloodshed, destruction, and intense emotions accompanying the conflict – together with what seemed to be an interminable "cold war" following in its wake – eventually arrested any serious belief in inevitable human progress; yet the majority of Americans who remained on the "home front" had prospered and, therefore, were able to put the war behind them quickly. This was not true, of course, of those mourning lost loved ones; of those veterans who had experienced more suffering, hardship, and brutality than would most people in two lifetimes; or of those still bearing severe physical, mental, or emotional scars. However, the war ended on a note of jubilation. The fighting had ended, the separation from those who had served overseas was over, and the nation was prosperous. Industries were retooling for a consumer economy, and thousands of former military men were enrolling in colleges under the "G.I. Bill." If a certain uneasiness concerning the future lingered and the swallowing of Eastern Europe by the Soviet Union and the fall of China in 1949 to a communist regime cast a pall over the peace, the nation, nevertheless, proceeded to disarm as quickly as possible. Americans worried more about the rising cost of living, securing good and affordable housing, and delays they were experiencing in being able to replace worn-out equipment or to purchase a new car than about what was going on in the rest of the world. While the forging of a United Nations Organization by the free nations of the world to keep the peace was trumpeted in the media, most Americans remained relatively unconcerned. They had enough of war and involvement abroad; they wanted to put all of this behind them – to obtain or retain good jobs, make money, raise their families, and pursue the "American dream."

Some concerns and frustrations were aired, of course, but on the whole Americans were optimistic, looking toward the future with confidence. Certainly, they were in no mood to look back on the warnings of historical theorists such as Oswald Spengler (d.1936), Vilfredo Pareto (d.1923), Pitirim Sorokin (1889-1968), and Arnold Toynbee (1889-1975).

Spengler was a German historian and philosopher whose *magnum opus, The Decline of the West* (2 volumes, 1918-1922; translated in 1926-1928) asserts that every civilization, like a living organism, passes through a life cycle – from birth to youth, maturity, old age, and death. During its adolescent years, it grows very rapidly, vigorously expanding its boundaries. By middle age, it begins to settle down, and eventually it decays and dies. The process is inexorable. Nothing man can do will avert or prevent it. Western culture, as Spengler saw it, was already in decline and might not last beyond the end of the century.

Not quite so pessimistic was Italian economist and sociologist Vilfredo Pareto, who saw cycles of liberty and authority repetitively alternating throughout history. In his own day, he recognized a swing toward authoritarian rule – a realty he saw take place when Benito Mussolini (r.1922-1945) seized power in September of 1922, shortly before Pareto's death.

Russian-born Pitirim Sorokin, a naturalized American citizen who taught sociology at the University of Minnesota and later at Harvard, echoed Spengler and Pareto in stating that Western civilization is in decline. In his work entitled *Social and Cultural Dynamics* (4 volumes, 1937-1941), Sorokin adopts Spengler's paradigm of a living organism whose eventual senility and death are inevitable; yet he attributes the decline of the West to its materialism and loss of values, thus creating an anomaly. He categorizes civilizations as being either ideational or sensate. The ideational civilization considers reality as being non-material and everlasting with predominantly spiritual needs and ends; on the other hand, the sensate civilization looks at reality as an evolutionary process of constant change, progress, and transformation that focuses principally on material concerns. In the latter case, a civilization traverses a number of stages to disintegration, though there is almost endless variety in how reality is manifested within different countries and time periods. It is clear, however, that Western civilization has passed its zenith and is in the sensate stage – that of post-maturity – in which freedoms gradually are being lost to be superseded by force and fraud in "all inter-individual and inter-group relationships."

The cyclical interpretation of history was also espoused by British historian Arnold Toynbee in his monumental *A Study of History* (12 volumes, 1934-1961). In it, he notes that of the 21 civilizations (Toynbee focuses on civilizations or culture groups rather than nations) in the history of mankind, only one – that of the West – remains, and it is decaying. Once emerging, a civilization develops and grows stronger as it successfully responds to the difficulties – the challenges – it encounters. In overcoming each obstacle, it becomes more able to meet the next one and to flourish. History moves through a rhythmic pattern of challenge and response, and civilizations are able to surmount challenges thanks to the efforts of a minority of creative, determined people. In its first stage, a civilization has to overcome the physical and external obstacles confronting it and gain command over the environment. Once this is accomplished and people begin to enjoy the fruits of their success, they become affluent. Then apathy sets in until, eventually, a sort of hardening of the arteries occurs. No longer does government allow as many changes as in the past, and freedoms are infringed upon until death finally occurs. The demise may come because of an intractability of institutions, or sometimes it may be the result of the intransigence of classes or of the religious parochialism of those legalistically adhering to powerless forms, traditions, and rituals. In decaying civilizations, standardization and rigidity, rather than diversity and flexibility, rule.

Unlike Spengler, Toynbee does not believe that the demise of a civilization is inevitable. Human beings still have the ability to choose and act. If they respond properly and with sufficient strength and dedication to the disintegration they observe, there is hope. In the case of the West, there must be a return to its cultural roots – Christianity – if it is to survive; yet Toynbee remains somewhat imprecise regarding the importance of the Christian faith, taking an equivocal stance that leaves the impression that one religion is not necessarily superior to another.

In the postmodern culture of the present day, the historical canons of the past are rapidly disappearing. Reality, even historical reality, is not critically dependent upon evidence provided in primary documents or reliable secondary sources as in the past; for, according to deconstructionists Jacques Derrida and Michel Foucault (inspired by Darwinian existentialist premises), to believe in absolute truth is absurd. Even factual statements found in writings or records of the past are susceptible to bowdlerization or reinterpretation. They may be disregarded or vandalized at the whim of the deconstructionists, who may proceed to create their meaning practically *ex nihilo*. Speculation, opinion, and fantasy may be paraded as scholarship; for language, in effect, determines reality, which in turn becomes a social construct. No longer content to manufacture reality for themselves, contemporary deconstructionists would fabricate it for society at large while recognizing that it is unstable and transient. Today's reality may be tomorrow's falsehood; for innumerable meanings may be assigned to any given text as the original author's intent is deconstructed and given a totally different meaning (or a number of meanings), proving that his was not the final word. Indeed, there is no final word.

Even linear chronology, a hallmark of Jewish and Christian historiography, would be destroyed by deconstructionists, because linear thinking allegedly inhibits "pluri-dimensional symbolic thoughts," thereby distorting the unity of reason. One can but wonder who is really destroying reason when it is interpreted as whatever will lead to a desired end. What confusion! What absurdity! Without recognition of God, there are no absolutes, no truth – everything is relative, subject to any interpretation, no matter how extreme, ridiculous, or unsubstantiated it may be.

It is interesting to recall that cyclical views of history have prevailed or have attained prominence in periods or in cultures not recognizing a Creator God – for example, among Oriental civilizations, the ancient Greeks, the humanists of the Italian Renaissance, the 18th-century "enlighteners," or adherents to some contemporary world view, thought pattern, philosophy, assumption, or false religion derived from or commensurate with the Darwinian theory of evolution. Such ideologies idolize the state, history, science, humanity, or other "deities," rendering a Creator God superfluous or irrelevant; or they "divinize" a process like Marxism or economic determinism, historicism, or naturalism, which remove moral constraints, thereby making man a victim rather than a sinner, and allowing him to act as he chooses or wills.

On the other hand, the linear view of history arises from a biblical understanding that there is a transcendent and personal God, who after bringing into being the cosmos and everything in it – including the earth and its atmosphere, plant and animal life, and mankind – continues to govern history and infuses it with meaning. God's purpose is being worked out, though man's input is important. History is not the senseless sequence and blind recurrence of events that cyclicists presume. While both Spengler and Toynbee postulated cycles moving forward within a linear schema in which they periodized civilizations from their beginnings to their ultimate demise, the former accepted blind recurrence of cycles that move civilizations inexorably toward their doom, while the latter believed Western man still could avert disaster, if only he would, by returning to his Christian roots. Spengler's pessimism is not ill-founded, and Toynbee's slender ray of hope is doomed to extinction; for natural man lacks the power to save himself and, according to the Bible, will refuse to return to God. Christian historians – at least biblically-minded Christian historians – should be aware of this fact, because they have an advantage over their secular counterparts: not only do they have the evidence from the past and developments in the present to guide them, but they have in God's Word a revelation of what the future holds. According to Scripture, individuals who trust in Jesus Christ and groups of believers will escape eternal death and the worst cataclysmic horrors of the final days (whether by avoiding them, being preserved in the midst of them, or death), but cultures, civilizations, and nations as we know them will be destroyed at Christ's second coming. He is the *Alpha* and the *Omega*, the Beginning and the End, and it will be through His intervention alone that our present world system will be terminated and His everlasting dominion will be established.

As we consider the task of the historian and, in particular, of the Christian historian, let it be said that any historian should incorporate new facts that he discovers. Even without new facts, the historian may have good reasons for wishing to present fresh thoughts that do no violence to the existing evidence. Most professional historians write about the past from the perspective of their own time though they may make a concerted effort to identify with the thought patterns and culture of those about whom they are writing. All of these techniques are acceptable and doubtless desirable in so far as they go, but the veracity of what is written will probably be determined as much by the historian's industry and integrity as by his methodology. The careful historian should do what he can to put aside personal biases and use his sources honestly and fairly, presenting on the basis of his expertise, knowledge, and regard for truth what he believes they reveal. His interpretations should be judicious and supported by the evidence; yet inevitably they will flavored by his personal experiences and world view.

The Christian historian should do more. He should view all events – past, present, and future – in the light of eternity. To be sure, by definition, history does not deal with contemporary affairs or the future, but a proper regard for them will affect what one writes concerning the past; and the more one knows about all eras, the more he is able to enrich his readers. For a historian to refrain from bringing to bear the fullness of his knowledge is to deprive the reader in some measure, perhaps even in a manner detrimental to him. At the same time, for a historian to write in the light of eternity is not to evangelize (that is not his task), but simply to present the truth, as he knows it, as cogently and completely as he can. To do so, he must have a mastery of all his sources, including the Word of God, recognize God's purpose and plan for mankind, and be able to set forth past events as illuminated by that plan. Thus, God's revealed truth, as well as the Christian historian's knowledge of the past and present, can enable him to bring special benefits and blessings to his readers as he writes, openly and without dissembling or special pleading, in the light of eternity.

Chapter XVI

SCRIPTURAL PRINCIPLES APPLICABLE TO HISTORY: "THE CREATION PRINCIPLE"

Christian historians should not only attend God's Word for their personal lives but commit to apply it to their writing and teaching; for God is the Creator of the universe, time, and history; and He has established laws or principles by which men should conduct themselves to help effect His eternal purposes. The principles applicable to individuals are also, by and large, applicable to peoples and nations; yet, surprisingly, the average Christian – even one careful to observe God's precepts in his own private life – has not realized that they are equally relevant to large corporate bodies. Moreover, the biblical principles pertaining to human society often overlap: indeed, they always complement one another and are never antithetical. Because they are Divinely given, to try to list them all would be presumptuous, to explicate them in a comprehensive manner impossible. Only when the Lord inaugurates His personal rule on earth will mankind fully understand His ways. Only then will "the earth be full of the knowledge of the Lord as the waters cover the sea" (Isaiah 11:9; cf. Habbakuk 2:14). Even now, however, the spiritually-minded person whose heart yearns for godly rule can learn to conduct himself in harmony with the principles governing man and his history. For that reason, we shall try to elucidate, if only imperfectly, some of these Divine decrees.

First, let us look at the "Creation Principle." "In the beginning," we are told, "God created the heavens and the earth" – the cosmos and the entire natural order (Genesis 1:1; cf. Psalm 102:25 and John 1:3). Notwithstanding what reprobate men may think – notwithstanding the views of ancient philosophers such as Aristotle, Plotinus, and Lucretius and modern proponents of Charles Darwin's theory of evolution, Almighty God is the Creator of the universe and all living things.

Just as the Great Designer brought everything into being by His Word (Genesis 1:3, 6, 9, 14, 20, 24, 26; Psalm 33:6; John 1:1-3; Hebrews 11:3; and II Peter 3:5), so He also sustains all things by His Word and governs all to the furtherance of His eternal purpose and the glory of His name (Psalm 19; Psalm 33:4-11; Psalm 119:89-91; Isaiah 40:6-8; and Hebrews 1:3). Ancient Israel recognized this truth. Moses taught the Hebrews that the Law was "inscribed by the finger of God" (Deuteronomy 9:18); the Israelites were commanded not to add to or subtract from the commands of their God (Deuteronomy 4:2) and that observing His Word or commandments brought life and prosperity (Deuteronomy 8:1-9 and 30:15-16); and prophets of the Lord God appealed to an oft-erring or apostate nation by saying, "Hear the Word of Yahweh."

Surely the God who called into being everything there is (outside Himself) by His Word still cares for His masterpiece. The Father, the great "I Am"; Jesus Christ the Son, who is the same yesterday, today, and forever (Hebrews 13:8); and the Holy Spirit, who brooded over the primeval waters and effected God's creative edict constitute an omnipotent, omniscient, omnipresent Godhead that tenderly watches over and cares for the entire creation. Contrary to all evolutionary process-oriented views of the universe, time, man, and history – all things – are the handiwork of God who is absolutely sovereign. Thus history can only be understood in terms of the Creator and the inalterable laws He established in the universe. As we realize this truth, we should share the enthusiasm of the little girl who listened enthralled as her grandmother read aloud the creation story. As the grandmother closed the Bible story book, she hugged the child who seemed lost in thought and said, "Well, dear, what do you think of it?" "Oh, I love it," responded the youngster. It's so exciting! You never know what God is going to do next!"

There are several aspects to the "Creation Principle," and the one stated above – that God as Creator is also the Supreme Law-giver – should be self-evident. In the early years of this country's existence, America's thinkers and leaders predicated their belief in the rule of law on Romans 13:1 and 4: "...there is no authority except that which God has established: the authorities that exist have been established by God..." as His servants "to do you good." This doctrine, inherent in Christian theology, was proclaimed by Catholics and Protestants alike. For example, Thomas Aquinas's "Treatise on Law" (*Summa Theologica*, Questions 90 -97) repeatedly insists that all law emanates from God and must serve "the common good," and that "every human law has just so much the nature of law as it is derived from the [God-given] law of nature: ... if at any point it deflects from the law of nature, it is no longer a law but a perversion of law" (Question 95, Article 2, Obj. 4. See also Question 96, Article 4). The same assumption is implicit in English common law; and as early as 1215, the *Magna Carta* enunciated the concomitant premise that, because God was the Author of all law, no human beings – not even kings – were exempt from it. These biblical precepts, taken for granted by the English settlers who established themselves on America's eastern seaboard, were reinforced by Sir William Blackstone's *Commentaries on the Laws of England* (4 volumes, 1765-1769), which nurtured generations of American jurists and lawyers from the late colonial period until after the Civil War. Blackstone taught that all human law is derived from a universally-applicable "law of nature" revealed by God in Holy Scripture; therefore, any legislation or man-made law not in accord with this law of nature is invalid. In the strictest sense of the word, therefore, men do not "make" laws, but rather ascertain how God-given principles can be adapted and promulgated for a particular exigency or situation. Since all man-made laws partake of the Divinely-ordained law of nature to which every man's conscience bears witness (cf. Romans 2:15), no lawbreaker can claim immunity from a statute by pleading ignorance of it. Laws predicated on immutable moral principles may be reworded or expanded to meet different or changing situations, but the moral absolutes themselves remain forever the same.

Unfortunately, the reliance on the law of nature and nature's God that undergirded our nation from its inception began to deteriorate as the evolutionary premises of Charles Darwin were adopted by American legal scholars. Charles William Eliot (1834-1926), President of Harvard from 1869 to 1909, decided to verify Darwin's theory and to enshrine scientific method in all forms of knowledge. Accordingly, he selected Christopher Columbus Langdell (1826-1906) as Dean of the Harvard Law School. Langdell hired like-minded professors who would teach the "scientific" case method, whereby legal principles would be educed from the study of individual court decisions and the supposed precedents they established. Within a generation, this methodology spread across the country, aided by noted jurists such as Oliver Wendell Holmes, Jr. (1841-1935), Louis Brandeis (1856-1941), and Roscoe Pound (1870-1964), who (like German legal scholar Friedrich Karl von Savigny, 1779-1861) believed that law must not be externally imposed but reflect citizens' mores and desires. Law, they insisted, need not be derived from eternal verities but should evolve in a "living," "progressive" process to suit the changing cultural and ethical attitudes of society – which, in recent years, has been determined by sociological inquiries. Thus, the creature has circumvented the Creator and arrogated unto himself the right to create law.

It would appear that Darwin's evolutionary theory, one of history's greatest hoaxes, has usurped God's authority. However, that theory is not grounded in reality, and God will not be mocked. His law, built into the universe, will ultimately prevail, while man's pridefully concocted ethical systems will continue to "devolve" (not "evolve") until they collapse under the weight of their own lies and duplicity.

Neither an evolutionary nor a naturalistic paradigm for ethical conduct can succeed – a fact that should be abundantly apparent to any insightful observer of contemporary society. Without a return to biblical absolutes and God-honoring legal principles, our nation will remain adrift without a moral compass. Evolutionary thought can provide no stability, for it is based on falsehood rather than actuality: it sets forth a relativistic ethic that is constantly degenerating or, even worse, a postmodern existentialism that recognizes neither right or wrong nor any moral obligations.

Naturalism or "nature worship" is equally bankrupt, however *avant garde* it may appear to be. Modern man's proclivity to consider himself a part of the natural order and to submit to or accommodate himself in a pseudo-Taoist fashion to the dictates of "Mother Nature" is idolatry – a substitution of the created order for the Creator. According to the Bible, the sin of our original forebearers in forsaking God's Word and rebelling against it brought a death sentence upon them and their progeny and subjected the entire creation to a curse (see for example, Genesis 3:17-19 and Romans 8: 19-22). Therefore, man is no longer perfect, as He was created to be, nor is the natural order. Neither can provide a flawless standard for rectitude, virtue, or moral integrity, and all of man's attempts to ignore God or to obviate the necessity for a Supreme Being by replacing Him with self-exaltation, false imaginations, and worship of "created things" inevitably end in futility, hopelessness, despair, disaster, and eventually everlasting death and punishment (see, for example, Roman1:18-32). The truth that God is both Creator and Supreme Law-Giver remains forever intact, and man disregards it to his peril and ultimate ruin.

Man is whole only when he receives Jesus Christ into his heart and abides in Him; for he is incomplete without the One who created him to fellowship with Himself (cf. Genesis 3:8; I Corinthians 1:9; and I John 1:3-6). Scripture tells us that man was created as a perfect being – made in God's image and capable of uninhibited, intimate communion with Him. Once man sinned, however, he experienced spiritual death (that is, his spirit was separated from God), and his sense of guilt prevented him from desiring fellowship with his Creator (Genesis 3:8-10). Still, the Lord God continues to reach out to man and make preparation for his full restoration. By reason of man's fall into sin, every person born into this world is flawed; yet the image of God in him has not been effaced (see, for example, Psalm 8:4-10 and Psalm 139: 13-14, written centuries after creation, in which David praises the Creator for how he is made): God's law is still implanted in his heart (Romans 2:15), and there remains in him, in the words of a perceptive observer, "a God-shaped vacuum" – a yearning for love and fulfillment that can be satisfied only by the indwelling presence of the living God. As Aurelius Augustine put it, "Thou hast created us for Thyself, and our heart cannot be quieted till it may find repose in Thee" (*Confessions*, Book I, chapter 1).

Let us consider, therefore, a second aspect of the "Creation Principle" – that "God created man in His own image (Genesis 1:26-27). What does it mean to be made in the image of God? Throughout the Christian era, theologians have presented theories and discussed what constitutes the image of God in man; yet perhaps there is room for still another explanation that has Scriptural backing. Christians believe in a trinitarian Deity – Father, Son, and Holy Spirit; and many accept this doctrine while counting it an incomprehensible mystery. Why should this truth be so perplexing? Is not man – made in the image of God – also tripartite: body, soul (mind), and spirit? Some may object that this is an erroneous comparison, since Jesus himself said: "God is spirit, and His worshipers must worship Him in spirit and in truth" (John 4:24). Certainly genuine worship must involve man's spirit, and God does not have a body like men; however, one could still maintain that the human soul (or mind, speaking generically) – man's essential being – is tripartite, consisting of the intellect, the emotions, and the will.

Who created these closely inter-related components in man, and are the same constituents present in God? Who can doubt their presence in our Lord, who was both fully God and fully man – a man "tempted in every way, just as we are – yet was without sin" (Hebrews 4:15)? Nevertheless, some people may be so argumentative to contend that Jesus manifested the attributes of intellect, emotions, and will out of His humanity; therefore, let us look for Scriptural evidence of these personal faculties in the Father and the Holy Spirit. Intellect, or mental ability, connotes knowledge and understanding – Divine attributes repeatedly attested to in the Bible (a sampling might include Job 21:22; Job 37:16; Psalm 44:20-21; Psalm 94:9-10; Psalm 139:2-4; Isaiah 11:9; Ezekiel 37:3; Matthew 11:25-27; Matthew 24:36; Luke 16:15; Acts 15:8; Romans 11:33; I Corinthians 3:19-20; and Colossians 2:2-3).

The will of God is equally supported. The Lord God willed to create the cosmos and all it contains, including man, but His will is also frequently mentioned throughout Scripture. Here are a few references from the New Testament: Matthew 6:10; Matthew 7:21; Matthew 12:50; Luke 22:42; John 4:34; John 6:38-39; Romans 8:27; Romans 12:2; Galatians 1:4; Ephesians 6:6; Philippians 2:13; Colossians 1:9; Colossians 4:12; I Thessalonians 4:3; I Thessalonians 5:18; Hebrews 10:5-10 & 36: Hebrews 13:21; I Peter 2:15; I Peter 4:1-2 & 19; I John 2:17; and I John 5:14.

Strong emotions are also manifested by the entire Godhead, anger and jealousy (examples: Exodus 4:14; Exodus 20:5; Numbers 11:10; Numbers 12:9; Deuteronomy 13:17) – though Holy Writ says that He is "slow to anger" (Psalm 30:5; Psalm 145:8; and Hebrews 1:3) and longsuffering (Romans 15:5). Perhaps the preeminent emotion that comes to mind when we think of the Lord is love, the quintessence of His being. "God is love," we are told in I John 4:8; indeed, the preceding precious verse indicates that He is the Source of love. How matchless, how beyond description is God's love – the love that sent Jesus to dwell among men in human flesh (John 3:16) and constrained Him to give His life for you and me! Though often spurned (Hosea 3:1), He has loved His chosen ones with an everlasting love (Jeremiah 31:3). We can rest in the love (Zephaniah 3:17) that he has poured out for all mankind and is effectual for those who receive Him (Romans 5:5-8 & Titus 3:5-7). Nothing can separate us from His love (Romans 8:38-39). The assurance and reality of that love enables us to obey our Lord's commands to overcome the lusts of the flesh and to demonstrate His love to others in practical, effective ways (I John 2:5, 15-17; I John 3:16-18).

Truly the love of God is better than life (Psalm 63:3) – beyond human comprehension! How inadequately we respond to it! How we need to be filled with His Spirit (the Third Person of the Holy Trinity, who thinks and possesses a will and emotions – see, for example, Acts 13:2; Acts 15:28; Acts 15:28; Romans 8:14; and Ephesians 4:30) that we may fellowship with Him as our most beloved friend, rest in His love, and draw strength from the joy of His presence (Zephaniah 3:17; Nehemiah 8:10)!

As we abide in Christ and contemplate His nature, God reveals Himself ever more fully to us. However, even the cursory discussion above should confirm to us God's essential make-up as a spiritual being – the Supreme, ever-living *Alpha* and *Omega*, possessing, in perfect fullness, all the personality traits (He is not a force, but a person) known to man. Although the image of God in us was tarnished by original sin, we are made in His likeness. Animals are not. They have a body and a soul: they are capable of thinking (up to a point), they have emotions, and they have a will; but they do not have a spirit. Only God and man are spiritual beings, and humans manifest a higher order of intelligence and the other soulish personality traits than any animal. It is important to recognize that man is a special creature made in the likeness of his Creator; for herein lies his worth – not in what he appears to be or even in what he can do. He does not need to pump up his self-esteem: he is of inestimable intrinsic worth, because he is formed in the very image of the God of the universe and can, by accepting Jesus Christ as Lord of his life, walk in the spirit – conducting himself in a godly manner, rather than allowing the fleshly (animal-like) appetites to govern him.

A person assured that he is created in God's image recognizes his own dignity, that of his fellow men, and the inestimable value of human life. It is not so with persons seeing no purpose for their existence apart from what they are able to create for themselves. In such cases, self-promotion may become a major aim. For example, elitists imbued with a Darwinian mind-set may feign compassion for the "poor," the "weak," and the "disadvantaged," or the "oppressed" to win adherents who will enable them to win victories in the political arena. By speaking in behalf of all manner of "victims" (cf. Judas's pretended concern for the poor in John 12:5-6), they may manage to fund "humanitarian programs"– many of them self-perpetuating, wasteful, and largely ineffectual – at public expense. In actuality, they may care little for the underprivileged for whom they purport to speak and whose expectations they arouse. Their main concern is to burnish their image as champions of the downtrodden in order to enhance their own power, even if they rob productive citizens and engender class hatred in the process.

In other cases, persons may express their Darwinian ethic by shamelessly acting on the premise that the strong have a logical right, even an obligation, to overcome the weak; for this is in accord with the "survival of the fittest" principle that carries forward the natural evolutionary process. Why, then, should a powerful, pleasure-seeking man hesitate to ravish a beautiful woman unable to resist him, or why should he be considered guilty of a crime? How can his act be called immoral if he is simply following his natural instincts and exerting his natural energies to prevail in the struggle for life and realization of pleasure? Perhaps even killing and disposing of a victim could also be rationalized under such an ethic, especially if it is a "blob of tissue," a "non-person" – a helpless, unborn baby. Even better, why not harvest the organs of the unborn and any tissues or substances that scientists can experiment with or use for treating Parkinson's disease or manufacturing skin lotions and cosmetics? After all, if man is no more than an animal, are such actions any more immoral than slaughtering cows to supply Burger King restaurants with ground beef or killing minks for their furs?

Would it not also make sense to give the aged and seriously ill the opportunity to "die with dignity?" Why not pass legislation to make doctor-assisted suicide legal? Should not persons in constant pain have this option to end their suffering, and would it not benefit society if unproductive, dependent old people, whose "quality of life" must surely be wretched, were "mercifully" given a lethal injection? On and on the arguments go, devoid of moral considerations; for life is considered merely accidental. If there is nothing beyond this present existence and there is no Creator God, why not simply terminate the "useless," miserable, terminally ill and anyone else who wishes to end a "meaningless" existence in a world without purpose?

The mental and emotional wounds inflicted by these diabolical thought-patterns are incalculable. Without God, life has no purpose, nor does anything have any value or make any sense: everything, as the existentialists contend, is absurd. Is it any wonder, therefore, in view of the evolutionary nonsense in which school children are indoctrinated and upon which our world view is based, that pessimism, hopelessness, despair, suicidal impulses, mental and emotional disorders, drug abuse, alcoholism, dysfunctional families, crimes, immorality, and perversion are rampant?

Under a Darwinian ethic or one based on modern psychology, one need not accept responsibility for his actions, because he is simply carried along by natural impulses too great for him to curb. Essentially, this is the inane argument presented by proponents of school-based clinics (in effect, "sex clinics") and promoters of so-called "safe sex": that abstinence education will not inhibit young people from being "sexually active," because, it is alleged, "they are going to do it anyway"; therefore, fornicators should be taught how to copulate with minimal risk by using condoms provided for them. Unfortunately, ideas of this sort have become more or less conventional in contemporary society because several generations have forsaken biblical truth. Even the church has tried to appear "relevant," "understanding," and "up-to-date" by adopting the latest theories from the "social sciences" – especially sociology and psychology/psychiatry, both founded by godless men on non-Scriptural, evolutionary premises.

We have previously shown (pp.91-92) how Auguste Comte, the "father of sociology," deprecated the religious and metaphysical experiences of man's supposed primitive evolutionary stages and sanctified "positivistic" or "scientific" methodology. In like manner, Sigmund Freud reflected the God-denying Darwinian ideology of his age in his studies of the human psyche by ignoring the "manufacturer's manual," the Bible, and delving into the recesses of man's unconscious mind. Acknowledging the influences of a person's heredity, Freud stressed the power of certain drives, common to all animals, to shape and define human personality and behavior. Among these drives were hunger, thirst, sex, fear, curiosity, and aggression – some of them basic, some not. The sexual urge, however, went far beyond an impulsion to procreate, according to Freud. Indeed, the *libido*, as he termed this drive, constituted psychic energy, which was the driving force behind all human actions. Early in his career, he used hypnosis to induce patients to recall scenes from early childhood no longer retained in the conscious mind. Later, he rejected hypnosis in favor of dream analysis and other techniques, but his efforts to plumb the depths of the unconscious mind to discover traumas experienced in early years never abated.

Mental or behavioral maladjustments, Freud was convinced, stemmed chiefly from religious beliefs – "the obsessional neurosis of humanity." Another cause for disorders lay in a boy's deep resentment of his father, resulting in an "Oedipus complex" in later life that would adversely affect a man without his being aware of it. All of a person's unconscious drives arose from the *id* – the deepest segment of the human psyche, composed of both the pre-conscious (containing latent knowledge not yet realized) and the unconscious, the repository of repressed ideas. Knowledge of the pre-conscious could be tapped in one's sleep, often in dreams; but to bring up repressed ideas or memories from the unconscious into the conscious mind would probably require psychoanalysis to overcome the *ego* – man's reason or conscious self – which doubtless had found them too painful to handle and, therefore, had repressed them and did not want to retrieve them. The *ego*, Freud believed, was concerned with how to cope with the drives, some quite embarrassing, emerging from the *id*. Therefore, it would try either to keep them from emerging (which was futile and would probably result in some form of mental disorder) or it would endeavor to gratify the drives without incurring societal disapprobation.

Freud insisted that man's fundamental drives must be satisfied in one way or another lest he manifest some extreme behavior, but the *ego* must be careful to vent the drives in a manner tolerable to his *superego* – comprised of his ethical standards, his mores, and ideals that society had helped to mold. If, to placate the *superego*, the *ego* emphatically stifled natural drives arising from the *id*, without allowing them to be expressed in some socially acceptable way, mental disorder could result. Therefore, it was important for the psychiatrist to administer psychoanalysis circumspectly to enable the *ego* to achieve a progressive "conquest of the *id*" – in other words, to restrain passionate, potentially hurtful drives or to shape them according to reason and common sense to norms acceptable in society. Coincidentally, according to Freud, psychoanalysis may serve to restore the *ego* obsessed with guilt feelings instilled by the *superego*, by eliminating or alleviating those feelings. In effect, then, feelings of remorse were largely attributable to the *superego's* reaction to thoughts and impulses arising from the *id* that were often beyond the control of the individual; therefore, it was fruitless to deal with the question of guilt or innocence: what was necessary was to eradicate or temper guilty sentiments.

Obviously, Freud's view of guilt is contrary to biblical doctrines. According to Romans 3:23-25 and 5:12-21, man is guilty of sin and must repent and receive Jesus Christ – the Divine Sacrifice for the sins of all mankind – into his heart. A holy God holds everyone responsible for his own misdeeds (Deuteronomy 24:16 & Jeremiah 31:30), and feelings of guilt can serve a redemptive purpose – that of convicting sinners and leading them to salvation. Cleansing from sin and liberation from guilt through new birth in Jesus Christ is needed – not salving or eliminating guilt feelings (Romans 6:22-23; Romans 8:1-2; I John 1:7b-10; I John 2:2).

Carl Jung (1875-1961), one of Freud's early associates, went even further, asserting that a person was not only influenced by his individual unconscious but by a collective unconscious common to all mankind. Because of these powerful influences, Freudian psychoanalysts maintain, no one can be held entirely responsible for his misdeeds or deviant behavior.

Although many modern psychiatrists purport to reject Freudian methodology and are more concerned with behavior that can be observed than with unconscious drives, they are just as anxious as Freud or Jung to mitigate individual responsibility. For example, behaviorists such as John B. Watson (1878-1958) and B.F. Skinner (1904-1990) attribute man's conduct largely to environmental and social factors. In fact, according to Watson, it is possible to ascertain how an individual will act or to predict what type of person he will be by considering what environmental or social influences are exerted upon him; and Skinner believes that a system of instant or delayed rewards or punishments (stimuli to attain desired responses) can modify behavioral patterns. He contends that positive or negative reinforcements for various types of conduct (devotees of transactional analysis speak of "warm fuzzies" to encourage desirable traits and "cold pricklies" to discourage undesirable ones) can be employed in such a way that the subject – the person whose behavior is being altered – will think he is changing of his own volition. To Skinner, social engineering is both feasible and desirable; but it may be wondered what right a programer who is himself shaped by environmental and social influences has to mold the personalities of others, and by what standards the changes are to be effected.

In certain instances, behavioral methodology is effective and not contrary to Scripture. There is no doubt that rewards and punishments are permissible (Deuteronomy chapter 28 bears this out) and that a person's associations and environment can exert a telling influence on him. Yahweh commanded the ancient Israelites to drive out or exterminate all the inhabitants of Canaan and not to intermarry with them (Exodus 34:12-16; Numbers25:1-8; Numbers 34:50-56; Deuteronomy 7:16; Joshua 11:20; & Joshua 23:12-13), because He wanted to preserve them as a holy people, uncontaminated by the Canaanites' demonic, pagan practices, so that Israel would fulfill its Divine destiny of carrying God's laws and message to the peoples of the earth and bringing forth the Savior of mankind. Moreover, the book of Proverbs advises choosing wise rather than foolish companions (Proverbs 13:20 & Proverbs 28:7), and II Corinthians 6:14-17 warns believers not to be yoked with unbelievers. God's people, therefore, are expected to maintain a wholesome environment whenever possible. The Apostle Paul recognized, however, that, short of death, it was not always possible to cut oneself off from evildoers outside of the church (I Corinthians 5:9-11), and to do so is probably not in accord with Christ's great commission. Nevertheless, Christians are not to be conformed to this present world (Romans 12:2), nor are they to entertain lustful thoughts or crave worldly things (I John 2:15-17). In short, by the power of the Holy Spirit, they are to act responsibly and live pure lives, even in the midst of an unfavorable environment.

Admittedly, behavioristic methods may superficially assuage destructive conduct, and Christian therapists may profitably employ a few carefully designed and limited stimulus-response techniques temporarily to help a patient participate in social activities or realize certain other minimal goals; but more is needed for permanent healing. As soon as possible, the patient should be weaned away from dependence on low-grade reinforcers and pointed toward the Great Physician, the Source of all truth, all worth, and all life. The therapist must humbly recognize his inability, aside from the Almighty, to bring about healing, while praying for his patient's eternal well-being and submitting to Divine guidance concerning how to foster wholeness in him. Unfortunately, most behaviorists depend too much on the methodology learned in graduate school and seem content, as therapy continues, to see minor improvement in the behavioral norms of their patients. Such is not a godly paradigm, nor is it clear whether psychiatric intervention of any sort is any more beneficial than simply allowing matters to take their course. In fact, there are statistical studies suggesting that psychologists and psychiatrists may have helped create the very problems they purport to treat and are continuing to enhance them. Few of these "professionals" understand the actual spiritual roots of the maladies and so-called neuroses they treat; yet they continue to enjoy tremendous prestige and have managed to secure governmental sanction of their monopoly over care of the mentally afflicted. In most instances, for a Christian counselor or therapist to bring biblical truths to bear in treating mental or emotional disorders would be very difficult and professionally risky. Any attempt to use techniques not officially prescribed – praying, sharing the Gospel with a patient, or ministering in any way to his spiritual needs (exorcism would definitely be out of bounds) – would be deemed "unprofessional" and "cockamamy," cause for censure, dismissal, or decertification.

All forms of psychological or psychiatric therapy – behavioristic or otherwise – ignore God, focusing on man and his supposed capacity, by one means or another, "to lift himself by his own bootstraps." For example, Erich Fromm (1900-1980) believes man can transcend self-estrangement and the dualistic bestial and intellectual characteristics of his nature through loving life, the world, and his fellow men. He writes, in *Escape from Freedom*, that a person capable of acting in a loving, compassionate, acceptable manner is almost like God.

Abraham Maslow's (1908-1970) answer to man's need to live beyond the mundane plain of self-preservation and security is "self-actualization" through constantly striving or experimenting to discover or "invent" himself by envisioning and then recognizing his potential as an individual. A self-actualized person will shun society's materialistic goals and status symbols, supplanting them with values of his own that require courageous movement rather than conformity and obsession with security. Involvement in creative activity and love of life characterizes such a person, who will be "surprised by joy" as he moves outside himself into "peak experiences." Certain facets of Maslow's prescription are alluring but unbiblical. For instance, non-compliance to social forces and pressure is admirable in particular situations; however, establishing one's own value system can lead only to tragedy: no one can be his own god; no one can stand alone without God, whom Maslow never brings into the self-actualization equation.

Similarly, Carl Rogers (1902-1987) – with his "non-directive therapy," conducted by listening to the patient's ideas and allowing him to work out his own "solutions" – affirms human free will in counterdistinction to the Freudian and behaviorist theories, but permits man to "actualize" himself, build up his self-regard, and create his own values, thereby assuming the prerogatives of Deity.

Rogers and like-minded modern psychologists recognize the therapeutic benefit of feeling good about oneself but often place more emphasis on building one's "self-esteem" – regardless of any harmful, hateful, or anti-social actions in which he may be engaging – than in dealing with deep personality problems. Denying that there are problems or whitewashing them with self-esteem therapy may salve a person's conscience, but it can abrogate legitimate twinges of guilt pressing him toward repentance or a determination to change or improve.

Man is not inherently good as Maslow, Rogers, and many other humanists believe. The Bible teaches that natural man is a sinner in need of salvation, not a person who simply needs to feel good about himself. No matter what we think or do (Isaiah 64:6), we can not manufacture self-worth: in fact, attempts to do so usually lead to an increased self-centeredness that may aggravate existing emotional deficiencies or personality quirks. Jesus rebuked prideful, self-satisfied, self-righteous persons and freely forgave those acknowledging their sins and crying out for help (Luke 18:9-14). A legitimate, positive, firmly-based self-regard comes from knowing that we are not the product of chance and not merely the best form of animal to have evolved but God's highest creation, bearing the Divine likeness, capable of creative thought and actions, free to make decisions and choices, and equipped for experiencing life deeply, fervently, and appreciatively through our emotions.

More than this, those who are in Christ Jesus spiritually experience His presence and the comfort and enablement of the Holy Spirit. They know that they are "the righteousness of God' in Christ (II Corinthians 5:21), that they are "more than conquerors" through Him (Romans 8:37), and that when they confess their sins, they receive forgiveness, cleansing, and restoration from the Father (I John 1:9) – not merely a "self-esteem" palliative. Complete wholeness is available only by abiding in the One who is our very life (Acts 17:28); without Him, we can never measure up to what we were created to be.

Still, man has a propensity to do things on his own and in his own way without seeking God, and even Christians – immersed as we are in today's decadent, secular culture – can be deluded into seeking help for mental or emotional maladies from psychiatrists, part of this world's priesthood. All of the psychological theories noted above possess a modicum of truth; yet Satanically-inspired lies and misguided notions of men far outweigh the morsels of truth observable in them.

Perhaps the most delusive psychology is that of Victor Frankl (1905-1987), who eclectically draws from Freud, other psychotherapists, existentialist philosophy, religious thought, and his own dehumanizing experience as an inmate in a World-War-II concentration camp to formulate his syncretic system, which he calls "logotherapy." Christians are generally sympathetic to Dr. Frankl's wartime suffering and attracted to his advice to view suffering as a redemptive agency that – along with doing a deed and experiencing a value – may endue a person with the will to transcend his circumstances in order to create meaning in his life. In the quest for meaning, he will discover himself, do his duty, and learn how to create values that can carry him through difficulties. Again, however, the emphasis is upon man's ability to exert "mind over matter" to effect his own salvation. Frankl, like all of the above-mentioned psychologists, is operating essentially on humanistic premises; and, in every case, the desired object is to realize one's potential through personal growth and fulfillment. The search for answers starts with man and his natural faculties – practically ignoring the spiritual dimension, though Frankl does leave room for it.

Any "truth" that fails to recognize the Creator – the Supreme Source of all truth – is only a partial truth, deficient at the very least, false and dangerously deceptive, and capable of deluding believers not well-grounded in God's word. Only a vital and thorough knowledge of Scripture is a sure antidote to cleverly-devised half-truths – a fact demonstrated by our Lord when He was tempted by the devil in the wilderness (Matthew 4:1-11; Mark 1:12-13; & Luke 4:1-13).

In so far as anything is true, that verity comes from the Creator God. Even non-believers incapable of comprehending spiritual truth, may discern through their mind many realities evident in the created order. Interestingly enough, even God-abnegating Sigmund Freud discovered, through his investigations of the human psyche, that man's mind was tripartite – consisting, he said, of the *id*, the *ego*, and the *superego*. Is it not amazing that he should apprehend to a remarkable degree the complexity of the human soul, verifying that human beings are in fact, as the Psalmist declares, "fearfully and wonderfully made?"

How man is constituted is beyond the ken of anyone, Christian or non-Christian, and there is a danger in trying to compartmentalize human faculties if, in so doing, we think we can understand (own) man completely and subject him to scientific analysis calculated to reduce him to animal or material status or impose unwarranted control over one upon whom the Creator has bestowed free will. Nevertheless, Scripture itself not only provides clues concerning the make-up and attributes of man, but indicates that we should take care to differentiate between soul and spirit so that we will conduct ourselves according to the spirit and not submit to the dictates of the mind or fleshly impulses. In I Thessalonians 5:23b, Paul says: "I pray God your whole *spirit* and *soul* and *body* be preserved blameless unto the coming of our Lord Jesus Christ" (KJV); and, in Hebrews 4:12, we read: "For the Word of God is living and active and sharper than any two-edged sword, and piercing as far as *the division of soul and spirit* ... and able to judge the thoughts and intentions of the heart" (NASB). There is a danger in confusing soul and spirit (which are almost inextricably affiliated); for Satan and his minions, as well as the Holy Spirit, have access to our soul (or mind) – constituted of the intellect (both conscious and unconscious), emotions, and the will.

Some people, especially those involved in the occult, mistake the voice of Satan, who is insinuating thoughts into the soul, for the voice of God. Such was the case with mass-murderer David Berkowitz, known as "Son of Sam," who after being apprehended in August 1977, claimed that God had ordered him to kill his victims. What he heard was not the God of the Bible but the god of this world (John 12:31 & II Corinthians 4:4) – the old deceiver the devil, or some demonic spirit.

Of course, God can speak to the mind, usually by way of our spirit – our faculty for communicating with Him to which Satan has no access; but the mind is also susceptible to perverse suggestions that appeal to the intellect, titillate or arouse the emotions, or challenge the will to action and is, therefore, open to pornographic temptations, occult beliefs, and all manner of demonically-inspired influences.

It is obviously difficult for sinful men to know that such impulses are from the Evil One, particularly if their consciences are seared (I Timothy 4:2) through continued rejection of God, rebellion against Him, or involvement in Satanic rites. The conscience is apparently closely united to the heart (Hebrews 10:22), the deepest segment of the soul, and Scripture tells us that the heart of natural man is "deceitful above all things, and desperately wicked ..." (Jeremiah 17:9, KJV; cf. Genesis 8:21 &Mark 7:21-23). "As a man thinks in his heart, so is he" (NKJ), and the heart of unregenerate man is the repository, like Freud's *id*, of all sorts of soulish and fleshly urges that we may try to keep suppressed or hidden, only to have them burst forth at unexpected times in loathsome, hateful, deceitful, immoral utterances and wicked, maleficent, even violently pernicious and fiendish deeds.

Outbursts of this nature and the concomitant rage and evil thoughts surging from the heart into the mind can be expected from persons having no relationship with Jesus Christ; for they can only resort to an iron will to try to inhibit them: after all, their spirit is effectively dead – separated from God their Maker and therefore inoperative. Wholeness can be attained only when the human spirit comes to life and becomes operative through the new birth that Jesus spoke of in John 3:5-6. In other words, belief in Jesus Christ is necessary – not merely a factual belief that there is a God (even the demons know that Jesus Christ exists and they tremble because of this knowledge, James 2:19), but a trusting, reliant, obedient belief – the heartfelt acknowledgment that Jesus Christ is not only the Son of God but one's personal Savior and Lord.

Full submission to God's will is imperative if a person is to experience victory over his soulish passions and thoughts. Many Christians want Jesus Christ as "fire insurance" against the time of their physical death, but they do not want to submit every aspect of their lives to Him, despite a biblical command to "be filled with the Spirit" (Ephesians 5:18). These "fence straddlers" will continue to manage their lives as they please – led by their own intellects, emotions, and willful desires, or even by fleshly lusts. After receiving Christ, a person is no longer a slave to his sin nature (he no longer has to sin); but to live victoriously, he must commit himself to allow the Spirit of God to rule and reign in his spirit and his total being. Man's revitalized spirit is his "God-communicator," enabling him to fellowship with his Lord, receive revelations from Him, and exercise godly intuition. This is intimated in Proverbs 20:27, which says that the "spirit of a man is the lamp of the Lord, searching all the innermost parts [the soul and heart] of his being."

As believers operate in the realm of the spirit instead of being programed or controlled by the mind (soul), they bring it into spiritual renewal (Romans 12:1-2; cf. Ephesians 4:23). "Spirit-filled" believers with transformed minds are comforted in adversity, experience joy and sweet communion with their Maker, are amenable and eager to be led into all truth, and are guided, motivated, and empowered by the Holy Spirit to live godly lives, pray effectively, witness for Christ, and perform the works they see the Father doing (John 14:16-17 & 26; John 15:26; Acts 1:8; Romans 8:5; Romans 8:26-27; Romans 15:19; I Corinthians 2:4; I Corinthians 12:7-11; I Corinthians 14:14-15; Galatians 5:16 & 22-26; Ephesians 3:16; Ephesians 6:18; Philippians 2:1; Philippians 3:3; I John 3:24; & I John 4:13). Thus, persons led by the Spirit of God are "heirs of God and co-heirs with Jesus Christ" (Romans 8:17) and are made complete in Christ just as the Creator intended. Followers of Christ, therefore, can be restored to the status that humanity enjoyed before Adam and Eve fell into sin – capable of fulfilling God's dominion and cultural mandates (see *infra.*, pp. 189-200) and his great commission to make disciples of all nations (Matthew 28:19-20).

Because man was created as a tripartite being, he is never satisfied with material things alone or even with pleasure, fame, and fortune for very long. (The book of Ecclesiastes confirms this.) We are told that "man shall not live by bread alone..." (Matthew 4:4); yet, all too often, professing Christians speak in materialistic terms, reflecting the attitudes of unbelievers as illustrated by the answer allegedly given by a Sunday School teacher to a small child's query: "Where did I come from?"

"Dust."
"Well," continued the child, "where am I going?"
"To dust," replied the teacher.

A few days later, the inquisitive child called from his upstairs bedroom: "Mama, Mama, come up here quick. There's someone under my bed either coming or going!"

Ambiguous statements or facile aphorisms are often unclear or only partially correct and may lead unbelievers to conclude that Christians share their attitudes and interests – in sports, television programs, and other trivial matters. We should be able to hold friendly conversations with unbelieving neighbors and friends on various topics in which they are interested, but we should be ready at any time to testify to our faith in a natural, compelling fashion. Indeed, we need to elicit questions from them that will turn conversations to matters of spiritual import. How thankful God's people should be to be tripartite beings just as He is Trinity. If we had no spirit, for instance, we might as well pursue those things the world deems important – pleasure, wealth, power, and fame; because, if we had no spirit, we could have no fellowship with God and could never rejoice in eternal life.

God created us as His regents on the earth, and we of all people should be faithful to carry out our Divinely-ordained mission. We are to be a "peculiar people," different from worldly-minded people and prepared to effect God's purposes. We are to be "salt and light" to the world, ready witnesses to the love and power of Christ – living epistles "known and read by all men" (Matthew 5:3-6; II Corinthians 3:2; Titus 2:14; I Peter 2:9), living expectantly, not in the light of things that are seen by our physical eyes, but in the knowledge that is spiritually discerned. "So we fix our eyes not on what is seen, but on what is unseen. For what is seen is temporary, but what is unseen is eternal" (II Corinthians 4:18).

Still, God's created order is one of substance, not *Maya* or illusory reality; therefore, it can be studied. Investigation is also encouraged by the biblical "Creation Principle" that the Creator and the creation are separate entities: God is not a part of nature. As a consequence, scientists wishing to subject nature to full and rigorous investigation are committing no sacrilege. Nothing is "off limits," because nature is not considered sacred as was the case in some Oriental civilizations at the time of the "scientific revolution" in the West. In view of this, the Western initiative and success in the realms of physical science and technology are understandable, as is also, perhaps, the slowness of most Eastern peoples in appropriating scientific methodology, educating their intellectuals instead in governmental and societal concerns. Moreover, in accord with the "Creation Principle," the Almighty created a structured, ordered universe, inculcating physical laws in nature that are absolute in the sense of being consistent and reliable – lending themselves to empirical study and application.

Who can doubt that "since the creation of the world God's invisible qualities – His eternal power and Divine Nature – have been clearly seen, being understood from what has been made" (Romans 1:20); or what child of God does not thrill to David's anthem of adoration and praise in Psalm 19:1-11?

"The heavens declare the glory of God;
And the firmament shows His handiwork.
Day unto day utters speech,
And night unto night reveals knowledge.
There is no speech nor language
Where their voice is not heard.
Their line has gone out through all the earth,
And their words to the end of the world.

"In them he has set a tabernacle for the sun,
Which is like a bridegroom coming out of his chamber,
And rejoices like a strong man to run its race.
Its rising is from one end of the heaven,
And its circuit to the other end;
And there is nothing hidden from its heat.

"The law of the Lord is perfect,
    converting the soul;
The testimony of the Lord is sure,
    making wise the simple;
The statutes of the Lord are right,
    rejoicing the heart;
The commandment of the Lord is pure,
    enlightening the eyes;
The fear of the Lord is clean,
    enduring forever;

The judgments of the Lord are true
    and righteous altogether.
More to be desired are they than gold,
    Yea, than much fine gold;
Sweeter also than honey and the honeycomb.
Morever by them your servant is warned,
And in keeping them there is great reward" (NKJV).

How true is this revelatory aspect of the "Creation Principle" – that much of the condign character and attributes of the Master Designer are evident in His handiwork: His majesty, infinite greatness, wisdom, omniscience, excellence, creativity, omnipotence, complexity, wholeness, love of variety, exactitude, faithfulness, constancy, changelessness, tranquility, loving-kindness, glory, infinite worth, sovereignty, providence, and all-encompassing pervasiveness (cf. Psalm 8; Psalm 24:1-2; Psalm 33:3-11; Psalm 65:5-13; Psalm 74:15-17; Psalm 89:1-2, 5-17; Psalm 102:12; Psalm 103:19; Psalm 104; Psalm 108:3-5; Psalm 148: 1-13; Colossians 1:15-17; and Hebrews 1:3).

Another "Creation Principle" – the revelation that God created the heavens and the earth – not only freed man from subjection to nature, but placed him at the apex of everything; for the Lord-God gave him dominion over the rest of creation, thereby encouraging scientific investigation and application as well as stewardship of resources. It follows also that, since man is God's highest creation and made in the Divine image, he is important. I Corinthians 6:3 states that someday we will judge the world and angels, and Hebrews 2:6-8 declares that, even in this world, man is crowned with glory and honor. If man is so important in the eyes of God, history is also important because it is the study of man. Nevertheless, if history merely glorifies man rather than recognizing or revering God as Creator and Sustainer, it denies the very Source of man's life, creativity, personality, and dignity. Therefore, when man humanistically tries to exalt himself, he actually diminishes himself because it is in God that we "live and move and have our being" (Acts 17:28), and we are told in Luke 14:11 that "everyone who exalts himself will be humbled, and he who humbles himself will be exalted."

Finally, let us note still another "Creation Principle": that born-again Christians – trusting not in their own righteousness, eminence, or ability but solely in the righteousness of Jesus Christ – are "created in Christ Jesus to do good works," which God created in advance to be accomplished "to bring all things in heaven and on earth together under one head, even Christ" (see Ephesians 2:10 & 1:10; cf. Matthew 28:19-20). In other words, Christians have a significant God-given mission, a holy purpose to carry out in this world. They have a special role in history.

Charlotte Cushman has said that when God conceived the world, that was poetry. He formed it – that was sculpture. Then He gave it variety and colored it – that was painting; and, finally, crowning all, he peopled it with living beings, and that was His grand, eternal drama. It is that drama that we study as history.

QUESTIONS TO PONDER

1. Why does God's creation of the universe presume His sovereignty over it?

2. In the minds of our nation's founding fathers, how did law originate? What was its basis? How could it be known?

3. When did American jurisprudence begin to change? Why?

4. Why can evolutionary premises never provide a stable, enduring foundation for law and ethics? Why can not naturalism provide such a foundation?

5. Should we be concerned that the truth that God created the universe, the entire natural order, and mankind is not being taught in the "public schools" of this nation? Why, or why not?

6. Genesis 1:26 informs us that man is created in the image of God. What does this mean? In what way is man created in God's likeness? Why is it important for us to know that we are made in the image of God? In

respect to the wholeness of the human personality? In respect to human conduct?

7. How does the biblical view of man's personality differ from that presented by modern psychologists and practiced by psychiatrists? Are there any points of agreement? How have the postulates of modern psychology affected our society? What should we as Christians do, if anything, to bring solutions to the personal and societal problems we see around us?

8. For what purpose was man created? According to those who believe in the evolutionary origins of man through natural selection, what is man's purpose?

9. What comfort should we derive from knowing that there is a transcendent, all- powerful, personal Being who created everything?

10. Does appreciation of the created order motivate you to worship God? Would a non-believer be motivated in the same way? Why, or why not?

PERTINENT SCRIPTURES

Genesis 1:1-26; Genesis 2:2; Exodus 20:11; Psalm 8:3; Psalm 24:1-2; Psalm 33:4-11; Psalm 119:89-91; Isaiah 40:6-8, 26, 28; Isaiah 42:5; Isaiah 45:11-12, 18; Jeremiah 10:12-16; Jeremiah 27:5; Jeremiah 51:15; Acts 17:24-28; Romans 8:18-22; Romans 11:36; I Corinthians 8:6; II Corinthians 4:18; Colossians 1:15-17; I Thessalonians 5:23; Hebrews 1:2-3; Hebrews 4:12; James 1:17; II Peter 3:5; Revelation 4:11; and Revelation 14:17.

Chapter XVII

"THE PRINCIPLE OF INDIVIDUALITY AND DIVERSITY OPERATING IN UNITY"

Although all human beings are made in God's likeness and are equally precious to Him (John 3:16), every person is unique. Every man, woman, and child has distinctive eyes and fingerprints, DNA, and voice patterns. No one is physically the same, nor does anyone have a personality, interests, skills, and aspirations identical to those of someone else.[3] The Master Designer loves variety. He created distinct personalities and unique individuals for His purposes. He also deals in an individual way with persons – usually in conjunction with others – to influence the course of history and to effect His eternal plan. As we allow Him to have His perfect way with us, we achieve our highest fulfillment and joy; and He is able to use our distinctive personalities and gifts in a manner best suited to accomplish that part of His purpose for which we have been ordained (Psalm 139:13-16; Romans 9:21-24; Romans 12:4-30; Ephesians 2:10; & Ephesians 4:11-16). To be sure, many talented people are not submitted to God's will; yet, even they – like The Pharaoh who resisted the Lord

---

[3]Are duplicates absolutely precluded? Would the Lord God intervene to prevent the cloning of human beings? If not, would the clone be exactly the same as the individual from whom it had been cloned? From the time of Cain and Abel, man has played God by taking away human life and, in contemporary society, has followed demonic enticements to murder the unborn. God has not stopped this, though the murderer can expect retribution, even eternal punishment, if he does not repent and receive Christ into his heart by faith. Doubtless we will see the precious, aborted innocents in heaven. But would the Lord prevent, as at Babel, men from contravening His will? Would He stop men from cloning other beings in their image – from producing animals looking like men but lacking a spiritual component? Would that human-like animal be unable to have eternal life in fellowship with Jesus Christ and those who have accepted Him; or, would God supernaturally confer on such a creature the faculty to trust Him? Would it be possible for two beings looking exactly the same in every respect to be present in the hereafter with Jesus and His saints? In the light of the principle of individuality and diversity, what can we conclude concerning cloning of human beings? Every person is of inestimable value in the eyes of God, so much so that He sent His "only begotten Son" to die for the sins of mankind and save every person who will believe in Jesus Christ from eternal death to everlasting life (John 3:16). Scripture informs us that there is great rejoicing in heaven when a single sinner repents. The Lord knows His own by name (John 10:3), the very hairs of our head are numbered (Luke 12:7), and the Father in heaven hears and answers the importunate prayer of a person who trusts in Him (Luke 11:13; John 15:7; and James 5:16).

God and Moses, or Pilate – may be used by the Almighty to serve His ends. When a Christian fails to fulfill his Divine calling, he is the loser; for God raises up someone else to fulfill what must be accomplished, while the unsurrendered or contumacious person misses the opportunity and blessing of being a co-worker with God and also suffers the consequences of disobedience. It behooves every believer, therefore, to seek to know his spiritual gifts as well as his natural talents, but, above all, to be yielded to God and sensitive to the leading of the Holy Spirit.

Many scriptural admonitions and promises are given to individuals, and Israel and nations that are inclined toward God have received similar admonitions and promises (Deuteronomy 4:6-8; Deuteronomy 11:22-25; Deuteronomy 12:28; Deuteronomy 14:2; Deuteronomy 15:6; Deuteronomy 26:18; Deuteronomy 28:1; II Samuel 7:23-24; I Chronicles 17:21-22; II Chronicles 7:14; Psalm 33:12; Psalm 67:1-2; Psalm 72:17; Psalm 147:19-20; Proverbs 14:34; Nehemiah 1:8-9; Isaiah 2:2-4; Isaiah 26:15; Isaiah 55:5; Isaiah 65:1; Jeremiah 29:14; Ezekiel 36:24-27; Ezekiel 37:21-23; Haggai 2:7; Zechariah 2:11; Zechariah 8:22; Malachi 3:12; Galatians 3:8; & Revelation 15:4). We are individually held responsible for our actions (II Corinthians 5:10 & Revelation 22:12), and salvation itself is an individual matter. God has no grandchildren (Psalm 24:3-5): whoever "calls on the name of the Lord will be saved" (Joel 2:32; cf. Acts 2:21 & see also John 3:36). In actual fact, evangelism and grounding converts in the Word of God are more important than political activism or electing principled Christians to public office. While laws based on biblical principles may retard evil, foster conditions conducive to godly changes in society, and keep avenues for Christian witness and influence open by insisting that the free exercise of our Constitutional rights be respected, it is only when individual hearts are changed that society can be transformed. Jesus Christ commanded His disciples:

> "Go and make disciples of all nations, baptizing them in the name of the Father and of the Son and of the Holy Spirit, and teaching them to obey everything I have commanded you..." (Matthew 28:19-20).

Jesus was interested in changing men and women one by one from the inside out – not in compelling them to conduct themselves in a moral and godly

172

manner by force of law, not in trying to take the controls of government, the educational system, the media, and the fine arts to effect cultural change (though certainly Christians are to be "salt and light" in their culture and to try to bring it into harmony with God's Word); and He did not say: "Go and conquer nations and compel them to believe in Me." The Teutonic Knights used the wrong method to Christianize East Prussia – that is by exterminating its pagan inhabitants and bringing in "Christian" German settlers to take their place. Nor was it right for the church to sponsor a military crusade against the Albigensian heretics early in the 13th century. Other historical examples could be cited of attempts to impose religion – whether Christianity, Islam, or some other faith – by force of arms. In the case of Christianity, military ventures of this sort are contrary to our Lord's teaching and *modus operandi.*

God always respects the human conscience and will. He created man with the God-like faculty of free will, and He never violates it. As our good and loving father, He warns us against disobeying His Word. He knows that observing His eternal laws is the pathway to blessing, happiness, contentment, joy, and life, while ignoring them will bring misery, pain, unhappiness, destruction of character, and eternal death. He wants us to become everything we were intended to be and desires to spare us from suffering the terrible consequences of sin; nevertheless, He does not nullify the human will and coerce obedience to His directives and ways. Instead, He pursues the ungodly to convict them of sin, woo them, and bring them to Himself, while He guides and exhorts believers, fellowships with them when they seek Him in prayer and meditate upon His Word, and disciplines them when they go astray (Hebrews 12:4-11). In other words, God brings to bear every influence He can for our well-being as He tries to induce us to conform to His will, but He never overrides our will to force us to accept Him or His precepts. What an amazing God!

Contrary to the manner in which the Creator God respects our individuality, totalitarian regimes try to control every aspect of their subjects' lives, thus setting themselves in the place of God. They use ungodly means of manipulation and sometimes intimidation and compulsion to maintain control, and they demand strict obedience and adherence to the party line. This means of governing is not of God (certainly it is contrary to His servanthood principle, *infra* pp.193-195, 262, 273-274, 292); therefore, any government that tries to collectivize men by forcing them into a common mold is acting contrary to God's will, because God endowed man with the freedom to make his own decisions. Any regime that attempts to take away free will – that attempts to bind man's total being to the will of the state – is not of God but of the Evil One. Any state that tries to dominate or control its citizens' thoughts and actions through intimidation and to compel total compliance to its mandates (through indoctrination, "brainwashing," oppression, punishment, propagation of lies, or other coercive tactics) is assuming prerogatives and powers that God himself does not exercise over man. God wants man to serve Him voluntarily – out of love; it is Satan who tries to exercise absolute control over man. Therefore, states that resort to totalitarian means of domination are demonic in their means and anti-Christ in their aims, since they are seeking to supplant God's authority with their own. In the final analysis, of course, totalitarian governments can be certain only of controlling men's actions, not their thoughts; therefore, their anti-God machinations are doomed to ultimate failure. In ancient times, Nimrod began centralizing and building cities, most notably Babylon (Babel). At Babel, men ignored God's command to fill the earth as they determined to remain where they were – in a centralized, regimented society. It was an exercise in futility; for as they pridefully began to construct a tower unto heaven, God confused their language and dispersed them.

This incident helps illustrate the difference between man-glorifying, rebellious individualism, which usually eventuates in collectivistic humanism as occurred at Babel, and the principle of individuality whereby a person recognizes his dependence on God and willingly and submissively uses his God-given talents for the edification of his fellow men. Individualism is essentially self-serving, deleterious, and divisive. Everyone does "his own thing" just as did Israel during the period of the judges when "everyone did as he saw fit" (Judges 17:6). People determined to do whatever they want to do are ungovernable unless forced into line by an entity powerful enough to keep them under control, trampling on their God-given liberties and rights in the process. Thus failure to respect Divine laws prepares the way for a collectivistic, totalitarian state that supplants the Lord God as the Source of all blessings.

The founders of our nation recognized every man's worth as a creature made in the Divine image and his capacity, under the God of all wisdom, to govern himself and, in concert with his fellow citizens, to govern a nation subject to Divinely-inspired laws insuring liberty and justice for all the inhabitants of the land. Admittedly, the ideal was not perfectly followed; and, to the extent that certain segments of society – especially slaves – were deprived of their God-given rights, the individuality principle was disregarded and the liberty of everyone was attenuated. (Many of today's societal problems can be traced back to our national sin of recognizing the enslavement of human beings made in God's likeness.) During a period of horrifying warfare and carnage and the years that followed, humanistic, Darwinistic currents subverted the biblical principles and standards implanted in our culture, causing us to look more and more to society itself and to civil government, not only as the fountainhead and interpreter of law, mores, and rights, but as the guarantor of livelihood, economic prosperity, education, and "proper" cultural expression – the answer to every problem or potential problem.

Because we have held too lightly the legal and cultural premises that at one time undergirded our society, individualism has largely superseded the original tenets of godly individuality and self-government upon which our nation was founded. Today we accept government largess as our due and are moving steadily into socialism and, if the present administration has its way, into a form of fascism.[4] So we see how our beloved nation, by moving away from God, is relinquishing its birthright of individual rights and liberties bestowed by the Creator and guaranteed by the United States Constitution and most state constitutions for a mess of humanistic, socialistic stew that provides no sustenance and, under the guise of insuring security and equity, is leading toward ever more intrusive civil government, abrogation of individual liberties and national sovereignty, and some system of global governance.

Even the church has been deeply influenced by the humanistic, secular spirit of the age. Thinking itself prosperous, it has departed from its "First Love" – the Lord Jesus Christ – following Him "afar off" and in a lukewarm fashion while conforming itself to the supposed wisdom of the world, contrary to the admonitions of the early apostles (Romans 12:2; I John 2:15-17; Revelation 2:4-5; & Revelation 3:15-17). Nevertheless, individual parishioners – even within apostate bodies – are beginning to recognize a need for revival

---

[4]See Appendix II: "Ideological Political Spectrum."

through a return to biblical Christianity, to which a faithful remnant throughout the ages has adhered.

The desire to serve God with all their heart, soul, and strength has led lay people, as well as ministers and priests, to yearn for a powerful visitation of the Holy Spirit. Some of them are beginning to re-examine the example of the early churches – individualistic in character, suiting the particular needs of their constituents and carrying out their evangelistic and discipleship mission in a variety of creative ways. In effecting this mission, church bodies are increasingly recognizing the necessity for conducting themselves in harmony with the "Principle of Individuality." Every born-again Christian is important, and those acknowledging Jesus Christ as Lord of every aspect of their personal lives are especially equipped to minister to the needs of the church. To each one has been entrusted at least one, often several spiritual gifts (not to be confused with the natural talents or abilities with which we are born into this world) that are to be exercised for the edification of the body of Christ, particularly that great segment of Christians with whom a person is closely affiliated. God has ordained that Christ-centered individuality be demonstrated within the church, whose members are blessed by a diversity of gifts operating in harmony under the aegis, power, and direction of the Holy Spirit for the benefit of all members (Romans 12:4-8; I Corinthians 12:4-11; & Ephesians 4:11-16). Individuals with different spirituals gifts are to operate in concord with other believers just as the various members of the physical body act in harmonious unity, complementing the functions performed by all the other members, for the welfare of the entire body. So it is that God-given individuality is not for self-aggrandizement or glorification but for ministering to God's people, and the individual gifts attain their fullest expression and effectiveness as they operate in unity with the gifts of other church members.

There is to be complete unity of spirit and purpose, but not uniformity of means. Uniformity of methods, functions, and gifts is stagnating and self-defeating: diverse individual spiritual gifts are often needed to minister even to one person's spiritual needs or to a particular spiritual problem. Therefore a uniform approach is usually ineffective, while a diversified approach by individual Christians – operating in unity under the anointing of the Holy Spirit – brings results, serves God's purpose, and reflects glory upon our risen Lord. As Christian brothers and sisters, we are to be of one spirit (Acts 1:14), praying with and for each other, loving and appreciating one another, relying on each other, and serving one another in accordance with our Lord's instructions to His disciples (John 13:13-17). In His high-priestly prayer, Jesus petitioned the Father in behalf of His disciples and all believers throughout human history:

> "My prayer is not for them alone. I pray also for those who will believe in Me through their message, that all of them may be one, Father, just as You are in Me and I am in You. May they also be in Us so that the world may believe that You have sent Me. I have given them the glory that You gave Me, that they may be one as we are one: I in them and You in Me. May they be brought to complete unity to let the world know that You sent Me and have loved them even as You have loved Me" (John17:20-23).

Individuals doing what they can do best in cooperation with others can accomplish almost anything – for good or for evil. Again, let us recall an event cited above. In Genesis 11:11-19, we read how the Lord God looked down upon the rebellious humanists who had disregarded His command to populate the entire earth and take dominion over it and were engaged in forming and retaining, in a locale of their choosing, a homogenous society and culture under one government. To symbolize their determination and unity of purpose, they began to construct a tower that was intended to reach to the heavens. Yahweh's response is informative:

> "If as one people speaking the same language they have begun to do this, *then nothing they plan to do will be impossible for them.* Come, let Us go down and confuse their language so they will not understand each other" (verses 6 & 7).

Here we see God himself recognizing the power of human beings acting in unity to attain their goals. Only His intervention by confusing their language created disunity and caused them to scatter abroad.

We see, then, that even non-believers acting in unity can, in the short term, accomplish incredible things. Adam Smith (d.1790) foresaw the efficacy of a division of labor working in a complementary fashion within a free enterprise economic system, and rulers and nations throughout history have applied the principle of unity successfully (Alexander the Great's coalition of Macedonians and Greeks is one example, while Vietnam's ouster of French and ultimately American armed forces in establishing a nationalistic communist regime might be cited as another). However, the United States today is rent by disunity, having rejected the God of unity and biblical principles in our public life. Permanent unity can be realized, of course, only by honoring the person and precepts of Almighty God, the Creator and Sustainer of everything, in whom all wholeness resides. Satan, on the other hand, is the author of disunity and deception. Although he can prompt peoples of diverse backgrounds or interests to cooperate temporarily by engendering or exploiting in them a hatred for some common object of animosity (the vehement hostility of the different Arab states for the nation of Israel provides an example), he can not forge permanent unity, because it is his very nature to promote disbelief, distrust, contumacy, dissension, factionalism, rebellion, destruction, devastation, and death. If Israel were to cease to exist tomorrow, the Arab states would soon be fighting one another; for the unholy cause that draws them together would be no more.

As we have seen, the Bible teaches the effectiveness of diverse individual efforts operating in unity, but it also encourages individual initiatives. We are told in **Ezek.** 22:30 that the Lord God looked for one faithful man to stand in the gap on behalf of the land of Israel. We should be encouraged to know that He often saves by a few dedicated people rather than by many and chooses individuals, sometimes unlikely persons, to carry out His designs. He used Noah to save mankind from extinction; He used Abraham to bring His blessings to all who are faithful; He used Joseph to preserve the lives of his relatives who became the nation of Israel; He used Moses to lead his chosen people out of bondage in Egypt toward the promised land; He used David – a man after His own heart – to establish the nation of Israel on godly principles and to bring forth a royal lineage to which the Savior of mankind was born; He used Esther to save Jewish exiles in Persia from extermination; and He used Nehemiah to rebuild the walls and fortifications of Jerusalem for the Jews who had returned to their homeland. Or consider the importance of Saul of Tarsus who, as the Apostle Paul, carried the Gospel to the Gentiles and wrote more than half of the New Testament. God uses individuals in a mighty way to effect His purposes.

It is not surprising, therefore, that God calls both individuals and nations to an obedient walk with Him – not to conformity with the world. Godly nations are not to conduct their policies according to expediency as all other nations of the world do, and God's people are to be a "peculiar" treasure, a holy people, consecrated to Him (Exodus 19:5; Deuteronomy 14:2; Deuteronomy 26:18; Psalm 135:4; Titus 2:14; & I Peter 2:9). We are not to be like the lady who after suddenly acquiring wealth headed straight for a sophisticated boutique, an exclusive millinery shop, and an expensive beauty parlor. Upon returning home, she waltzed into the living room all powdered, painted, perfumed, and decked out in the latest fashion to bask in her husband's admiration. You can well imagine her pleasure at his greeting:

"Honey, you look like a million."
"Really?" she asked. "Like a million dollars?"
"No," replied the disappointed husband. "Like a million other women."

As persons or as a nation, would that we would not seek to emulate the world but rather trust in God, allowing Him to work the miracle of committed individuality in us and to demonstrate that He is more than sufficient in every situation.

QUESTIONS TO PONDER

1. What Scriptures reveal that the Lord God is interested in every individual?

2. Is our eternal salvation an individual or collective matter?

3. What force or means for transforming society does God recommend and sanction? What means does Satan use to influence society?

4. What do Romans 12:4-6, I Corinthians 12:4-31, Ephesians 4:11-16, and Philippians 2:1-4 teach us about individuality in the Christian? Why has God created us with different personalities and gifts? What should be our attitude concerning our individuality? How should we exercise or

manifest it? To what purpose? Does Satan promote individuality of any sort? Does he desire that men and women exercise freedom of will?

5. Why should believers be careful to foster Christian unity but not uniformity?

6. Why is maintaining unity of spirit and purpose important for God's people?

7. Name five or six biblical characters whom God used to further His grand design for His people. Did any of them help change the course of history?

PERTINENT SCRIPTURES

Genesis chapter 1; Exodus 2:1-10; Exodus chapter 3; Exodus chapters 19-20; Exodus 31:1-11; Exodus chapter 24; Exodus chapter 35:30 through chapter 36:15; Exodus 37:1-9; Exodus 40:5; Numbers chapter 13; Numbers 27:12-33; Judges chapters 4 through 8 and 13 through 16; Ruth; I Samuel chapters 16 through 31; II Samuel chapters 1 through 24; I Kings chapters 1 and 2:1-11; Nehemiah chapters 1 through 13; Esther chapters 1 through 10; Psalm 24:3-5; Psalm 139:13-16; Proverbs 2:1-13; Joel 2:32; Luke 10:38-42; Luke 19:1-10; John 4:3-42; Acts 8:5-8, 14-17, & 26-34; Romans 9:21-24; Romans 12:4-15; I Corinthians 12:4-30; Ephesians 4:11-16; and Hebrews 2:4.

Chapter XVIII

"THE SABBATH PRINCIPLE"

Can our secular attitudes and activities be distinguished from those of the world? Are we simply maintaining a godly facade while denying by the way we live the reality and power of God? (Cf. II Timothy 3:2-5). Just as the Lord God rested from His work of creation on the seventh day, so He instituted one day in seven as a hallowed day in which man was to rest from his labors (Genesis 2:2-3). His people, the Israelites, were not to remain idle but to work six days a week, while ceasing everyday activities on the seventh day, which was to be set aside to worship their Creator and to rest (Exodus 20:8-11; Deuteronomy 5:12-15; Leviticus 23:3; and Ezekiel 46:3). The seven-day week was part of the order of the universe; and the people of Israel were commanded to observe the Sabbath as a holy day and time of repose. They were to desist from their daily toil on the strength of Yahweh's promise that the material provisions or produce they acquired during the rest of the week would suffice for their needs (Exodus 16:22-30). The Israelites were to keep the seventh day as a lasting covenant unto their God – the great I Am – devoting themselves to public worship, study, meditation, and spiritual and physical refreshing while abstaining from labor and commercial activities (Nehemiah 10:31; Nehemiah 13:16-18; Jeremiah 17:21-27; and Amos 8:5). Desecration of the Sabbath was tantamount to breaking the Mosaic covenant and could incur the death penalty (Exodus 31:12-17 and Exodus 35:2-3; cf. Ezekiel 20:12-13, 19-24). National disregard for Yahweh's prescribed Sabbaths and sabbatical rests for the land could bring dire consequences – dispersion of the Hebrews among the nations and ruination of their lands and cities (Leviticus 26:27, 33, & 40-45; and Jeremiah 17:27). As a matter of fact, the Kingdom of Israel was conquered by the Assyrians and its people were scattered after 721 B.C., and Judah spent seventy years in Babylonian captivity so that the land would enjoy the sabbatical rests of which it had been deprived for almost five centuries (Leviticus 26:27-35 and II Chronicles 36:20-21).

It is interesting that the Lord God prescribed not only a weekly Sabbath rest for His people, but a rest for the soil every seventh year (Leviticus 25:1-34;

Leviticus 26:34-35; and Ezekiel 22:8 & 26), thus demonstrating His concern for the entire creation. God's people are not to squander natural resources or exhaust the soil. They are to use them to satisfy their needs while properly managing and conserving them (Genesis 1:29 and Genesis 2:4-17). There is a biblical sense, therefore, in which Christians are environmentalists, enjoined as good stewards to use and preserve (not abuse) the resources God has entrusted to their care.

Such beneficent superintendence pays handsome dividends as the Creator knew full well. In establishing the Sabbath rest for man, for example, God was providing what was best for him: He himself had rested on the seventh day of creation, and He knew that people made in His image required a weekly day of relaxation and refreshment. Sabbatical stipulations were never intended to be onerous but were meant for the well-being of mankind. As our Designer and Maker, God knows our strengths and weaknesses, our desires and needs, our capacities and limits better than do we ourselves; and He prescribed a weekly day of rest as an act of love. Jesus himself attested to this, declaring that the "Sabbath was made for man, not man for the Sabbath" (Mark 2:27; see the entire passage and compare it with Matthew 12:1-13 and Luke 6:1-11).

Jesus's pronouncement was not unprecedented. The prophet Isaiah had proclaimed blessings upon persons who would maintain justice, do what was right, keep the Sabbath, and hold fast to God's covenant (Isaiah 56:1-2, 4-5). He even emphasized a specific promise in this regard:

> "If you turn away your foot from the Sabbath, from doing your pleasure on My holy day, and call the Sabbath a delight, the holy day of the Lord honorable, and shall honor Him, not doing your own ways, nor finding your own pleasure, nor speaking your own words, then you shall delight yourself in the Lord; and I will cause you to ride on the high hills of the earth, and feed you with the heritage of Jacob your father. The mouth of the Lord has spoken" (Isaiah 58:13-14 NJK; cf. Jeremiah 17:24-26).

What are we to make of this? Do special blessings attend nations that observe a weekly day of rest as the Bible prescribes, and are nations cursed that flout His Word? The founding fathers of this nation were careful to observe one day a week as a day of rest and worship consecrated to Almighty God, as the so-called "Blue Laws" handed down through generations by inhabitants of the New England states and other regions originally settled by pious colonists have attested. Today, however, most of these laws have been eliminated or are regarded as curious anachronisms not to be enforced or taken seriously. Although the first day of the week, "Sunday," is still one of two weekly "days off" the majority of employees can anticipate and the day when Christians (with the exception of Seventh-Day Adventists) attend church, it apparently is not considered a holy day even by the vast majority of believers. Christians and non-Christians alike frenetically pursue pleasure, do their shopping, "catch up" with chores and work projects around the home, and engage in sports or other everyday activities on "the Lord's day" without compunction, at least not after attending worship services. Are we merely observing religious rituals and forms while our hearts are cold toward God?

Ancient Israel and Judah were severely punished and their people uprooted, scattered, persecuted, and killed because they acknowledged Yahweh with their lips and in their rites and religious observances without obeying His commandments or inclining their hearts toward Him (Isaiah 29:13; Matthew 15:8-9; and Mark 7:11-13). Jesus recognized the hypocrisy of the religious leaders of His day and denounced silly, empty legalism. When His disciples were criticized for "threshing" on the Sabbath because they separated a few kernels from the standing grain and ate them as they were passing through a field, Jesus proclaimed Himself "Lord of the Sabbath." On the same day, He healed a man with a shriveled hand, declaring that "it is lawful to do good on the Sabbath" (Matthew 12:1-13 and Luke 13:10-17). He taught that human need takes priority over strict interpretation of the law and that God's people can work on the Lord's day in certain circumstances such as unforeseen emergencies (Luke 14:1-5). Performance of necessary functions and deeds of mercy are not prohibited by Scripture (John 7:21-24); and, presumably, recreation of an edifying nature is appropriate if one's spiritual focus is maintained and not sacrificed to unworthy pursuits. However, such teaching hardly gives believers *carte blanche* to disregard or desecrate the appointed day of rest and worship as the vast majority of modern Americans do, manifesting a cavalier attitude, even a legalistic one ("I attend church most Sunday mornings: isn't that enough?") toward God's ordained "Sabbath Principle."

Although Christians are no longer bound by ceremonial law of the Old Testament (Galatians 3:13), which pointed toward a Savior to come, God's moral laws have never been abrogated. Jesus himself declared that He came not to abolish the law but to fulfill it (Matthew 5:17). Indeed, our Lord taught that the law did not merely enjoin abstinence from evil deeds, but that man's thoughts and attitudes also must be pure (Matthew 5:21-22, 27-28). If keeping the law was required of those chosen by Yahweh and covenanted with Him to reveal His ways to the nations, if our Lord had to keep the law perfectly to be able to take the punishment for our sins upon himself, and if the law was a "schoolmaster" to lead people to Jesus Christ (Galatians 3:24-25, KJV; cf. Romans 7:7), then certainly it should be taken seriously by all believers – not as a means of salvation but as a willing and loving submission to the desires of our Savior and the will of the Father.

Even the specific day to be set aside for rest and honoring God is of little consequence so long as one of seven is regularly observed for His glory and one's own benefit – spiritually, emotionally, mentally, and physically. The ancient Hebrews observed the seventh day, the Sabbath, as Yahweh instructed them to do, and so do modern observant Jews. On the other hand, the church (with minor exceptions) sets aside the first day of the week,"Sunday" or "the Lord's day," for corporate worship and rest from the toil and cares of the week to commemorate Jesus Christ's resurrection from the dead and His appearance to His disciples on that day (John 20:1-19 and I Corinthians 16:2). Nevertheless, Paul makes it clear that the day of observance is not so important as is the spirit of the celebration, stating in Romans 14:5-6:

"One man considers one day more sacred than another; another man considers every day alike. Each one should be fully convinced in his own mind. He who regards one day as special, does so to the Lord. He who eats meat, eats to the Lord, for he gives thanks to God; and he who abstains does so to the Lord and gives thanks to God."

Paul comments further in Colossians 2:16-17:

"Therefore, do not let anyone judge you by what you eat or drink, or with regard to a religious festival, a New Moon celebration, or a Sabbath day.

These are a shadow of things that were to come; the reality, however, is found in Christ."

It is also a reality, of course, that a weekly day of rest was stipulated by the Creator to meet the needs of our earliest ancestors (Genesis 2:2-3) and was later declared to the children of Israel as a part of their covenant with the Lord in the "Ten Commandments," by which they were to regulate their morals and conduct. Curiously enough, modern Christians who honor their parents and would at least give lip service to the prohibitions against idolatry, the misuse of God's name or profanity, murder, adultery, theft, libel or perjury, and even covetousness, often act as if the injunction to keep one day a week unto the Lord is no longer relevant. Admittedly, the blood sacrifices and ceremonial laws of ancient Israel no longer pertain, having been fulfilled by Christ's once-and-for-all-time sacrifice on the cross (Hebrews 10:1-8), but do we dare arrogate unto ourselves the prerogative of God in passing judgment on His commandments by arbitrarily picking and choosing which to obey or ignore? What impudent idolatry! When we dispense with biblical rules or principles set forth for our well-being, we must be prepared to suffer the consequences.

In 1793, during the French Revolution, a new revolutionary calendar was instituted – one of a number of measures calculated to destroy the influence of the church and foster the cult of reason. It mandated a ten-day week featuring nine rather than six workdays that violated the Divinely-ordained "Sabbath Principle." The experiment was a disaster for several reasons. Ironically, productivity, which might have been expected to increase because of the three additional workdays per week, declined drastically. After his rise to power, Napoleon Bonaparte – shrewdly aware of economic, religious, social, and political realities militating against continued imposition of the revolutionary calendar – eventually quashed it and restored the Christian calendar in 1806.

Some students of prophecy say that the Antichrist in the time of the end will institute a calendar that will virtually preclude the Jews from keeping the holy feasts to Yahweh prescribed in Leviticus chapter 23. As early as 1954, the Secretary-General of the United Nations proposed "world calendar reform" that would have disrupted the seven-day week, posing an affront to several major religions, including Christianity and Judaism. Since that time, other proposals for reforming the calendar have emerged, and it will be interesting to see what further initiatives may be forthcoming from individual nations or the United Nations. In the final analysis, of course, any attempts to set aside the natural order built into the universe will bring suffering, turmoil, and ultimately calamity.

Our nation is still enjoying countless blessings stemming from the righteous seeds planted and watered by godly forebears, but we are also experiencing more and more the baneful consequences of our apostasy. The Lord God always honors His Word and His covenants with God-fearing nations and individuals. A striking example of how He protects and provides for those faithfully following His precepts was related to me by my wife, the daughter of a Kansas wheat farmer. A God-fearing man who lived his faith in a simple, uneffusive manner, Dad K. took his family to church on the Lord's day and abstained from work on that day except for tending to his animals and fowls. On one occasion in the midst of the wheat harvest, much of his ripe grain remained uncut at week's end, and thunder showers and possible hail were forecast for the weekend. Nevertheless, Dad K. brought his implements into the shed or places of shelter on his farmstead when he finished combining late Saturday evening. On the next day when the family was returning from Sunday worship services, they noticed that almost all of their neighbors, including Christian farmers, were out in the fields combining wheat, desperately trying to save their crops from the predicted storm. As the clouds continued to darken and move in, Dad K. humbly offered thanks at the dinner table for God's blessings and provision. Within minutes, the storm burst, and farmers rushed for shelter, some of them leaving their combines in the fields. Torrential rains accompanied by hail poured down on every side, bringing an end to the harvest and shredding standing grain. The ruinous effects were apparent everywhere after the storm lifted and farmers began to assess the damage – in most cases amounting to total loss of everything that had not been cut. But on Dad K.'s land it was a different story. The deluge that struck his neighbors' properties and croplands had stopped at the boundaries of his fields, by-passing them. His wheat crop was spared, his unwavering trust in God vindicated!

God blesses those whose heart is right, those who sincerely desire to conform to His principles. Conscious obedience is the key – the acid test of our love and trust of God (see Hebrews 3:12 through 4:13). Just as the Israelites who left Egypt under the leadership of Moses did not enter into God's intended rest for them in Canaan because of unbelief manifested in disobedience, so we

186

will not appropriate the fruits of victory if we are not submitted to the will of God. How can there be rest for us if God is directing us in one direction and we are willfully insisting on going in another? We can not live victorious lives without obedience, Therefore, whether the Sabbath rest spoken of in Hebrews 3:14 through 4:11 represents the peaceful, trusting victorious Christian life or our final abode with the Lord in heaven, obedience is required to attain it.

QUESTIONS TO PONDER

1. Who instituted one day out of seven as a day of rest?

2. Did God consider the keeping of the Sabbath by His people of Israel to be important?

3. In addition to ordaining a Sabbath rest for mankind, did God prescribe a sabbatical rest for any other part of the created order? Does this fact bear a message concerning how we are to treat our natural resources?

4. Was God being harsh and arbitrary in commanding Israel to set aside one day a week for rest and worship?

5. Why do Christians (with the exception of the Seventh-Day Adventists) observe the first day of the week rather than the Sabbath?

6. Should we become upset and angry because the Seventh-Day Adventists observe the seventh day rather than the first day of the week as the day of rest and worship?

7. Can persons and nations observing the "Sabbath Principle" and trying to do God's will expect special blessings from the heavenly Father?

PERTINENT SCRIPTURES

Genesis 2:2-3; Exodus 16:22-30; Exodus 20:8-11; Exodus 31:12-17; Exodus 35:2-3; Leviticus 23:2-3; Leviticus 25:1-34; Leviticus 26:27, 33-35; Deuteronomy 5:12-15; Nehemiah 10:31; Nehemiah 13:16-18; Isaiah 56:2; Isaiah 58:13-14; Jeremiah 17:21-27; Ezekiel 20:12-13, 19-24; Ezekiel 22:8-16, 26; Ezekiel 23:58; Ezekiel 44:24; Ezekiel 46:3; Amos 8:5; Matthew 12:1-13; Mark 2:23-28; Luke 6:1-11; Luke 13:10-13; Luke 14:1-6; John 7:21-24; John 20:1-19; Acts 20:7; Romans 14:5-6; I Corinthians 16:2; Galatians 2:16-17; and Hebrews chapters 4 and 5.

Chapter XIX

"THE DOMINION PRINCIPLE"

The Creator gave mankind dominion over all things on the earth and told married couples to be fruitful and multiply to replenish and subdue the earth (Genesis 1:26-30; Genesis 2:19-20; and Hebrews 2:6-8). Man was to serve as God's regent. However, Adam and Eve committed high treason by disobeying God's clear command *not* to partake of the tree of the knowledge of good and evil. This injunction was intended to safeguard man's innocence, his spiritual vitality, and his purity of soul, and to develop his character through obedience to the Lord God in making proper choices in the face of contrary inducements. However, our original forebears failed the test. Satan, the "Old Serpent," deceived Eve into attaining experiential knowledge, denying God's warning that eating the forbidden fruit would culminate in death and alleging it would open her eyes so that she would "be like God, knowing good and evil" (Genesis 3:4). The same wily inducements are being made today: "Hey, man, forget what those goody goodies say about the dangers of taking LSD! If you haven't tried it, don't knock it! You'll feel a rush you won't believe, and you'll see things you never saw before." One does not have to experience drugs to know their deleterious and ruinous consequences; yet thousands of young people and adults fall for that line. Unfortunately, in learning experientially of evil, they become insensitive to God's ways, endangering their souls and their very lives.

If naivety and hubris caused Eve to accede to Satan's blandishments, Adam did so in conscious disobedience to the Lord God (I Timothy 2:14). By their contumacious acts, our first ancestors turned the regency of the earth over to the Adversary, who became the "the god of this world" (John 12:31; John 14:30; John 16:11; II Corinthians 4:4; Ephesians 2:2; and I John 5:19). Nevertheless, man, as God's highest creation, has continued to exercise an imperfect dominion over the earth, its creatures, its plant life, and its resources

– a fact verified in Psalm 8:4-8, which speaks of man's superintendence of all of these things many centuries after man's expulsion from the garden of Eden.[5]

Dominion over the earth denotes caretaking and not spoiling or polluting the environment or engaging in unnecessary cruelty to animals; yet sinful men, greedy for financial gain or perhaps yielding to diabolical, domineering, sadistic urges, have sometimes ravished the land and mistreated living creatures. Satan worshipers sometimes engage in tormenting and slaughtering fowls, animals, and even fellow humans in their fiendish rites, thereby blatantly violating the "Dominion Principle."

Occasionally too, ignorance, negligence, or indolence cause men to abuse the created order or fail to take beneficial measures enjoined by the "Dominion Principle." Abstention from cultivating cropland, allowing it to become overgrown with weeds, mishandling fire in a dry forest, or refusing to tether or pen up potentially dangerous beasts are examples of careless or passive disregard of the Divine mandate. Sometimes inexpedient government regulations may impede proper management of lands or resources, and fear may hamper or preclude positive responses to certain problems.

The story is told of two hillbilly sweethearts, Jesse and Joany, who were walking hand-in-hand through a pasture one evening. Suddenly, Jesse saw a bull bearing down on them. Freeing himself from his lover's grasp, he dashed for safety. "Jesse, Jesse," the frightened girl cried. "Don't leave me, ya hear, Ya

---

[5]The creator God, of course, is the sole Source of all authority, and He retains ultimate control over the entire creation. Psalm 24:1 states: "The earth is the Lord's and everything in it, the world and all who live in it...." Therefore, God remains Supreme Ruler, retaining territorial control over the material earth, its products, and its populace; and men are still able to manage the created order, though admittedly the administration of sinful men is flawed. However, because of man's fall, Satan became the god of the world system, assuming a preponderant influence in civil governments and cultural systems (John 14:30) through reprobate people. When he tempted Jesus Christ in the wilderness, Satan offered Him "the kingdoms of the world and their splendor" if our Lord would only bow down and worship him(Matthew 4:8-9). Significantly, Jesus did not challenge the Devil's legal right to make this offer, but appropriated the spiritual high ground by declaring: "Away from Me, Satan! For it is written: 'Worship the Lord your God, and serve Him only'." Similarly, Christians must confront the enemy, not by trying to gain control over civil governments and culture in order to use them in Christ's service (though Christians are to be "salt and light" for the sake of winning the lost and discipling them in godly principles of righteousness), but by speaking God's Word and waging spiritual warfare (Ephesians 6:12).

sed you'd face death for me!" "Yeh, Ah did, Joany," the fleeing young man called over his shoulder, "but that thar bull ain't daid!"

Like many persons in threatening circumstances, Jesse did not take dominion or stand his ground in the face of opposition or danger. Dominion must be exercised: it is not automatic, and many times it can not be properly implemented in our own strength. Christians may repair to their "high tower" of refuge (Psalm 18:2-3) in times of peril, perplexity, need, sorrow, or disappointment – Jesus Christ, the Pure and righteous One, who by His sinless life, substitutionary death on the cross to pay the penalty for our sins, descent into hell, and resurrection from the grave, triumphed over the Evil One and seized the keys of death and Hades (Colossians 2:10-15 and Revelation 1:18). Today, He is at the right hand of the Father in heaven interceding for us. Everyone who believes in Him has His life, the life of the one who has conquered death and has dominion over all things. As members of His body (even if we are minor members, like an appendix or a toenail), we share in His dominion; for everything is under His feet, and the lowest members of the body could be no lower than that (see Ephesians 1:19-23; cf. Romans 6:1-14; and Colossians 2:13-15).

The original dominion mandate (which we shall use synonymously with "Dominion Principle") was entrusted to both Adam and Eve (Genesis 1:26-30), because the Lord God realized Adam could not effect it alone: he needed a suitable helpmate, companion, and partner in reproduction to accomplish the Divine prescription by forming a family and carrying out God's purpose (Genesis 2:20-24). Thus, the family was instituted as the basic unit of society. A man and woman were to produce children and affectionately nurture them. The family was to protect and provide for their sustenance and teach them in the formation of character – by example, precept, and loving discipline – so that they could one day transmit to their own children a foundation for virtuous conduct and the knowledge of how to govern themselves as individuals, as family members, and as responsible persons living under authority in a godly, stable and law-abiding society.

Actually, families were purveyors of culture and civilized conventions even before the Lord God established civil authority for the purpose of encouraging goodness, punishing evildoers, and protecting society from internal and external disturbances and disorders (see God's covenant with Noah in Genesis 9:1-16 and Romans 13:1-7; I Timothy 2:1-6; Titus 3:1-2; and I Peter 2:13-17). Composed of a man and a woman and their offspring (or adopted children), the family is the basic unit of any civilized society; therefore anything that weakens the family undermines the entire social edifice. God himself ordained and sanctioned marriage, because He wants godly offspring who will carry out His agenda (Malachi 2:14-16). For that very reason, demonic forces today are trying to break up marriages and destroy the family by every imaginable means – by redefining what a family is and applauding alternative arrangements of all sorts; prompting the civil government to impose confiscatory inheritance taxes; rendering the public increasingly insensitive to pornography, homosexuality, fornication, and adultery; and condoning conception out of wedlock. The welfare system has also encouraged promiscuity by providing government funds for single mothers whose boyfriends or spouses are not living with them. In addition, the income tax code has discriminated against married couples as opposed to those living together in sin. Moreover, no-fault divorces have enabled spouses to separate much more readily than in the past, working to the detriment of spouses desiring to save their marriages – usually women who may suffer tremendous economic loss as well as emotional devastation. Divorce has become epidemic in our nation, often being viewed as a convenient option for mates terming themselves "incompatible."

Broken families affect all of society: in fact, the cost of divorce in aggravated social problems and the increased revenues required to deal with them is incalculable. Children of divorced couples are generally more inclined than are children living in a stable home with a father and a mother toward suicide, anti-social behavior, breakdown of self-control, violent crimes, lack of focus in school, drug and alcohol abuse, sexual promiscuity and deviance, and severe emotional disturbances of all kinds. In view of the heartrending, frequently tragic consequences of broken families, the traditional Christian view of matrimony as a covenant between one man and one woman for a lifetime or until the death of one – the type of marriage ordained and sanctioned by the heavenly Father – looks better and better. Commitment to one another and to the family is essential if our society and culture are to endure. Therefore, honoring one's marriage vows and maintaining a faithful, committed, caring relationship with one's mate goes a long way toward effecting God's dominion mandate. Senator John Ashcroft fondly recalls his father's admonition : "The best thing a man can do for his kids is to love their Mom."

Another bulwark of the social order is the church – comprised of Christian families and singles – who, by purposefully and harmoniously working in unity and in the power of the Holy Spirit, can carry out the dominion mandate. The New Testament uses several similes to describe the church, including a building composed of "living stones" and a living organism, "the body of Christ." In I Peter 2:5-10, God's saints are characterized as "living stones," a chosen race, a royal priesthood, a people of God's own possession. The picture depicted here is of a structure built upon a biblical foundation with Jesus Christ constituting the chief cornerstone. As "living stones," we are joined together by the mortar of love according to the Divine Architect's plan in perfect union (I John 4:7-21 and I Corinthians 13). Godly order prevails throughout the entire structure as each stone occupies its God-ordained place in relationship to all of the others and fulfills its proper function. The Lord himself has ordered and arranged it all. He has ordained that we should be interdependent – just as members of an organic body (Here we encounter a second simile, explicated in Romans 12:5-16; I Corinthians 12:12-31; and Ephesians 4:11-16) – and that certain stones (or bodily organs) shall have more prominent positions or functions than others though every one is necessary. As members of one edifice, we are to accept the design of the Chief Architect and as members of His body (the other analogy), we are to submit to His chosen and anointed leaders and to give preference to one another in love (Philippians 2:1-8; Romans 12:10; Ephesians 5:21; and I Peter 5:5). Each believer is a temple of the living God and, as such, should function under the motivation and power of the Holy Spirit in harmony with fellow Christians and, above all, in strict obedience to the Father.

During His sojourn on earth, Jesus said:"Truly, truly ... the Son can do nothing of Himself unless it is something He sees the Father doing; for whatever the Father does, these things the Son also does in like manner" (John 5:19, NASB). What a spirit of obedience to the father! What a spirit of humility, self-denial, and servanthood is manifested in this statement and in our Lord's every act! We are to walk in the same way, and we can by faith. We can not do so in our own strength, our own diligence, our own self-discipline, our own perseverence, but only by relying on the Spirit of God and trusting implicitly in our Divine Master (Romans 8:4; Galatians 4:16; and Galatians 5:25). Such devotion involves self-denial (Mark 8:34-38 and Luke 9:23-26) and the same spirit of servanthood that we observe in Jesus Christ (John 13:34; I Corinthians 9:19; and Galatians 5:13).

A faithful Christ-like life is impossible unless we consistently and regularly commune with the risen Savior and feed on His Word. As we do this, we will be equipped for the task of effecting God's dominion mandate. We can not afford to focus on the discouraging, depressing, sordid, demoralizing, and faith-destroying news of dishonest dealings, extortion, corruption, and deception in high places or accounts of violent crimes, substance abuse, debauchery, lewdness, perversion, abortions, child abuse, treachery, embezzlement, irreligion and the like. All too often, we become overwhelmed by such news – to the point that we may come to believe it is futile to do anything. This is precisely the attitude the Adversary wants us to adopt. He would have us remain inactive and silent, passive and apparently acquiescent; but we must keep our eyes on our Supreme Commander – Jesus Christ, the Author and Perfecter of our faith – and persevere in the mission assigned us. We must continue, under the guidance and enablement of the Holy spirit, to be "salt and light" by speaking God's truth, testifying to our faith, ministering to needs close at hand about which we *can* do something, and joining with like-minded people and godly organizations to promote reforms and to reclaim our culture. Boldness and persistence are required of "soldiers of the King of kings," as well as the ability to endure hardship, criticism, scorn, and persecution in the spirit of Christ, and a determination to please God rather than men.

In seeking to fulfill the God-given cultural mandate, we must keep in mind not only who He is, His nature, and His eternal purposes and commands, but the nature of what He expects us to accomplish. Godly culture is characterized by perfect wholeness – not merely in the sense that it is healthy, positive, edifying, and attuned to the Divine will and purpose – but also in the sense that it is not fragmented, disjointed, contradictory, unbalanced, one-sided or less than all-encompassing. As the Source of all life, reality, and culture, God must be recognized as the wellspring and core of everything; otherwise, civilization becomes at best a distorted caricature or grotesque counterfeit of what He intended it to be. All things, all knowledge, all events in the entire universe are perfectly and harmoniously joined together in the infinite wisdom of the Almighty, though man in his finite fallen state can not fully apprehend it, and even nature – flawed by man's fall – does not accurately reflect it. Nevertheless, we should appropriate, by His Spirit and through His Revelation in Jesus Christ and the inspired Word, everything we can discover or know about the "Father of lights with whom there is no variableness or shadow of turning" (James 1:2).

We must acknowledge, honor, and trust in a personal Creator-Sustainer God who never changes and whose eternal law is perfect, universally applicable, and immutable – from age to age the same (Psalm 19:7; Psalm 119:142, 144, 151-152, & 160; and Hebrews 13:8). Only by applying eternal verities rather than the "evolving" opinions or evanescent tastes of society can we become worthy, effective instruments (and collectively a redemptive force) to fulfill the Divine purpose.

Doing the will of the Lord must be paramount, and we must proceed to redeem our culture solely in His strength and in His ways. Although we are admonished to destroy false "arguments and every pretension that sets itself against the knowledge of God" and to "take captive every thought to make it obedient to Christ" (II Corinthians 10:5), we must undertake this task by His methods and in His spirit.

First of all, we need to deal with our own sins and our own thought-life (our motives should be pure and our attitudes humble) before proceeding to refute anti-Christian speculations and ideologies. In doing so, we should realize that the "anger of man does not achieve the righteousness of God" (James 1:20, NASB) and that we do not struggle against flesh and blood, but against the rulers, against the powers, against the world forces of this darkness, against the spiritual forces of wickedness in the heavenly places" (Ephesians 6:12, NASB). Are we careful to put on all of our spiritual armor? Are we skillful and obedient in wielding the offensive weapons afforded us – the Word of God and praying *always* in the Spirit? (see Ephesians 6:13-18a). Furthermore, do we conduct the battle according to God's campaign strategy? Do we get our battle orders each day from the Lord of Hosts, or are we going forth to do battle according to our own plan and in our own strength? Are we, for example, relying primarily on worldly wisdom – on knowledge attained at institutions of higher learning or knowledge gleaned from personal experience? If so, may we not unwittingly fall into the Enemy's trap of employing fleshly, humanistic means to combat evil.

There is nothing good of the flesh. This statement is not to be misconstrued in a Manichean sense of refusing to propagate the race, abstaining from eating meat, and considering the physical body and all its appetites abhorrent, but is simply a renunciation of carnal methods to promote biblical ideals or to attack humanism, ostensibly in the service of God.

Soon after receiving Jesus Christ as personal Savior, we may have put to death what we deem to be the abominable deeds of the flesh – fornication, drunkenness, debauchery, brawling, gossiping, and the like. However, in our human weakness, we may wrongly use what we consider to be good and admirable fleshly attributes, talents, or traits to advance the kingdom of God. One believer, for example, may take such pride in his courage, candor, and forthrightness in denouncing evil that he needlessly antagonizes non-believers and wounds fellow Christians with his tongue; another may mistakenly consider a personal weakness such as obstinacy to be a virtue, terming it courage, constancy, or fidelity. Not that God can not use our personal traits to His glory, but we must submit them to him to employ as He wills.

Nothing prompted by our fallen, fleshly nature – whether it appears beneficial to God's service or not – is pleasing to the Lord. All of our righteousness, we are told in Isaiah 64:6, is as filthy rags. After all, if we should achieve success through our own efforts, to whom would go the glory? The fact is that we can not glorify God by relying on our own methods and expending our energies as we see fit; for, in doing so, we are not depending on Him but exalting ourselves. No matter that we give lip service to God's enabling power and purport to be doing His will: if we are not following biblical principles and have not ascertained the Lord's *modus operandi* in dealing with the specific matter at hand, and furthermore if we have not worshipfully, prayerfully, and obediently submitted to His battle directives, we are acting as self-reliant humanists – trying to be our own God while posing as followers of Jesus Christ. He is *all* our righteousness; for He is the Truth, the Light of the world, the Source of all worth, all justice, all righteousness. To be sure, in Jesus Christ we are "the righteousness of God" (II Corinthians 5:21), but anything that we attempt in our own will or in our own strength and ability – even when we are involved in what we conceive to be the work of God – is done in a spirit of prideful humanism.

We may ask God's blessing upon our well-intended efforts to please Him. We may even sincerely believe that we are glorifying God (Saul of Tarsus did when he went about persecuting Christians), but if we have formulated our own battle plan to fight the forces of evil, we may be just as sinful as the forces against which we are contending; because we are presuming that we are intelligent enough, courageous enough, and spiritual enough to carry out God's work for Him. In this unconscious supposition, we are ignoring the necessity of reliance on God and in effect glorifying ourselves.

Victory has to be won in God's way, so that it is His victory alone (remember Gideon's army). It is wrong for us to decide how to carry out God's work and then, as an afterthought, to ask Him to bless our endeavor and give it success. We can not contend with evil in our own way and expect God's almighty power to work in behalf of our efforts. To do so is tantamount to insolent insubordination. We are not to use carnal weapons to engage in spiritual warfare; rather we must use God's weapons and take our orders from him. A soldier does not decide how to attack the enemy and then demand that the commanding general give him air support and other assistance; the good soldier listens attentively to orders issued by the general and communicated to him by his superior and proceeds to implement them.

How many times do we as Christians try to be our own generals only to suffer defeat? The fact is that God can not afford to have us win in His name by humanistic means. He is a jealous God, and to him alone belongs the honor and glory for every success. To plan and execute "God's work" without seeking, receiving, and obeying His directives is to bury Him under a heap of gangrenous rags of self-sufficiency and self-righteousness.

Thank God that we are not automatons! We have been given the freedom to choose God and His way or to follow our own devices. However, we can never be fully free and victorious, as He intended us to be, until we submit wholeheartedly to Him. Such submission, of course, does not issue from compulsion. Feodor Dostoyevsky's "Grand Inquisitor" did not recognize this truth. In fact, he berated Jesus Christ for allowing men to exercise free will and for not proscribing their liberty in order to impose social justice and give them material benefits. Atheistic humanists and self-styled "liberals" are doing the same thing today; yet we must not stoop to fight them with fleshly weapons – the very means that we find abhorrent in them. We must freely choose to follow Jesus Christ in both purpose and means. Jesus loves all mankind – that includes atheists and humanists; and by God's grace we must love them too, even when we detest their deeds. At the end of Dostoyevsky's mini-masterpiece, Jesus Christ, without a word, kisses the bloodless lips of the Grand Inquisitor – not to indicate acquiescence to his ideas or approval of his distorted reasoning – but to prove that God loves all men and paradoxically allows free choice even to those who denounce Him for doing so.

The Divine purpose in this world will be realized only when it is ardently effected in the spirit of our Lord and according to His directives. May God grant us the grace to confess our fleshly, intellectual inadequacy, to submit to His will, and to welcome His discipline and commands. May we renounce pride – taking into captivity every false and arrogant thought – and then go forth in the wisdom and strength of the Lord alone, confessing that we are the righteousness of God in Christ, that we can do all things through Christ who strengthens us (Philippians 4:13), and that we are "more than conquerors," but only "in Jesus Christ," our Savior, our Lord, our Supreme Commander.

Until Jesus Christ returns to claim His own and to renew all things, let us remain faithful to our cultural mandate – thinking God's thoughts after Him and obeying His commands to multiply and replenish the earth; to exercise dominion over it; to proclaim the Gospel of Jesus Christ; and to carry His salvation, healing, and wholeness to the nations – thereby doing our part to effect the will and grand design of our Savior and Lord.

QUESTIONS TO PONDER

1. Do we have to experience something to know it or know about it? Why or why not? Are there any dangers that may attend acquisition of knowledge by experience?

2. We know from Scriptures that our original forebears, by disobeying God, allowed Satan to usurp regency over the earth. Does this mean that man is no longer able to exercise dominion over the earth as God originally commissioned him to do? Do we share in Christ's triumph over Satan through our Lord's crucifixion and resurrection? Can we exercise the authority that we have in Jesus Christ?

3. Is the Creator God still concerned about His creation? About all of His creation? Should we have a similar concern?

4. How does marriage and the family enter into the dominion mandate? Do broken families attenuate attempts to fulfill the dominion mandate?

5. What is the church's role in mankind's endeavor to exercise dominion and carry out God's cultural mandate? How should God's people go about this?

6. Why must God not be discarded from culture or marginalized?

7. Why must the dominion mandate be effected by godly methods? What methods and attitudes should be avoided? What ones should be employed?

PERTINENT SCRIPTURES

Genesis 1:26-30; Genesis 2:19-24; Genesis 9:1-16; Psalm 8:4-8; Psalm 119:142, 144, 151-152, & 160; Malachi 2:14-16; Mark 8:34-38; Luke 9:23-26; John 5:19; John 12:31; John 13:34; John 14:30; John 16:11; Romans 6:1-14; Romans 8:4; Romans 13:1-7; Romans 12:15-16; I Corinthians 9:19; I Corinthians 12:12-31; I Corinthians chapter 13; II Corinthians 4:4; II Corinthians 5:21; II Corinthians 10:5; Galatians 4:16; Galatians 5:13; Galatians 5:25; Ephesians 1:19-23; Ephesians 2:2; Ephesians 4:11-16; Ephesians 5:21; Ephesians 6:10-18; Philippians 2:1-8; Philippians 4:13; Colossians 2:10-15; I Timothy 2:1-6; Titus

3:1-2; Hebrews 2:6-8; Hebrews 13:8; James 1:2; I Peter 2:5-10 & 13-17; I Peter 5:5; I John 5:19; and Revelation 1:18.

Chapter XX

"THE SIN PRINCIPLE" AND "THE PRINCIPLE OF GOD'S GRACE"

What is sin? Noah Webster's *American Dictionary of the English Language* (1828 edition) defines sin as "the voluntary departure of a moral agent from a known rule of rectitude or duty, prescribed by God; any voluntary transgression of the divine law, or violation of a divine command; a wicked act; iniquity. Sin is either a positive act in which a known divine law is violated, or it is the voluntary neglect to obey a positive command, or a role of duty clearly implied in such command. Sin comprehends not actions only, but neglect of known duty, all evil thoughts, purposes, words, and desires, whatever is contrary to God's commands or law...." *The Westminster Shorter Catechism*, used for years in many Presbyterian Churches, says: "Sin is any transgression of or want of conformity unto the law of God." In I John 5:17, we are told that "all unrighteousness is sin" (NASB). Since righteousness denotes moral and spiritual perfection, anything short of perfection is sin. Even our thoughts and attitudes are open to God and may be sinful or imperfect. Jesus taught that being angry with a brother or looking lustfully at a woman were spiritually equivalent to committing murder or adultery (Matthew 5:21-28). Furthermore, Romans 14:23 teaches that "whatsoever is not of faith is sin"; therefore, if we doubt in our mind or conscience whether a thing is right, it is sin to us. James 4:17 presents a further dimension reflected in the two definitions given above: "therefore, to him that knoweth to do good, and doeth it not, to him it is sin" (KJV). This precept is generally referred to as "sin of omission," though the terminology can be misleading. A young pupil was asked by his Sunday School teacher: "What is a sin of omission?" "I don't know," replied the lad. "Maybe that's a sin you should have done but didn't."

At any rate, the biblical standard for righteousness is a stringent one. The Apostle Paul taught that righteousness and right standing with God could come only through faith in the altogether righteous One, Jesus Christ; for all [others] have sinned and fall short of the glory of God..." (Romans 5:22-23). Although humanists would have us believe that man is inherently good, both our experiences and observations in everyday life demonstrate the fallacy of this view. Even infants soon manifest inclinations to do as they please, regardless of what they are directed to do, and to evince self-centeredness, selfishness, and anger that belie their sweet, innocent appearance.

The Bible teaches that since our original forebears disobeyed their Creator, their rebellious nature has been transmitted to their progeny – the only exception being Jesus Christ, the God-man, who was conceived not by human agency alone, but by the interaction of the Holy Spirit and a virgin chosen by God (Matthew 1:18-24 and Luke 1:26-38).

Although we have inherited the propensity to follow our own soulish inclinations (those of the mind, constituted of the intellect, emotions, and the will) or fleshly urges rather than to obey God, we are still free moral agents, responsible for our own choices and actions. Some people, even in antiquity, so yearned to walk with God – Enoch, Noah, and Job are examples – that He enabled them to do so, but these were the exceptions rather than the rule, and even they, though accepted by God, were not without sin.

Not only are we prone to follow our own ambitions and desires rather than God, but the "ancient serpent" or "dragon," Satan (Revelation 12:7-9), who seduced our first parents into disobeying the Lord God (Genesis chapter 3), is going about "like a roaring lion, seeking whom he may devour" by inducing people into sinful, destructive practices (I Peter 5:8, KJV). At one time, this enemy of our soul was Lucifer, the light-bearing star of the morning and guardian cherub of God, but he lost his position of trust when he pridefully attempted to usurp the honor, glory, and authority of Almighty God (Isaiah 14:12-15 and Ezekiel 28:11-19). Since his fall, he and the fallen angels (demons) have continued in rebellion against the Lord God, trying to destroy His greatest creation – man – and, through him, to take over dominion of the earth in order to bring it into conformity with his destructive thought patterns and death-dealing cultural activities.

We have already seen the first act in this drama when our first ancestors yielded to the "serpent's" temptation, but let us take further note of the crafty, insidious, and subtle *modus operandi* of this "father of lies." For one thing, he tempted Eve, apparently in the absence of Adam (Genesis 3:1), and he continues to this day to isolate, whenever possible, individuals from persons or agencies capable of providing godly support, or to set probable supporters at odds in order to "divide and conquer" them independently. Notice also that the serpent guilefully cast doubt on God's love and instilled discontent with existing circumstances (idyllic as they were) when he asked Eve: "Did God really say 'You must not eat from any tree in the garden'?" Of course, Eve replied that she and her husband were permitted to eat of all the trees in the garden except one, but the serpent's insinuation that the Creator was arbitrary and restrictive in not allowing them full liberty and personal enjoyment was not lost on her. Her attention became focused not on God's bountiful liberality, but on His one proscription; and she apparently began to view this restriction not as evidence of God's desire to spare her suffering and tragedy, but as an unwarranted deprivation from something desirable. At least, she did not cease talking to her tempter: she continued to listen to him even after she was aware that he was impugning God.

Do we not do much the same today? When we are tempted to do something contrary to God's Word, do we not sometimes contemplate the prospective pleasures or advantages the suggested course of action may bring rather than dismissing the thought and praying to God for strength to resist the temptation? We can not stand against the enemy of our soul in our own strength but only in the power of His might. To appropriate this, we must live in close communion with Him and in submission to His will, just as Jesus did.

Our Lord used the Word of the Father to rout the enemy when He was tempted in the wilderness (Matthew 4:1-11), not adding to that Word or subtracting from it. On the other hand, Eve added to God's command not to eat fruit from the tree of the knowledge of good and evil the words "and you must not touch it" (Genesis 3:2). There is always a danger in playing fast and loose with the Word of God or doubting its exactness rather than standing firmly and immovably upon it. Israel's first king was rejected by Yahweh for putting his own construction on God's Word spoken to him through the prophet Samuel (I Samuel 15:1-23), and the man of God from Judah who courageously prophesied against the apostate king of Israel suffered death when he paid attention to the fabrication of another prophet rather than adhering to the Word God had given him (I Kings 13:1-32). Our nation has allowed the secular, pragmatic, often God-denying ideas of men to influence or determine policies rather than acting on principles grounded in God's Word. We are already suffering the results, and utter calamity will overtake us unless we repent.

Like many of our contemporary political, intellectual, and cultural leaders and people everywhere, Eve pusillanimously listened to Satan's lie (Genesis 3:4-5) that disobedience would not eventuate in death – that it is possible and even desirable to break Divine commandments: that individuals or a society can sin and get away with it. "You will not surely die," the serpent said. Likewise, believers taking a stand for biblical truth are likely to hear: "You don't really believe that a loving God would punish society for upholding 'the right of choice' for pregnant women, do you? You're too intelligent to believe that!" Or it may be that a drug dealer will say: "Hey, man! Snort some of this and your whole consciousness will be expanded. You'll experience sensations and sights that'll blow your mind!"

In a similar manner, Satan appealed to Eve's pride (his own pride had brought him down, Isaiah 14:13-14), saying: "... God knows that when you eat of it [the forbidden fruit] your eyes will be opened, and you will be like God [Elohim], knowing good and evil" (Genesis 3:5).

"Come on, don't listen to all those outmoded religious ideas," we might hear today. "Live it up! Do your own thing!" As Eve looked at the forbidden fruit and saw that it was pleasing to the eye and allegedly able to give her wisdom, she came to rely on her reason rather than standing on God's Word. She picked some of the fruit and ate it. Such actions inevitably have an affect on others (see pp.231-232) – in this case on her husband, to whom she handed some of the fruit. Although Adam was not deceived into partaking of it (I Timothy 2:12-14), he apparently loved the creature (Eve) more than the Creator (cf. Romans 1:25) and fell into the same sin as his wife, except that he deliberately broke God's commandment. How often do we yield to the creature rather than to the Creator – to peer pressure, for example, or to a desire to please men whom we see with our eyes rather than God whom we do not see? (Cf. I Thessalonians 2:4.)

The immediate result of Adam and Eve's sin was a loss of innocence (just as sin in our lives – sexual intercourse before marriage, for instance – brings a loss of innocence that can never be fully recovered in this life). For the first time, they knew they were naked (perhaps they had been covered by God during their primeval state of innocence with the light of righteousness (see Job 29:14, Psalm 104:2, Daniel 12:3, and Matthew 13:43), and they tried to cover themselves with fig leaves sewn together (Genesis 3:7). Likewise, people today try to conceal their moral and spiritual nakedness by stitching together religious good deeds, philanthropy, good moral living, and other "fig leaves" when only the shed blood of Jesus Christ – symbolized by the animal skins with which the Lord God clothed our first forebears (Genesis 3:21) – can cover our transgressions (Hebrews 9:11-28) and reconcile us with an all-righteous God.

Did Adam and Eve gain wisdom as Satan said they would when they partook of the forbidden fruit? In a sense they did, but at what a price! They learned experientially of the sorrow, despair, and guilt brought about by disobedience and rebellion. How much better it would have been for Adam and Eve to have submitted themselves wholeheartedly to God's will, to have obeyed and trusted Him perfectly (not through reason but through fellowship with Him in the spirit) until they attained godly knowledge and wisdom without experiencing evil, anguish, pain, and death. Sadly, mankind attained the ability to discern the difference between good and evil according to the plan of the evil one, not in God's way. As a result, far from being freer, our first ancestors became slaves of sin, unable by their own efforts to make themselves right with their Maker; for they suffered immediate spiritual death (separation from their Divine Source of life and loss of fellowship with Him) and therefore conducted themselves under the guidance and impulses of their impaired minds (souls, consisting of the intellect, emotions, and will) and their fleshly instincts. Eventually, they also experienced physical death, and their progeny have experienced the same forms of death.

Ever since the fall of mankind, we have been subject to sin and death, unable to save ourselves; therefore, humanists believing in the essential goodness of man are deluding themselves. Their attempts to do righteous things may seem admirable, but they can not save a person from eternal death, and all relativistic ethical systems are based on false premises and doomed to tragic failure. The fact is that nobody can live as God intended him to: no one by simple force of intellect or will or by doing "good deeds" can make himself right in God's eyes.

A person must recognize his sinful state before he can turn away from it and experience the salvation available through Jesus Christ (John l4:6; Acts 4:l2; and I John 5:l2). By predisposing us to strive to improve ourselves, humanistic attitudes inhibit us from repenting of our sins. In much the same way, an alcoholic may try to solve his drinking problem or deny that he has one, insisting that he is not as bad off as others. Such a person can not overcome his addiction. Some alcoholics joke about their slavery to drinking. One may say: "I can give up alcohol anytime I want to. I've given it up hundreds of times." Another may laughingly state: "I drink only once a day – a fifth of whiskey before breakfast," and still another may joke: "I can't remember a time during the past twenty years when I wasn't under the 'alfluence' of 'incohol,' but I've never become an alcoholic." Perhaps not. Perhaps he is just a habitual drunk. What does the terminology matter? The fact is that before an alcoholic can be helped, he must acknowledge his problem; and before we can be delivered from the bondage of sin, we must take sin seriously, recognizing it for what it is – rebellion against God – and repent, crying out to Jesus Christ for mercy, forgiveness, and salvation.

When a person gives "the devil a foothold" by allowing sin to take root in his life (Ephesians 4:27), there is a continuous and inexorable degeneration in his character, and sin gains dominion over him (see Romans l:2l-32). The only way "to break the yoke" is to repent, renounce sin, turn to Jesus Christ for salvation and deliverance, and allow Him full sway.

Demonic powers have even established themselves over certain areas of the earth, because inhabitants of these particular regions have given entry to them or encouraged them in one way or another. In Daniel l0:l0 to ll:l, we read that the demonic "prince of Persia" for three weeks withstood an angel sent by God to answer the petition of the prophet Daniel. Demonic activity is still evident today. Bizarre occurrences and disorientation have been experienced by pilots flying through the so-called "iron triangle" in the Caribbean, and a number of ships and aircraft have mysteriously disappeared. In Haiti, occult, animistic beliefs and practices have mingled for more than two centuries. Voodoo came in with the first West African slaves brought to the island of Hispaniola, and Haiti's revolutionary leaders invoked demonic forces to assist them in their war for independence from France early in the l9th century. Even in the post-World-War-II era, President Francois Duvalier employed voodoo and paramilitary police to instill fear in the masses and enhance his autocratic rule. It is little wonder that superstition, poverty, disease and anarchy have plagued Haiti over the years and that it remains the most backward and impoverished nation in the Western Hemisphere. Much the same could be said of India whose teeming population has been kept in demonic thralldom by Hinduism and other unholy influences in spite of its republican form of government. Proverbs 14:34 states: "Righteousness exalts a nation, but sin is a reproach to any people" (NKJV). Our nation should heed this scriptural truth; for we have been going in the wrong direction for most of this century, testing the patience of a loving, merciful, but altogether righteous God.

The Almighty has graciously extended His unmerited favor – His grace – to all mankind, but millions continue to spurn Him. In the presence of our disobedient original ancestors, the Creator-God cursed the serpent, stating to him: "I will put enmity between you and the woman, and between your offspring and hers; He will crush your head and you will strike His heel" (Genesis 3:15). The offspring of the woman is, of course, Jesus Christ, the "last Adam" – sired by the Holy Spirit and born of a virgin – who overcame every temptation and kept the Divine law perfectly so that He could die in our place, taking the punishment for our sins upon himself. Whoever accepts His sacrificial death and believes in his heart that God has raised Him from the dead will have eternal life (cf. Romans 10:9; I Corinthians 15:22 & 45; and Hebrews 9:28).

Although God's grace has been offered to everyone just as a radio beam is broadcast to everyone within a particular listening area, not all will receive Him as personal Savior and Lord any more than will all potential listeners to a local radio station tune in to its programs. Nonetheless, salvation through Jesus Christ is available to everyone, and those who trust in Him, making Him Lord of their lives, become children of God – "heirs of God and co-heirs with Christ" (Romans 8:17 & 21). However, He is not the Father of those who refuse to accept Him, despite the popular fable of "the fatherhood of God and the universal brotherhood of man." Jesus emphatically proclaimed to some of the religious leaders of His day that if God were truly their Father, they would love Him – the One sent by the Father. That they rejected Him was quite evident, Jesus asserted, because they did not pay attention to what He was saying. Therefore, they were not God's children but belonged to their father, "the devil," spouting his lies and carrying out his desires (see John 8:31-47).

The Gospel of reconciliation was, of course, offered first to the Jews, then to the Gentiles (Romans 1:16 & Romans 2:10). Indeed, centuries before Jesus Christ walked the earth, God reached out in love to men and women who would follow His ways. Enoch, Noah, and Job have already been mentioned. Yahweh chose another man of faith, Abraham (Genesis 12:1-3), and later the nation of Israel (Deuteronomy 7:6; Deuteronomy 14:2; Deuteronomy 26:18; I Kings 3:8; I Chronicles 16:13; Psalm 105:6; and Isaiah 44:1) to be to Him a consecrated people who would reveal His way of righteousness to mankind and proclaim the coming of the Messiah.

However, few of the chosen people of Israel recognized the Messiahship of Jesus of Nazareth; few accepted this itinerant Preacher-Teacher and "Suffering Servant" as the king they were expecting, and the vast majority rejected Him (John 1:1-3 & 10-12). Nevertheless, Jesus Christ (Messiah) was God's "only- begotten Son," born on earth of a Jewish maiden in the form of human flesh to demonstrate God's love to men, to show them the way to abundant and everlasting life, and to be the Way, through His propitiatory death and resurrection, for all those accepting His atonement for sin, to appropriate and experience eternal life. God's mercy is boundless; He does not want anyone to perish (I Timothy 2:3-6 and II Peter 39), and His saving grace is extended to nations as well as individuals (Matthew 28:19 and I Peter 2:9-10). The latter passage makes a collective reference to the redeemed, and Psalm 33:12 declares: "Blessed is the nation whose God is the Lord, the people whom He has chosen for His inheritance." Our American forefathers sought to establish such a nation, and our land is still benefiting from many of the blessings accrued from our godly beginnings. Let us not presume upon His mercy, however, or take His grace for granted. If He punished His chosen people Israel for their sins, He will surely punish us for ours. Therefore, may we repent of our personal and national sins and turn to the One who will graciously pardon us and heal our land (II Chronicles 7:14).

QUESTIONS TO PONDER

1. What is sin? According to the Bible, how did sin enter God's creation? What are the effects of sin?

2. Does the Bible support the humanistic premise that man is essentially good and that if he is educated properly, he will do what is right? Does empirical evidence substantiate this premise?

3. If all of us have sinned and the good deeds we do are no better than "filthy rags" (Isaiah 64:6), is there any hope for us?

4. Does God hold nations as well as individuals responsible for their sins?

5. How should nations deal with the problem of sin?

PERTINENT SCRIPTURES

Genesis chapter 3 and 12:1-3; Exodus 19:6; Deutronomy 7:6; Deuteronomy 14:2; Deuteronomy 26:18; I Samuel 15:1-23; I Kings 3:8; I Kings 13:1-32; I Chronicles 16:13; II Chronicles 7:14; Job 29:14; Psalm 33:12; Psalm 104:2; Psalm 105:6; Proverbs 14:9 & 34; Isaiah 14:12-15; Isaiah 44:1; Ezekiel 28:11-19; Daniel 10:10 through 11:1; Daniel 12:3; Matthew 1:18-24; Matthew 4:1-11; Matthew 5:21-28; Matthew 13:43; Luke 1:26-38; John 1:1-3 & 10-12; John 3:16; John 8:31-47; John 14:6; Acts 4:12; Romans 1:16 & 18-32; Romans 2:10; Romans 3:23; Romans 4:13-16; Romans 5:7-23; Romans 6:5-23; Romans 8:17 & 21; Romans 11:6; Romans 14:23; I Corinthians 15:22 & 45; II Corinthians 5:21; Ephesians 2:8-10; Ephesians 4:27; I Thessalonians 2:4; I Timothy 1:15; I Timothy 2:3-6 & 12-14; Titus 3:5-7; Hebrews 9:11-28; I Peter 2:9-10; I Peter 5:8; II Peter 3:9; I John 1:7-8; I John 5:12 & 17; and Revelation 12:7-9.

Chapter XXI

"THE PRINCIPLE OF GOD'S DEALING WITH MAN IN HISTORY"

As Creator, the Lord God is the Author of history, and throughout the ages His hand has been evident in the affairs of mankind. Many incidents may be cited from the Bible. In it, we read of the expulsion of Adam and Eve from the garden of Eden to prevent our guilt-laden ancestors from partaking of the tree of life that would have trapped them in a hopeless situation – everlasting physical existence as sinners separated from God (Genesis 3:22-24). We are also told how people became so corrupted and evil that God sent a flood to exterminate them, saving only righteous Noah and his family (Genesis chapters 6 through 8); and later (Genesis 11:1-9), when the earth's inhabitants refused to carry out God's dominion mandate to replenish the earth and manage it (deciding instead to unite in one place as one people and build a city with a tower that would earn them universal renown), He confused their language and scattered them throughout the earth. Time and again, the Lord God guided and protected Abram (later Abraham), a man of tremendous faith despite his imperfections – sometimes from his own folly (Genesis chapters 12 through 23) – promising to bless all the nations of the earth through him.

God was preparing a people for himself, a people that were to separate themselves unto Him and demonstrate His ways to all mankind. These descendants of Jacob (later Israel) were to eradicate the iniquitous, demonized inhabitants of Canaan and to follow Yahweh in holy obedience as a people chosen by Him to bring forth the Savior of the world. He delivered them by His servant Moses from bondage in Egypt (Exodus chapters 2 through 12), supernaturally led them by a pillar of cloud by day and fire by night (Exodus 13:21-22), enabled them to walk through a seemingly impassable sea by parting the water for them; made a covenant with them and gave them His laws, directives for proper worship, and a viable government; and eventually led the second generation victoriously into their promised inheritance (Exodus chapters 14 through 40 and the books of Leviticus Numbers, and Joshua).

Unhappily, the Israelites strayed from the Lord, intermarrying with the inhabitants of the land and adopting their pagan practices. Because of their apostasy, the Lord allowed them to be oppressed by various enemies; yet when the inconstant Hebrews cried out to Yahweh, He again and again raised up leaders to rescue them and finally permitted them to have a king (Judges and I Samuel). The Kingdom of Israel, founded about 1,000 B.C., expanded and grew strong under King David, the "sweet Psalmist of Israel," war hero, and "man after God's own heart" (I Samuel 13:14 and Acts 13:22). His son and successor, King Solomon, built a magnificent temple in Jerusalem and dedicated it to the worship of the one Eternal God; but, despite an auspicious beginning, he fell into idolatry; and after his son Rehoboam acceded to the throne, the Kingdom was divided into the Kingdom of Israel, consisting of the northern ten tribes, and the Kingdom of Judah, made up essentially of the tribes of Judah and Benjamin.

From the time of its formation, the northern kingdom was unfaithful to the Divine covenant. It was finally conquered by Assyria (722-721 B.C.) and exited from the annals of history. Thanks to a number of godly kings, Judah fared better, but eventually departed from the covenant with Yahweh. Although it preserved time-honored religious ceremonies, it lapsed into contumacy, idolatry, and perverse practices. Repeated and persistent prophetic warnings of impending punishment fell on deaf ears, and God's prophets were persecuted. At last, the Lord prompted Babylon's King Nebuchadnezzar to sack Jerusalem (586 B.C.), destroy Solomon's temple, and take the bulk of the people of Judah into captivity. Nevertheless, He remembered them during this trying period; and when their hearts turned to Him again, He intervened through His human agent – King Cyrus of Persia (which along with the Medes had conquered Babylon) – to allow the captive Jews to return to the homeland set aside for them (538 B.C.). The temple was rebuilt, proper worship restored, and the walls of Jerusalem reconstructed.

For a period of time, under the Persians and later the Greeks, the Jews were able to maintain their faith without undue interference. Eventually, however, one of the Greek successor states resorted to Hellenization and tried to stamp out all vestiges of Jewish worship and practice (c.175-164 B.C.). The Jews resisted, and a priestly family, the Maccabees, led a successful revolt, winning independence for Judah, though the Hasmonian dynasty founded by the Maccabees degenerated after about 135 B.C. and engaged in determined

Hellenization. Discontent continued after Rome conquered Palestine in 63 B.C. but did not immediately erupt into open rebellion.

It was in this political and cultural maelstrom that God's greatest intervention to that point occurred: the first advent of Jesus the Messiah. His life was exemplary, His message revolutionary, His death and resurrection in fulfillment of many Old Testament prophesies redemptive, liberating, and world-changing. The full impact of Christ's first coming to earth is beyond all comprehension and doubtless will never be fully assessed, unless perhaps after His second advent when He will rule and reign as "King of kings and Lord of lords."

It is through Jesus Christ alone that God's eternal purpose is being worked out and will ultimately be fulfilled. One should never suppose, however, that the Bible is the only redolent testimony to Divine intervention in human history; for examples of such interventions are numerous in so-called secular history and literature. Take, for example, the conversion of the Emperor Constantine (r.312-327). Less than a decade prior to Constantine's taking the reins of Empire, the Dalmatian Emperor Diocletion (r.284-305) had styled himself "most sacred lord" while unleashing a ruthless persecution of Christians in the year 303. Believers were hunted down in cave and forest and, after being apprehended, were burned alive, thrown to wild beasts, or executed by other equally brutal means. The terrible persecution had continued after Diocletion's abdication in 305, with churches being closed or demolished, sacred books destroyed, and efforts made to compel believers to offer libations to the gods.

Soon after Diocletion's abdication, warfare broke out between several aspirants to the Imperial purple. One of these was the young general Constantine, who successfully dealt with clandestine plots calculated to bring him down and marched southward into Italy to confront his chief rival, Maxentius. While preparing for battle (according to church historian Eusebius), he called for God's assistance and observed a cross of light shining above the sun at high noon. Emblazoned on it were the words "*in hoc signo vinces* – in this sign you will conquer." Again that night, Jesus Christ appeared to him with the same sign, telling him to make a likeness of it to carry into battle. Constantine did just that, and on October 26, 312, he won a decisive victory over his rival. In the following year, he joined with his co-ruler in issuing the famous Edict of

Milan, which guaranteed full religious toleration for Christians. In 325, now sole Emperor, he convened the Council of Nicaea, which upheld the doctrine of the Holy Trinity, outlawed Arianism, and drafted the Nicaean creed. Thus, God enabled His church to endure in a hostile, pagan environment in spite of persecution, to prevail, and to maintain an orthodox witness to the world.

Crises have always attended the church, however, and a major one presented itself in the waning years of the Roman Empire as it began to contract in the late 4th and 5th centuries, evacuating Britain and various frontier outposts. Would Christianity survive in the British isles or for that matter in continental regions threatened by barbarian hordes? A Christian Roman Briton named Patrick (d. 461) knew what he must do when, in his dreams, he heard Ireland calling. As a teenager, Patrick had been a slave herdsman for six years in "the Emerald Isle" after being captured by Celtic pirates. Managing to escape to the continent, he had received training in monastic seminaries. Now in his late forties, he sensed God's tug on his heart to return as a missionary to Ireland – a country of wild tribesmen hardly touched by the Gospel. Circumstantially commissioned to succeed Palladius who had served barely a year as Bishop of Ireland before his untimely death, Patrick arrived in the spring of 432, shortly before Easter. Near Tara, he confronted a local chieftain whose court was preparing to celebrate the annual Druid rites and confounded his magicians by miraculously igniting a fire. The frightened and awed ruler was converted, and Patrick spent the remainder of his life traveling throughout the country, baptizing thousands (many of them sons and daughters of Irish chieftains), founding monasteries to train Christian leaders, and superintending the fledgling church from his see at Armagh.

God's hand on the Celtic church became more and more evident in the succeeding centuries as Celtic monks – among them St. Columba (521-597) and St. Columbanus (c. 540-615) – penetrated into Scotland, the islands around Britain, and as far as Iceland, Britain itself, and the vast regions of Europe, including what is today modern France, parts of Germany, and northern Italy, founding teaching abbeys and stirring up the flames of faith. In fact, Christianity in Europe may have dwindled and died in the wake of Rome's collapse had it not been for the fervent and able Celtic missionaries, though in point of fact God never abandons His people or leaves them without a witness.

Next to the first advent of Jesus Christ, the opening of the "New World," North and South America and the islands in proximity to them, may have been God's most significant intervention in human history to date. Certainly the great Genoan sea captain who, under the auspices of Ferdinand and Isabella of Spain, opened it up to missionary activity was convinced that he was Divinely called to carry forth the "great commission" of our Lord, quoting it in his *Book of Prophecies*.[6] While unaware of the full significance of his first voyage to "the Indies" in 1492, Columbus reflected on that expedition some months later:

> "So since our Redeemer gave this victory to our most illustrious King and Queen, and to their famous realms, in so great a matter, it is fitting for all Christendom to rejoice and make celebrations and give solemn thanks to the Holy Trinity and with many solemn prayers for the great exultation which it will have in turning of so many peoples to our holy faith, and afterwards for the temporal benefits which henceforth will bring great refreshment and gain, not only to Spain, but to all Christians."[7]

Admittedly, diseases carried by the Spaniards proved deadly to segments of the native populace, and Columbus proved to be a better navigator than a colonial administrator, eventually inaugurating an economic system calculated to provide incentives for wealthy investors that resulted in exploitation and enslavement of the Indians. Nevertheless, like ancient Israel's King David, Columbus remained cognizant of his Divine calling. Conscious that his name, Christopher, meant "Christ Bearer," he referred to God's "hand" upon him and believed that his chief purpose was to carry the Gospel of Jesus Christ to far-off lands and islands. In pursuit of this goal, he entreated Pope Alexander VI (r.1492-1503) to send forth "priests and monks ... suitable for the work,... because I trust in our Lord to divulge his Holy name and Gospel throughout the

---

[6] As found in *Christopher Columbus's Book of Prophecies* (reproduction of the original Manuscript with English translation by Kay Brigham; Barcelona: Libros Clie, 1991), 214. This remarkable book – released by TSELF, Inc., 3585 NW 54th St., Fort Lauderdale, FL 33309 – provides the full text of Columbus's "Prophecies," a work virtually unknown on this side of the Atlantic until made available to English readers by Kay Brigham one year after the publication of her unique biographical study entitled *Christopher Columbus: His Life and Discovery in the Light of His Prophecies* (Barcelona: Libros Clie, 1990).

[7] From Columbus's 1493 letter to Santangel, presented in Brigham, *Christopher Columbus...*,p. 39.

Universe."[8] If the Spanish record in the New World was far from being beyond reproach, God is more than able to use flawed instruments to effect His will.

Four years after Columbus's death, a Dominican priest named Anton Montesino set foot in Hispaniola and courageously denounced the colonial regime's harsh treatment of the natives, challenging the colonists to treat them with the love of Christ. Upon returning to Spain, Montesino pleaded with King Ferdinand for humane treatment of the Indians, and laws were subsequently promulgated that assured them legal protection.

Whatever may be said of Spanish hegemony in the New World, the nominally Christian regions of the world were almost doubled, and church missions, schools, universities, hospitals, and charitable institutions did exercise a civilizing influence on society. Moreover, two new continents were opened to colonization, development, and eventually the formation of independent nations that have helped change the course of history.

Moral and religious issues as they affect history are seldom clear-cut; for such considerations may be subordinated to perceived national interests or a desire to gain advantage over a rival dynasty. So it was that when Turkish Grand Vizier Kara moved an enormous army against the Holy Roman Empire early in 1683, Habsburg Emperor Leopold I (r.1658-1705) was able to elicit the support of relatively few German princes, since many of them perceived that centralization of Imperial power could attenuate or override their own political prerogatives. At the same time, Pope Innocent XI's appeal to "the most Christian King of France" to join forces against the Moslems received a half-hearted response, because it ran counter to King Louis XIV's policy of maintaining an Ottoman alliance as an eastern counterpoise to the Habsburgs, easing their pressure upon France. Therefore, the most Leopold could expect from France was non-aggression against his western frontier.

At the same time, one religious matter – the Catholic Emperor's suppression of Hungary's constitution and persecution of its Protestants – caused a Hungarian nationalist leader to cooperate with the Turkish invaders. The Emperor sent a hasty appeal to his ally, King John Sobieski of Poland, but

---

[8]Quoted in Brigham, *Christopher Columbus....* p. 124.

Imperial forces under Duke Charles of Lorraine were only with difficulty able to prevent the Turks from blocking the Poles' route of advance.

In the meanwhile, Ottoman forces almost 200,000 strong marched towards Vienna and invested the city on July 14th, 1683. Although the Polish king was a redoubtable Turk-and-Tartar fighter, he was in his 60th year and needed to be hoisted onto his steed. Nevertheless, he set forth with what troops he could muster and moved posthaste toward Vienna. He was joined en route by the Duke of Lorraine, who placed himself under Sobieski's command, and advanced on the beleaguered Imperial capital, which had recovered from the plague only five years earlier. The combined force numbered only about 80,000, and the city seemed doomed. Indeed, the Emperor and his court had abandoned it, leaving its defense to a paltry 13,000 soldiers commanded by Count Rudiger von Starhemberg. Confident of their military superiority, the Ottomans were digging their entrenchments ever closer to the heavily outnumbered defenders, inexorably closing the noose on them.

Fervent prayers ascended from the besieged city as the situation continued to degenerate throughout the month of August, almost to the point of hopelessness. Then, in early September, news that a relief force was approaching heartened the besieged inhabitants but hardly concerned the Ottoman commander who expected the city's capitulation within three days. But John Sobieski was not to be underestimated. He approached Vienna through the rugged Kahlenberg heights rather than by the easier, more obvious route, taking the Turks by surprise. The combined Polish and German forces engaged the Ottomans on September 12 and, though outnumbered three to one, put them to flight, causing them to abandon baggage and luxury items.

The Polish king was hailed as deliverer by the city's grateful inhabitants who crowded in to catch a glimpse of him, to kiss his feet, or to touch his horse. *Te Deums* were offered in the Stephensdom, with the Archbishop taking his text from John 1: 6: "There was a man sent from God, whose name was John." Although rifts soon began to develop between the victorious allies, the Turks were steadily pressed back during the succeeding years until hostilities were terminated in 1699. The Moslem threat to Europe was ended.

In the 20th century, too, there have been dramatic incidents of Divine intervention though the skeptical modern mind generally attributes them to chance or to men's extraordinary efforts. To be sure, men and women were involved in these astounding incidents, either as prayer warriors or active participants, because in most instances God uses human beings – whether actively or passively, consciously or unconsciously – to effect His purposes. Human nature being what it is, however, recipients of Divine intervention may initially express gratitude to the Almighty only to recall the event in different terms later, perhaps out of timidity or deference to the skeptical, humanistic climate of our times. Needless to say, succeeding generations become even more likely to minimize any supernatural aspect of an event, so that eventually success or failure is attributed solely to natural causes or circumstances, and history is left all the poorer. If we have no awareness of God's hand in the affairs of this world, they are meaningless.

Today it is difficult to recapture the sense of awe, apprehension, and uncertainty accompanying the outbreak of World War II. The world was stunned in August 1939 to learn of the Ribbentrop-Molotov pact between Nazi Germany and the Soviet Union, though the terms were not immediately known. It was soon apparent, however, that the two aggressive totalitarian regimes would stop at nothing to expand their territories and enhance their power. On September 1, Germany seized Danzig, Poland's outlet on the Baltic Sea, and unleashed a coordinated land and air attack on its Slavic neighbor. Great Britain and France, honoring their treaties with Poland, declared war on Germany but were woefully unprepared to intervene. In a *Blitzkrieg* that startled the world, Hitler's *panzer* divisions (motorized infantry units) and Stuka dive bombers struck from every quarter, making short work of Poland's ill-equipped, obsolescent army, which after September 17 was caught between the advancing *Wehrmacht* and a Soviet invasion from the east. The hapless Poles were quickly overwhelmed, and their country was partitioned by the German and Russian aggressors in accord with a secret protocol of their "non-aggression pact."

The Soviets, no longer fearful of possible German objections, annexed the Baltic states and attacked tiny Finland, which after a valiant struggle was forced to surrender. In the spring of 1940, Nazi Germany also moved to forestall having her ships bottled up unable to negotiate the straits between the Baltic and North seas and to obtain ports from which to conduct naval operations by overrunning Denmark and Norway and pressing Sweden, from which she received substantial quantities of iron ore, to remain favorably neutral.

While this was going on, Great Britain and France feverishly were mobilizing their armed forces, but were in no state of readiness to launch an attack on Germany. The world watched as Hitler began to digest his Scandinavian conquests and, disregarding the neutrality of the Lowland nations, simultaneously smashed through Luxemburg, the Netherlands, and Belgium – forcing their surrender – and through northern France to the coast. These lightening thrusts cut off three French armies and a British expeditionary force that had been sent to bolster (futilely as we have seen) the crumbling Dutch and Belgian defenses. The situation was extremely grim. Destruction or capitulation of the Allied armies appeared imminent. Hitler believed total victory was within his grasp, and the British and French governments recognized that loss of nearly 340,000 trapped soldiers – 198,000 of them British veterans and officers whose continued service was sorely needed – would be a crushing blow.

The only alternative to disaster was to abandon all heavy equipment and to evacuate as many soldiers as possible, but prospects were not good. Realistically, the British Navy did not know if a rescue operation could succeed but hoped to withdraw 45,000 troops from the port city of Dunkirk before the Germans overran the beaches. In this crucial exigency, however, men and women of God were earnestly praying – none more zealously than the faculty and students of the Bible College of Wales, whose founder and head Rees Howells called for daily corporate intercession from 7 P.M. until midnight. While British Christians were beseeching Almighty God to intervene, German Field Marshal Gerd von Runstedt halted his five armored divisions just thirteen miles from Dunkirk, giving the allies time to strengthen their perimeter defenses and begin to withdraw their troops. From May 26 to June 4, the evacuation proceeded, with the Royal Air Force providing cover for over 1,000 carriers, naval vessels and private boats of every sort – tugboats, barges, channel steamers, sailboats, fishing vessels, yachts, and even lifeboats – to ply their way across the English Channel and return with their precious human cargo. Amazingly, the weather cooperated. On occasion the channel was unusually calm enabling small craft to make the perilous round trip, a virtual impossibility had the seas been churning. Moreover, during part of this critical period, the *Luftwaffe* was grounded by inclement conditions. Truly God is able to deliver!

The rescued men were to form the nucleus of new forces that would one day defeat the Third Reich.

Great Britain was saved from invasion during World War II because of God's mercy and because it suited His overall purpose. Britain was pulled back from the brink of disaster, thanks to the intercession of Christians who stood in the gap, just as in the post-war era it has been saved from economic collapse because Christians – including a ladies group, the Lydia Fellowship – have interceded for the nation. The spiritual and moral fabric of Great Britain had been dangerously weakened in the years between the two great wars – a period of religious skepticism and indifference, of a hedonistic quest for pleasure, and of widespread acceptance of homosexuality in her great universities. The Empire had been replaced by a new "Commonwealth" arrangement; a constitutional struggle had attended Edward VIII's announcement that he intended to marry Wallis Warfield Simpson, a twice-divorced American woman, that had resulted in his abdication; the nation had suffered economic distress (as had most of the Western World); passivist sentiments had contributed to an indecision in foreign affairs verging on appeasement; and pragmatism had triumphed over principle as the government reneged on its promise, made in the Balfour Declaration of November 2, 1917, to assist world Jewry in establishing a homeland in Palestine. In fact, in a 1939 White Paper, the British had practically rescinded the pledge by declaring that only 75,000 Jews could enter Palestine during the next five years and, after that, none at all without Arab consent. Jewish rights to purchase property were also drastically curtailed, because 95% of the land was placed off-limits to prospective Jewish buyers. Restriction of Jewish immigration into Palestine caused thousands trying to leave Hitler's Germany to suffer incarceration in concentration camps and ultimately execution.

Nonetheless, thousands of Palestinian Jews volunteered for military service against the Axis powers in World War II, and Jewish factories in Palestine produced shipbuilding tools and cranes, air compressors, hydraulic jacks, electric transformers, tie blocks, ships' propellers, anti-tank mines, and a variety of other war materiel. By way of contrast, the Palestinian Arabs took care not to offend the Axis powers until Allied victory was certain. Only then did they declare themselves to be on the side of the Allies to be assured favorable treatment in the peace settlement and membership in the United

Nations Organization. Much the same must be said of other states of the Middle East. Egypt, Syria, and Lebanon were more or less pro-Axis until the end of the conflict, while Iraq actually concluded a treaty with Nazi Germany.

Notwithstanding the Moslem states' obstructionism and collaboration with the enemy and the Jewish support for the Allied war effort, British policy regarding Jewish immigration did not immediately change, nor was the United States, under Franklin Delano Roosevelt, likely to protest British policy. However, after Roosevelt's death in 1945, the new President, Harry S. Truman, openly sympathized with the Zionists, both for humanitarian and political reasons; and he urged the British government to admit 100,000 Jewish refugees. At last, Britain agreed to submit the question of Jewish immigration to an Anglo-American committee. It is highly unlikely that anything of this sort would have occurred had Franklin Roosevelt been alive. Be this as it may, the British found the committee's recommendation for a lenient immigration policy unacceptable. The situation in Palestine degenerated quickly as Jewish and Arab terrorists rendered peacekeeping extremely difficult and the frustrated Jews undertook more determined measures to force the British out. In 1947, Great Britain referred the problem to the United Nations, which proposed partitioning Palestine between the Jews and the Arabs. After further haggling and turmoil, the British finally agreed to withdraw; and, with the support of the American President (who helped push the petition plan through the United Nations) and the Soviet Union, which wanted a socialist client state in the Middle East, the independent nation of Israel came into being on May 14, 1948.

It was one thing to establish a new nation; it was another to maintain independence and even nationhood itself in the face of the rancorous armed opposition of the surrounding Arab states. Armed mercenaries and guerrillas attacked isolated settlements and outposts even before completion of the British withdrawal. For their part, the British refused to cooperate with United Nations' efforts to effect a smooth transfer of authority. Indeed, it would almost appear that British Prime Minister Ernest Bevin wished to sabotage the partition plan, perhaps believing that chaotic conditions and determined Arab resistance would cause the new nation to be stillborn and bring about the succession of an Arab client state. At any rate, at the very moment when the Arab nations and Egypt were openly mobilizing for war, Great Britain continued to sell them arms, while at the same time trying to obstruct the efforts of the Israeli Haganah to forge a military force capable of defending the nation. British naval vessels in the Mediterranean even halted ships bearing arms to Israel until President Truman pressed the British Prime Minister to remove the blockade and "give the Jews a chance!"

The plight of Israel appeared desperate. With a population of 650,000, it was surrounded by 30,000,000 potentially hostile Arabs in Transjordan, Syria, Lebanon, Yemen, Iraq, Saudi Arabia, and Egypt (which strictly speaking is not Arab) – all bent on eradicating it. Moreover, not all Israeli territory was contiguous. Under the partition agreement, there were numerous Jewish settlements located in Arab territories, fragile enclaves that were almost impossible to defend. A miracle was needed, and a miracle occurred. Arms were procured from France and from Czechoslovakia, a Soviet satellite, and with courage born of desperation and unshakable belief in their cause, the Israelis blunted the uncoordinated Arab attack and rallied to assume the offensive. In a fierce conflict interspersed with two transient truces, Israel seized the initiative, consolidating its territories and forcing thousands of Arabs to flee. Eventually, about 600,000 were dispossessed. Refused permanent residence by their Arab brothers, they crowded into refugee camps that became hotbeds of restlessness, rage, and intrigue. On Israel's southern frontiers, Israeli engineers refurbished an ancient Roman road unknown to the Egyptians and, in late December of 1948, launched a surprise attack on one of their strongholds in the Sinai that broke the back of Egypt's military effort.

When a cease-fire was arranged by U.N. negotiator Dr. Ralph Bunch on February 24, 1949, Israel found itself in a much more defensible position than would have been the case under the original partition arrangement. (Surely the hand of God may be seen in this.) The surrounding states – especially Syria and Egypt – almost choked on their rage, and a group of young Egyptian army officers began plotting to overthrow pleasure-loving King Farouk.

Israel's first Knesset met on February 14, 1949 and elected longtime Zionist leader, the elderly and infirm Dr. Chaim Weizmann, President of the Republic. However, it was Prime Minister David Ben-Gurion, white-maned leader of the Mapai or moderate socialist party, who nurtured and guided the nation during its formative years. The task was far from easy; for not only was Israel encircled by enemies but her own population was culturally, politically, and linguistically quite diverse, and as many as a thousand new immigrants were arriving daily. To obviate a complete confusion of tongues, a newspaper editor named Eliezer Ben-Yehuda expanded the ancient Hebrew tongue from less than 8,000 words to almost 100,000 and devoted his life to breaking down the opposition of rabbis who believed Hebrew should remain solely a sacred language. The effort was successful, and today Israelis share a common language based upon the tongue of their ancient forefathers. (See Jeremiah 31:23.)

There are remarkable affinities between Old Testament prophecies and present conditions. Isaiah 35:1 says: "The wilderness and the solitary place shall be glad for them; and the desert shall rejoice, and blossom as the rose" (KJV). Since their return to the promised land, the Jews have transformed a denuded, eroded wasteland into fertile cropland. They have drained marshes, washed salt deposits out of the soil, fertilized and irrigated barren lands, and constructed plants to remove salt from sea water. Agricultural production has soared. The nation now produces most of its own food and exports millions of dollars worth of citrus fruit – a truly remarkable transformation. Reference to it is given not only in the passage quoted above but in other prophesies as well. Note, for example, Ezekiel 36:29-30, which after stating that the land will produce abundant grain, mentions that "the fruit of the tree" will be multiplied. This has literally taken place. More than 83,000,000 trees were planted during the first sixteen years of nationhood, and the planting of eucalyptus, pines, and fruit trees – as well as indigenous tamarisk, sycamore, and myrtle trees – has continued. Furthermore, both Isaiah (54:3) and Ezekiel (36:33) prophesied that urban living would be reestablished, and that is exactly what has happened. In 1948, Tel Aviv was the only city of more than 100,000 inhabitants, and only nine others boasted more than 10,000 people. Today, this situation has completely changed. As Israel's population continues to grow toward the 6,000,000 mark, it is, indeed, becoming a nation of city dwellers.

We have previously noted that Harry Truman became President of the United States at an opportune moment for the Zionist cause. The Kremlin's support for the fledgling Jewish nation – in extending instantaneous *de jure* recognition, in urging its satellites to fall in line, and in encouraging Czechoslovakia to provide armaments to Israel at a critical juncture – was also of the utmost importance. It is hard to imagine how the modern state of Israel could have become a reality without such assistance. Can God's hand be seen in these unusual occurrences?

One can only wonder also at the manner in which Germany (West Germany at that time) providentially hastened Israel's economic development. Under an agreement signed with Ben-Gurion in 1952, the Bonn government promised to deliver $850,000,000 worth of equipment and goods in reparations. Many ships in Israel's merchant marine were built and equipped in German ports, and Israeli factories benefited from the importation of machines, tools, and technical equipment of all sorts from West Germany. Truly the ways of God are past finding out!

Repercussions of the Israeli war for survival and independence continued to be felt throughout the Middle East but especially in Egypt where young officers blamed the defeat on a corrupt monarchy and staged a coup on July 23, 1952 that ousted King Farouk. Although General Mohammed Neguib became the titular head of the new regime, its actual ruler was Colonel Gamal Abdul Nasser who soon charged Neguib with attempting to assassinate him and took over undisputed control of affairs.

Nasser gave Egypt a renewed pride in nationhood. Moreover, he capitalized on the anti-Israeli passions of the Arab nations to form a coalition opposed to the existence of the Jewish state. He also bargained with both the U.S. and the Soviet Union to secure funds and technical assistance for the construction of a gigantic hydroelectric dam at Aswan. Failing to procure the aid he sought from the United States, he turned to the Soviets for the desired assistance. Then, piqued by what he construed to be Western arrogance and buoyed up by his personal popularity, Nasser announced nationalization of the Suez Canal in 1956, eleven years short of the date when Britain's leasehold was due to expire. The outraged British and a French government frustrated by the loss of Indo-China and most of her North African possessions joined with Israel to teach Nasser a lesson. Late in October, Israel struck into the Sinai Peninsula and quickly took over the area around the Gulf of Aqaba, thereby opening a trade route by way of the Red Sea and the Indian Ocean for her merchant ships, which had been denied passage through Suez by Egypt. The Israeli thrust also abruptly terminated the terrorist raids of the vicious Egyptian *fedayin*. In fact,

Israel's lightening attack effectively secured her major objectives within a few days.

Britain and France fared far worse. American President Dwight Eisenhower denounced the Anglo-French attack and urged the United Nations to secure a withdrawal of aggressor forces from Egyptian soil. The humiliation was too much for Britain's Prime Minister Sir Anthony Eden and estranged U.S. relations with France. The United States also affronted Israel by compelling her to return the Gaza Strip, which was to be demilitarized, to Egypt.

The entire episode severely strained the Western alliance, allowing the Soviet Union to suppress a popular revolt in Hungary without fear of Western opposition aside from a barrage of meaningless protests. Moreover, the Western democracies were discredited in the eyes of Third-World countries.

Despite Great Britain's humiliation, she continued to intervene occasionally in the volatile Middle East through the early 1960s, but late in the decade when she withdrew her forces from Aden, destabilizing forces could no longer be kept in check. Egypt's Nasser, heavily armed with modern Soviet weapons, announced in May of 1967 that the Gulf of Aqaba was closed to Israeli shipping, and his Syrian, Jordanian, and Iraqi allies began marshaling troops on Israel's borders. Propaganda emanating from Cairo proclaimed: "Our people have been waiting twenty years for this battle. Now they will teach Israel the lesson of death! The Arab armies have a rendevous in Israel!"

Faced with this threat and cut off from vital oil shipments by Egypt's blockade of the Strait of Tiran, Israel decided upon a preemptive strike. On June 4, Israeli fighter-bombers caught Nasser's air force on the ground, demolishing it, and simultaneously attacked Jordanian, Iraqi, and Syrian airfields. Within six days, Arab forces were routed, and Israel took the Sinai; the Golan Heights near Syria; Judea and Samaria, which had been occupied since 1948 by Jordan; and, most dear to Jewish hearts, the old sector of Jerusalem. At last, the nation of Israel possessed a contiguous, defensible territory.

Predictably if not logically, the Palestinian Liberation Organization (PLO), founded by Yasser Arafat in 1964, demanded that the "West Bank" (Judea and Samaria) be converted into a separate Palestinian state – a demand never voiced during the nineteen years it had been under Jordanian control. Interestingly enough, the trouble-making PLO, which temporarily took refuge in Jordan was expelled by King Hussein in 1970. The ousted Palestinians fled to Lebanon, from whence they have continued to foment strife and terrorism.

After the Six-Day War, the enmity between Israel and her Arab and Egyptian neighbors mounted. Furious at both Israel and the United States, Nasser moved closer to the Soviet Union before his sudden death in September of 1970. His successor, Anwar Sadat, was less flamboyant but no less determined. He declared himself willing to negotiate for a permanent peace with Israel on terms that the Jewish nation could not accept. For a time, Sadat hoped to obtain further Soviet assistance and support, but he became disillusioned with Moscow's self-serving policies and terminated the alliance, aligning himself instead with the oil-producing states on the Persian Gulf.

As events were soon to prove, the Soviet Union was continuing to fish in the troubled waters of the Near East while dictator Muammar Gadafy of Libya incessantly incited the Arab nations to wreak bloody vengeance on Israel. He also raised the price of Libyan oil, prompting the Organization of Oil-Exporting Countries (OPEC) to follow suit, so that, by the end of 1973, the price of crude oil stood at four times that of the previous year. Western nations dependent on Arab oil were now increasingly careful not to affront the oil-producing states; thus Israel became more and more vulnerable.

This was the situation when on October 6, 1973, while Israel was observing Yom Kippur (The day of Atonement), Egypt and Syria hurled their armored divisions without warning into Israeli territory. Although the Israeli intelligence service had provided information concerning military build-ups along the nation's northern and southwestern borders, its communiques were discounted or misinterpreted, while Soviet spy satellites kept Egyptian and Syrian forces posted on the location and movements of the Israeli military. The surprise attacks initially succeeded. For two days, Israel suffered defeat after defeat, and her survival seemed to hang in the balance. Defensive positions on Mount Hermon were quickly overrun by the Syrians, while the small, trip-wire contingents posted near Suez were overwhelmed or by-passed by the invading Egyptians. Confusion reigned as Israel's defenses crumbled, but then a double miracle occurred: the waves of Syrian tanks overrunning the Golan suddenly stopped one mile short of Israel's command headquarters as did also the Egyptian armor once it penetrated Israel's Bar-Lev defense line. Had the Syrians and Egyptians pressed on, Israel's disorganized, piece-meal defensive forces almost certainly would have been destroyed and the war lost, but unexpectedly the Israelis were accorded a new lease on life – the opportunity to regroup and reorganize.

In spite of the massive influx of arms received by Egypt and Syria from the Soviet Union, a British and French embargo on war materiel en route to Israel, and the perfidy of all her Arab neighbors and the World Council of Churches, Israel fought back. To its credit, the U.S. administration, already embroiled in the Watergate scandal, airlifted modern arms and equipment to Israel that helped turn the tide. Many would insist, however, that it was only by an act of God that Jordan refrained from hostile action against her Jewish neighbor. Had the Hashemite kingdom attacked, the Israeli cause would have been practically hopeless.

As the Israelis began to rally on both the northern and southwestern fronts, titanic tank battles took place – one of them involving at least a thousand tanks, sometimes firing at point-blank range. Not only did Israel disperse the Syrians and advance to within 22 miles of Damascus, but she regained the initiative in the Sinai, effecting a daring crossing of the Suez Canal that trapped the Egyptian Army and opened the way to Cairo before American Secretary of State Henry Kissinger mediated a cease-fire.

The providential nature of the birth of Israel, its successes, and its uncanny ability to survive and flourish under the most adverse circumstances and bitter and powerful opposition has frequently been cited, and some Jewish and Christian observers appear to believe national Israel to be Divinely protected and, therefore, invincible. But God is not through with His "chosen people," be they Jews or Gentiles; and contemporary Israel is not what God predestined it to be. Much pain and sorrow, including military defeat, still lie ahead for the plucky nation. Only in the midst of a coming horribly bloody ordeal during three and a half years of unprecedented tribulation will its people recognize and accept their Messiah, Jesus Christ, as He returns to defeat the nations laying waste to Jerusalem, to judge evildoers, and to establish God's kingdom on earth. (See Ezekiel chapters 38 & 39; Daniel 12:1-4; Zechariah 12:2-11; Matthew 24: 1-33;

and Revelation 19:11-21 & chapter 20.) We shall examine this last-days' scenario in the final chapter.

Until the day of our Lord's final triumphant intervention in human history, we may take comfort in the knowledge that God's eternal plan applies to all mankind, not just to Israel or the Jewish people. He will continue to superintend the affairs of this world, intervening when necessary, to implement His plan and purpose for mankind and for His entire creation. Be assured that God *does* control history (Psalm 33:10-22 and Proverbs 21:1) and will bring its culmination in a manner that will serve His eternal purpose; yet in all His oversight and management, He does not attempt to mandate everything (Job 1:6-12). As the Master of History, God allows men freedom to exercise their own wills while, at the same time, He uses events – both good and bad – to carry out His will. He may use hard times, calamities, or trials to bring persons or nations to himself, as is seen in His dealings with ancient Israel and Judah.

The Lord of the universe may work through individuals such as Joseph, Moses, David, Cyrus, Nebuchadnezzar, the captive Hebrew slave girl serving in the household of Syria's General Naaman, or the poor widow who baked a little cake for Elijah. In most cases of which we are aware, God does use people or natural means to bless and nourish and protect and care for His people, to discipline them, to preserve them, or to effect His will among the nations; but He may, as He chooses, intervene supernaturally to the same ends (see, for example, Genesis chapters 6-8 and 19; Joshua 10:5-14 and II Kings 20:10-11; II Kings 6:8-23; Daniel chapter 3; and Acts 16:9-40). He is God – the Creator, Sustainer, and End of all things. His wisdom is unsearchable, beyond human understanding; His holiness, virtue, and character pure, perfect, unimpeachable, sublime; His knowledge and might infinite; His law altogether righteous, absolute, universal, unchanging, and incontrovertible; His resources and creativity limitless; and His love constantly active, incomprehensible, and everlasting.

Battles are continuously being waged in the spiritual realm that affect world affairs (Daniel 10:2-13 & 20-21 and Ephesians 6:10-19) although this is not apparent to the average man in the street, certainly not to the natural man. As Christians, however, we should always be on the alert for the Adversary. Our Lord and Supreme Commander expects us to be co-workers with Him to effect His purpose (II Corinthians 6:1); therefore, it is important for us to be continually filled with His Spirit and to act correctly in difficult situations in order to be channels of redemption and blessing (Psalm 22:3; Psalm 41:1-3; Psalm 107:22; Psalm 150; Isaiah 58:5-14; Matthew 5:10-12; II Corinthians 4:8-11 & 16-18; Philippians 4:4; II Thessalonians 5:16; James 1:2-4 & 12; and I Peter 4:12-19). Praising God during adversity, prayerfully interceding in harmony with His will, acting in obedience to His Word and the impulse of the Holy Spirit, doing His deeds and extending compassionate assistance and succor to the helpless, downtrodden, and poor are ways that we can work with Him to bring good into trying situations. Properly handled, "... all things work together for good to them who love God, to them who are called according to His purpose" (Romans 8:28, KJV). Regardless of the trial or need, we can rest in the bedrock certainty of His care and the assurance that through Him all things are possible. "The race is not to the swift or the battle to the strong, nor does food come to the wise or wealth to the brilliant or favor to the learned; but time and chance happen to them all" (Ecclesiastes 9:11, KJV). "'Not by might nor by power, but by My Spirit,' says the Lord Almighty" (Zechariah 4:6; see also Psalm 58:10-11). If we remain faithful, no weapon forged against us will prevail (cf. Isaiah 54:17).

At the return of Jesus Christ, the Creator God's eternal purpose will be fulfilled; His direct and universal sway will be restored and His entire creation made perfect (Romans 8:19-23). Let us, therefore, be steadfast and, with implicit trust and thanksgiving, sing His praises among the nations (cf. Psalm 57:9 and Psalm 108:3)!

QUESTIONS TO PONDER

1. Does God intervene in human affairs?

2. In the biblical account of God's dealing with His people, what instances of Divine intervention are recorded? Think of several examples.

3.   Does God still intervene in human affairs? If so, how? Can you think of any examples?

4.   How can the remarkable affinities between Old Testament prophecies and some of the things taking place in the modern world be explained?

5.   How can the concept of God's controlling history be reconciled with the doctrine of man's free will?

PERTINENT SCRIPTURES

Genesis 3:22-24; Genesis chapters 6 through 8; Genesis 11:1-9; Genesis 21:1-7; Exodus 13:21-22; Exodus chapters 14 through 40; Leviticus; Numbers; Joshua; Judges; I Samuel; II Kings 6;8-23; II Kings 20:10-11; Job 1:6-12; Psalm 22:3; Psalm 33:10-22; Psalm 41:1-3; Psalm 57:9; Psalm 58:10-11; Psalm 107:22; Psalm 108:3; Psalm 150; Proverbs 21:1; Ecclesiastes 8:11; Isaiah 54:12; Isaiah 58:5-14; Jeremiah 31:23; Ezekiel chapters 38 & 39; Daniel chapter 3; Daniel 10:12-13 & 20-21; Daniel 12:1-4; Zechariah 4:6; Zechariah 12:2-14; Matthew 5:10-12; Matthew 24:1-33; Acts 13:22; Acts 16:9-40; Romans 8:19-23 & 26-28; II Corinthians 4:8-11 & 16-18; II Corinthians 6:1; Philippians 4:4; II Thessalonians 5:16; James 1:2-4 & 12; I Peter 4:12-19; Revelation 19:11-21; and Revelation chapter 20.

Chapter XXII

"THE LAW OF THE LAND PRINCIPLE" AND "THE LAW OF NATURE"

The universe as God originally created it reflects not only the majesty but the will of the Creator. By Him all things consist and in Him "all things hold together" (Colossians 1:16-17; cf. Job 34:14-15, Ephesians 1:10, and Hebrews 1:3). Therefore, the very land itself, even in its current unregenerate state, cries out against violations of God's holiness and will (law). This fact is evident to those contemplating the brief account pertaining to the second generation of humanity. In Genesis 4:1-16, we read how Adam and Eve's eldest son Cain murdered his younger brother Abel several thousand years before the Lord God made known His law through Moses that would have required a murderer to be put to death. Had that law been in place, our original progenitors would have been required to execute their own son, which would have shattered family harmony. It was the Creator God himself, therefore, who announced to Cain "the law of the land": "Your brother's blood cries out to Me from the ground," which "opened its mouth to receive your brother's blood" but will "no longer yield its crops for you" (Genesis 4:10-12). Moreover, God made Cain a wanderer in the earth unable to remain in the Divine presence: thereby Cain incurred eternal punishment. Something of the connection between man and the created order and the manner in which it is affected by the sins of mankind is revealed in Job 5:17-23, Isaiah 24:4-6, and Romans 8:19-22. This connection is dramatically depicted in Leviticus chapter 18, which prohibited the Israelites from engaging in sexual sin of any kind – incest, fornication, adultery, homosexuality, bestiality – or sacrificing children to Molech in the same spirit that our contemporary society hedonistically pursues sexual pleasure and aborts the helpless babies that are produced. All of these activities are abominable in the sight of the Lord, who warned Israel:

> "Do not defile yourselves in any of these ways, because this is how the nations that I am going to drive out before you became defiled. Even the land was defiled; so I punished it for its sin, and the land vomited out its inhabitants. But you must keep My decrees and

My laws. The native-born and the aliens living among you must not do any of these detestable things, for all these things were done by the people who lived in the land before you, and the land became defiled. And if you defile the land, it will vomit you out as it vomited out the nations that were before you" (Leviticus 18:24-28).

Have you ever wondered why the Lord God commanded Israel not only to dispossess the heathen inhabitants of the land of Canaan but to obliterate them and in some cases even their animals? It is because the tribal nations who had occupied the land for centuries had refused to repent despite every warning from God and every inducement that a merciful Creator had offered them for generation after generation. Not only were these people absolutely incorrigible, but they were demonized (as were their livestock sometimes): God could extend them no further mercy because they irrevocably rejected it. As long as they continued to exist, they posed a severe spiritual threat to Israel – chosen by God to live in purity before Him, to reveal His ways to the nations, and to bring forth the Savior of mankind. Therefore, these demonized people – men, women, and children – and even demonized animals must be eradicated lest they contaminate God's people and lead them into demonic practices that would bring the Lord's displeasure and their destruction. (Demon worship is referred to in Leviticus 17:7 and Deuteronomy 32:17.) The Israelites were commanded by Yahweh to avoid defilement from the peoples He was driving out before them (Leviticus 18:24). The Canaanites had defiled the land until it "vomited" them out: if the Israelites became so disobedient as to act in the same manner and thus defile the land, it would likewise spew them out (Leviticus 18:25-28; cf. Isaiah 64:6-7). That is the "law of the land."

No people in any age has been dispensed from "the law of the land." Therefore, there is no sin or crime that does not have baneful, often tragic consequences. Every infraction of God's law is contrary to the "law of the land" whether government authorities think so or not. Those violating the law of the land will surely be punished, as will also the society that overlooks evil practices. This principle applies to so-called "victimless crimes" such as sodomy and homosexual relations between consenting adults. These actions are violations of God's "law of the land," and individuals or nations committing them will suffer punishment. The biblical account of the destruction of Sodom and

Gomorrah (Genesis 18:16 through 19:29) and the tragic decimation of the tribe of Benjamin for protecting homosexuals from being brought to justice (Judges chapters 19 through 21) seem to indicate that the civil government or society that allows or protects immorality and sexual perversion will be brought down: and, in the Greek and Roman civilizations, social toleration of sexual promiscuity and perversion contributed to their decline and overthrow. In modern times, much the same could be said of the Weimar Republic, and the deleterious affect of sexual permissiveness and perversion in Great Britain has been mentioned. What can promiscuous, licentious, invert-tolerating America expect?

In point of fact, of course, God's law for His creation is much broader than the "law of the land," which is actually subsumed under the "law of nature." The law of nature (God's will) is known to man in four ways: first of all through observation of the natural order, whose wonderful intricacies, interrelationships, complexities, wonders, organization, and completeness requires a Creator (Psalm 19:1-4 and Romans 1:20). It is easy for us, even those of us who are believers, to take the miraculous wonders of nature for granted, without giving much thought to the One who created it all, while evolutionary naturalists may believe, as did Carl Sagan, that matter is all there is, or ever was, or ever will be. The latter view was held by a friend of Sir Isaac Newton, who adamantly resisted the great scientist's acclamation of an omniscient, omnipotent Creator. Upon entering Newton's laboratory one day, he beheld with awe a planetarium driven by a hand-operated crank that demonstrated the marvelously coordinated, interacting movements of the earth and all the then-known planets circling appropriately in their respective orbits around the sun. Pointing to the apparatus, he asked Newton: "Who made the planetarium?"

"No one," relied Newton without looking up from his work.

"O, come now. Tell me who made it."

"Nobody," responded the laconic Newton.

"You must be jesting," said the friend. "It surely required a great designer and mechanic to fashion something so complex and intricate!"

"Quite so," Newton replied, "but is not the universe much more complex and intricate? Does it not require a Creator?"

However, if the natural order demonstrates the reality of a Creator and reveals – in a partial, indirect way – some of the ways of God, we should remember that nature can not provide an absolute moral standard for mankind because it is flawed – rendered imperfect by the fall of man (Romans 8:19-22).

This brings us to the second manner in which the law of nature is made known to man: the implantation of God's law (His will) in the human heart (the deepest segment of the mind). (See Romans 1:19 and Romans 2:14-15 and compare with Deuteronomy 6:6-9, which indicates that positive law is based on God's law; Psalm 37:30-31; and Psalm 40:8.) If non-believers do what is required by the Divine law "written on their hearts" (Romans 2:14-15), how much more responsible for observing God's will is the believer, whose spirit is alive to God (Proverbs 20:27).

Thirdly, God's very nature, reflected imperfectly in the natural order, is seen clearly in the nature, character, love, power, and ways of His only-begotten son, Jesus Christ (John 1:1-14; John 14:8-11; and Galatians 4:4-5). "In the past God spoke to our forefathers through the prophets at many times and in many ways," says the writer of Hebrews, "but in these last days He has spoken to us by His Son, whom He appointed heir of all things, and through whom He made the universe [which demonstrates that there is a God and testifies in a general, indirect way to His nature and ways]. The Son is the radiance of God's glory and the exact representation of His being, sustaining all things by His powerful Word..." (Hebrews 1:1-3a).

Fourthly, in addition to making known to man what America's founding fathers called "the law of nature and nature's God" in creation, in the human heart, and through the life of His Son, God has stipulated His will and ways in a much more specific manner in Holy Writ (II Timothy 3:16 and II Peter 1:20-21; cf. Psalm 119:11, Mark 12:24, Luke 24:27 & 44-47, John 5:39, Acts 17:2-3 & 11, Acts 18:28, Romans 15:4, and Romans 16:25-26). According to the great English jurist William Blackstone, Scripture is the foundation for the law of nature, to which all people everywhere and in all times should adhere; therefore, if anyone is unsure of what "the law of nature and nature's God" is, he may repair to the Bible to understand the immutable and universal laws upon which all valid human laws must be based.

To do otherwise – to enact or promulgate positive laws on the shifting sands of public opinion or sociological studies – is folly, a denial of the Creator and the laws He has instituted and inculcated throughout His entire creation. All of man's laws that are lawful must be subject to God's higher law. Our forefathers understood this principle very well and, on the strength of it, established the premise that ignorance of a law is no excuse for disregarding or breaking it, since positive laws are based on "the law of nature and nature's God" – eternal principles known to all men. In this respect, the founders of our nation concurred with the axiom of Thomas Aquinas that "every human law has just so much of the nature of law, as it is derived from the law of nature. But if at any point it deflects from the law of nature, it is no longer a law but a perversion of law" ("Treatise on Law," *Summa Theologica*, Question 95, Article II, Obj. 4).

The "law of the land" subsumed under "the law of nature and nature's God" sets a higher standard than any positive laws calculated to prohibit incest or to impose penalties for sexual deviance or misconduct and does not countenance so-called "victimless crimes," which, in actuality, corrupt and undermine the entire social order. As for "the law of nature and nature's God," it is not a license to do what seems natural, nor is it a purely intellectual construct as some defenders of natural law maintain: it is a Divinely-prescribed law – God's will as revealed in the natural order, implanted in the heart of man, clarified and fulfilled in Jesus Christ, and spelled out in Holy Scripture. It alone is the source of all true law, and it alone will prevail when our Lord and Savior returns to planet earth to establish His kingdom. Until then, the wise will do well to attend it, for any person or nation consistently violating it will suffer the consequences – confusion, decomposition from within, and ultimate ruin.

QUESTIONS TO PONDER

1. Does the created universe and its life reflect in any ways the personality, majesty, beauty, holiness, justice, and provision of the Creator?

2. Is there a sense in which the natural order opposes anything that is contrary to God's will? Is it possible for us to obtain inerrant ethical guidance from nature? Why, or why not?

3. Can homosexual relations carried on privately between consenting adults be considered "victimless crimes"?

4. In what four ways has God revealed himself and His laws to men?

PERTINENT SCRIPTURES

Genesis 4:1-16; Genesis 18:16 to 19:29; Leviticus 17:7; Leviticus chapter 18; Deuteronomy 6:6-9; Deuteronomy 32:17; Job 5:17-23; Job 34:14-15; Psalm 19:1-4; Psalm 37:30-31; Psalm 40:8; Psalm 119:11; Proverbs 20:27; Isaiah 24:4-6; Isaiah 64:6-7; Mark 12:24; Luke 24:27 & 44-47; John 1:1-14; John 5:39; John 14:8-11; Acts 17:2-3 & 11; Acts 18:28; Romans 1:19-20; Romans 2:14-15; Romans 8:19-22; Romans 15:4; Romans 16:25-26; Galatians 4:4-5; Ephesians 1:10; Colossians 1:16-17; II Timothy 3:16; II Peter 1:20-21; and Hebrews 1:1-3.

Chapter XXIII

"THE PRINCIPLE OF THE DIVINE COMMISSION TO BELIEVERS"

Redeemed men, women, and children share in God's concern for people and nations deceived by Satan, who since the sin of our original forebears has been known as the prince or god of this world (John 12:31; John 14:30; John 16:11; II Corinthians 4:4; Ephesians 2:2; Ephesians 6:12; I John 4:4; and I John 5:19) – the God-hating, money-driven, pridefully assertive, self-centered and self-aggrandizing realm of humanistic endeavor comprising what we call the "world system." Through His death and resurrection, Jesus Christ triumphed over the Enemy (Colossians 2:15), and we are to trumpet that victory to all who have not heard, so that they may be freed from the bondage to the Evil One. Before departing from this earth, our Lord proclaimed to his followers:

> "All authority in heaven and earth has been given to Me. Therefore go and make disciples of all nations, baptizing them in the name of the Father and of the Son and of the Holy Spirit, and teaching them to obey everything I have commanded you. And surely I am with you always, to the very end of the age" (Matthew 28:18-20).

Have we taken our Divine charge seriously? We should, because Christ commanded us to carry it out and because He will not return to rule and reign on this earth until the "gospel of the kingdom" is preached "in the whole world as a testimony to the nations" (Matthew 24:14). God has placed in our hands the means of changing the world system – the only means that will work: winning people one by one to Jesus Christ, who alone can change their hearts, and training and discipling them to walk in His ways. As recipients of His grace and members of His body, and with the assurance that He is with us, we should obediently and eagerly serve as His ambassadors, seizing every opportunity to further His work in our society and throughout the world. Evangelism is not an option offered to us but a divinely-imparted imperative as essential as prayer to the believer. We were born in Christ to reproduce by sharing our faith with others – men, women, and children victimized by the Enemy who need to hear the liberating, life-giving "good news" of Jesus Christ.

Christ's "great commission" can not be accomplished in our own strength regardless of our convictions, zeal, plans, or efforts. Consider, for example, Christ's first converts. His intimate disciples believed wholeheartedly in Him, especially after His resurrection. They even received the Holy Spirit when Jesus breathed on them (John 20:22) before ascending to the Father; but, though "born again," they were not prepared to carry the truths of their Lord's teaching, substitutionary death, resurrection, and ascension to their own people (let alone to the Gentiles) until they were endued with power through baptism in the Holy Spirit (Acts 1:4-5 & 7-8; and Acts 2:1-41). After the astounding events of Pentecost, Spirit-filled believers acted in ardent obedience to God's will and with His power flowing through them. Their unquestioning devotion may be illustrated, if only very inadequately, by an incident occurring on January 21, 1930 as Great Britain's King George V was addressing the London Arms Conference. The message, carried abroad by radio, was heard in America only because Harold Vidian, overseeing the broadcast, picked up the bare ends of an electrical wire that had been accidentally severed and served as an electrical conductor, allowing the current to flow through his body until the King completed his address. Just so, it is only as believers abide in the Vine, allowing His life to flow through them, that unbelievers will be touched and born into the kingdom of God.

The very commitment to lay aside conventual wisdom or reliance on natural faculties and to trust implicitly in Jesus Christ – meditating on His Word, communing with Him, and resting in Him – can not be realized without loving surrender of self in mystical union with Him. Only through intimate fellowship with our Lord will His likeness emerge and be evident to those about us; only through such fellowship can we escape from an intellectual approach to Him that leads to legalism, striving to do "the right things" and to live a good life, and erecting false facades of piety. After a young university-educated intellectual accepted Jesus Christ as his personal Savior, he daily spent hours with his Lord, and his ardor and enthusiasm seemed boundless. Within a short time, he entered seminary to prepare for full-time ministry; but in the middle of the second year, he confided to a spiritual mentor: "The very effort of analyzing Jesus's philosophy and putting it into words has removed that mystical portion where man and God become as one in spirit." How sad, but how true!

Our faith, however strong and vibrant, can become sterile if we begin to reduce our encounter with the Almighty to reasoned explanations or theological formulae. "Abide in Me," the Savior tenderly continues to entreat us; yet our busy schedules or the allures of this world so frequently divert us. Little wonder that we are often barren, for only through fellowship with Him can we know His heart and be equipped and empowered to do His bidding; and only through spiritual fellowship does "the fruit of the Spirit" – love, joy, peace, patience, kindness, goodness, faithfulness, gentleness, and self-control – develop appropriately so that we may be "green and fruitful" branches.

Mature, vibrant, Spirit-filled believers should be "salt and light" in their communities, living godly lives and testifying to what God has done for them. Matthew 5:16 states: "Let your light so shine before men that they may see your good works and glorify your Father in heaven" (NKJ). Christians who do good works without saying anything about the Savior are not letting their "light" shine. Many non-believers may likewise do worthy, helpful, humanitarian deeds; and if Christians performing kind and benevolent deeds do so without letting their "light" – Jesus Christ, the "light of the world" (see John 8:12; cf. Matthew 5:14: Christ's followers are to be light-bearers in society) – shine through in such a way that people *see* their good works as a practical expression of Christ's love, they merely reflect credit on themselves. For instance, a Christian workman who consistently performs his duties well and even goes beyond what is required of him might be asked by a fellow employee, "Hey, Dick, why work so hard? You're getting the same pay as I am. No need to knock yourself out!" If the Christian timidly replies, "Oh, I don't know: I've always enjoyed working; I like to keep busy," he fails to shine his "light." Instead of capitalizing on an opportunity to testify to his faith by saying something like "The Bible tells me to do my best in everything I undertake," he has accepted *for himself* the backhanded compliment of a co-worker. Good works are necessary, but a verbal testimony is also needed in such a case.

By the same token, if a person constantly speaks about how wonderful it is to know Jesus but does shoddy work and evinces a "me first" attitude in his actions, he has no testimony worthy of the term. For a Christian, good work or, more appropriately, "good works" and letting his "light" shine by pointing to Jesus Christ as the motivator of his deeds, are complementary. Both are necessary. A forthright testimony enables hearers to recognize the reason for a person's competent, unassuming, honest, painstaking work or benevolent acts so that honor is reflected on Jesus. Righteous deeds without an unashamed verbal testimony can be self-exalting or at least valueless as evidence of God's redeeming grace, while telling others about Jesus and living a careless, worldly life is counterproductive, egoistic hypocrisy. A life-bearing testimony has a strong impact when moral rectitude, integrity in fulfilling responsibilities, and humble, unobtrusive acts of kindness characterize the speaker's life. "Good works" and spoken words of commitment to the Lord are powerful evangelistic tools when carried out and expressed under the direction and unction of the Holy Spirit.

Granted, not every Christian possesses the "gift of evangelism," but every believer can pray for the lost and plant and water "seeds" by words and deeds, that may take root and grow until other workers reap the harvest. A spirit of cooperation with those of "like precious faith" should typify our endeavors to carry out our Lord's great commission, which incidentally involves not only converting the lost but training and mentoring converts. Regardless of the nature of our personal talents or vocations, each of us, in one way or another, can participate in bringing unbelievers to Jesus Christ; doing the will of the Father (which may be different for one individual than for another); bringing all governments, societies, and cultures under His dominion; and praying in anticipation for restoration of God's entire creation to its original perfection (Acts 3:21; Romans 8:21; II Peter 3:13; and Revelation chapter 21). In other words, we are God's ambassadors to every nation and people (II Corinthians 5:20) and co-workers with Him to effect His great commission (I Corinthians 3:9; II Corinthians 5:20; and II Corinthians 6:1). While on earth, our Lord said: "I tell you the truth, anyone who has faith in Me will do what I have been doing. He will do even greater things..., because I am going to the Father" (John 14:12).

To do these prescribed works, we must rely on the Holy Spirit to bring conviction in the hearts of men, women, and children; to prepare them to receive the Word of God; and to nurture the truth presented to them until they accept it and grow into living examples of God's love and grace. Without the blessed Third Person of the Holy Trinity, we can accomplish nothing; yet so often we barely tap into His infinite strength, wisdom, and resources. Why do we ignore the Apostle Paul's admonition to "be filled with the Holy Spirit" (Ephesians 5:18) or His command to "pray *in the Spirit on all occasions*" (Ephesians 6:18)? How can we obey this injunction unless we have a prayer language conferred by the indwelling Holy Spirit? On many occasions, of course, the Holy Spirit motivates us to pray in a certain manner in our native tongue, but to be certain of praying *in the Spirit on all occasions*, we must yield ourselves unreservedly and totally, including our tongue (the hardest member to control – James 3:5-7) to the Holy Spirit, allowing Him to pray through us though our minds remain "unfruitful," that is, we do not intellectually understand what we are praying (I Corinthians 14:14-15). If the disciples of Jesus, who wholeheartedly believed in Him, were told to wait in Jerusalem until they received the power of the Holy Spirit before they went forth to evangelize, should we not also yearn for that power and pray to be filled with God's Spirit? Is it right to plan and inaugurate evangelistic campaigns largely according to ideas conjured up in our minds or by employing Madison Avenue techniques? How presumptuous our prayers for God to bless *our efforts* can be! We are called to join in with His plan and to rely on Him to "give the increase." It is "not by might nor by power, but by My Spirit, says the Lord Almighty" (Zechariah 4:6).

The people of God constitute "a chosen people, a royal priesthood, a holy nation" called to "declare the praises of Him" who called us "out of darkness into His wonderful light" (cf. I Peter 2:9). This is the Divine commission to the people of God; yet we should walk humbly and gratefully in the knowledge that we have been grafted into the "olive root," God's chosen people of Israel. Gentile believers are not the only ones intended to constitute a holy nation. Indeed, they are "wild olive" shoots grafted into the "olive root," the God-fearing people of Israel chosen to carry out God's designs (Romans 11:11-24).

How interesting that nations as well as individuals are commissioned to effect the Divine purpose! Scripture tells us how ancient Israel was set apart by Yahweh to demonstrate His ways to the other nations and to prepare for the coming of the Savior of mankind. Admittedly, Israel turned from God and ignored His commandments on many occasions; nevertheless, this chosen people was used of God to convey the Holy Scriptures to the peoples of the earth, and Jesus the Messiah was born of a Jewish mother. Thus Israel has been wondrously used to minister to peoples and nations as well as to individuals.

Similarly, the United States, founded as a covenant nation under God, has been mightily used to spread the Gospel of Jesus Christ throughout the world, though we have not remained true to our commission.

Even at home, within the confines of the United States, Christ's "royal priesthood and holy nation" – Christians – have become apathetic, compromising with the world and depending on Mammon or education or intellectual ability to further their own ends rather than being "salt and light" in an increasingly materialistic, humanistic, eudaemonistic, secular culture. The desire to be accepted by the world has compromised our witness and discredited and attenuated our influence. "Tolerance," perhaps our nation's most touted virtue, has been carried to absurd extremes – to the point of accepting all sorts of bizarre, unbiblical beliefs, doctrines, practices, and ungodly public policies. The situation will not be remedied by political or governmental means (though certainly Christian lawmakers, judges, and administrators may help to retard evil and to keep avenues open for evangelism) but only in a manner familiar to our forefathers: carrying forward Christ's great commission to bring people into the kingdom of God and to nurture and train them according to His revealed Word. Only when we repent of going our own way and, with prayerful reliance on God, courageously and persistently proclaim the Gospel and propagate biblical principles in this land – in government, education, the media, and culture – will our Lord allow and enable us to succeed. Only then, will the plunge towards disaster be halted and our institutions and our society be restored to health.

QUESTIONS TO PONDER

1. What constitutes the "great commission"?

2. Can we carry out the great commission on our own? What is essential?

3. Is testifying to what God has done in one's life sufficient? Is it enough simply to be faithful, competent workers and to do good and benevolent deeds?

4. Is Christ's "great commission" to be carried out exclusively by believers possessing a "gift of evangelism"?

5. What is "praying in the Spirit"? Why are Christians commanded to pray in the Spirit on all occasions?

6. Are nations as well as individuals used to effect God's purposes? Explain.

7. What does the Divine commission have to do with public policy? With human history?

PERTINENT SCRIPTURES

Zechariah 4:6; Matthew 5:14 & 16; Matthew chapter 10, especially verses 32-33; Matthew 24:14; Matthew 28:18-20; Mark 16:15-18; John 8:12; John 12:3; John 14:12 & 30; John 16:11; John 20:22; Acts 1:4-5 & 7-8; Acts 2:1-41; Acts 3:21; Romans 8:21; Romans 11:11-24; I Corinthians 3:9; I Corinthians 14:14-15; II Corinthians 4:4; II Corinthians 5:19-20; II Corinthians 6:1; II Corinthians 10:4-5; Ephesians 2:2; Ephesians 5:18; Ephesians 6:12 & 18; Colossians 2:15; James 3:5-7; I Peter 2:9; II Peter 3:13; I John 4:4; I John 5:19; and Revelation chapter 21.

Chapter XXIV

"THE PRINCIPLE THAT THE SOVEREIGN GOD IS NO RESPECTER OF PERSONS OR NATIONS"

Rich and poor, bond and free, educated and uneducated, privileged and non-privileged: all who believe in Jesus Christ – whatever their background, condition, color, gender, or other differences – have eternal life; and all who do not believe, do not have eternal life. "He who has the Son has life; he who does not have the Son of God does not have life" (I John 5:12). God's love is extended to everyone, but not everyone will accept Him. Those who do not by faith accept His redeeming sacrifice will not receive His salvation though His mercy is extended to everyone. God plays no favorites: He shows no partiality, and He expects his people to show no partiality. God's perfect justice does not allow for favoritism, especially in judgment. Moses clearly enunciated this principle in Deuteronomy 1:16-17:

> "...I charged your judges...: 'Hear the disputes between your brothers and judge fairly, whether the case is between brother Israelites or between one of them and an alien. Do not show partiality in judging; hear both small and great alike. Do not be afraid of any man, for judgment belongs to God.'"

Similarly, King Jehoshaphat of Judah instructed the judges of the land:

> "Now let the fear of the Lord be upon you. Judge carefully, for with the Lord our God there is no partiality or bribery" (II Chronicles 19:7).

Most people in our society understand that the wealthy and powerful may seek and obtain preferential treatment, which is an abomination to the Lord God (cf. Deuteronomy 10:17-18; II Chronicles 19:7; Psalm 72:1-4 & 12-14; Proverbs 29:14; and Isaiah 10:1-2). How many realize that it is equally sinful and detestable to favor the poor at the expense of the rich? Leviticus 19:15 plainly states: "Do not pervert justice; do not show partiality to the *poor* or favoritism to the *great*, but judge your neighbor fairly."

In personal injury cases, lawyers for plaintiffs characteristically go after the "deep pockets" – persons, agencies, or corporations with copious sums of money that a jury may be inclined to hold responsible simply because of their ability to pay a settlement. The same incentive appears to fuel litigation against firms or individuals known to be heavily insured and thus able to pay a lucrative settlement, whereas lawsuits against potentially insolvent parties could be unprofitable, even costly, and therefore not worth the effort to try to obtain compensation for losses or damages regardless of the legitimacy of the claim. Is this not a form of unrighteous discrimination? What also of so-called "affirmative action" legislation that sanctions special privileges on the basis of one's "minority" status? Do job quotas, preferential admission to institutions of higher learning, and other privileges based on who people are rather than on their performance not promote inequality of opportunity? Is not this an unconstitutional, institutionalized form of discrimination contrary even to the stated aim of President John F. Kennedy's Executive Order # 10,925 and the Civil Rights Act of 1964 to insure *equal opportunity* to all on the basis of one's qualifications *without regard to a person's race, creed, gender, or national origin*?

More importantly, does the preferential treatment of particular groups not contravene the spirit of the scriptural injunction not to "show partiality to the poor or favoritism to the great"? Injustice in the guise of compensating for previous mistreatment, wrongs, and injustice is nonetheless unjust (Deuteronomy 25:13-16; Romans 3:8; and I John 5:17). God hates laws and policies that pervert His principles, regardless of the rationale advanced in their support. Kind intentions and noble ends do not justify employment of unrighteous means, and two wrongs can never produce what is right. "God is no respecter of persons" (Acts 10:34b-35, KJV). In the RSV it reads: "God does not show favoritism" and in the NASB: "God is not one to show partiality, but in every nation the man who fears Him and does what is right, is welcome to Him." The point can not be missed. Romans 2:11 says: "... God does not show favoritism," and the same message is given in Ephesians 6:8-9.

Elsewhere the principle is stated in somewhat different terms. For example, in Galatians 2:6, the Apostle Paul declares: "as for those who seemed to be important – whatever they were makes no difference to me; God does not judge by external appearance...," and Colossians 3:25 states that "he who does wrong will receive the consequences of the wrong which he has done, and that without partiality" (NASB). A God-fearing police officer heeded this biblical admonition when, during a raid, he discovered his own teenaged daughter among those consuming illicit drugs. Shocked to the core of his being and deeply dismayed, he nevertheless, with aching heart, booked her along with the others caught in the bust. Even his wife could not understand how he could treat their daughter with such "legalistic indifference," but with the passage of time both she and the daughter, delivered from substance abuse, came to appreciate his principled and impartial act for what it was – obedience to God's Word and an affirmation of his implicit faith in a loving heavenly Father capable of redeeming any situation. Would that all modern-day Christians would take God's Word as seriously as did he!

God's absolute impartiality is manifested toward nations as well as persons. Consider the following aspects. First of all, both persons and nations have God-given missions to perform, some of which transcend this present earthly life (Israel and the United States of America have already been cited as examples); yet even a chosen nation will be chastened if it falls away from God (Romans chapter 11, especially verses 19-24). Furthermore, God is no respecter of persons in that He may effect his will through anyone whom He chooses – through the righteous or the unrighteous. He used a pagan nation, Babylon, to punish His people for their sins, and He later used the King of Persia to restore a large remnant of the Jews to their ancestral land. Amazingly, the prophet Isaiah foretold the restoration in explicit detail about two centuries before it occurred:

> "The Lord God says of Cyrus, 'He is My shepherd and will accomplish all that I please; he will say of Jerusalem, "Let it be rebuilt," and of the temple, "let its foundations be laid.""'

> "This is what the Lord says to his anointed, to Cyrus, whose right hand I take hold of to subdue nations before him and to strip kings of their armor, to open doors before him so that gates will not be

shut: I will go before you and will level the mountains; I will break down gates of bronze and cut through bars of iron. I will give you the treasures of darkness, riches stored in secret places, so that you may know that I am the Lord, the God of Jacob My servant, of Israel My chosen, I summon you by name and bestow on you a title of honor, *though you do not acknowledge Me*. I am the Lord, and there is no other; apart from Me there is no God. I will strengthen you, *though you have not acknowledged Me*, so that from the rising of the sun to the place of its setting men may know there is none besides Me. I am the Lord, and there is no other" (Isaiah 44:28 through 45:6).

This prophecy and one by Jeremiah were fulfilled as foretold. II Chronicles 36:22-23 states: "In the first year of Cyrus, King of Persia, in order to fulfill the Word of the Lord..., the Lord moved the heart of Cyrus King of Persia to make a proclamation throughout his realm and put it in writing:

'This is what Cyrus King of Persia says: "The Lord, the God of heaven, has given me all the kingdoms of the earth and he has appointed me to build a temple for Him at Jerusalem in Judah. Anyone of His people among you – may the Lord his God be with him, and let him go up".' "

The record is repeated and expanded upon in the book of Ezra, which after recounting Cyrus's permission for the Jews to return to Jerusalem to rebuild their temple, notes the invitation to those wishing to remain in Persia to provide "silver and gold, ... goods and livestock, and... freewill offerings for the temple of the Lord in Jerusalem" (Ezra 1:1-4). We are told that those who remained behind responded by bestowing money and valuable gifts upon the returnees, and the Persian King returned to them the sacred articles of gold and silver that had been confiscated by the King of Babylon from the former temple (Ezra 1:5-11). These are incidents of momentous proportions and import, demonstrating God's foreknowledge of events and His moving the hearts of rulers to carry out His will (cf. Proverbs 21:1).

The account of how Cyrus the Great was used to effect a Divine purpose is quite striking but not surprising to Christians believing in the absolute sovereignty of a Creator God who, by eternal decree, gives meaning to every occurrence and controls history according to His perfect, comprehensive plan. Although there is much that the human mind can not comprehend concerning God's foreordination of events and how He chooses and uses certain people to effect His will, the Bible teaches it. The Apostle Paul cited Exodus 7:3 and 9:16 to verify that Yahweh raised up the Egyptian Pharaoh of the exodus and hardened his heart so that only by Divine miracles – signs and wonders that would strengthen Israel's faith and glorify God's name "in all the earth" – was he forced to let the Israelites depart (Romans 9:17).

God bestows His mercy and compassion on anyone according to His desires; for as the Creator, He has the right to use the "same lump of clay" to make "some pottery for noble purposes and some for common use" (Romans 9:16-21). Jesus himself taught that "no one knows the Father except the Son and those to whom the Son chooses to reveal Him" (Matthew 11:27b) and told His disciples: "You did not choose Me, but I chose you and appointed you to go and bear fruit – fruit that will last" (John 15:16). In other words, the sovereign God predestines individuals (and also nations, as mentioned above) to serve His eternal purposes (see also Acts 2:23 and Acts 9:15).

The Pauline epistles state this truth very emphatically (see additionally Romans 8:29-30; Ephesians 1:5 & 11; and II Timothy 1:9); yet Paul also insists that God shows no favorites and that men who turn against Him are "without excuse" (Acts 2:9-11 and Romans 1:20-32). There is no difference, he says, between Jew and Gentile. The "same Lord is Lord of all and richly blesses all who call upon Him, for everyone who calls on the name of the Lord will be saved" (Romans 10:13). Again, he states in I Timothy 2:3-4 that "God our Savior... wants all men to be saved and to come to a knowledge of the truth." It would appear, therefore, that while God is sovereign and predestines some to salvation and conformity to His image and hardens others (Exodus 9:12; John 12:40; and Romans 9:18) so that they can not serve Him, He never takes away a person's freedom of choice: every individual makes his own decision to receive or reject Jesus Christ. One commentator observes that just as sunshine melts wax and hardens clay, so the sunshine of Christ's redeeming love, extended to all men, has a different effect on those with tender, receptive hearts than on those with calloused unteachable hearts, who eventually become completely hardened and impervious to the Gospel. Therefore, just as the God of the universe controls history while allowing mankind freedom of action, so He predestines individuals and nations to carry out His designs while permitting them to make their own choices. Although He wants all human beings to accede to His perfect will for their lives. He never compels compliance: He has created them as free moral agents, not automatons, and therefore will never override what they will to do.

Throughout the historical books of the Old Testament, there are accounts of how Yahweh used wicked tribes or nations to discipline and chasten His chosen people when they turned away from Him (in addition to the books of Judges, I & II Kings, and I & II Chronicles, see the prophecies in Isaiah 63:10; Isaiah 65:6-7; Jeremiah 20:4-5; Jeremiah 21:8-14; and Jeremiah 25:7-14). Our nation should take note, for "... to whom much is given, from him much will be required" (Luke 12:48, KJV). Like apostate Israel and Judah of old, the United States has turned its back on God, shamelessly squeezing Him out of our public schools and institutions as much as possible and using ridicule, intimidation, and subtle forms of persecution to muzzle or tone down Christians who challenge "sacred cows" of academia or try to propagate their views in the public arena. "Liberals" are using tax monies to fund all manner of evil causes and to perpetuate discrimination in many forms – economic, cultural, and social – while hypocritically decrying it. Add to this the shedding of innocent blood in millions upon millions of abortions, the immorality that is rampant in the land, our self-exalting idolatry, and the cavalier attitude toward Divine commandments and callousness toward the things of God (to mention but a few of our national sins), and it becomes apparent that we will experience God's chastening hand. Indeed, judgement, as I Peter 4:17 informs us, begins with the "family of God," and perceptive, spiritually-minded Christians know that it has already begun in our land.

Thank God, however, that "mercy triumphs over judgment" (James 2:13b). Our Lord is altogether merciful, and His mercy and pardon are extended impartially. If a person or nation that is suffering His just judgment for sin repents, He will relent, forgive, and restore that person or nation (see II Samuel chapters 11-12; I Kings 21:27-29; II Kings 22:16-20; Daniel 4:25-27: Jeremiah 18:7-10; Jeremiah 26:13; Ezekiel 18:30-32; Jonah 3:4-10; Jonah 4:10-11; and Acts 3:19). If we confess our sins, He is faithful and just to forgive our sins and to cleanse us from all unrighteousness" (I John 1:9, NKJ). More than that, if

Christians will humble themselves and pray and seek God's face and turn from their wicked ways, the Lord will hear from heaven, forgive their sins, and heal their land (II Chronicles 7:14; cf. Genesis 18:20-33).

We must not take God's mercy and forgiveness lightly, however. With unwavering impartiality, God turns His back on persons or nations that ostentatiously observe pious rituals or give mere lip-service to His sway (Isaiah 29:13-14; Ezekiel 33:31; and Matthew 15:7-9). He requires trustful obedience. In Exodus 20:2-5, believers in the one true God are commanded not to engage in idolatry of any sort. We are not to put our trust in anything that relegates our trust in God to second position, for we are to "have no other gods before Him" (Exodus 20:3). We are not to rely on our own abilities, science, wealth, armies, influence in high places, or any other thing instead of trusting Him. If we do not have implicit trust and faithfully exercise it, we are engaging in idolatry to some degree and are disobeying God's intentions. No matter what our confession of faith may be, if we are not obedient, God is not pleased – and He will not be mocked (Galatians 6:7). I Samuel 15:22 tells us that "to obey is better than sacrifice," and John 14:15 states: "If you love Me, you will keep My commandments" (cf. John 14:21 & 23 and John 15:10). Obedience is essential. A declaration of faith without works is dead (James 2:17). In Matthew 21:28-31, we learn that courtesy or genteel manners do not take the place of obedience. There are even those who use the name of Jesus but do not belong to Him (Matthew 7:21-23); but those who do the will of the Father will be accepted. Jesus said: "Whoever does God's will is My brother and sister and mother" (Mark 3:35). Our Lord's true followers will be known "by their fruit" (Matthew 7:16). Persons and nations that trust in God, carry out His will, and respect His laws shall prosper; but those who ignore the "law of the land," the law of nature established by the Creator, will suffer punishment. As Proverbs 8:35-36 proclaims, whoever "finds me [wisdom], finds life, and obtains favor from the Lord; but he who sins against me wrongs his own soul; all those who hate me love death."

In all things and over all peoples and nations the sovereign Lord of the universe reigns supremely and impartially. All authority and all human rights flow from Him, not from civil government; and those who are truly wise will give Him their allegiance. "The Lord sits enthroned over the flood; the Lord is enthroned as King forever. The Lord gives strength to His people; the Lord blesses His people with peace" (Psalm 29:10-11). "Blessed is the nation whose God is the Lord" (Psalm 33:12; cf. Psalm 144:15). How thankful we should be that this promise is given by an impartial God, so that it pertains to every nation that will acknowledge His sovereignty and obediently follow and serve Him!

QUESTIONS TO PONDER

1. How is God's impartiality in His treatment of people and nations manifested?

2. Does God expect His people to be impartial in their treatment of others? Can anyone but God be completely impartial? Should Christians uphold biblical exhortations to impartiality as their ideal and pursue that ideal in practice?

3. Does our government observe the biblical principle of impartiality to all citizens? How, or how not?

4. How should God's impartiality prompt us to be obedient to His will? Will God force us to do His will?

5. If God is absolutely impartial, how can He predestine some people to receive eternal salvation through Jesus Christ while allowing others to reject Him? Is God impartial in His provision of eternal salvation?

6. Can we please God in our own way? What is required to please a sovereign God?

7. What are the consequences of living as we please? What are the consequences of trusting in Jesus and obediently submitting to His will?

PERTINENT SCRIPTURES

Genesis 18:20-33; Exodus 7:3; Exodus 9:12; Exodus 20:2-5; Deuteronomy 1:16-17; Deuteronomy 10:17-18; Deuteronomy 25:13-16; Leviticus 19:15; I Samuel 15:22; II Samuel chapters 11-12; I Kings 21:27-29; II Kings 22:16-20; I Chronicles 9:1; II Chronicles 7:13-14; II Chronicles 19:7; II Chronicles 36:22-23; Ezra 1:1-11; Ezra 6:22; Psalm 29:10-11; Psalm 33:12; Psalm 40:6-8; Psalm 51:15-17; Psalm 72:1-4 & 12-14; Psalm 144:15; Proverbs 8:35-36; Proverbs 21:1; Proverbs 29:14; Isaiah 1:11-20; Isaiah 10:1-2; Isaiah 29:13-14; Isaiah 40:15-17, 21-24, & 28-31; Isaiah 41:10; Isaiah 44;28 through 45:7; Isaiah 63:10; Isaiah 65:6-7; Jeremiah 7:22-29; Jeremiah 18:7-10; Jeremiah 20:4-5; Jeremiah 21:8-14; Jeremiah 25:7-14; Jeremiah 26:13; Jeremiah 27:6-7; Ezekiel 4:25-27; Ezekiel 26:7-14; Ezekiel 29:19-20; Ezekiel 30:10-11 & 24-25; Ezekiel 33:31; Daniel 4:25-27; Hosea 6:6; Jonah 3:4-11; Micah 6:6-8; Matthew 7:16 & 21-23; Matthew 11:27; Matthew 15:7-9; Matthew 21:28-31; Mark 3:35; Luke 12:48; John 12:40; John 14:15 & 21-23; John 15:10 & 16; Acts 2:9-11 & 23: Acts 3:19; Acts 9:15; Acts 10:34b-35; Romans 1:20-32; Romans 3:8; Romans 8:29-30; Romans 9:16-21; Romans 10:13; Romans chapter 11; Galatians 2:6; Galatians 6:7; Ephesians 1:5 & 11; Ephesians 6:8-9; Colossians 3:25; I Timothy 2:3-4; II Timothy 1:9; James 2:13b-17; I Peter 4:17; I John 1:9; and I John 5:12 & 17.

Chapter XXV

"THE PRINCIPLE OF SOWING AND REAPING"

Closely affiliated with the principle that God is no respecter of persons or nations is the God-ordained principle (or law of nature) governing sowing and reaping. It has several aspects: one negative, another apathetic, and still another positive. On the negative side, we are told in Scripture that "those who plow [stir up] iniquity and sow trouble harvest it" (Job 4:8, NASB), those who sow iniquity reap vanity (Proverbs 22:8), those who sow the wind "reap the whirlwind" (Hosea 8:7, NASB), and those who stir up wickedness reap "injustice" (Hosea 10:13); for "whatever a man sows, that he will also reap" (Galatians 6:7, NKJ). If a person sows to his own flesh, he will "of the flesh reap corruption" (Galatians 6:8a). Nothing prompted by our carnal nature – whether it appears to be beneficial for God's service or not – is pleasing to the Lord. *All* our fleshly endeavors, *all* our righteous acts done in the flesh are as filthy rags in the sight of God (Isaiah 64:6). Doing things in our own human strength, according to our own plans, or with our own abilities without regard for God, is nothing more than prideful humanism. We may even sincerely believe that we are glorifying and serving God (Saul of Tarsus did when he went about persecuting Christians), but if we are operating in our own way and in our own strength, we are not relying on God but attracting commendation to ourselves. In doing so, we stand in danger of becoming just as humanistic as those whose ungodly, humanistic attitudes we purport to deplore.

As Christians, we are called upon to take up our cross daily and follow Jesus (Matthew 10:38; Mark 8:34; Luke 9:23; and Luke 14:27). Taking up the cross does not mean putting up with one's mother-in-law or sanctimoniously and ostentatiously suffering through some trial that comes our way. No, taking up the cross is purposely crossing out the self-nature and yielding oneself fully to the will of the father. That's what Jesus did. Remember that the cross is an instrument of death. Our "old man" (Romans 6:6, NKJ) is to be put to death. We can not do this on our own: whoever heard of someone's crucifying himself? But we can allow God's Spirit to execute, with the willing cooperation of our spirit, the old fleshly nature. Scripture tells us that this old nature was crucified with Christ "so that the body of sin might be done away with, that we should no longer be slaves to sin:

> "Now if we died with Christ, we believe that we will also live with Him. For we know that since Christ was raised from the dead, He cannot die again; death no longer has mastery over Him. The death He died, He died to sin once and for all; but the life He lives, He lives to God.

> "In the same way, count yourselves dead to sin but alive to God in Christ Jesus. Therefore, do not let sin reign in your mortal body so that you obey its evil desires. Do not offer the parts of your body to sin, as instruments of wickedness, but rather offer yourselves to God, as those who have been brought from death to life; and offer the parts of your body to Him as instruments of righteousness. For sin shall not be your master, because you are not under the law, but under grace" (Romans 6:8-14).

In the book of Galatians, we learn that "those who belong to Christ Jesus have crucified the sinful nature with its passions and desires," so that we may live by the Spirit of God (Galatians 5:24-25). The point is emphasized in Galatians 2:20 where Paul writes:

> "I have been crucified with Christ and I no longer live, but Christ lives in me. The life that I live in the body, I live by faith in [or of] the Son of God, who loved me and gave himself for me."

In the light of this truth, we are to walk in newness of life by the Spirit of God; for if we sow to the flesh, we will reap to the flesh such things as "sexual immorality, impurity and debauchery, idolatry and witchcraft, hatred, discord, jealousy, fits of rage, selfish ambition, dissensions, factions and envy, drunkenness, orgies, and the like" (Galatians 5:19-20). Not only individuals but nations can sow to the flesh – just as our nation has been doing – and reap corruption.

It is possible, of course, not intentionally to sow anything or to sow very little. II Corinthians 9:6 speaks to this. It says that "he who sows sparingly shall also reap sparingly, and he who sows bountifully shall also reap bountifully" (NASB). Here we see the principle of proportionate return in operation. A person or nation can even carry sparse planting of seeds to the extreme of not voluntarily planting anything – good or bad. In Ecclesiastes 11:4, we read that "he who watches the wind will not sow and he who looks at the clouds will not reap." There are young married couples today, even Christian couples, who are doing their utmost to avoid having children, often acting on the premise that they do not want to bring offspring into such an evil world when times are so uncertain. However, God's mandate to "be fruitful and multiply, fill the earth and subdue it," exercising dominion "over every living thing" (Genesis 1:28; cf. Genesis 9:7, NKJ) has never been rescinded; and to disregard it intentionally is disobedience.

How small is the faith of those who refrain from "planting" as the Father has instructed! Cannot God be trusted to protect and provide for us and the progeny He would have us bear? If we expect to enjoy God's blessings to the fullest, it is incumbent on us to obey His Word and observe His commandments. We will not have a desired harvest if we do not plant.

The story is told of a slothful southern farmer who spent the spring and summer sitting day after day in a rocking chair on his front porch, sometimes rocking and sometimes dozing with a battered old straw hat tipped down over his eyes. During one of his waking periods, a stranger happened by to ask directions and, after receiving the desired information, pleasantly asked,

"How is your cotton coming on?"
"Ain't got none," was the reply.
"Didn't you plant any?" asked the stranger.
"Nope," said the farmer. "Afraid of boll weevils."
"That so? Well, how's the corn crop?"
"Didn't plant none. Feared we wouldn't have 'nuff rain."
"My, my," said the stranger, still trying to be pleasant. "How are your potatoes?"
"Don't got none: scairt of potato bugs – lot of 'em this year."
"I see," said the stranger. "What then did you plant?"
"Nothin'," answered the farmer, "just playin' it safe."

Jesus told a parable (Matthew 25:14-30) about a man who entrusted sums of money to several of his servants before departing on a trip. Upon his return, he summoned the servants to render an accounting. Two of them reported making a profit – for which they were commended and rewarded; but the third servant simply returned what had been committed to him, saying, "Master, I knew that you are a hard man, harvesting where you have not scattered seed. So I was afraid and went out and hid your talent in the ground. See here is what belongs to you."

Angered and disturbed by the servant's temerity, the master of the household replied, "You wicked, lazy servant! So you knew that I harvest where I have not sown and gather where I have not scattered seed? Well then, you should have put my money on deposit with the bankers, so that when I returned I would have received it back with interest." Not only did the outraged master rebuke the indolent servant, but he had him severely punished and consigned the returned talent to his most profitable servant.

Clearly, our Lord wants us to promote His interests and objectives with the money and talents He has given us, and he will not be satisfied with excuses. God expects us to plant good seeds and to count on having a good crop. When we fail to plant, negative forces come into play as the "weeds" begin to take over. Just so, when good men fail to use the gifts God has given them, they are acting contrary to God's will and will suffer negative results. We harvest in proportion to what we plant, and neglecting to plant is tantamount to planting weeds.

Furthermore, we should take care to plant seeds where the Lord would have them planted, rather than simply going into areas that are already well cared for, or blithely throwing out seeds as we drive down the interstate highway (Matthew 7:6). Certainly, we should be ready in any circumstances to testify, at our Lord's leading, to our faith, but ordinarily our witness – in word and deed – will be most productive among friends, neighbors, or others who know us or work with us. We are to plant in good soil.

The question may also arise: "Are we equipped and willing to backpack into wilderness areas, as the Lord may lead, to break new ground or plant in virgin soil that is off the beaten pathway?" It is easier, of course, to do our planting in the pleasant areas where the "nice" people live, but are we willing to answer the "Macedonian call" (Acts 16:9) to go into rugged, possibly hostile territory where the gospel has seldom, if ever, been disseminated or nurtured

One young man who answered such a call was a former missionary and assistant pastor in the Hampton Roads area of Virginia. Deeply concerned about the people living in the nearby crime-ridden and drug-infested inner city, he appealed to couples in his church to take up residence in the problem area, to live among its inhabitants (just as Jesus Christ came to dwell among men) to bring the loving, practical message of salvation to bear. Couples and families took up the challenge, some of them selling nice suburban homes to move into the inner city; and God honored their obedience. As they showed friendship to their new neighbors and inaugurated ministries to their everyday needs, teaching ministries, and athletic programs, the community began to change. Crime and drug activity drastically declined, and, best of all, many persons of every age received the Lord. What a dramatic example of God's love in action!

It would have been far easier, of course, for church members simply to take food and clothing into the inner city occasionally – perhaps at Thanksgiving or Christmas – and to distribute Gospel tracts, but it would also have been far less effective. These Christians were called to a difficult walk of faith – to follow their Lord in implementing the "incarnation principle" of living among the people they wished to serve, identifying with them, befriending them, and ministering to them in Jesus's name.

Does human history bear out the "principle of sowing and reaping"? Yes! Many illustrations from sacred and secular history could be cited, but we will touch briefly on only a few. In our country's early years, "bad seeds" were planted as slavery was recognized and permitted to continue until officially terminated by a horribly bloody and incredibly destructive Civil War that left indelible scars on the nation – moral decay, economic maladjustment, political corruption, and a legacy of hatred, emotional distress, and irrational prejudices. Our society is still reaping the bitter, baneful harvest of slavery: racial tensions, a misguided and poorly implemented welfare system that perpetuates poverty and contributes to the breakdown of the family, out-of-wedlock pregnancies, crime and drug addiction, contempt for the law, and many other less apparent contemporary problems.

Consider also the "bad seed" planted by the Kennedy administration when, in the summer and autumn of 1963, it supported, through the CIA and Ambassador to the Republic of Vietnam Henry Cabot Lodge, Jr., a military coup against the country's President, Ngo Dingh Diem, who was brutally assassinated. Only three weeks later, President Kennedy himself was murdered, while in Vietnam the Communist "National Liberation Front" assumed the offensive. Massive infusion of American manpower and assistance, after 1965, to the Republic of Vietnam was ultimately of no avail; but, for ten more years, the bloodshed continued until, in April 1975, the United States "reaped the whirlwind," being forced to withdraw ingloriously from a debacle whose repercussions are felt even today.

Planting no seeds can be equally disastrous. After Portugal withdrew from Angola in 1975, the newly independent African nation was rent by civil strife between three contending factions. Viewing the situation with alarm, President Gerald Ford urged American intervention to assist pro-Western forces against the Soviet-backed Popular Movement for the Liberation of Angola (MPLA), but Congress prevented the President from taking action (from "sowing the seeds" that may have thwarted Soviet designs). Therefore, "weeds" sown by Moscow were allowed to take root. With the assistance of Cuban troops and East German advisers, the MPLA managed to establish a Soviet client state that, though challenged by Jonas Savimbi's National Union for the Total Liberation of Angola (UNITA), managed to maintain itself, owing to American passivity and the financial support of the Gulf-Chevron corporation, whose payments for Angolan crude oil were to constitute about 96% of the Communist regime's revenue. Notwithstanding some temporary armistices, factionalism and civil strife continue in this rich but divided African country.

Despite criticisms of the "ugly American" or U.S. imperialism heard around the world today, American missionaries have scattered and planted copious "seeds" of a positive nature throughout much of the world, and even our government has sown "seeds" that have produced beneficial fruit. As previously noted, for example, the Truman administration, despite opposition from the U.S. State Department, served as midwife at the birth of Israel in 1948; and, during the Yom Kippur War of 1973, when Israel's survival hung in the balance, the United States airlifted about $2.2 billion worth of arms to the desperate Jewish state that helped turn the tide. The arms were flown in over the objections of

Great Britain and America's NATO allies, helping to counter the massive assistance the Soviet Union was supplying to Syria and Egypt. For a time, in fact, Soviet intervention seemed imminent; but President Richard Nixon, though troubled by the Watergate scandal, ordered a worldwide alert of United States military forces, and Moscow backed off. To be sure, American policy immediately began to shift as Secretary of State Henry Kissinger pressed Israel to stop short of total victory, quickly brokered a cease-fire that saved the Egyptian Third Army, and (with an eye to insuring continued availability of Arab oil) inaugurated a policy of "even-handedness" in the Middle East that has continued in various guises through successive administrations, frequently to the detriment of Israel.

Nevertheless, for much of the first twenty-five years of Israel's existence, the United states planted "good seeds" from which we have reaped the benefits of a stalwart democratic ally in the Middle East (the only stable state in the region with the possible exception of Egypt), significant information concerning weaponry, intelligence reports, solid opposition to international terrorists and warnings of their plans and activities – but, more importantly, the incalculable blessings God has promised to people and nations that bless His people (Genesis 12:3 and Numbers 24:9b). In recent years, our policy in the Middle East has been determined more by perceived expediency than principle, causing us to coddle the oil-producing Arab states, appease the PLO, and urge Israel to give up territory, including the so-called "West Bank," for peace. Thus, the United States is sowing "bad seeds" as well as "good seeds" – a dangerous practice that could have unhappy results.

Another example of planting some "good seeds" but not our best "seed corn" may be seen in our attempts to bolster nations vulnerable to the inroads of communism. For example, the "Truman Doctrine" and its spin-off – the Marshall Plan – provided funds that may have forestalled communist coups in Greece and Turkey after World War II and to have stimulated economic recovery in a number of war-ravaged countries of Europe. Initially, the aid seemed to have a stabilizing effect. Unfortunately, subsequent grants in foreign aid and international monetary and banking loans have not been entirely successful and some even appear to have been counter-productive, helping to foster or prop up inefficient, corrupt socialistic regimes and promoting supra-nationalism. As time goes on, more and more "tares" or "weeds" (Matthew

13:24-30) are being planted through the International Monetary Fund and the World Bank, so that the original noble intent of bolstering free enterprise economies through short-term assistance has been turned on its head. In these last days, we can expect more and more people and nations to be serving Mammon; yet Christians are to persist in planting, watering, and fertilizing the true Word despite the "thorns" and "weeds" sown by the Enemy (Matthew 13:38-39), which must not be allowed to choke out the truth.

As we saw in the last chapter, all Christians are called to be co-workers with Jesus Christ. Some, like the unprofitable servant in the parable of the talents (Matthew 25:14-30 and Luke 19:12-27), may ignore the call and perhaps even rationalize that someone else will carry it out or maybe the Lord himself will supernaturally bring about the desired results, "reaping" where nothing has been sown. However, God has ordained that His servants will be involved, so that they grow in faith and character and derive unexpected rewards for their service, while giving human form and expression to His Love and full provision for downtrodden, hurting people. The unprofitable servant in the parable falsely accused his master of reaping where he had not sown, and was unwilling to assist him to make a profit. As a man of authority, the master was doing exactly what he should – committing sums of money to his servants to invest for the sake of earning additional wealth. The servant was contumacious. Like some Christians who do not discern how the "body of Christ" works, he did not accept the fact that God has ordained and prepared some to be overseers and some to be workers. He would not accept the role assigned him by his master, apparently resenting the fact that the master asked him to invest the talent instead of investing the money directly for himself. In like manner, many Christians like to receive the benefits of being in the family of God, but do not want to be co-workers with Jesus Christ.

Certainly, it can not be said that our Lord and Savior Jesus Christ has reaped without sowing. No, He planted His all – His very life – in order to obtain a desired harvest. By laying down His life to take the punishment due for our sins, He gained eternal life for everyone who will believe in Him. What a bountiful harvest He has realized and is continuing to realize! One day, from all the peoples and nations of the earth, every knee will bow before Him (either in worship and adoration or in fear and trembling), and every tongue will confess that Jesus Christ is Lord!

As believers act in obedience to the Father, their efforts will be rewarded. We are told in Psalm 97:11 that, through Jesus Christ, "light is sown like seed for the righteous...," and this seed will bring forth much good fruit. Not that any righteousness resides in our natural selves, but those who trust in our Lord for salvation are "the righteousness of God in Christ Jesus" (II Corinthians 5:21; cf. Romans 3:21-22 and I Corinthians 1:30). He is our righteousness, so that in Him we stand blameless (not sinless but blameless, see Jude 24) before the Father. Moreover, as we sow not to the flesh but to the Spirit, we will, of the Spirit, reap eternal life (Galatians 6:8) and manifest the fruit of the Spirit – love, joy, peace, patience, kindness, goodness, faithfulness, gentleness, and self-control" (Galatians 5:22-23).

The fruit of the spirit will be evident in the lives of Christians rooted in God's Word and nurtured and enlightened by the "Son shine" of the Holy Spirit. This "fruit," like a heavy-laden stalk of grain, will multiply exponentially, affecting all of society; where wheat is copious and healthy, it is difficult for weeds to take root. Consequently, it is incumbent upon Christians to be productive. Christ's great commission applies: "...make disciples of all nations, baptizing them in the name of the Father and of the Son and of the Holy Spirit, and teaching them to obey everything I have commanded you...." If the ground is properly prepared, fertilized, and cultivated; if Christians are nourished on the Word to follow Divine precepts; the philosophies of the world will atrophy, and where they continue to exist, they may be easily spotted. The danger today is that undernourished Christians not grounded in the Word look much like the weeds dwelling in their midst. For this reason, the Antichrist is able to deceive many anemic believers who are easily deluded by religiosity, church attendance, supposed "good works," and references to the Bible, however inappropriate or inexact they may be. Even Satan, we are instructed, comes as "an angel of light," and we know that deception will be pervasive in the end time – something which we see on every side today. For this reason, Jesus cautioned against trying to tear out the weeds prematurely (Matthew 13:28-29). He advised leaving them till the harvest when the angels would root them out, gather them in bundles, and burn them before harvesting the wheat. No doubt the angels' task will be rendered less difficult than otherwise would be the case by the fact that weed stocks do not bear proper fruit. This truth will be especially apparent if the wheat is bearing plump, full, well-nourished grain produced by regular feeding on the Word of God. Weeds, on the other hand will tend to be crowded out by well-nourished grain and in any case can not assimilate God's Word to produce godly fruit. Just as the parables of Jesus could be understood properly only by people who followed Him closely and yearned to know the secrets of the kingdom (Matthew 12:10-17) while curious onlookers, pretended followers, and critics remained ignorant, uninformed, and impervious to the truth, so the unsaved today and even believers who are apathetic or inured to spiritual principles found in the Bible and to the life-changing work of the Holy Spirit, will not comprehend Divine Wisdom and Truth. Indeed, worldly Christians and persons posing as followers of the Lord may be difficult to distinguish from unbelievers; consequently, the burning of the "tares" and the in-gathering of those who truly love Jesus Christ must await the end-time harvest.

Godly individuals and nations will reap "in due season" if they do not grow weary (Galatians 6:9). When a farmer plants grain and fertilizes it, he does not expect instantaneous results. Certainly, he would not plant on one day and dig up the seeds on the following morning to see if they are growing. Every good farmer knows that a period of time – a "due season" – must pass before he can begin to harvest. In the meanwhile, he will faithfully watch, wait, and pray – fertilizing and irrigating, if necessary, in anticipation of an abundant harvest. In like manner, the person or nation that plants "good seeds" of any kind and nurtures them, trusting God for a good harvest, will not be disappointed. Those who plant spiritual seeds according to God's Word will discover that what they planted and watered will be vastly multiplied in a bountiful harvest that will bring salvation, healing, and blessings to untold multitudes of people, and even to nations. Therefore, "sow with a view to righteousness. Reap in accordance with kindness; break up your fallow ground, for it is time to seek the Lord until He comes to rain righteousness on you" (Hosea 10:12).

The principle of sowing and reaping pertains to all phases of personal and national life, though a number of modern-day evangelists have tended to focus on the economic aspect by citing passages such as Malachi 3:8-12, Matthew 19:29, and Mark 10:29-30. Regarding finances, it should always be remembered that God is our Source, not man; therefore, when we give to persons or to organizations, we are not to expect something back from them, but to believe that God will recompense us.

Furthermore, we sow not only money but time, labor, service, love, and many other things. Indeed, we are called to be servants of others just as Jesus was, which brings us to the subsidiary principle of Christian servanthood.

Above all, Christians must realize that they are servants of God and, as such, are to further His kingdom and His will – not their own. The compensation received in this world is unimportant compared to the rewards to be expected from the Lord to His good and faithful servants (cf. Isaiah 49:4 and Matthew 25:31-46). Therefore, in recognition of the One to whom they belong, Christians are to plant seeds of righteousness in the humble, submissive spirit of servanthood (Philippians 2:3-11) and, whenever possible, avoid quarreling and resentment while gently and patiently teaching God's ways, thereby sowing "seeds" that may lead unbelievers to repentance, a knowledge of truth, and eternal life (II Timothy 2:24-26; cf. Romans 12:5-21).

As servants of Jesus Christ, Christians must realize that they are not greater than their Master who came "not to be served but to serve" and gave "His life as a ransom for many" (Mark 10:42-45; cf. John 3:16 and John 13:12-17). Christ told His disciples to follow His example, seeking to serve others rather than lording it over people under their influence or authority. "Whoever wants to be great among you," Jesus said, "must be your servant" (Matthew 20:26; cf. Mark 10:44).

Under our system of government, our nation, state, and local leaders are to be "public servants," but today the spirit of Antichrist is evident as our elected and appointed officials seek, not only to "feather their own nests" and further partisan interests, but to implement humanistic policies in this nation and throughout the world. Ultimately their hubris will bring them down, but, in the meanwhile, they are doing incalculable harm to our nation and the kingdom of God. The Apostle Paul knew well the cost of discipleship. Perhaps no one but the Lord himself has been required to suffer the deprivation, physical hardships and punishments, and humiliation that he had to bear while planting and nourishing the Gospel throughout the Mediterranean world of his day; yet because he considered himself to be a "bond-slave" of Jesus Christ, he ministered, according to the "principle of servanthood," to people of every type and background, stating in I Corinthians 9:19-23:

"Though I am free and belong to no man, I make myself a slave to everyone, to win as many as possible. To the Jews I became like a Jew, to win the Jews. To those under the law I became like one under the law (though I myself am not under the law), so as to win those under the law. To those not having the law I became like one not having the law (though I am not free from God's law but am under Christ's law), so as to win those not having the law. To the weak I became weak, to win the weak. I have become all things to all men so that by all possible means I might save some. I do all this for the sake of the gospel, that I may share in its blessings."

In the Spirit of our Lord, may we do the same – sowing "good seeds" in humble submission to His will, that He may obtain a bountiful harvest, while we receive His approbation and at last an eternal reward beyond comprehension!

QUESTIONS TO PONDER

1. The Bible teaches us that we will reap whatever we sow. Does this principle have both positive and negative aspects?

2. If we plant seeds "to the flesh" (that is, for fleshly pleasure or gratification), what kind of harvest can we expect? Is it possible for Christians to plant bad seeds even while they are serving the Lord? Can our egos sometimes ruin the "good deeds" we perform in the name of the Lord? In the light of Matthew 16:24, Mark 8:34, Luke 9:23, Luke 14:27, and Galatians 5:24, what is the antidote to egoistic pride? What does taking up the cross of Jesus mean?

3. Owing to apathy, sloth, disobedience to God, or self-centeredness, there may be people who do not take the time or make the effort to plant anything. What is the result of not planting anything?

4. Is the place where we plant as important as the quality of the seeds being planted? How can we know where to plant for best results?

5. When we obediently plant spiritual seeds where God directs us to plant (sowing to the Spirit), what kind of harvest may we expect?

6. Are there examples from biblical and secular history that illustrate the efficacy of the "principle of sowing and reaping"? Give several examples from the Bible and at least one from secular history.

7. Are all Christians to be involved in planting or nourishing good seeds in expectation of a harvest pleasing to our Lord? What kind of harvest may be expected?

8. Does the "principle of sowing and reaping" apply not only to proclaiming the Gospel but also to such mundane matters as our personal finances? Does it apply to any other areas?

9.   Explain the "principle of servanthood or servant-leadership." Whom are we to serve above all? Is "servant leadership" common in today's world?

PERTINENT SCRIPTURES

Genesis 1:28; Genesis 9:7; Genesis 29:3 & 23; I Kings 2:3; II Chronicles 21:5-6 & 10-20; II Chronicles 22:2-9; II Chronicles 24:18; Job 4:8; Job 35:9-13; Psalm 1:1-3; Psalm 41:1-3; Psalm 97:11; Psalm 126:5; Psalm 128; Proverbs 3:9-10; Proverbs 11:25; Proverbs 18:9; Proverbs 19:17; Proverbs 22:8 & 29; Proverbs 28:27; Ecclesiastes 11:4; Isaiah 49:4; Isaiah 64:6; Isaiah 65:6-7; Jeremiah 25:12-29; Jeremiah 50:29-32; Ezekiel chapter 7; Hosea 8:7; Hosea 10:12-13; Hosea 12:2; Micah chapter 2; Malachi 3:8-12; Matthew 7:6; Matthew 10:38; Matthew 13:24-30 & 38-39; Matthew 19:29; Matthew 20:25-28; Matthew 23:1-12; Mark 8:34; Mark 10:29-30 & 35-45; Luke 6:13; Luke 9:12-27; Luke 19:12-27; John 3:16; John 13:12-17; Acts 16:9; Romans 3:21-22; Romans 6:6-13; Romans 12:5-21; I Corinthians 1:30; I Corinthians 7:20-24; I Corinthians 9:19-23; II Corinthians 5:21; II Corinthians 9:6-7; Galatians 2:20; Galatians 5:19-25; Galatians 6:7-9; Ephesians 6:7-8; Philippians 2:3-11; and II Timothy 2:24-26.

Chapter XXVI

"THE PRINCIPLE OF HUMILITY"

Any servant leader and anyone living by the principle of servanthood must either be a sincerely humble person or a shameless hypocrite. Admittedly, there are persons who may exhibit what might be called the "Hollywood syndrome" – pretending to be humble in order to enjoy all the more the plaudits of vocal admirers; but God who sees the heart of man quickly distinguishes between false humility that ostensibly denigrates self in comparison with others and genuine humility that recognizes one's unworthiness in the eyes of God and cries out to Him for mercy. The difference is partially illustrated in Jesus's parable, found in Luke 18:9-14, about the self-righteous Pharisee and the lowly, contrite tax collector who were praying in the temple. The Pharisee's prayer was hardly self-effacing but evoked comparisons with persons who were wrongdoers or despised: "God, I thank you that I am not like other men – robbers, evildoers, adulterers – or even like this tax collector. I fast twice a week and give a tenth of all I get."

Now it is altogether fitting and proper to enter God's presence with thanksgiving and praise (Psalm 100 and Ephesians 5:20), and Christians are exhorted to "...give thanks in all circumstances..." (I Thessalonians 5:18). The Pharisee, however, was apparently more concerned with making a favorable impression on human listeners than to offer heartfelt gratitude to the heavenly Father. Doubtless he gained the recognition he sought – the admiration of men – as his reward (compare with Matthew 6:16), but God knew the pride in his heart. The attitude of the tax collector, on the other hand, was quite different. Bowing his head in shame and beating his breast, he uttered the anguished, honest, desperate prayer of a penitent: "God, have mercy on me, a sinner." It was his prayer that touched the heart of God; for Jesus declared: "I tell you that this man, rather than the other, went home justified...," because "everyone who exalts himself will be humbled, and he who humbles himself will be exalted."

The Pharisee's prayer was similar to some testimonies, purportedly to a work of God's grace in one's life that lack genuine spiritual depth or a ring of authenticity and celebrate the speaker's role in effecting a change of heart or character rather than demonstrating the Lord's ineffable love and power.

What society terms humility is often nothing but false humility, sometimes manifested in seemingly unpretentious and deferential attitudes or speech. For example, in response to a well-deserved expression of appreciation, a person may deny or denigrate the accomplishment or talent for which he is being complimented. Such contrived "humility" may be prompted by shyness, embarrassment, or perhaps even by a desire to receive additional affirmation or accolades. When a dinner guest tells the hostess "this is the best chocolate mousse I've ever tasted," she may coyly reply: " Oh, it was not as good as usual. Perhaps I should have used less sugar than the recipe called for. Jacqueline Bergan's mousse is much better – always just right."

Comparing one's accomplishment with that of someone else in a self-deprecating manner is not humility. One should be able to acknowledge a compliment gracefully without drawing undue attention to it – perhaps with a simple "thank you!" Making a comparison with someone else is out of place, as is also offering excuses such as those made by Ring Lardner's fictional baseball outfielder Frank X. Farrell, known to his teammates as "Alibi Ike." During a practice session, he made a "whale of a catch" of a fly ball, and the manager, Carey, called out, "Nice work!" Farrell's response was that he could have caught the ball with his back turned only he slipped when he started after it and, besides that, the air currents fooled him.

> "I thought you done well to get to the ball," said Carey.
> "I ought to been settin' under it," said Ike.
> "What did you hit last year,?" Carey asked him.
> "I had malaria most of the season," said Ike. "I wound up with .356."
> "Where would I have to go to get malaria?" said Carey, but Ike didn't wise up.

Pretending to be humble does not make one so. True humility is grounded in an implicit recognition of God's perfection, sovereignty, and mercy, and confidence in His unfailing love and His willingness and ability to assist His children. A truly humble person will not downplay his own accomplishments, but express heartfelt adoration and thanks to God for every success. A person engaging in false humility may secretly be harboring prideful thoughts, but humility will naturally flow out of an intimate relationship with the Father. Unless we recognize the hand of God in our affairs, pride is unavoidable; for humans are idolaters by nature and disposed to satisfy the desires of the flesh by pursuing "self-gratification" and "self-actualization" or "self-realization." In doing so, they lay themselves open to insinuations from the Adversary "to look out for number one," live up to one's "highest potential," develop "self-esteem," and make a sensational impression on one's friends and associates through good grooming, appropriate dress, and attainment of knowledge, wealth, a prestigious position, fame, power, or any number of other alluring, self-centered goals. Let us all beware! Overweening pride caused Lucifer and one-third of the angels to revolt against the God of the universe (Isaiah 14:12-14), and this one-time guardian angel has appealed to human pride – in our first ancestors and in every person born into this world – to instigate rebellion against the Creator-God.

Noah Webster's *American Dictionary of the English Language* (1828 edition) gives nine meanings for the word "pride," two of which are pertinent to this discussion: "(1) Inordinate self-esteem; an unreasonable conceit of one's own superiority in talents, beauty, wealth, accomplishments, rank or elevation in office, which manifests itself in lofty airs, distance, reserve, and often in contempt of others, and (2) Insolence; rude treatment of others; insolent exultation."

Such pride is anathema to the Lord, who "opposes the proud but gives grace to the humble" (James 4:6 and I Peter 5:5; cf. Psalm 31:23; Psalm 109:21; Proverbs 15:25; Proverbs 16:5; Isaiah 2:12; Isaiah 13:11; Jeremiah 50:31-32; and Malachi 4:1). The verity of this statement and that found in Proverbs 16:18: "Pride goes before destruction, a haughty spirit before a fall" is confirmed by numerous incidents related in the Bible. For instance, Numbers 12:1-15 tells of how Moses's siblings – Miriam and Aaron – contemptuously criticized him for marrying a "Cushite," probably out of jealousy because Yahweh had conferred a special prophetic gift on their brother, the Israelite leader. The Lord rebuked them and struck Miriam with leprosy, which was healed only because of Moses's intercession.

Likewise, King Rehoboam's haughty response to the leaders of Israel caused the northern ten tribes of the nation to secede from following the house of David, initiating a rift not to be mended until the end times (see II Chronicles 10:3-16).

Another monarch, godly King Uzziah of Judah, became proud as he experienced success and tried to assume the prerogatives of the priesthood by burning incense on the altar consecrated for that purpose. Heedless of the warnings of the priests, Uzziah was stopped only by Divine intervention. He became a leper and remained one until his death (II Chronicles 26:16-21).

The boasting of still another monarch – this one a foreign conqueror, King Nebuchadnezzar of Babylon – was silenced by Yahweh, who took away his sanity and divested him of his authority, humbling him to the point of eating grass like a cow until he turned his eyes toward heaven in repentance and acknowledged the God of the Hebrews as sovereign Lord of heaven and earth (Daniel chapter 4 and chapter 5:18-21).

From all of the foregoing examples, it may be seen that nations as well as individuals are affected when leaders pursue prideful, self-exalting policies. In fact, the annals of history are replete with princes and conquerors whose prideful ambitions led them on until both they and their followers or nation suffered the consequences. Napoleon Bonaparte was such a ruler. "To honor the Emperor [Napoleon] is to honor God himself," his new catechism declared; and on one occasion, as he basked in the aura of his accomplishments, he let his male secretary know that, because of his loyal service, he too would "be immortal." Napoleon's ambition for conquest was insatiable, causing much needless bloodshed and eventually his own downfall and that of his adopted country.

Similarly, Adolf Hitler brought Nazi Germany to ruin as a result of his arrogant, demonically-inspired quest to conquer Europe. In seeking to prove that he could succeed where the French conqueror had failed, he waited to launch his attack on the Soviet Union until late June of 1941 – on the very day of the year that Napoleon had begun his ill-fated campaign against Czarist Russia in 1812. The results were equally disastrous.

The prideful will to conquer has characterized many of the world's renowned military commanders, but not all of them. We read in the Bible of the incredible exploits of Israel under General Joshua – exploits that Joshua himself humbly and correctly attributed to Yahweh. In his retirement speech, he reminded the people of Israel that it was the Lord their God who had driven out before them "great and powerful nations." "No one has been able to withstand you," he said, because the Lord your God fights for you, just as He promised." Joshua made no attempt to take credit for the victories; instead, he offered praise to God and led the nation into a covenant with Him, to observe all His commandments (Joshua chapters 22 and 23).

David too was a humble leader, trusting implicitly in Yahweh; yet there is no scriptural basis for believing he lacked confidence in exercising his God-given abilities. When volunteering as a young man to engage in personal combat with the giant Philistine champion Goliath, he informed the king that, by Divine help, he had been able to kill a lion and a bear; and after his astounding victory over Goliath, he continued to conduct himself discreetly, though acclaimed a national hero. When King Saul jealously turned against him, David resourcefully evaded him; indeed, on two occasions, he refused to take the life of the monarch endeavoring to kill him, saying that he would not touch "the Lord's anointed." How difficult it must have been for him not to take matters into his own hands, especially in view of his awareness of having been Divinely chosen to succeed Saul! Once he became king, David's humble and unwavering trust in the Lord God continued to be evident in his submission to His will – in plans for battle, in acceptance of words of rebuke for his sins of adultery and murder, and in his remorseful repentance. Humility was also manifested in David's restraint of an army commander who wanted to put a Benjaminite to death for cursing the king and encouraging rebellion, and in his ready acknowledgment of responsibility for the sin that brought a plague upon the land (see I Samuel chapters 16 through 31 and the book of II Samuel).

In our own land, George Washington is an exemplar of Christian humility, serving as General of the Continental Army without pay, doing his utmost to hold the army together and to obtain supplies from a parsimonious Continental Congress, inspiring his troops, sharing their perilous and arduous lives, admonishing them to fear God and practice Christian virtues, and regularly humbling himself in earnest supplication and occasional fasting and prayer before the One in whom he trusted. In May of 1778, shortly after the Netherlands and France concluded treaties of alliance with the insurgent Americans, Washington issued orders to his troops at Valley Forge:

"It having pleased the Almighty Ruler of the Universe propitiously to defend the cause of the United American states, and finally by raising up a powerful friend among the Princes of the earth, to establish our Liberty and Independence upon a lasting foundation; it becomes us to set apart a day for gratefully acknowledging the Divine Goodness, and celebrating the event, which we owe to His benign interposition."[9]

The following heartfelt prayer of Washington expresses very well his faith and humility:

"Almighty God; we make our earnest prayer that Thou wilt keep the United States in Thy holy protection; that Thou wilt incline the hearts of the citizens to cultivate a spirit of subordination and obedience to government; and entertain a brotherly affection and love for one another and for their fellow citizens of the United States at large. And finally that Thou wilt most graciously be pleased to dispose us all to do justice, to love mercy, and to demean ourselves with that charity, humility, and pacific temper of mind which were the characteristics of the Divine Author of our blessed religion, and without a humble imitation of whose example in these things we can never hope to be a happy nation. Grant our supplication, we beseech Thee, through Jesus Christ our Lord. Amen."[10]

Washington's sincerity and humility are revealed even more clearly in the following prayer:

---

[9]Quoted in Mark A. Beliles and Stephen K. McDowell, *America's Providential History* (Charlottesville, VA: Providence Foundation, 1989), p.158

[10]"George Washington's Prayer for America" (The Washington Memorial Chapel at Valley Forge, Pennsylvania) as quoted in Catherine Millard, *The Rewriting of America's History* (Camp Hill, PA: Horizon House Publishers, 1991), p.67.

"O most glorious God... I acknowledge and confess my faults, in the weak and imperfect performance of duties of this day. I have called on Thee for pardon and forgiveness of sins, but so coldly and carelessly that my prayers are become my sin and stand in need of pardon. I have heard Thy holy word, but with such deadness of spirit that I have been an unprofitable and forgetful hearer.... But, O God, who art rich in mercy and plenteous in redemption, mark not, I beseech Thee, what I have done amiss; remember that I am but dust, and remit my transgressions, negligences and ignorances, and cover them all with the absolute obedience of Thy dear Son, that those sacrifices (of sin, praise, and thanksgiving) which I have offered may be accepted by Thee, in and for the sacrifice of Jesus Christ offered upon the cross for me."[11]

Contemporaries attest to Washington's exceptional modesty and wisdom as a man who listened carefully to advice, sagaciously pondering it before reaching a decision. Attributes of this sort are rare; yet they reinforce our portrayal of a man who eschewed pride – a man who knew how to listen before responding in accord with the biblical admonition "to be quick to hear, and slow to speak and slow to anger; for the anger of man does not achieve the righteousness of God" (James 1:19-20, NASB).

Throughout the ages, humility has been valued. Confucius (c.551-479 B.C.) considered it to be "the solid foundation of all the virtues," and John Ruskin (d.1900) believed that "the first test of a truly great man is his humility." To speak of humility or to give utterance in a lowly, unassuming manner is, of course, easier than *being* meek. The great Renaissance painter Raphael Sanzio (d.1520) was doubtless aware of this; for, while painting sacred scenes, he kept a lighted candle on his cap to prevent his shadow from falling on his work.

How many people can you name who do not want their friends, associates, or the public at large to see their contributions in their chosen vocations or give them credit for doing a good job? If we perform our daily

[11]As quoted in Peter Marshal and David Manuel, *The Light and the Glory* (Old Tappan, NJ: Fleming H. Revell Company, 1977), pp. 284-285.

work with diligence and integrity, we will probably receive some recognition or tokens of appreciation for doing so; but we are not to work for the purpose of achieving acclaim, and we must be wary of insincere encomiums. "Flattery," it is rightly said, "is like fine perfume: it may be sniffed but not swallowed" (cf. Proverbs 26:28 and Proverbs 29:5). The Christian's supreme purpose – even beyond that of providing for his family – should be to glorify God (I Corinthians 10:31; cf. II Corinthians 10:17; Philippians 1:9-11; and Hebrews 13:20-21) in the confident knowledge that He will provide for every need as promised: "But seek first the kingdom of God and His righteousness, and all these things [food, clothing, housing – the "necessities" of life] shall be added to you" (Matthew 6:33, NKJ).

In putting the Lord first in our lives and in doing our utmost to know and carry out His will and glorify Him, we assume a position of humble submission and implicit trust – relying upon God as a little toddler depends completely upon his parents or those caring for him. Is not this exactly what Jesus taught? In Matthew 18:4, we read:

> "I tell you the truth, unless you change [stop trying to attain personal recognition] and become as little children, you will never enter the kingdom of heaven. Therefore, whoever humbles himself like this child is the greatest in the kingdom of heaven."

Jesus exemplified humility – coming to earth as a "bond-servant" in human flesh and "being found in the appearance as a man, He humbled himself and became obedient to the point of death, even death of the cross" (Philippians 2:7-8, NKJ). Shortly before His sacrifice to atone for the sins of mankind, Jesus took a final meal – the passover supper – with His disciples, knowing that one of them would betray Him to be executed; yet secure in His Father's love, He got up from His place, took a towel and a basin of water, and humbly knelt down to wash the feet of His disciples. After resuming His seat, He told them:

> "You call Me Teacher and Lord; and you are right; for so I am. If I then, the Lord and the Teacher, washed your feet, you also ought to wash one another's feet. For I gave you an example that you also should do as I did to you" (John 13:13-15, NASB).

Is the church today carrying out our Lord's affectionate instruction, ministering to our Christian brothers and sisters, or going further, getting down where hurting and needy people are to treat them as He would – cleansing and bandaging their wounds, feeding them, providing them with clothing and shelter – in the name of Jesus? Thank God, some church bodies are, and this is as it should be; for the church, unlike civil government, is called to follow the "law of love" (Romans 13:8) as manifested in compassionate service. If the majority would do so, no doubt we would witness a tremendous revival and reformation in our society. People who see genuine Christian love in action that goes beyond the Old Testament exhortation "to act justly, and to love mercy, and to walk humbly with ... God" (Micah 6:8) are often surprised but deeply touched. Christ ordained that His church (not civil government) should be a redemptive force in the world. Oh that the church would be everything our Savior intended it to be, functioning in the power of the Holy Spirit!

Unfortunately, there are all too many church bodies today that do not give more than lip-service to the Lordship of Jesus Christ and are caught up in perpetuating themselves, in administrative and organizational matters, and in impressive rituals rather than in ministering Christ's love in practical ways; and many of those who do assist the downtrodden do so from purely humanitarian motives without mentioning the name of Christ or communicating His love. Indeed, practical action must be accompanied by love, and that will never be present where humility is lacking. Both were beautifully and inextricably blended in the compassionate ministry of an off-duty Catholic nurse who visited an elderly Protestant lady dying of cancer three times a week to cleanse the stinking cancerous flesh and change her bandages.

The risen Lord wrote to the church of Laodicea, one of the churches typifying the contemporary church, saying that it was "lukewarm – neither hot nor cold" and, therefore, He was about to spit it out of His mouth:

> "You say 'I am rich and do not need a thing' [compared to other congregations perhaps – a comparison likely to engender a prideful attitude]. But you do not realize that [by ignoring Me – see Revelation 3:20] you are wretched, pitiful, poor, blind, and naked" (Revelation 3:16-17).

A prideful church of this type is worse than useless, because it masquerades as something it is not and may arouse or foster resentment in non-believers already skeptical concerning tax exemptions enjoyed by religious organizations. Benjamin Franklin opined: "Pride that dines on vanity, sups on contempt." How true! A church that becomes self-satisfied and ingrown tends to view with disdain poorer or less sophisticated bodies – let alone society at large, which desperately needs to experience the truth and love of Jesus Christ expressed through His people.

Ecclesiastical bodies, probably more than any other entities, should give both spiritual and physical expression to Christ's love, compassion, and humility, which are inseparably bound together. Moreover, individual Christians should exemplify these virtues not only because the Bible enjoins them to do so (see, for example, Proverbs 16:19; Mark 12:30-31; Luke 6:27-36; John 15:17; Romans 12:10-13; Galatians 5:13b-14; Hebrews 10:24; and I Peter 3:8), but also because of the wonderful promises to those who conduct themselves with godly humility. The prophet Isaiah proclaimed:

> "For thus says the High and Lofty One, who inhabits eternity, whose name is Holy: 'I dwell in the high and holy place, with him who has a contrite and humble spirit, to revive the spirit of the humble, and revive the heart of the contrite ones'" (Isaiah 57:15).

As we have seen, pride and arrogance have serious, sometimes deadly consequences for individuals, rulers, or even nations indulging in them. The proud will suffer humiliation. On the other hand, the humble can expect multiple blessings. Proverbs 29:23 tells us: " A man's pride brings him low, but a man of lowly spirit gains honor" (cf. Proverbs 16:19); and Luke 14:11 states that "everyone who exalts himself will be humbled, and he who humbles himself will be exalted." This truth is reiterated throughout the Old and New Testaments. In Proverbs 22:4, we read: "Humility and the fear of the Lord bring wealth and honor and life" while James 4:10 states: "Humble yourselves before the Lord and He will lift you up."

In view of these biblical verities and the generally Christian tenor of the American colonies, it is not surprising that, faced with the ominous possibility of war with the mother country in the wake of the "Boston Tea Party" and

Britain's punitive "Intolerable Acts" of 1774, they not only prepared for action in defense of religious and civil liberties, but humbly besought Almighty God. The Connecticut Assembly designated a day for "humiliation and prayer," New York urged ministers of the gospel to lead their congregations in fasting and prayer for God's "interposition" and "deliverance," and the colony of Virginia set aside a day for "fasting and prayer." John Hancock declared before the "Provincial Congress" of Massachusetts:

> "We think it is incumbent upon this people to humble themselves before God on account of their sins, for He hath been pleased in His righteous judgment to suffer a great calamity to befall us, as the present controversy between Great Britain and the Colonies.... [It is necessary] also to implore the Divine Blessing upon us, that by the assistance of His grace, we may be enabled to reform whatever is amiss among us, that so God may be pleased to continue to us the blessings we enjoy, and remove the tokens of His displeasure, by causing harmony and union to be restored between Great Britain and these Colonies."[12]

Bolstered by their reliance on Almighty God and convinced that their cause was just and righteous, our forefathers brought into existence a new nation committed to the premise that "all men are created equal" and "endowed by their Creator with certain unalienable rights." Most of the founders of this nation were God-fearing, determined, and humble men. Would that the same spirit of faith and humility would animate our nation today – a nation that sadly has departed from the God of our fathers and the way of humility in its worship of power, clever schemes, influence-peddling, and money. May we – starting with the people of God – humbly and earnestly seek the face of our Maker in prayer, repent of our sins, and follow His principles and precepts so that our society and culture may be redeemed, revitalized, and reformed, and our nation be motivated as never before to honor and serve the life-giving God of the universe!

---

[12] Quoted in Marshall and Manuel, *The Light and the Glory*, p. 269.

QUESTIONS TO PONDER

1. Is there a relationship between the principle of servanthood and that of humility?

2. How can false humility be distinguished from true humility? What attitudes characterize false humility? True humility?

3. Are people naturally humble? By whom or by what standard does the humble person measure himself? In whom is his confidence?

4. Can pride and "self-esteem" be dangerous? Examples? What is the only biblical basis for "self-esteem"?

5. Is it possible for nations as well as individuals to be adversely affected by pride? Examples?

6. Is it possible for a humble, meek person to be a strong, effective leader? Examples? Are truly humble people dependent upon a Higher Power? On whom are the prideful depending?

7. Is the humble person willing to listen to counsel? Does the truly humble person seek recognition from others? Whose approbation does he seek?

8. Does our Lord commission His followers to undergo anything or do anything He has not experienced or done? Does He commission them to do anything for which they are not enabled?

9. How can the church have a Christ-like, redemptive impact on society? Is this possible without humility?

10. In what ways is pride injurious, not only to the prideful person or agency, but to society?

11. Do words and deeds flowing from a humble spirit have greater influence than they ordinarily would?

12. Can the humble expect a reward? If so, from what quarter?

13. Is it sufficient for Christians to want to restore the spiritual climate of our nation to that of its early years?

PERTINENT SCRIPTURES

Numbers 12:1-15; Joshua chapters 22 and 23; I Samuel chapters 16 through 31; the book of II Samuel; II Chronicles 10:3-16; II Chronicles 26:16-21; Psalm 31:23; Psalm 100; Psalm 109:21; Proverbs 15:25; Proverbs 16:5 & 19; Proverbs 22:4; Proverbs 26:28; Proverbs 29:5; Isaiah 2:12; Isaiah 13:1; Isaiah 57:15; Jeremiah 50:31-32; Daniel chapters 4 and 5; Malachi 4:1; Matthew 6:16 & 33; Matthew 18:4; Mark 12:30-31; Luke 6:27-36; Luke 14:11; Luke 18:9-14; John 13:13-15 & 17; Romans 12:10-13; Romans 13:8; I Corinthians 10:31; II Corinthians 10:17; Galatians 5:13-14; Ephesians 5:20; Philippians 1:9-11; Philippians 2:7-8; I Thessalonians 5:18; Hebrews 13:20-21; James 1:19-20; James 4:6 & 10; I Peter 3:8; I Peter 5:5; and Revelation 3:16-17 & 20.

Chapter XXVII

"THE PRINCIPLE OF NOT BEING UNEQUALLY YOKED"

In all probability, no scriptural principle is held more lightly than the prohibition against being "unequally yoked together with unbelievers" (see II Corinthians 6:14-18, especially in the NKJ); yet, the propensity for God's people to engage in idolatrous associations or compromising unions with unbelievers goes back to antiquity. As a matter of fact, a cryptic reference to the antediluvian "sons of God" having intercourse with the "daughters of men," who bore "giants" and "mighty men ..., men of renown," may indicate that fallen angels copulated with human women (see also Jude 6-7) or, more likely, alludes to intermarriage between the progeny of godly Seth and the godless descendants of Cain. In either case, the result was tragic; for men and women became so evil that God determined to extirpate them (with the exception of righteous Noah and his family) from the earth (Genesis 6:6-8, 13 & 17) with a flood.

Calamity likewise overtook the family of Abram's nephew Lot, who chose to live near Sodom and eventually in it (Genesis chapter 19). Although the lives of Lot, his wife, and two daughters were supernaturally spared when God's judgment of "fire and brimstone" destroyed the wicked cities of Sodom and Gomorrah, his wife perished as they were escaping and the daughters got their bereaved and bewildered father drunk and committed incest with him, resulting in the nations of Moab and Ammon – implacable enemies of the descendants of Abraham.

Abraham himself momentarily began to doubt the promise of the Lord to make his offspring plentiful and a blessing to the peoples of the earth (Genesis 12:2-3 and Genesis 15:2-5) and yielded to the entreaties of his wife Sarah to have a child through her Egyptian maidservant Hagar. The product of this "unequal union" was Ishmael, whose descendants have been hostile to those of Isaac, whom Sarah eventually bore to Abraham (Genesis chapter 16 and Genesis 22:1-20). Is it not extraordinary that the current animosities between the nation of Israel and her Arab neighbors can be traced back to the extramarital liaisons of Lot and Abraham?

From the time of their deliverance from Egyptian bondage, the Israelites were commanded to retain their liberty and purity as a people separated unto the Lord. They were not to make a covenant with the people of the promised land or "play the harlot with their gods" (Exodus 34:15-17, NKJ). Nevertheless, God's covenant people disregarded Yahweh's command to drive out the heathen living in the land lest they become as pricks in their eyes and thorns in their sides (cf. Joshua 23:11-13). Even before entering the land, Israel indulged in the detestable fertility rites of the Moabites, and thousands died of a plague before a righteous priest and other God-fearing leaders executed the perpetrators, assuaging God's wrath (Numbers 25:1-18).

This pattern of disobedience continued as God's chosen people settled down in the promised land. Not only did they fail to exterminate the demonized inhabitants of Canaan and allow them to retain enclaves within pacified territories, but they began to intermarry with these heathen peoples and adopt their religious and cultural practices.

Certainly, the Canaanites that the Israelites spared during the conquest did become snares and "thorns in the sides" to them (cf. Psalm 106:34-42). In the book of Judges, we read how, time and again, the people of Israel fell away from the Lord. Even several of the judges whom God raised up to deliver them during periods of repentance were far from being pure vessels. The strong man Samson, for example, was filled with lust for Philistine women, frequently engaging in "unequal yoking"; and his affair with Delilah caused him to break his Nazarite vow and suffer imprisonment and blinding of his physical eyes. (His spiritual acuity was also affected; for sin always involves loss of spiritual vision.)

Nevertheless, Yahweh used imperfect vessels to rescue his people when they came before Him in contrite repentance. Unfortunately, Israel's interludes of repentance were short-lived. I Samuel 2:12-25 & 27-36, I Samuel 3:11-18, and I Samuel chapter 4 tell of how even spiritual leaders – the sons of Eli the high-priest – engaged in adultery and desecration of the Lord's sacrifices, thus merging the holy with the unholy. As a result, these apostate priests met a violent end, and the aged Eli died in great sorrow, knowing that the ark of God had been captured by the enemy.

All was not lost, however. In their distress, the people of Israel began to return to Yahweh, who restored the ark to their care and raised up the prophet Samuel to renew the covenant with His chosen people, teach them His ways, and begin to deliver them from their oppressors. Urged by the people to give them a king, Samuel did so within the context of the covenant with the Lord, thereby inaugurating the Kingdom of Israel. It was soon apparent, however, that Israel's first monarch – King Saul – possessed a flawed character. He was not careful to carry out the Lord's commands, upon one occasion sparing the life of an Amalekite king – a scion of the line of Esau through his "unequal union" with a pagan wife.

Saul's successor, King David, was "a man after God's own heart" in spite of personal weaknesses and sins; but his son Solomon, whose early humility and wisdom were astounding, was led astray by his many foreign wives, demonstrating once again the folly of marriages between the people of God and the followers of pagan deities.

Interestingly enough, the Bible does not prohibit marriages between various ethnic groups – what society terms "inter-racial marriages" – but only unions between believers and non-believers. Obviously, the Lord cares nothing about differences in pigmentation of the skin, physiognomy, or facial features of people He has created; rather, He looks at the hearts of men and women and prescribes that Christians should not be joined in holy matrimony with non-Christians, who may lead them astray or at least cause them to mute their Christian witness.

The condition of the heart is of the utmost importance to God; therefore, He forbids not only intermarriage with unbelievers but "unequal" alliances or binding ties of any sort. When King Asa of Judah, normally a God-fearing monarch, made a treaty with the godless king of Syria to force a hostile nation to desist from attacking Judean strong points and withdraw its army (see I Kings 15:17-22 and II Chronicles 16:1-9), he was rebuked by the prophet Hanani; and Asa's son and successor, King Jehoshaphat, was likewise reproved for concluding an alliance with wicked King Ahab of Israel. Subsequently, he suffered loss of his merchant marine because of a treaty with Ahab's successor (see I Kings 22:1-4 and II Chronicles 19:2).

Actually, the "yoking" between Judah and apostate Israel brought much more than a few temporary setbacks; for the worship of Baal – introduced into Israel by the Sidonian princess Jezebel, Ahab's queen – was now extended into Judah and could not be completely eradicated, notwithstanding the determined efforts of King Joash and the high-priest Jehoiada and several succeeding rulers (II Chronicles 24:2 & 15-24, II Chronicles 28:1-4, and II Chronicles 33:1-9).

In the light of these biblical examples, should any nation purporting to trust in God make an alliance with an evil, God-denying nation? Did the Lord ever excuse Israel or Judah because of supposed political expediency? How, then, can the World-War-II alliance between the Soviet Union and the United States of America be excused? Could not the two nations have been co-belligerents against Nazi Germany without a formal, binding agreement? Were the results of the alliance restricted to the realm of foreign policy? What has been the fruit of this alliance for the people of the former Soviet Union? For the people of the United States? For the people of the world? Is its influence continuing to be felt? if so, in what ways?

Definitive answers to these questions can not be given since there is no possibility to go back to January 1, 1942 and abrogate the "Declaration by the United Nations" by which twenty-six nations – including the Soviet Union and the United States – entered into a military alliance against the Axis Powers. Although it was handled as merely an executive agreement signed by President Franklin D. Roosevelt and, therefore, never submitted to the United States Senate for ratification as prescribed under the Constitution, the agreement bound together disparate nations against a common enemy. While the signatories officially acknowledged the principles of the Atlantic Charter of August 14, 1941 and pledged themselves "to defend liberty, independence and religious freedom, and to preserve human rights and justice in their own lands as well as other lands ...," the communist U.S.S.R. predictably did as it pleased without any restraints or serious objections from its allies. The consequences – religious, political, economic, social, cultural, moral, and attitudinal – are now irrevocably part and parcel of modern history.

"Unequal yoking" has broad connotations – prohibiting wedlock with unbelievers, alliances with ungodly nations, religious syncretism, acceptance of false and profane ideologies, and business partnerships that could undermine a believer's witness or integrity. If a Christian finds some of the practices of his business associates dishonest or disreputable, he should be able to go to them privately and voice his objections. Should wrongs continue to be perpetrated, the Christian must disclose and oppose them at the risk of being cashiered or forced to resign; for Ephesians 5:11 instructs followers of Jesus Christ to have "nothing to do with the fruitless deeds of darkness, but rather expose them," and II Corinthians 6:14-17 commands:

> "Do not be unequally yoked together with unbelievers. For what fellowship has righteousness with lawlessness? And what communion has light with darkness? And what accord has Christ with Belial? Or what part has a believer with an unbeliever? And what agreement has the temple of God with idols? For you are the temple of the living God. As God has said: 'I will dwell in them and walk among them. I will be their God, and they shall be My people.' Therefore, 'come out from among them and be separate,' says the Lord. 'Do not touch what is unclean, and I will receive you'."

This does not necessarily mean that a person can not work for a company whose policy-makers and managerial staff are not totally composed of born-again Christians, but it does mean, at the very least, that a believer should disassociate himself from the company if its policies are ungodly or unethical or its business practices are dishonest. In some cases, it may be that a board member is able to set or influence policies in a moral, upright, principled mode of administration. On the other hand, should he be unable to exert sufficient authority to move things in an honorable and ethical direction, and if he is "*unequally* yoked" to the point of having to implement fraudulent, unscrupulous, or immoral practices, he should protest and, if necessary, resign. There is no concord between Christ and the Evil One (cf. II Corinthians 6:15).

Disregarding or scorning biblical injunctions against "unequal yoking" inevitably brings suffering, sometimes catastrophe. When ancient Israel and Judah ignored Yahweh's prohibitions in that regard by allowing pagans to settle down in their midst, intermarrying with them, and adopting significant features of their religious practices and culture, the Lord God raised up the Assyrians and Babylonians to punish them. Israel fell to Assyria in 721 B.C., and Judah was humbled by the Babylonians under Nebuchadnezzar. In 597 B.C., the Babylonians conquered Jerusalem and transported about ten thousand Jews, including the prophet Ezekiel, to Babylon. Although the Kingdom of Judah continued to exist under Nebuchadnezzar's appointee, King Zedekiah, the people of Judah proved incorrigible. Ignoring the warnings of Jeremiah the prophet, they persisted in their wickedness and rebelled against their overlord. Babylonian forces invested Judah's capital in 588 B.C. and, after a siege of almost two years, it fell in July of 586 B.C. The city was plundered, the temple was burned, and the leading citizens were led away into Babylonian captivity (II Kings chapters 24 & 25, II Chronicles chapter 36, and Jeremiah 39:1-10).

Jeremiah, who was permitted to stay in the land, joined a remnant of Judeans under Nebuchadnezzar's appointee, Gedaliah, who was treacherously murdered. Fearing retribution, the remaining princes of Judah asked Jeremiah to pray for guidance from the Lord and promised to heed whatever word he would give. However, when the prophet told them to remain in the land and serve the King of Babylon, they broke their word and fled to Egypt – making an unholy arrangement with that nation that brought disaster (Jeremiah chapters 40 through 44). The remnant that migrated to Egypt has simply disappeared from the pages of history.

In the meanwhile, the prophet Ezekiel was speaking forcefully to the Judean captives in Babylon. In chapter 16:15-22 & 32-34 and in chapter 23:4-49, Ezekiel recalled the sins of Israel and Judah in unequally yoking themselves with unbelievers. He termed it harlotry, because they had turned away from their "husband" – the one true God – and had used the precious gifts and blessings God had conferred upon them to entice and entertain pagan lovers.

Israel had been delivered over to the Assyrians, Ezekiel insisted, because she had lusted after them – "their warriors clothed in blue, governors and commanders, all of them handsome young men, and mounted horsemen" – apparent references to Israel's political overtures to Nineveh and her spiritual prostitution (Ezekiel 23:5-10). Judah went even further, looking at "men portrayed on a wall" – Chaldean military officers – just as lustful persons in our contemporary society might resort to arousal through voyeurism or pornography before trying to arrange assignations calculated to satisfy their lustful cravings (Ezekiel 23:14-22). A probable reference to pornography is also made in Ezekiel

16:17, and both political and cultural prostitution is described in chapters 16 and 23 – whoredom that went beyond the usual practice of harlots, for Israel and Judah paid lovers to come in to them without receiving a *quid pro quo*. Can a parallel be drawn to the foreign assistance schemes of the United States?

The ultimate consequences of such national prostitution are horrendous – terror, pillaging, burning and killing by "a mob" (Ezekiel 23:46); yet our nation pursues all manner of accommodations with Moscow, Peking, and third-world Marxist dictators and has opened our society to Eastern cults, New Age philosophy, and pagan thought patterns. Moreover, we are shedding innocent blood, literally sacrificing the children borne of our harlotry in abortion mills (cf. Ezekiel 16:36 and Ezekiel 23:39). Our nation has not been forced into submitting to these iniquitous practices: it has not been raped or violated against its will – complicity is involved. Like ancient Israel and Judah, we have not honored our "wedding vows," the marriage covenant made by our founding fathers; we have not cleaved with faithful, loving heart to our "husband" – who, as stated in our national anthem, is "the Power that hath made and preserved us a nation!"

No doubt it is too late for our nation to escape the judgment of God; nevertheless, we know that "mercy triumphs over judgment" (James 2:13b). Therefore, if we renounce our unholy alliances, repent of our religious and cultural syncretism, and contritely turn to the only true God, He will forgive our sins and purify and heal our land (cf. II Chronicles 7:14 and I John 1:9).

QUESTIONS TO PONDER

1. What constitutes "unequal yoking" according to Scripture? Are "interracial marriages" prohibited?

2. Does the principle of abstaining from "unequal yoking" apply solely to proposed marriages between believers and unbelievers, or does it have a broader application?

285

3. Does disregard of God's prohibition against "unequal yoking" lead to serious consequences?

4. Is it God's will for believers to curry favor with the godless?

5. Is the principle of abstaining from "unequal yoking" pertinent to our personal lives? If so, how?

6. Does the principle of not being "unequally yoked" have any relevance for us today, as a people and as a nation? Of what applications can you think?

7. As citizens of the United States, what must we do to break the power of evil evident in our land?

PERTINENT SCRIPTURES

Genesis 6:6-8, 13 & 17; Genesis 12:2-3; Genesis 13:5-13; Genesis 15:25; Genesis chapter 16; Genesis 18:16-33; Genesis chapter 19; Genesis 21:1-21; Genesis 22:1-20; Exodus 34:12-17; Numbers chapters 22 through 25; Numbers 33:55; Joshua 23:11-13; Judges 1:28-36; Judges 2:1-5; Judges chapter 16; I Samuel 2:12-25 & 27-36; I Samuel 3:11-18; I Samuel chapter 4; I Samuel 15:1-29; I Kings 15:17-22; I Kings 16:31-33; I Kings 22:1-4; II Kings 8:16-18 & 29; II Kings 9:16-27; II Kings 11:1; II Kings chapters 24 and 25; II Chronicles 7:14; II Chronicles 16:1-9; II Chronicles 19:2; II Chronicles 20:35-37; II Chronicles 22:2-10; II Chronicles 24:2 & 15-24; II Chronicles 25:6-7 & 13; II Chronicles 28:1-4; II Chronicles 33:1-9; II Chronicles chapter 36; Psalm 106:34-42; Proverbs 1:10-15; Jeremiah 39:1-10; Jeremiah chapters 40 through 44; Jeremiah 46:2; Ezekiel 16:15-22 & 32-36; Ezekiel 23:4-49; Matthew 10:12-15; I Corinthians 5:9-13; I Corinthians 6:15-17; II Corinthians 6:14-18; Ephesians 5:6-11; II Thessalonians 3:6; James 2:13b; II Peter 2:15-16; I John 1:9; Jude 6-7; and Revelation 2:14-16.

Chapter XXVIII

"THE PRINCIPLE OF GOVERNMENT AUTHORITY"

The Creator is the Source of all authority: "there is no authority except that which God has established. The authorities that exist have been established by God" (Romans 13:1); therefore, any temporal authority denying God's primacy and absolute authority eviscerates itself. As already shown in Chapter XVI dealing with the "Creation Principle," man is made in the Divine image and is a free moral agent. As such, he should be schooled and disciplined from birth to love God supremely and his fellow man as himself, to respect God's precepts and human law based on the "law of nature and nature's God," to accept responsibility for his actions, and to learn and practice self-discipline. "Better a patient man than a warrior," states Proverbs 16:32, "a man who controls his temper than one who takes a city."

A person who does not respect authority is a rebel against God and society and a law unto himself – in effect an idolater who confuses his own ability, might, or cleverness to achieve what he wants to do with the right to do it. No free society can exist if its citizens refuse to recognize lawful authority. Where self-government is absent, anarchy results, necessitating coercion – the exercise of force, violence, compulsion, raw power, or totalitarian measures – for society to survive. Since the impact of Darwinian thought, with its celebration of the "survival of the fittest" and evolving laws and mores devoid of any objective, "supernatural" standards, the pagan concept of "might makes right" has become increasingly acceptable, though perhaps couched in more sophisticated terms. We speak of "political power," the "clout" of special-interest groups, and the "sovereign state" in a manner tacitly recognizing civil government as the granter and guarantor of all "rights." ("Civil rights" rather than "unalienable God-given rights" is the assumption and parlance of our day.) We confuse "power," the ability of government to force compliance to its will, with "authority" to govern in accord with Divine moral mandates conferred by a Supreme Being. Without a biblical view of authority, man becomes the ultimate arbiter (through the institutions he creates and the manner in which he applies the law) of "right and wrong," and individual liberty ceases to exist; but "where the Spirit of the Lord is, there is freedom" (II Corinthians 3:17). Thus, inculcation of eternal truths in the individual conscience fosters self-government, and a nation's affirmation of the biblical paradigm for law and ethics is the surest guarantee of liberty and equality for *all* its citizens, not just for Christians and Jews.

Besides bestowing on man a capacity for self-government and the concomitant authority and obligation to tend and govern the natural order (cf. Genesis 1:26-28 and Psalm 8:5-6), the Creator instituted at least four corporative authorities to assist him in carrying out his responsibilities: the family, the church, the state, and private, voluntary organizations. Additionally, there are lines of authority depending upon a person's position: master over servant, teacher over student, employer over employee, and other arrangements. Each type of God-given authority has its own function and delimited realm of jurisdiction outlined in the Bible. When an institution arrogates powers beyond those allotted by God, it becomes perverted, corrosive of legitimate authority, and destructive; conversely, an institution refusing to exercise its Divinely-ordained responsibilities abrogates its moral duty, thereby placing the entire established order in jeopardy.

Society's most basic and essential institution is the family. Men and women were created to have children and carry out the Creator's dominion mandate to rule over the earth and subdue it (Genesis 1:27-28 and Psalm 8:4-8). Will and Ariel Durant, authors of the popular *The Story of Civilization* in eleven volumes, correctly recognize the family as "the nucleus of civilization," and former President Ronald Reagan avers:

> "Strong families are the foundation of society. Through them we pass on our traditions, rituals, and values. From them we receive the love, encouragement, and education needed to meet human challenges. Family life provides opportunities and time for the spiritual growth that fosters generosity of spirit and responsible citizenship."[13]

---

[13]Excerpted from the "Proclamation of National Family Week," November 15, 1984.

Children receive their first and perhaps most influential training in morals, character formation, and government with its underlying principles within the home. At its best, the family – consisting of a husband, wife, and at least one child – provides protection, ministry for spiritual and physical ills, companionship, identification, mutual care and nurturing, acceptance and understanding, training in virtue as well as basic attitudes and skills, opportunities for intellectual growth and emotional stability, sustenance and care, an inheritance, and even cultural outlets that stimulate self-development and creativity.

Unfortunately, families in our nation today are being upset and all too often destroyed because husbands and wives do not observe God-given order, and parents do not exercise authority within the home according to biblical directives. The results are a mounting crime rate, wholesale divorces, teenage suicides, psychological maladjustments, the feminist movement, alienation between genders and generations, and possibly increasing homosexuality, incest, rape, violence in the home, child abuse, and spousal abuse.

The authority structure within the family is set forth in I Corinthians ll:1-l6, Ephesians 5:22 to 6:4, I Timothy 2:ll-l5, and I Peter 3:l-9. Man, male and female, is made in God's image and is accountable and responsible to Him; and husband and wife are also mutually accountable to one another "out of reverence for Christ" (Ephesians 5:2l). Required are mutual faithfulness, respect, and consent in matters affecting the marriage covenant; for they are "one flesh." Man is to be woman's protector, nurturer, and provider. His responsibility and accountability before God is greater than that of the woman and, concomitantly, his authority within the home. Nevertheless, as head of the household, he is not to dominate his spouse but to fulfill his God-given responsibilities to her and to love and nurture her as Christ loves and nurtures the church (Ephesians 5:25-33). On her part, the wife is to submit to her husband "as to the Lord," in a gentle, quiet, appealing manner just as Sarah submitted to Abraham (I Peter 3:l-6); yet she is not to be servile, compelled by her husband to do something contrary to God's Word. The husband secure in his manhood need not be domineering. Conscious of the obligations the Lord has laid upon him, he will be careful to observe them, loving his wife as he loves himself and as Christ loves the church, even to the point of giving his life for her (Ephesians 5:25 & 33). He is not to resort to "macho" tactics, but to cherish the helpmate God has given him. By the same token, a wife confident of her husband's fidelity and loving care should have no difficulty in honoring and supporting him and in conducting herself with amiable and affectionate modesty, prudence, and grace. Both spouses should promote the well-being of the other in the bond of loving commitment: the husband must give no place to vaunting himself at his wife's expense or to crudity, malicious acts, threats, browbeating, and cruelty; and the wife must not nag, manipulate, or play the demanding, strident feminist game.

Husband and wife should support one another and cooperatively manage their household in a manner pleasing to God, nurturing and training their children – not provoking them to anger, but consistently disciplining them whenever necessary in love, and instructing them in the way of the Lord (Ephesians 6:4). In return, parents may expect obedience and respect from their children (Ephesians 6:1-3) as they experience the integrity, truth, and genuineness of their parents' lives and the benefits of observing God's ways.

In societies where respect for parents has traditionally been deeply ingrained, and where the father has been recognized as the head of the home, many of the baneful problems resulting from a permissive society such as ours have been averted or minimized. In China, for example, until modern times, Confucianism, though certainly not Christian, inculcated a respect for the father and one's elders and superiors that resulted in a generally stable society; and, among American Chinese, it is only in recent years as this tradition has been breaking down that Chinese-American young people have become involved in crime, vandalism, drugs, and attendant problems.

On the other hand, reverence for the father to the point of obsessive veneration of ancestors was carried too far (humanism always eventuates in idolatry); and Chinese rulers in assuming prerogatives as "fathers" of their people were out of harmony with biblical principles, which do not permit a mingling of family and state authority. The father is to act out of loving concern for his family, while the ruler, with the welfare of his subjects in mind, must concern himself primarily with maintaining law and order, administering righteous and impartial justice, and protecting the land from foreign enemies. As bearer of "the sword," the civil ruler or magistrate dare not allow personal feelings or relationships to sway his judgment of the law. Therefore, Confucian emperors not strictly observing jurisdictional boundaries were not in line with God-given principles for exercising authority, nor were the Confucian *literati*, the mandarins, who advised them and served as magistrates. The concept of developing "perfect men" or at least "highly superior men" (the *chün-tzu*) to govern resulted in the rule of men rather than the rule of law, leaving room for all sorts of corruption and arbitrary rule. Ironically enough, however, the United States, which has always prided itself upon limiting its leaders and protecting its citizens by the rule of law rather than men, has – through the idolatrous, humanistic, and evolutionary doctrine of case law – fallen into the trap of judge-made law. Thus, we have come to the rule of men (who can virtually act as little gods) rather than the rule of law, which our Constitution sought to guarantee.

According to God's Word, the state is ordained for the well-being of those under its authority; therefore, citizens are to submit respectfully to their public officials (the magistrates), who are God's servants to them for good (Romans 13:4-5; cf. Exodus 18:21, Deuteronomy 16:18-20, Proverbs 24:21-22, Daniel 2:20-21, Daniel 4:17, Titus 3:1, and I Peter 2:13-17). The state is to protect society by wielding the sword against foreign enemies and domestic criminals, maintaining law and order according to eternal principles revealed in the Bible and observed in the natural order, including capital punishment (cf. Genesis 9:6, Exodus 21:12-14; Leviticus 24:17 & 21, Deuteronomy 19:11-13; and Romans 13:4). It is to protect the innocent, reward the righteous, and punish evildoers, administering justice lawfully and impartially (Isaiah 5:23 and Isaiah 10:1-2) and to provide a climate and framework within which other God-instituted authorities may operate according to the Divine will by facilitating their efforts while refraining from usurping duties properly belonging to them. On the other hand, if the state exceeds the legitimate bounds of its authority, encroaching into jurisdictional areas not assigned to it and perhaps even infringing on its citizens' "unalienable rights," protests should be lodged through proper channels to curb its usurpations. Citizens are to "render to Caesar" the revenue to enable the state to fulfill the legitimate responsibilities placed upon it (Luke 20:25), but they should demand accountability, resisting the state's attempts to assume authority not granted to it in Holy Writ.

For example, the civil government may promulgate and enforce laws designed to uphold public morals whose violation poses a danger to society, and it may punish unlawful behavior but not alleged thoughts or intentions. The church, however, must influence public morality through example and religious and moral teaching, but it can exert disciplinary measures only on its members (I Corinthians 5:1-13) through exclusion of the offending or sinful member from fellowship, not by coercion or the sword, the symbol of civil authority. Rather it is the staff that symbolizes ecclesiastical authority, and the purpose of the staff is to comfort, encourage, exhort, warn, correct, and restore, not merely to inflict punishment in the manner appropriate to the civil authority. Unfortunately, the contemporary church often shirks its responsibility to discipline erring members, manifesting a flaccid, sociologically-based tolerance under the guise of "love." Little wonder that the spiritual authority of the church is so lightly regarded – to the point of being considered irrelevant, ineffectual, and even ludicrous.

The chief responsibility of the church, of course, is to lead men, women, and children to eternal life in Jesus Christ and make disciples of all the nations (Matthew 28:18-20). The church is also authorized to build up and equip the saints for ministry and works of service (Ephesians 4:12-13) that will strengthen and unify God's people and enable believers to be effective evangelists and preceptors of righteousness.

Externally, the church is to proclaim the message of God's love and salvation by speaking His words and performing His deeds, preaching and teaching (Deuteronomy 4:14 and Deuteronomy 5:31), and ministering to the spiritual and physical needs of people. Internally, the church is to promote its members' spiritual growth, nurturing them in the faith and preparing them to be Spirit-inspired-and-empowered servants (such preparation will doubtless include edifying praise and worship that invokes the Lord's presence, vivifies the participants, and provides musical and esthetic expression of a faith and adoration to be manifested in society); to teach the full counsel of God – biblical principles, doctrines, and moral living that will enable them to be overcomers in this world; and to minister to the poor, the downtrodden, the sick, the fatherless, the widow, the prisoner, the castaway, the despised, the dejected, the depressed, the afflicted, the friendless, the lonely, the emotionally ill, and the spiritually destitute. Essentially, therefore, the internal activities of the church should equip God's people to carry the Gospel effectively to neighbors, communities, the nation, and the world in every possible way – through preaching and teaching, but also through acts of kindness intended to meet the physical and practical needs of hurting people (cf. Matthew 5:1-16 & 43-48; Matthew 6:1-4; Matthew (9: 35-38; Matthew 10:1 & 5-8; Mark 16:15-18; Luke 4:18-19; Luke 6:27-36; Luke 9:1-2;

Luke 10:27 & 30-37; Luke 14:33-35; Luke 22:26; John 12:24-26; John 15:4-12; Romans 1:16-17; Romans 15:1-7; I Corinthians 1:10; II Corinthians 7:1; II Corinthians 9:6-11; Galatians 5:16-25; I Timothy 4:13; II Timothy 2:15; II Timothy 4:2 & 5; Hebrews 2:4; Hebrews 13:1-3; James 1:27; James 2:14-17; James 5:19-20; I Peter 2:9; I John 2:5-6; I John 3:17-18; 1 John 5:2-4; and Jude 20-23).

The foregoing exposition has noted that attending to people's needs is part of the ministry of the church though the family and righteous individuals are also to help the needy, and private organizations may play a role (Leviticus 19:9-10; Leviticus 25:35-40; Deuteronomy 14:28-29; Deuteronomy 15:4-11; Deuteronomy 16:9-15; Deuteronomy 24:17-21; Deuteronomy 26:12-19; Psalm 41:1-3; Proverbs 19:17; Proverbs 22:9; Proverbs 31:20; Luke 14:12-14; Acts 6:1-4; II Corinthians 9:6-11; Galatians 2:10; I Timothy 5:3-16; James 1:27; and James 2:1-17). According to the Bible, the state has no such responsibility: it is to "bear the sword," safeguarding society and administering justice, but is not to involve itself in acts of love such as those that can be offered by individuals, the family, the church, and charitable agencies. When the "sword bearer" intrudes into jurisdictions not given to it, confusion results. For example, failure to help the poor is not a crime, though contrary to God's word; therefore, the civil government can not coerce people to perform acts of kindness and charity. Moreover, when the "sword bearer" oversteps its rightful bounds and involves itself in charity, it must require recipients to prove their need, and this necessitates subjecting them to intrusive, humiliating questions and supervision. Of necessity, the state overseeing welfare dispenses relief grudgingly and without compassion; therefore it can not meet recipients' spiritual or emotional needs and sometimes even forbids its agents to render such ministry of their own volition because of a misguided interpretation of the so-called "separation of church and state." Furthermore, state control and management of the welfare system leads recipients to believe that they are *entitled* to the benefits received (otherwise they would not be obtaining them), and it may engender attitudes of hopelessness, self-loathing, dependency, and an underlying antipathy toward society at large.

Assistance to human need should be given in love. The "sword bearer" can not do this. Indeed, when civil government exceeds its jurisdiction by involving itself directly in public welfare instead of merely providing a favorable climate for individuals, the church, and private agencies to function effectively in their charitable endeavors, resentment against recipients almost inevitably arises from burdened taxpayers who not only resent the waste, the exorbitant administrative costs involved, the inefficiency and counter-productivity of programs they view as being promoted and managed by self-serving government bureaucrats but may criticize the poor, even those deserving of assistance, as "parasites" or "deadbeats."

How much better it would be to follow a biblical paradigm that encourages individuals, the religious community, and private entities to distribute assistance to the homeless, destitute, or downtrodden in a loving, Christ-like, non-judgmental spirit. In Leviticus 19:9-10, the Israelites were commanded not to harvest the corners of their fields or pick up fallen fruit, because the needy and the stranger were to be allowed to harvest them (see also Leviticus 23:22). Deuteronomy 24:20-21 went even further, prescribing that the owner of an olive tree or vineyard should refrain from picking more than one crop, so that what was left could be picked by the "alien, the orphan, and the widow." Moreover, at the end of every third year, farmers were to bring out a tithe of their products and deposit it within the gates of a local town to help support the Levites, aliens, orphans, and widows (Deuteronomy 14:28-29). Debts were to be remitted every seven years among the Israelites, individuals having more than enough for their needs were commanded to give to the less fortunate, and slaves were to be set free in the seventh year of service and sent on their way with liberal provisions unless they opted to remain as permanent bond servants (Deuteronomy 15:1-18). Even land that had been sold from the family inheritance was to be reclaimed every 50th year, which was a "year of jubilee." Therefore, sons of fathers who may have lost family property because of hardship could expect that the owner holding it would restore it in the year of jubilee (Leviticus 25:10-16 & 26-34). Furthermore, an Israelite was not to exact interest payments from a fellow countryman, and if a needy countryman and his family agreed to serve as indentured servants, they must be treated leniently and released from any further obligation in the year of jubilee (Leviticus 25:35-43). Israelite families were to care for their own and even take care of their relatives and the needy whenever possible (Leviticus 25:46-49; Numbers 26:7-11; Psalm 41:1-3; Psalm 72:12-14; Psalm 82:3-4; Psalm 146:7; and Psalm 147:3 & 6). In the New Testament, the head of a family who did not provide for his own was to be considered worse than an unbeliever (I Timothy 5:8), and in I John 3:17 we read: "If anyone has material possessions and sees his brother in need but has no pity on him, how can the love of God be in him?" (Cf. James 2:15-16). Christians were expected to help other Christians, both on an individual basis and through the church (Acts 4:32 & 34-37, Acts 5:1-11, and Acts 6:1-4). Believers were even told to give assistance to non-believers (Romans 12:20 and Galatians 6:10). Therefore, welfare was to be handled by God's people, on an individual basis and corporatively through the church, but welfare is not to be supplied by the state.

If the exact means of providing for the needy in our modern industrial society may differ somewhat from those employed in the rural society of ancient Israel or the endeavors of the early church, the spirit of love and compassion characterizing charitable works should never be absent. Individuals hearkening to God's commands, churches desiring to minister to the totality of human need as a part of their evangelical outreach, and charitable organizations can render assistance effectively and in a merciful, tender, warmhearted manner. Christians should be especially adept at this, for they know the love of Christ experientially and should be attuned to His heart. Concern for "the whole person" – body, soul, and spirit – should be a priority with them though they may wonder how best to minister their Savior's love. Opportunities for serving people abound, however, through voluntary service or contributions to privately-sponsored soup kitchens, clothing depots, shelters, orphanages, schools, health-care facilities, prison ministries, day-care facilities, and crisis pregnancy centers. Individual initiatives may also be undertaken: visiting the sick in a local hospital, allotting land and seed and perhaps some tools to enable people to plant a garden, teaching people how to read or to perform certain minimal but important tasks, taking care of young children for a working parent, serving as an "elder brother" or "sister" or "grandparent" for emotionally-starved children, being a friend to a downhearted neighbor, visiting an elderly person, or engaging in myriads of other creative means of loving service. Beyond this, churches may wish to sponsor one or more facilities such as those mentioned above or, if strapped for funds, to partner with an organization such as the Christian Broadcasting Network's "Operation Blessing" in order to distribute food, clothing, or blankets to the needy in the name of Jesus Christ. Under a plan of this sort, material goods may be supplied by the larger agency, while the church does what it can, selects worthy recipients (a task that can be performed more effectively by local people than by an impersonal government agency), and distributes the supplies, providing in the process encouragement and spiritual help.

According to Scripture, civil government has not been given a direct role in dispensing "charity," though it is to provide favorable conditions for individuals, churches, and private organizations to carry out their God-ordained duties in this regard. The same is true concerning education, an obligation that God has placed primarily upon the family though the church is also authorized to play a significant role (see Genesis 18:19; Deuteronomy 4:9-14; Deuteronomy 6:1-2, 4-9 & 20-25; Deuteronomy 29:29; Proverbs 6:20-23; Proverbs 22:6; Matthew 23:1-3; Luke 2:46-47; I Timothy 4:13; II Timothy 1:15; II Timothy 3:14-17; and Titus 2:1-8 & 15). Parents are admonished to rear their children in "the nurture and admonition of the Lord" – to train them in the way they should go (Proverbs 22:6 and Ephesians 6:4). In ancient Israel, law, government, history, and literature as well as religion, moral philosophy, ethics, and music were to be presented in the home (Deuteronomy 4:9-10; Deuteronomy 6:1-8; Deuteronomy 29:29; Psalm 8:2; Psalm 51:6; Psalm 78:2 & 4-6; Proverbs 6:20-24; Proverbs 16:20; Proverbs 22:6; Proverbs 29:15-17; Matthew 21:16; Luke 18:18-21; and II Timothy 3:15). Authority given to the family and the church is not to be usurped by civil government. Even if the family and church do not fully perform their God-given responsibilities, the civil government must not take these responsibilities unto itself (see, for example, I Samuel 7:14).

Unfortunately, the state and federal governments in our land, particularly in the course of the last century, have usurped the educational responsibility belonging to the family and, in lesser degree, to the church – a responsibility that already had been gradually delegated to local government.

Government education (euphemistically termed "public education" though the public has little control over it) is based upon unbiblical premises just as sinful and destructive (if not as far advanced) as the indoctrination implemented through the educational system of Nazi Germany or the former Soviet Union. Sadly, our own nation is following the same path. Training for citizenship by state-certified teachers has been accepted by the vast majority of Americans to lie within the purview of the state, which has increasingly encroached on the rights of parents (witness courses introduced or being offered in "transcendental meditation," "quietism reflex," "values clarification," sex education, death and suicide education, and anti-nuclear education – to mention only a few), eliminated the influence of the church whenever possible, and engaged in shameless humanistic indoctrination that promotes slanted environmental theories based on pseudo-science, and one-world propaganda that flies in the face of sound scriptural teaching. In all cases, the state mandates what can and can not be taught, determines, to a significant degree, what methods and materials may be used, and attempts to exclude theistic religion. Any system that leaves God out of the equation (as does that imposed upon us by the ideological descendants of Edward Lee Thorndike, John Dewey, and their ilk) is doomed to failure and will bring catastrophe to those who accept it (Genesis 11:1-8 and Romans 1:18-32): how much more calamitous is a system established contrary to the will of God!

The fact is that the civil government is not to promote, administer, or regulate education. Its jurisdiction, according to the Bible, is limited to "bearing the sword" to punish evildoers, maintain the rule of law, and protect those under its authority (Romans 13:1-6 and I Peter 2:13-14). All authority is bestowed by God – the authority of civil government, the authority of the church, the authority of the family, and the authority of all other organizations or governing bodies. Each of these Divinely-ordained institutions has its specified realm of jurisdiction that can not be violated without ignoring, disobeying, or rejecting God's will and thus courting disaster. It is the family, not civil government, that God has charged with educating the young. Although parents may delegate to other agencies (the synagogue or the church, for example) the right to render assistance in the educational process, they can not escape their God-given mandate; for God holds them responsible for the children entrusted to their care (I Samuel 2:22-25 & 27-36).

Our early forefathers understood this very well. They likewise understood that "the fear of the Lord is the beginning of knowledge" (Proverbs 1:7): that all education must be biblically-based and that there is no knowledge or wisdom apart from the One who is "the Way, the Truth, and the Life" (John 14:6) and in whom all things hold together (Colossians 1:15-17). However, as the concepts of the European "Enlightenment" began to be assimilated toward the end of the 18th century and were blended into a religio-philosophic hodge-podge by the Unitarians, 19th-century Americans became susceptible to the deluding currents of transcendentalism, positivism, higher criticism of the Bible, Hegelianism, Darwinism, utilitarianism, pragmatism, and other alluring and heady ideologies or worldviews. In a spiritual sense, they "intermarried" with pagans as surely as had ancient Israel, and they gradually succumbed to the idea of tax-supported public schools, hailed by several educational theorists as "temples" erected to save the nation and humanity.

The messianic, humanist faith was expostulated and promoted by the most influential educational philosopher of the 20th century, John Dewey. He believed that education, properly applied, could redeem society. He discountenanced revealed or self-evident absolutes: experience alone determined reality, and values were valid only in terms of their consequences. One must, therefore, learn by doing, and teachers should be instruments for reshaping a given environment to promote learning. Ideas should be used for a utilitarian purpose, and various forms and means of human activity (collectively employed) should be applied to individual problems but, more importantly, to those of society.

In more modern times, the fallacious hypotheses of psychologists, sociologists, and theorists – from the likes of behaviorists John B. Watson and B.F. Skinner to "situational ethics" advocate Joseph Fletcher and moral relativists Sidney Simon and Lawrence Kohlberg, with their different formulae for determining personal values – have been freely propagated in the "public schools," and, in the last few decades, the influence of UNESCO, Planned Parenthood, the New Age Movement, and all manner of socialist utopians has been increasing.

Is there a solution, a way out? Yes, but not by trying to reform government education as many sincere and well-intentioned educators are proposing. Education that is funded and administered by civil government is contrary to God's established jurisdictional order and will inevitably result either in worship of the state or in idolatrous pursuit of a Satanic world government. By misinterpreting the First Amendment to our Constitution, the judiciary has sought to expunge theistic religion from government schools in the name of "separation of church and state." Notwithstanding the fact that all education is based on some form of religion, the government is perversely determined to remove the Judaic-Christian foundations of this nation's education and culture. It can hardly be otherwise under a government-sponsored educational system that purports to maintain religious neutrality in a pluralistic society. After all, to insure that neither evangelical Protestantism, Catholicism, Judaism, Mormonism, or other formal creeds do not predominate, all are officially excluded, permitting the noxious weeds of secular humanism to assume religion's normative foundational role. What a mockery of religious liberty!

Citizens should not be forced to pay taxes to support government schools that propagate a false religion. On the other hand, if by majority decision evangelical Protestantism were legislated into the curricula of the government schools, what of the religious rights of other groups, including secular humanists and atheists? Obviously, even on the basis of logic or pragmatic arguments, civil government should not be involved in education. In fact, it should get out of the business of education altogether, lowering taxes accordingly and rescinding all restrictive regulations, thereby creating a climate in which private schools can compete in a free market. Schools sponsored by all sorts of religious denominations and private organizations could then blossom forth to the betterment of education and the nation, and parents would be able to choose the school most suited to their children, insuring them a genuinely superior education while obviating or accommodating conflicting interests.

For more than two hundred years of our history when private education, mostly church-supported, prevailed, intellectual achievement was very impressive and the literacy rate was the highest in the world. Within certain geographical confines, parents had the freedom to choose what persons or schools would educate their children – a far cry from the situation imposed today by compulsory attendance legislation.

The monopoly enjoyed by the stultifying indoctrination mills popularly referred to as "public schools" must be broken and the entire "public education" edifice dismantled. Not only is government education unbiblical, it is excessively costly and inefficient (as is almost everything the government does), ineffectual at teaching genuine fundamentals and, more often than not, spiritually degenerate. Seeking to reform schools controlled by self-perpetuating and self-seeking "educationists" (not "educators," for they do not educate) steeped in unbiblical, evolutionary ideologies and wedded to a God-denying behavioristic methodology, is futile – like trying to sew new patches on old garments (Matthew 9:16). The entire, iniquitous system must be eliminated. Only then will true freedom of religious expression and intellectual growth and investigation be possible and God be able to bless the efforts of parents and private schools adhering to biblical patterns of jurisdiction.

Elimination of government schools can not take place overnight, however. Indeed, were they to be abolished too precipitously, chaos might temporarily reign (Exodus 23:29 and Deuteronomy 7:22). Nevertheless, with all deliberate haste, citizens should press Congressmen to eliminate the U.S. Department of Education, dry up funding for the National Institute of Education, and abolish all Federal regulation. At the state level, similar pressure should be exerted to break the ridiculous certification monopoly of the educational establishment, including teachers' colleges and separate education departments. (Pedagogy can be taught more effectively in the student's major area of concentration by requiring him to take one course in teaching methods and to experience a semester of practice teaching.) Under present conditions, teachers might be compared to medical doctors with most of their training in "bedside manner."

Some critics of the present system contend that certification is unnecessary and undesirable: that anyone should be free to advertise his qualifications and solicit students, allowing the free market to determine his ability to teach. However, should some form of certification be required, it should not be under government auspices and control (which is scripturally untenable), but under the supervision of a private agency open to parental input.

Citizens should also agitate at the state and national levels for tax reductions that would necessitate drastic cutbacks in funds earmarked for education. On the average, about 40% of a state's budget is expended on schooling. Vast sums have been squandered on education since 1964 with diminishing returns: as government expenditures have soared, student achievement as measured by standardized examinations has declined. Widespread opposition to school-building projects involving bond issues can be mounted, and within the Christian community, efforts can be made to teach biblical principles of jurisdiction that will call in question the legitimacy of government schooling and encourage parents to assume an informed, active, and perhaps more direct role in their children's education.

One option, home schooling, is a superior means of education and should be undertaken by any parents who can make an investment of time in their children's future. In the unlikely event that parents are not able to educate their children at home, they may wish to delegate this task (but not the primary responsibility) to a church school or some other sound, privately-supported institution. Keeping one's children at home or paying for their private education keeps them out of government schools, thereby protecting them from ungodly influences while, at the same time, assisting in the gradual dissolution of so-called "public education."

Constant vigilance will be necessary, of course; for the teachers' unions and the educational establishment will try to quash home schooling and to extend regulations over private schools. But parents are obliged to maintain their Divinely-ordained right to teach their offspring and to obey God rather than man where questions of jurisdiction arise.

Churches should take the lead in teaching biblical principles of jurisdiction that expose governmental infringement of parental rights to educate their progeny. Once believers become "salt and light" in our society and act in unity against Caesar's control of education, changes will be made; for both politicians and the public at large will be influenced. Parents should be entirely free to choose how and where their children will be educated, and be immune from supporting "public education" – unless, of course, they opt to enroll their children in government schools.

At present, various kinds of voucher schemes are being proposed, whereby the government would allot to parents a certain sum to be used to pay for schooling of their choice. However, the selection must be made from schools designated as government-approved or certified. Why should parents be so limited? Nowhere in God's Word is civil government granted the jurisdiction to impose educational standards. Since parents are responsible for training their children, they must be able to exercise full freedom of choice.

Some observers fear that vouchers given to parents may be construed by the U.S. Supreme Court as a grant to the school in which their children are enrolled, providing bureaucrats with a pretext to extend government regulations over all schools, "public" or private, that accept this indirectly distributed largess. These apprehensions are not without foundation as the U.S. Supreme Court's decision in the case of *Bob Jones University v. the U.S.* (1983) clearly reveals, and the very acceptance of vouchers may be interpreted as tacit recognition of the government's right to issue or deny them. Biblically, there is no such right. The government needs to get completely out of the education business. This is doubtless a shocking statement to many citizens conditioned to go along with the only system they have ever known, but it is nonetheless true.

Apologists for our present tax-supported brainwashing system known as the "public schools" will no doubt continue to feign deep concern for a hypothetical throng of parents who can not afford to educate their children privately. (After all, if Holy Writ, empirical evidence, and logic refute one's arguments, all that is left is a heart-wrenching emotional appeal.) Let it be said in response that even in colonial times special provisions were made to provide schooling for the impoverished, and the challenge to provide an education for the children of indigent parents should call forth a number of creative initiatives from churches and private organizations. Moreover, home schooling is a viable option that any parent can well afford, and there are various types of support groups for parents teaching their children in the home . There are also private schools and agencies willing to provide testing assistance, advice, and sundry types of special services for home schoolers at minimal cost. Never in the history of this nation have persons been unable to procure a basic education for lack of funds; on the other hand, thousands unhappily have failed to do so in the well-heeled but abysmally incompetent government schools. How do apologists dare voice a compelling state interest argument in behalf of these fatuous purveyors of ignorance, dependency, and socialism?

Innovative means of providing sound education for one's own children and those of the putatively needy are too numerous to mention here, but concerned Christians should seize every opportunity to offer schooling as one of their church's ministries to the indigent or disadvantaged, perhaps under the home missions budget. Individuals may also serve as volunteer tutors, teachers, or financial benefactors to needy families. The Bible says that "anyone who gives even a cup of cold water to one of these little ones because he is My [Jesus's] disciple...will certainly not lose his reward" (Matthew 10:42). Individuals should not hesitate to do what they can do even if their church does not operate a school, and a congregation unable to have a school of its own might consider subsidizing a private education for parishioners with two or more school-age children or for needy, unchurched families who would agree to enroll their children in a church school. The Apostle Paul said that he would use any and every means to win the lost. Should a church do any less?

During the 1980's, the Christian Broadcasting Network performed modern-day wonders with its "Sing, Spell, Read, Write" initiative. Similar programs could be undertaken by churches or private agencies; and perhaps cable network presentations especially designed for church schools and Christian home schoolers could be developed and implemented.

There are all manner of creative means of attacking the problems of education within the context of biblical principles. Why, therefore, do we limp along willing to settle for less, looking to civil government rather than God as our source of supply simply because we have become accustomed and conditioned to accepting the *status quo*? Have we accommodated ourselves to the worldly system principally for financial reasons, though we are loath to admit it? If so, God help us! In whom or in what do we put our trust? Let us remember the words of our Lord recorded in Matthew 6:24: "You cannot serve both God and Money!"

In point of fact, groups from the New Evangelical Left, including Evangelicals for Social Action and the publishers of *Sojourners* magazine and the *Otherside* magazine, have propagated their peculiar concepts of institutionalized sin and "social justice." Intimating that the well-to-do have prospered by taking advantage of the poor, they favor state redistribution of wealth – contrary to biblical principles of authority. Paradoxically, the New Evangelical Left advocates pacifism (another doctrine contrary to biblical teaching), thereby rejecting civil government's God-given authority to wield the sword, while at the same time endorsing socialistic solutions to "economic maladjustments" by state management of "public welfare," again distorting and violating jurisdictional boundaries established by God.[14] No wonder confusion prevails in our society when a segment of God's people facilely misconstrues the Bible's teaching concerning the Divinely-instituted spheres of authority.

Leaders in the family, the church, and the national, state, and local governments are accountable to God for exercising their authority lawfully and

---

[14]To examine this subject would take us beyond our discussion of the "Authority Principle." Those who would like to study it further, may wish to read Robert A. Morey's *When is it Right to Fight?* (Bethany House: Minneapolis, MN, 1985) and Francis Schaeffer, Vladimir Bukovsky, and James Hitchcock's *Who is for Peace?* (Thomas Nelson: Nashville, Camden, NY, 1983).

within prescribed jurisdictional bounds. Eli the high priest was censured for not disciplining his sons (I Samuel 2:12-17, 22-25, & 27-36 and I Samuel 3:11-14). Aaron's sons Nadab and Abihu perished for offering unauthorized fire before the Lord (Exodus 10:1-3), and both King Saul (I Samuel 13:7-14) and King Uzziah of Judah (II Chronicles 26:16-21) transgressed by usurping priestly prerogatives and suffered Yahweh's punishment.

Rulers are held responsible for the manner in which they rule as well as their conduct. Righteous rulers bring God's blessing to a nation: but conversely, the sins of rulers adversely affect the entire nation. For example, King David's sins of adultery and murder brought him much personal suffering (despite his repentance and the Lord's forgiveness), and criminal acts and treason on the part of several of his sons were injurious to the nation (II Samuel chapters 11-20 and 24). Israel's King Jeroboam I introduced pagan worship from which the nation never recovered (I Kings 12:26-33 and the remainder of I & II Kings), and later wicked King Ahab instituted Baal worship that affected both Israel and Judah in calamitous ways (I Kings 16:26-33 and sequel). On the other hand, godly monarchs such as Judah's King Hezekiah helped restore spiritual vitality, if only for a short period of time, and material prosperity (II Kings chapters 18 through 20 and II Chronicles chapters 29 through 32).

In a free nation like ours, men and women of God have the right to protest against evil actions and to work for righteous causes. As people of God, we need not only to intercede in behalf of our nation but to rise up and act. Drastic action was taken by Moses against the Israelites who were worshiping the gods of the Moabites (Numbers 25:1-5), and Phineas the priest executed an Israelite and his Midianite wife to stop a plague from which many of God's people were dying (Numbers 25:6-13). We are to be bold in exercising the authority that is ours in Jesus Christ rather than tolerate harassment from Satan (Acts 16:16-18). At the same time, we must not act or speak out of hatred for another person or in our own strength but only as motivated by the Spirit of God in an attitude of servanthood. If we speak as men-pleasers or as self-seekers, our words will lack authority; for, according to God's principle of authority, "whoever wishes to become great..." shall be a servant (Matthew 20:25-28, Luke 22:25-27, John 12:24-26, and John13:3-17).

God has established all authority – of the family, the church, civil government, and that exercised by private agencies and by individuals by reason of their positions. Christians must exercise authority properly and courageously as unto God, recognizing that they are His agents and, therefore, have a responsibility to Him and to their fellow men to exercise the authority entrusted to them.

A young high-school teacher, conscious of his obligation to maintain discipline in a difficult classroom situation for the sake of students desiring to learn, was disciplining a disruptive, unruly pupil by requiring him to remain in the classroom after school was dismissed for the day. About fifty minutes elapsed, with the young man in detention evincing a growing restlessness, when unexpectedly there was a knock at the door. Arising from his desk chair, the teacher opened the door and, seeing no one there, walked outside onto the porch overlooking a part of the campus. Suddenly he was confronted by three tall, rough-looking young men unknown to him. One of them, the apparent leader, planted himself in front of the classroom door and demanded, "When is Fred [the detainee] gittin' out?"

Aware that his colleagues had left school for the day, leaving him no hope for assistance, the teacher fought down the fear trying to arise within him and replied evenly, "That's none of your concern. He'll stay where he is until I decide to release him."

"Well, we want him out now, and he's gittin' out now!" said one of the hoodlums, while the leader brandished a steel rod and queried in a threatening tone, "Hey, man, what'cha think ya can do? What'cha gonna do if I decide to use this on ya?"

"Well, there's one sure way to find out, isn't there?" responded the teacher, looking him straight in the eye and stepping toward him. "Why don't you try it?"

Abashed by this unexpected response, the would-be tough guy hesitated for a split second, whereupon the teacher pushed him aside and brushed past the others with a terse, "Get out of my way!" Quickly he entered the room and latched the door behind him as the three frustrated potential assailants disappeared. The teacher's confident and bold assertion of authority appeared to have won the day, but surely the hand of God was with him, enabling him to prevail.

Authority must be exercised to be effectual. Had the young teacher not exercised his authority, it would matter little that he had the right to do so. If authority is not exercised, it remains useless and may be removed; for God wants his servants to use what he has entrusted to them. Moses surely recognized this when Yahweh ordered him to raise his staff over the sea that was blocking the Israelites' flight from a pursuing Egyptian army. What went through his mind at that moment, we do not know; but we do know what happened when he obeyed God's command: Israel walked through the sea on dry ground and their enemies were drowned when Moses again stretched out his hand and the waters overflowed them (Exodus chapter 14). Moses's successor, Joshua, met a similar test. Commanded by Yahweh to have the priests carry the ark of the covenant into the Jordan River, which was at flood stage, Joshua did not hesitate. He gave the order for the priests to advance into the river. Had he not done so, nothing would have happened. God's miracles occur only when we speak and act in faith. The obedience of Joshua in relaying the Divine command and that of the priests who implemented it moved the hand of God in behalf of Israel: the waters of the Jordan were heaped up as a wall, enabling the peripatetic tribal nation to walk across the river on dry land (Joshua chapter 3).

A Christian who claims to have faith but shrinks from speaking the word of faith or from acting on his alleged faith is like a skydiver who insists he has faith in parachutes, that he knows they work effectively and are perfectly safe, then refuses to jump. James 2:14-26 makes the same point from a somewhat different perspective, stating that "faith without works is dead." David the shepherd boy would never have prevailed over the giant Philistine warrior Goliath had he simply testified that his faith in God would give him the victory. No, he had to go forth to confront his foe in the authority of the Lord God, shouting to the Philistine:

> "You come against me with sword and spear and javelin, but I come against you in the name of the Lord Almighty, the God of the armies of Israel, whom you have defied. This day the Lord will hand you over to me, and I'll strike you down and cut off your head. Today

I will give the carcasses of the Philistine army to the birds of the air and the beasts of the earth, and the whole world will know that there is a God in Israel. All those gathered here will know that it is not by sword or spear that the Lord saves; for the battle is the Lord's, and he will give all of you into our hands" (I Samuel 17:45-48).

Having spoken these words – the words of God, not idle boasting – David went into action, and the Lord delivered the giant into his hand.

In like manner, Christians are to exercise the authority delegated to them from the Father through Jesus Christ (see Ephesians 1:19-23) to carry out the Divine will, knowing that victory can come only through God's power, not through their own abilities; knowing also that even when properly exercising the authority granted them, the immediate results may be unhappy or painful, seemingly futile. Such was the case with our Savior, whose death on the cross seemed to mark a tragic end to His ministry. Such also was the case with the deacon Stephen whose life was snuffed out by men enraged by his testimony about his Messiah; and what of Jim Elliott, missionary to the Auca Indians, whose young life was cut short by the very people to whom he was ministering? In each instance, however, it will be recognized that tremendous victories for the kingdom of God were won through the deaths of God's "only begotten Son" and the faithful and courageous servants mentioned above. The death and resurrection of Jesus Christ made available eternal life for the entire human race, the death of Stephen was a poignant testimony to Saul of Tarsus who later became the indomitable Apostle Paul, and the deaths of Jim Elliott and his comrades was used by God to bring a tribe of vicious headhunters to the Savior. The moving theme from *Man of La Mancha*, "The Impossible Dream," expresses a high and noble, unswerving dedication to worthy goals, but to be submissive to God's will and to be the agent of His grace, order, and blessing is far greater.

All authority bestowed by the Lord God is to be exercised for His glory and the furtherance of His purposes. When this delegated authority is faithfully executed, untold rewards obtain to the designated authority, but also to the society and nation that it serves and to the world.

QUESTIONS TO PONDER

1. Is there a difference between power and authority? Is authority self-generated or does it have a specific source? If the latter is the case, what is the source?

2. What happens when an institution arrogates to itself powers not given to it? What is the result when an institution fails to execute its authority? Why is maintenance of proper lines of authority important?

3. What different areas of authority have been established? Under what types of authority do we live? Does each type of authority have a different jurisdiction? Explain the duties and responsibilities of each. Are these jurisdictions sometimes confused in our contemporary society?

4. Are there particular areas in which civil government in our country has usurped authority? Is it all right for the civil government to assume responsibilities given to other authorities if they do not fulfill their obligations as they should?

5. As Christian citizens, we may be involved in exercising some degree of authority in one or more realms. Are we held responsible for the manner in which we exercise that authority? By whom? What is the result when we fail to exercise the authority conferred upon us?

PERTINENT SCRIPTURES

Genesis 1:26-28; Genesis 9:6; Genesis 18:19; Exodus 10:1-3; Exodus chapter 14; Exodus 18:21; Exodus 21:12-14; Exodus 23:29; Leviticus 19:9-10; Leviticus 23:22; Leviticus 24:17 & 21; Leviticus 25:10-16, 26-43 & 46-49; Numbers 25:6-13; Numbers 26:7-11; Deuteronomy 4:9-14; Deuteronomy 6:1-2, 4-9 & 20-25; Deuteronomy 7:22; Deuteronomy 14:28-29; Deuteronomy 15:1-18; Deuteronomy 16:9-15 & 18-20; Deuteronomy 19:11-13; Deuteronomy 24:17-21; Deuteronomy 26:12-19; Deuteronomy 29:29; Joshua chapter 3; I Samuel 2:12-17, 22-25 & 27-36; I Samuel 3:11-14; I Samuel 7:14; I Samuel 13:7-14; I Samuel 17:45-48; II Samuel chapters 11 through 20 & chapter 24; I Kings 12:26-33; I Kings chapter 16 to the end of the book; II Kings chapters 18 through 20; II Kings 21: 1-16; II Kings 22:1-2 & 13-20; II Chronicles 26:16-21; II Chronicles chapters 29 through 32; Psalm 8:2 & 4-8; Psalm 41:1-3; Psalm 51:6; Psalm 72:12-14; Psalm 78:2 & 4-6; Psalm 82:3-4; Psalm 146:7; Psalm 147:3 & 6; Proverbs 1:7; Proverbs 6:20; Proverbs 16:20 & 32; Proverbs 19:17; Proverbs 22:6 & 9; Proverbs 24:21-22; Proverbs 29:15-17; Proverbs 31:20; Isaiah 5:23; Isaiah 10:1-2; Daniel 2:20-21; Daniel 4:17; Matthew 5:1-16 & 43-48; Matthew 6:1-4 & 24; Matthew 9:35-38; Matthew 10:1 & 5-8; Matthew 10:42; Matthew 20:25-28; Matthew 21:16; Matthew 23:1-3; Matthew 28:18-20; Mark 16:15-18; Luke 2:46-47; Luke 4:18-19; Luke 6:27-36; Luke 9:1-2; Luke 10:27 & 30-37; Luke 14:12-14 & 33-35; Luke 18:18-21; Luke 20:25; Luke 22:25-27; John 12:24-26; John 13:13-17; John 14:6; John 15:4-12; Acts 4:32 & 34-37; Acts 5:1-11; Acts 6:1-4; Acts 16:16-18; Romans 12:20; Romans 13:1-17; Romans 15:1-7; I Corinthians 1:10; I Corinthians 5:1-13; I Corinthians 11:1-16; II Corinthians 3:17; II Corinthians 7:1; II Corinthians 9:6-11; Galatians 2:10; Galatians 5:16-25; Galatians 6:10; Ephesians 1: 19-23; Ephesians 4:12-13; Ephesians 5:21 through 6:4; Colossians 1:12-23 & 27-28; I Timothy 2:11-15; I Timothy 4:13; I Timothy 5:3-16; II Timothy 1:15; II Timothy 2:15; II Timothy 3:14-17; II Timothy 4:2 & 5; Titus 2:1-8 & 15; Titus 3:1; Hebrews 2:4; Hebrews 13:1-3; James 1:27; James chapter 2; James 5:19-20; I Peter 2:9 & 13-17; I Peter 3:1-9; I John 2:5-6; I John 3:17-18; I John 5:2-4; and Jude 20-23.

Chapter XXIX

"THE COVENANT PRINCIPLE"

In its inception, the United States of America was a covenant nation. Unfortunately, the concept of a "covenant nation" is little understood or even known today. However, from early colonial times until well into the 19th century, prominent churchmen and statesmen alike consistently compared the Lord God's covenantal dealings with ancient Israel to His dealings with another "chosen people" – settlers on this continent imbued with common Judaic-Christian values, rights, and interests, and destined to form a "holy commonwealth," a city on a hill." While this attitude was most clearly evident in New England, it was not absent from the other sections of the country. One of the best-known early examples of an appeal to the Supreme Authority as witness to an agreement mutually subscribed to for the creation of a political and social entity was the Mayflower Compact of 1620. Declaring themselves as having undertaken a voyage to plant a colony "for the glory of God and the advancement of the Christian faith and the honor of our King and country," the Plymouth settlers covenanted "to enact, constitute, and frame...just and equal laws, ordinances, acts, constitutions, and officers...." As its title denotes, this was a compact binding together by common consent all of the persons, Puritans and non-Puritans, about to found a small settlement in the New World. It was not merely a contract, that is, an agreement between relatively few persons making a commitment to effect some specific transaction of limited purpose. No, it was the strongest form of all *compacts*, a *covenant*, because it was composed and agreed to under the eyes of the Almighty, the Source and Guarantor of all authority.

The pattern is biblical; for not only did the Lord God make unconditional binding covenants with individuals – Noah (Genesis 8:20 through 9:17), Abram (Genesis 15:4-21), and David (II Samuel 7:5-16 and Psalm 89:1-37), for example – and an affiliate covenant with Abraham and his descendants (conditional on their total consecration to Him as symbolized in the rite of circumcision), but He extended the Abrahamic covenant to the entire nation of Israel at Mount Sinai (Exodus chapters 19 through 24). Conditions of the latter covenant were explicit: Yahweh would be Israel's God, Protector and Provider, and the Guarantor of her

Divinely-established destiny, but His chosen people were to worship Him alone, observe His commandments and appointed feasts, and maintain themselves as a holy nation separated unto Him for the furtherance of His purposes in history.

Similarly, when the Pilgrim community consciously combined "together into a civil body politic," they were forming a "social compact" almost seven decades before John Locke enunciated the concept on scriptural foundations found in the *Magna Carta* and English common law; and by invoking God as witness, they transformed a simple *compact*, requiring only the assent of those formulating it, into a *covenant* sanctioned by the sovereign God, which is reminiscent of ancient Israel's covenantal relationship with Yahweh.

The ancient Hebrews believed in personal responsibility before Almighty God. They were instructed to obey God's decrees and to consecrate themselves wholeheartedly to His worship and service and were warned of the consequences if they should violate the covenant (Deuteronomy 4:4-40; and Deuteronomy 28;l4-68; Leviticus 26:14-39). On the other hand, obedience to the covenant would guarantee continuance of the Lord's blessings (Leviticus 26:l-l3 and Deuteronomy 28:l-l3). Israel renewed the spiritual covenant on several occasions (see, for example, Deuteronomy chapters 29 and 30 and Joshua 24:1-27) but over the centuries failed time and again to honor it, incurring as a result Yahweh's discipline and punishment.

Nevertheless, the Divine covenant with Israel has not been terminated (see Romans chapter ll), and someday all of the "sons of Abraham" (John 8:39-44; Romans 4:llb-17; and Galatians 3:29), Jews and Gentiles alike, will experience together the joy of their salvation by reason of the "new covenant." This "new covenant" is not predicated upon keeping God's law perfectly but on the finished work of the promised Messiah, who kept the entire law perfectly and voluntarily bore the penalty for the sins of everyone, suffering crucifixion – a disgraceful and excruciatingly painful death inflicted upon felons – as the wrath of God the Father was poured out upon Him. Raised from the grave on the third day, Messiah Jesus met on numerous occasions with many of his followers before ascending into heaven to assume the seat of supreme authority with the Father and sending the Holy Spirit to reside within every person who accepts His sacred, once-and-for-all sacrifice by trusting in Him for forgiveness of sins and eternal life (John 3:16; Romans 10:9; Ephesians 2:8-9; and Hebrews 9:ll-l5 & 23-28). Covenants were customarily ratified by the symbolic shedding of blood, so that God's provision of a "sacred lamb" to die for the sins of men, women, and children (none of whom could keep the "covenant of God's law") is aptly termed "the new covenant" or "covenant of grace" (Jeremiah 31:31, Luke 22:20, Hebrews 8:6-13, Hebrews chapter 9, and Hebrews 10:1-18).

The culmination of the spiritual covenant in the life, death, and resurrection of Jesus Christ and the life we experience in Him through faith was of tremendous importance to the founders of this nation. Every colonial charter acknowledged God, and most encouraged the propagation of the Gospel. But if a personal adherence to the covenant of grace was deemed important and the concomitant covenantal body of believers – the church – was fostered, the often closely-affiliated idea of a "civil covenant" also pertained. While the spiritual and civil authorities were separate, each of these God-given jurisdictions complemented and supported the other; and a covenantal view of both seemed propitious and biblically sanctioned. Had not ancient Israel followed a covenantal paradigm in inaugurating a monarchy under King Saul? To be sure, the strapping young Benjaminite had been selected by God and anointed by the respected prophet-judge Samuel (see I Samuel 9:15 and I Samuel 10:1), but the people of Israel still had to accept him and confirm his right to rule (I Samuel 10:17-25 and I Samuel 11:14). The same was true of David, Saul's successor, who had been Divinely designated and anointed for kingship (I Samuel 16:1-13) long before the elders of Israel made a solemn covenant with him, enabling him to exercise royal authority (I Chronicles 11:3).

Thus, Israel's monarchs assumed the throne by reason of a solemn covenant with the people they were to govern, with the understanding that both parties were to observe the Divine will. "If you fear the Lord and serve and obey Him and do not rebel against His commands, and if both you and the king who reigns over you follow the Lord your God – good! But if you do not obey the Lord, and you rebel against His commands, His hand will be against you, as it was against your fathers" (I Samuel 12:14-15).

Accordingly, religious and civil covenants were closely identified. In fact, it would appear from II Chronicles 11:17 that royal coronation rested upon a dual covenant: one an oath before God by monarch and people that they would be true to their Divine Sovereign; the other a compact between king and people requiring just and godly rule. According to the Huguenot author of *Vindiciae contra tyrannos* (1579) and Scotsman Samuel Rutherford in *Lex Rex* (1644), the foregoing biblical passages established a mutual obligation on the part of the people and their ruler, subject to Divine oversight. If infractions of the covenant should occur, protests were in order, though mere incompetence and dereliction of duty should be borne with patience. On the other hand, a ruler's infringement of the covenant by abrogating or violating God-given moral law, trampling on his people's natural and lawful rights, resorting to tyrannical acts, and perverting justice rendered the compact void, releasing the people from their oath of obedience. Although the people as a whole were not to take matters into their own hands, the lesser magistrates were obliged to resist a tyrannical prince and to replace him, if possible, with one who would uphold the covenant.

It is obvious that these views, grounded in biblical covenant theology and amplified by John Locke, provided justification for the Declaration of Independence, the founding document of our nation. Moreover, most state constitutions were drafted in covenantal terms that reveal the influence of the old colonial compacts. Although the United States Constitution, promulgated with the appended "Bill of Rights" twenty-five years after the birth of our nation, does not explicitly mention God (such reference had already been made in the nation's founding document), its provisions accord with biblical principles. The concept of the separation of powers, the requirement that the chief executive be a natural-born citizen, the premise that he may be removed from office for "treason, bribery, and other high Crimes and Misdemeanors," and the provision that nobody be convicted for treason without his confession in open court or the testimony of at least two witnesses are examples. Beyond such specific stipulations and despite similarities to a charter, the Constitution has assumed a covenantal aura that makes it more than simply a legal contract, thanks in no small part to the appendage of the First Ten Amendments guaranteeing citizen's rights (adopted in December 1791). This inherent spiritual element is recognized in the solemn inaugural ceremony requiring an elected President to place his hand on the Bible and swear in the presence of God and man to uphold and defend the Constitution. It is also evident in similar oaths required of Congressmen, federal judges, and other public officials.

For about two hundred years, our nation's religious heritage and her covenant-based founding documents were revered. Looking back upon the nation's founding, Secretary of State John Quincy Adams proclaimed on July 4, 1821:

"The highest glory of the American Revolution was this: it connected, in one indissoluble bond, the principles of civil government with the principles of Christianity.... From the day of the Declaration.... [the American people] were bound by the laws of God, which they all, and the laws of the Gospel, which they nearly all, acknowledged as the rules of their conduct."[15]

In 1891, the United States Supreme Court (*Church of the Holy Trinity v. United States*) declared:

"Our laws and our institutions must necessarily be based upon and embody the teachings of the Redeemer of mankind. It is impossible that it should be otherwise; and in this sense and to this extent our civilization and our institutions are emphatically Christian...: this is a religious people. This is historically true. From the discovery of this continent to the present hour, there is a single voice making this affirmation...: we find everywhere a clear recognition of the same truth... this is a Christian nation."

Even liberal justice William O. Douglas, speaking for the U.S. Supreme Court in the case of *Zorach v. Clauson* (1952), asserted that "...we are a religious people and our institutions presuppose a Supreme Being."

Sadly, however, the Hebrew prophet Isaiah's statement (Isaiah 29:13) that "these people honor Me [God] with their lips, but their hearts are far from Me" (restated by our Lord as recorded in Matthew 15:8 and Mark 7:6) is apropos to our contemporary society. God's sovereignty in the affairs of state is neither acknowledged by the majority of our people nor does it enter their minds that we were founded as a "covenant nation" and, therefore, are still bound to protect and preserve the covenant with God and the integrity of the compact between citizens and their public servants. Instead, we have tried to discourage or eliminate any

---

[15]Quoted in "Letter from Plymouth Rock," November 1983 (published by the Plymouth Rock Foundation of Marlborough, New Hampshire).

reference to God in our "public schools" and the public arena and to introduce all manner of fashionable individual "rights" contrary to God's Word and never imagined by our forefathers. Furthermore, we have misinterpreted and misapplied the Constitution to conform with current opinions and faddish "isms" while adopting a supercilious attitude toward Holy Writ and scriptural moral standards, disdain for biblical absolutes, and contempt for any person or agency bold enough to assert their veracity and pertinence or to endeavor to act upon them. The church has been marginalized, in many instances co-opted, and biblical precepts are scorned as irrelevant or even "hateful."

These corrupt, corrosive, and God-denigrating currents were surely in Presidential candidate Ronald Reagan's mind when he stated in 1980: "The time has come to turn to God and reassert our trust in Him for the healing of America.... Our country is in need of and ready for a spiritual renewal...."[16]

Our nation, like ancient Israel, is a covenant nation, though we have turned our back on the God of our fathers. Let no one be deluded. The fact that there are more Christians in this land than anywhere else and that we are still preaching God's Word at home and proclaiming it overseas will not palliate the Almighty or avert judgment for our individual and national sins. If Israel, His chosen people, did not escape judgment when the nation fell into apostasy and sin, how can we escape? If God did not spare the native stock (Israel). He will not spare the branches grafted into the root (Romans 11:17-22).

Our nation and many other nations – especially Third World nations – are looking to the wrong source, putting their trust in man rather than their Maker. Elihu in Job 35:9-13 speaks to this perverse attitude of heart, noting that when the poor cry out against their oppressors but refuse to recognize God as their source, He gives no heed to them:

> "Men cry out under a load of oppression; they plead for relief from the arm of the powerful. But no one says 'Where is God my Maker, who gives songs in the night, who teaches more to us than to the beasts of the earth and makes us wiser than the birds of the air?' He does not answer when men cry out because of the arrogance of the

---

[16] Quoted in *Letter from Plymouth Rock*, November 1983.

wicked. Indeed, God does not listen to their empty plea; the Almighty pays no attention to it."

Individuals and nations who do look to God and seek His righteousness in these harrowing times will be satisfied and blessed (Matthew 5:6 & 10 and Matthew 6:33-34). God honors those who honor Him. Persons who honor the Lord in their lives are about to come into their heritage. They will be diligent in their work (Proverbs 10:4; Proverbs 18:9; Proverbs 22:29; Galatians 1:10; Ephesians 6:5-8; and Colossians 3:22-24), performing even arduous or routine and boring tasks as unto the Lord – not working, as do "men-pleasers," only when a supervisor is around. Moreover, many will receive superior educations in the home or in private Christian schools and will apply Christian principles in their everyday lives, enhancing their opportunities for "success" in the most positive sense of the term. Many will prosper and be promoted to positions of leadership. The same applies to nations.

The admonition of Matthew 5:16 (NASB): "Let your light shine before men in such a way that they see your good works and glorify your Father who is in heaven" applies both to individuals and to covenant nations. Certainly it has applied to Israel – the nation chosen by God to teach His ways to all mankind and provide salvation through the Messiah. It should also apply to the United States – a nation conceived in covenant principles, blessed by God, and used to spread the light of the Gospel throughout the world. But we have departed from the covenant; therefore we will suffer the consequences of our sins. Yet God's mercy triumphs over judgment (cf. James 2:13); and, out of our affliction, misery, degradation, anguish, and spiritual torment can come restoration if we will repent, even at this late hour, and return to our covenant-keeping God.

At this very moment, a titanic spiritual, intellectual, and cultural struggle for the soul of this nation is being waged, which will determine if our children and grandchildren and all subsequent generations will enjoy the God-given liberties we have known. The pervasive powers of Mammon, vested interests, the media, and Antichrist are strong. Will we repent in time, renounce our sins, accept God's revealed Truth, and see to it that righteousness will prevail in our institutions, society, and culture, so that we may insure to ourselves and to our posterity the blessings attending a faithful covenant nation?

QUESTIONS TO PONDER

1. In your mind, what does a covenant entail?

2. What is the difference between a contract, a simple compact, and a covenant?

3. Compare the covenant God made with Noah in Genesis 8:20 through 9:17 with that made with Abram in Genesis 15:4-18. Are there any common elements?

4. God has made covenants not only with His faithful servants, but with nations. As you reflect on God's covenant with the nation of Israel (Deuteronomy 4:4-40), what elements stand out?

5. Has God ever broken or terminated His covenant with Israel? Did the manner in which Israel observed the covenant oblige God to keep His end of it? (Psalm 25:10 and Psalm 103:17-18.)

6. Why did God establish the "new covenant" as mentioned in Matthew 26:28, Luke 22:20, II Corinthians 3:6, and several passages in Hebrews (including Hebrews 8:6-13 and Hebrews 13:20)? Are there similarities between the "new covenant" and the "old covenant"? Are there any distinguishing characteristics?

7. Have any nations besides Israel consciously founded themselves on covenant principles? Examples? Evidence?

8. Are covenantally-founded nations immune to the adversities, defeats, and sufferings that other nations undergo or are they perhaps even more likely to experience Divine discipline?

PERTINENT SCRIPTURES

Genesis 8:20 through 9;17; Genesis 15:4-21; Genesis 17:1-24; Exodus 6:2-5; Exodus chapters 19 through 24; Leviticus 26:9-45; Deuteronomy 4:4-40; Deuteronomy 5:2-21; Deuteronomy chapters 28 through 30; Joshua 24:1-27; I Samuel 9:15; I Samuel 10:1 & 17-25; I Samuel 11:14; I Samuel 12:14-15; I Samuel 16:1-13; II Samuel 7:5-16; I Chronicles 11:13; II Chronicles 11:17; II Chronicles 29:10; Job 35:9-13; Psalm 25:10; Psalm 33;12; Psalm 89:1-37; Psalm 103:17-18; Psalm 105:8-11; Psalm 111:9; Psalm 115:9-15; Proverbs 10:4; Proverbs 18:9; Proverbs 22:29; Isaiah 29:13; Jeremiah 31:31; Matthew 5:6 &10; Matthew 6:33-34; Matthew 15:8; Matthew 26:28; Mark 7:6; Mark 14:24; Luke 22:20; John 3:16; John 8:39-44; Romans 4:11-17; Romans 10:9; Romans chapter 11; II Corinthians 3:6; Galatians 1:10; Galatians 3:29; Ephesians 2:8-9; Ephesians 6:5-8; Colossians 3:22-24; Hebrews 8:6-13; Hebrews chapter 9; Hebrews 10:1-18; Hebrews 12:24; Hebrews 13:20; and James 2:13.

Chapter XXX

"THE PRINCIPLE OF PRAISE"

"Clap your hands, *all you nations*; shout to God with cries of joy!" (Psalm 47:1.) "Shout with joy to God, *all the earth*! Sing the glory of His name; make His praise glorious!" (Psalm 66:1-2.) "Praise our God, *O peoples*, let the sound of His praise be heard" (Psalm 66:8).

To all too many people, praising God is merely a pious gesture that may make a person feel better as he offers adoration, either privately or in public assembly; but Scripture informs us that the Lord inhabits (or is enthroned upon) the praises of His people (Psalm 22:3). If we yearn for His presence, if we want to experience victory in our personal lives or the life of our church or of our nation, we should praise Him. "How blessed are the people who know the joyful sound! O Lord, they walk in the light of Thy countenance. In Thy name they rejoice all the day, And by Thy righteousness they are exalted. For Thou art the glory of their strength, And by Thy favor our horn is exalted" (Psalm 89:15-17, NASB).

In the presence of the Lord is "fullness of joy" (Psalm 16:11, NASB). As the New International Version puts it, "You have made known to me the path of life; You will fill me with joy in Your presence, with eternal pleasures at Your hand" (Psalm 16:11) and with the strength attending the "joy of the Lord" (Nehemiah 8:10). Spiritual deliverance from oppression can come when we praise God for His salvation and His mighty deeds (Psalm 86:12-13). As the Spirit of praise arises within us and fills our beings, the immediacy, wonder, and sweetness of His presence carries us beyond praise into heartfelt worship – unreserved and supreme adoration and homage for whom He is. Where the Spirit of the Lord is, there is liberty, deliverance from every demonic entity or influence, and victory over forces of the Enemy and the problems of this world.

Confidence in the sure and imminent deliverance of the Lord is joyously expressed in Psalm 108:1-6:

"My heart is steadfast, O God;
I will sing and make music with all my soul.
Awake harp and lyre!
I will awaken the dawn.
I will praise You, O Lord, among the nations;
I will sing of You among the peoples.
For great is Your love, higher than the heavens;
Your faithfulness reaches to the skies.
Be exalted, O God, above the heavens,
and let Your glory be over all the earth.
Save us and help us with Your right hand,
that those You love may be delivered."

Psalm 95:1-2 exhorts God's people to praise and honor their Lord:

"Come, let us sing for joy to the Lord;
let us shout aloud to the Rock of our salvation.
Let us come before Him with thanksgiving
and extol Him with music and song."

This exhortation approximates a command in Philippians 4:4: "Rejoice in the Lord *always*. I will say it again: Rejoice!" Hebrews 13:15 reiterates the need for offering thanksgiving and praise *at all times*, not just when we feel like doing it: "let us *continually* offer to God *a sacrifice of praise*...." Such a "sacrifice" is fitting when we are most discouraged and disinclined to offer thanks and praise to the Heavenly Father; it is also often most efficacious in times of great distress and need. Psalm 50:14-15 & 23 confirms this:

"*Sacrifice* thank offerings to God (cf. Psalm 107:22), fulfill your vows to the Most High, and call upon Me in the day of trouble; I will deliver you, and you will honor Me.... He who *sacrifices* thank offerings honors Me, and he prepares the way so that I may show him the salvation of God."

The Apostle Paul and his missionary companion Silas offered a "sacrifice of praise" to their Lord after being imprisoned in the Macedonian capital of Philippi for preaching the Gospel and casting a spirit of fortune-telling out of a slave girl. Mercilessly flogged and incarcerated in a miserable cell with shackles on their feet, God's faithful emissaries, undismayed by their painful predicament, prayed and sang hymns to the glory of the Lord of the universe ("songs of deliverance" as it turned out: see Psalm 32:7). Their "sacrifice of praise" (surely evidence of lunacy or futile bravado in the estimation of their incredulous fellow prisoners) moved the hand of God. A violent earthquake shook the prison to its foundations, opening all the doors and striking off all the fetters so that the terrified jailer, knowing that he would forfeit his life should the prisoners escape, prepared to kill himself. At that very instant, God's "bond slave" became master of the situation, shouting, "Don't harm yourself! We are all here!" The awe-stricken jailer, still trembling, fell down before Paul and Silas and then, leading them toward his abode, earnestly asked, "What must I do to be saved?" They replied, "Believe in the Lord Jesus Christ and you will be saved – you and your household" (Acts 16:22-34).

What an evangelistic service took place in that household in the middle of the night, and what a lasting affect it had! Paul, who previously had wanted to go into Asia Minor, was assured by this marvelous deliverance that he was to continue his ministry in Europe, and henceforth he carried out his Divine commission with confident fervor. Thus, a turning point in history – leading to the evangelization of Europe and the West – was precipitated by Paul's obedience to the "Macedonian call" and his offering, with his co-worker, a "sacrifice of praise" in the midst of great adversity!

Praise and worship invoke God's presence; demonstrate implicit trust in Him; put to flight doubt, fear, and despondency; engender in the worshiper faith and an expectant, confident spirit; and, therefore, unleash God's power, just as flipping a switch will precipitate the flow of a powerful electrical current to effect a particular purpose.

Praise is much more than simply a private exercise or even a ritual celebration in churches and synagogues of God's sovereignty, greatness, and love: it is our lifeline to the Creator of the universe and the key to rejuvenation of our society and institutions. That the principle of praise is applicable in matters of national import is seen in an incident related in I I Chronicles 20:1-29. A hostile coalition was ready to attack the nation of Judah during the reign of godly King Jehoshaphat, who proclaimed a fast and led the nation in prayer.

Encouraged by a Word from God spoken through one of the prophets, the king sent out a male "choir" to lead his armed forces against the enemy. As these singers lifted up their voices in praise and adoration to Yahweh, the Lord caused dissension in the ranks of the hostile armies so that they began to destroy one another. In fact, God's people did not even need to wield the sword but only to gather the spoil; for the enemy was wiped out by Divine agency, and God's people jubilantly praised their Almighty Deliverer.

Salvation belongs to the Lord! Let us pray that our nation will repent and turn to the eternal God with unfeigned praise and purified hearts! His "ear" is always open to the contrite of heart, and His "arm" is always ready to intervene in their behalf. Therefore, let His people rejoice in Him, leading the nation in sincere, exultant praise!

> "Sing joyfully to the Lord, you righteous;
>> it is fitting for the upright to praise Him.
> Praise the Lord with the harp;
>> make music to Him on the ten-stringed lyre.
> Sing to Him a new song;
>> play skillfully, and shout for joy.
> For the word of the Lord is right and true;
>> He is faithful in all He does.
> The Lord loves righteousness and justice;
>> the earth is full of His unfailing love.
> By the word of the Lord were the heavens made
>> their starry host by the breath of His mouth.
> He gathers the waters of the sea into a heap;
>> He puts the deep into storehouses.
> Let all the earth fear the Lord;
>> let all the people of the world revere Him.
> For He spoke, and it came to be;
>> He commanded, and it stood firm.
> The Lord foils the plans of the nations;
>> He thwarts the purposes of the peoples.
> But the plans of the Lord stand firm forever,
>> the purposes of His heart through all generations.
> Blessed is the nation whose God is the Lord,

the people He chose for His inheritance" (Psalm 33:12).

QUESTIONS TO PONDER

1. Beyond lifting our spirits, do praise and worship of God bring any practical benefits? Explain.

2. What types of changes are brought about by praise and worship? Why?

3. Is there a difference between praise and worship? If so, how would you explain the distinction?

4. Can any major changes in situations or occurrences in history be attributed to praise and worship?

5. Does the Bible teach that nations as well as individuals should praise the Lord?

PERTINENT SCRIPTURES

II Chronicles 20:1-29; Nehemiah 8:10; Psalm 16:11; Psalm 22:3; Psalm 32:7; Psalm 33:1-12; Psalm 40:3; Psalm 47; Psalm 48:1-3; Psalm 50:14-15 & 23; Psalm 51:15; Psalm 66:1-2, 8, & 20; Psalm 71:6-8; Psalm 79:13; Psalm 86:12-13; Psalm 89:15-17; Psalm 95:1-2; Psalm 100:1-5; Psalm 106:1-3; Psalm 107:22; Psalm 108:1-6; Psalm 147:1-12; Psalm 148; Psalm 149; Psalm 150; Jeremiah 17:26; Matthew 21:16; Acts 16:22-34; Romans 15:7-13; II Corinthians 1:3-7;

Ephesians 1:1-14; Philippians 4:4; Hebrews 13:15; Revelation 5:13-14; and Revelation 7:11-12.

Chapter XXXI

"THE PRINCIPLE OF DILIGENCE AND PERSEVERENCE"

The Bible exhorts God's people to be diligent in their work, persistent in prayer, and perseverant in trials and in their walk with the Lord. Matthew 11:12 tells us that "the kingdom of heaven has been forcefully advancing, and forceful men lay hold of it." Moses was a forceful man though meek, and so was Jesus. They were determined, single-minded, courageous, indomitable, diligent, and persistent in proclaiming and doing the will of the Father.

Throughout history, heroes and heroines of the faith have possessed and manifested these same qualities: Jeremiah the prophet (d. 584 B.C.), the deacon Stephen (first century), Paul the Apostle (died about 67 A.D.), Athanasius (d.373), Augustine's mother Monica (4th century), Winfrith of Nursling ("St. Boniface," d.755), Pope Gregory VII (r. 1073-1085), Jan Hus (d.1415), William Tyndale (d.1536), Martin Luther (d.1546), Francis Xavier (d. 1552), "Brother Lawrence" (17th century), William Carey (1761-1834), David Livingstone (d.1873), Charles Finney (d.1875), George Müller (d.1898), Hudson Taylor (d.1905), Presbyterian pastor Bob Childress (d.1956), Nelson Bell, Richard Wurmbrand, Nora Lamb, and Joni Erikson Tata to mention only a few representative examples.

The "father of our nation," George Washington, lacked adequate support from the Continental Congress during the War for Independence and lost a number of battles against the British, but he persevered until victory was attained and continued to provide stable, godly leadership for the infant United States during his two terms as President.

Diligence and perseverence are virtues ordained by God. Proverbs 10:4 informs us: "Lazy hands make a man poor, but diligent hands bring wealth"; Proverbs 18:9 declares: "One who is slack in his work is brother to one who destroys"; Proverbs 12:24 states: "Diligent hands will rule, but laziness ends in slave labor"; and Proverbs 22:29 puts forward the axiom: "Do you see a man skilled [or diligent] in his work? He will serve before kings; he will not serve before obscure men." The New Testament emphatically reiterates the principle of diligence and persistence. In Matthew 7:7-8, we read:

> "Ask [and "keep on asking"] and it will be given to you; seek [and "keep on seeking"] and you will find; knock [and "keep on knocking"] and the door will be opened to you. For everyone who asks ["keeps on asking"] receives; he who seeks ["keeps on seeking"] finds; and to him who knocks ["keeps on knocking"], the door will be opened" (see also verses 9-11).

Luke 11:9-10 states the same thing, and the preceding verses (5 through 8) illustrate the point with the story of a man who goes to a friend's home in the middle of the night to ask for food to set before an unexpected guest. Although the disgruntled householder at first refuses to arise from bed to answer the request, he ultimately does so because of his friend's importunity.

The point is further emphasized in verses 11-13:

> "Which of you fathers, if your son asks for a fish, will give him a snake instead? Or which if he asks for an egg, will give him a scorpion? If you then, though you are evil, know how to give good gifts to your children, how much more will your Father in heaven give the *Holy Spirit* to those who ask Him!"

The parable of the unjust judge lends further corroboration to the principle that God's people should persist in prayer, for although the unrighteous judge time and again refused to take up the cause of a poor widow, he finally relented because of her persistence: "Even though I don't fear God or care about men," he reasoned to himself, "yet because this widow keeps bothering me, I will see that she gets justice, so that she won't eventually wear me out...!" Commenting upon this illustration, Jesus assured His followers that, though a godless and corrupt judge may only reluctantly yield to importunate entreaty, their petitions would be welcomed by a loving Father and answered quickly (Luke 18:1-8).

Still, God sometimes may delay answering petitions for our own good. He is sovereign, and He alone knows what is best for us. Only a careless human parent would hand a sharp knife to a small child begging for it, but would wait

326

until the child was old enough and sufficiently mature to handle a knife without endangering himself. God is not a cosmic Santa Claus who can be manipulated to bestow everything we want whenever we want it. He wants to develop positive Christian traits in us that will glorify Him, make us spiritual overcomers, and enhance our ability to help others and be useful citizens – traits such as faith, submission to His will and to lawful authority, patience, commitment, industry, and perseverence. These are not attained effortlessly or instantaneously: maturity in the Lord or in this present life does not come easily. God may lavish blessings upon us at times but confer them slowly and discreetly at other times, in accord with His wisdom and eternal purpose; but He wants us to come before Him with trusting, childlike expectation and to be sufficiently serious in our prayer requests to persevere.

Unlike many human parents, God is not irritated but rather pleased when we continue to come to Him with sincere and heartfelt requests. An eight-year-old boy was pestering his dad for a wrist watch. After hearing his son's request for the umteenth time, the father finally said, "Billy, I don't want to hear any more about your wanting a watch!" At dinner that evening, every member of the family was asked to recite a favorite Scripture verse. When Billy's turn came, he said, "My verse is Mark 13:37: 'and what I say to you, I say to all, *watch!*'."

Who can doubt that because of his persistence, Billy eventually received the watch he desired? If the burden for presenting a particular petition does not go away, we should persist in offering it with unflagging faith. Just as we are not to become "weary in doing good," because we "will reap if we do not give up" (Galatians 6:9), so we should not yield to discouragement in the prayer closet. When Daniel's insistent plea for understanding was not answered immediately, he did not cease to pray; and after considerable delay owing to demonic interference, he received the answer for which he had been yearning.

God's heart is always open to us, though our faith sometimes begins to waver when nothing appears to be happening in response to repeated petitions. In such cases, it might be helpful simply to praise Him for what He has already done for us and thank Him in advance for the anticipated answer (see Philippians 4:6 and Mark 11:24). Certainly our spirits will be uplifted and attuned to our Lord's will as we extol and thank Him; and anxiety, which can hinder our prayers, will be banished. We can then rest in the peace of His presence and the assurance that He will do what is best for us.

As Christians, we are to "consider it pure joy" whenever we encounter trials, knowing that the testing of our faith develops perseverence and perseverence brings us to spiritual maturity (cf. James 1:2-4). As Paul states elsewhere, "We rejoice in our sufferings, because we know that suffering produces perseverence; perseverence, character; and character, hope" (Romans 5:3-4), enabling us to be overcomers in this world.

Without the struggle, we would not be prepared for survival, let alone for triumphant living. An author looked up from his work and peering through the window, saw a cocoon on the back deck of his home. Out of curiosity, he went out, picked it up, and placed it gently on the sill of his study window. For a number of days, he almost forgot about it until one morning his eyes were drawn to the cocoon where something quite amazing was occurring. Something was trying to emerge. The cocoon was being assaulted from within! A titanic struggle for new life was taking place! But each time the struggling moth seemed about to come forth, its efforts were frustrated. Impatiently, the writer reached into the top drawer of his desk, procured a small scissors, and snipped the remaining strands of the cocoon to assist the emerging butterfly. Sadly, however, as it tried to spread its beautiful wings, it suddenly expired. Several days later, the writer related the incident to a friend, an amateur naturalist, who tersely remarked, "You killed the butterfly."

"No, no, quite to the contrary. I tried to help it – it was going through such a terrible struggle!"

"Just so, you killed it," his friend repeated. "The struggle is absolutely necessary to release certain fluids essential for the butterfly's survival. You interfered with the natural process, causing it to die."

When handled properly, trials strengthen us and cause us to grow in our faith and to succeed in the everyday business of living. As weight lifters are apt to say, "No pain, no gain." There is no substitute for overcoming difficulties through hard work, diligence, and persevering effort.

The principle of diligence and perseverence, like many of the other principles, has both a natural and a spiritual relevance and is applicable to non-believers as well as to believers. On the football gridiron or the battlefield, victory is seldom won without a determined, persistent effort. John Paul Jones, generally acclaimed as the founder of the American Navy, evinced an indomitable, triumphant spirit when with his ship sinking beneath his feet he replied to a British captain's suggestion that he surrender with the words, "Sir, I have not yet begun to fight!"

Union General Ulysses S. Grant manifested much the same resolute attitude during the "wilderness campaign" against General Robert E. Lee's Confederates when, despite very heavy losses, he dispatched the message to Washington on May 11, 1864: "I propose to fight it out on this line if it takes all summer."

While stubbornness in waging war or standing alone in defending honorable principles may be considered admirable or advantageous in certain situations, it is usually thought of as a pridefully motivated vice, inconsistent with the biblical concept of meek and persevering strength in the service of righteousness and justice. The Lord God was ready to destroy the Israelites for being a "stiff-necked," disobedient people (Exodus 33:3 and Deuteronomy 9:6 & 13-14); yet pertinacity in following Him is a virtue, and perhaps the stubbornness of the Jews has enabled them to endure as a people.

Jesus admonished His followers to be steadfast, telling them: "All men will hate you because of Me, but he who stands firm to the end will be saved" (Matthew 10:22). In respect to the end of the age, He also stated: "Because of the increase of wickedness, the love of most will grow cold, but he who stands firm to the end will be saved" (Matthew 24:13).

The message, therefore, is to persevere in adhering to Jesus Christ and biblical precepts, but persistence in pursuit of beneficial or praiseworthy goals is also to be encouraged. William Wilberforce (d. 1833) spent his Parliamentary career courageously doing everything in his power to eliminate commercial traffic in slaves and human bondage within the British Empire. His perseverence paid off, though he died one month before all of his anti-slavery agenda were realized. Blessings have also redounded to mankind because of the persistence of other noted personages: Noah Webster expended thirty-six years in compiling a dictionary; Thomas Edison performed hundreds of fruitless experiments before discovering the tungsten filament that enabled him to introduce the incandescent light bulb in 1879; Tuskegee Institute's George Washington Carver persevered with his research until he discovered scores of uses for peanuts, sweet potatoes, and soybeans and many products from cotton waste that improved the economy and the condition of black people; and Robert E. Peary failed seven times to discover the North Pole before reaching it and claiming it for the United States on his final expedition.

The premise of the efficacy of industry and perseverence is sound. It has been proven many times over and in virtually every realm of human endeavor. Certainly, determination and tenacious dedication to a goal are essential to the success of any great athlete, successful politician, noteworthy musician, or heroic figure; and God's people need to be actively involved in trying to influence society, government, and culture. Refusal to become involved is tantamount to countermanding the Creator's dominion mandate and will incur his disapprobation.

It is a sad commentary on our lack of perseverence when political operatives are prone to believe that opinions or protests from Christians can be taken lightly. Christian activists may be upset about a particular issue, it has been observed, but they will not be around for "the long haul."

Even nations, as we have seen earlier, are created to serve God's predestined ends; and God's people, of all people, should be about their Father's business, proclaiming His Good News, doing His work, demolishing "arguments and every false pretension that sets itself against the knowledge of God," taking "captive every thought to make it obedient to Christ" (II Corinthians 10:5), and endeavoring to extend His spiritual dominion and principles throughout the earth (Matthew 28:18-20) by His prescribed methods and enabling. Although the times are evil, we are to persevere until our Lord's return. In this wicked, God-denying, spiritually-blind world, we are to be "steadfast, immovable, always abounding in the work of the Lord," being assured that labor of that sort in never in vain (cf. I Corinthians 15:58).

QUESTIONS TO PONDER

1. Is indolence pleasing to God? Is failure to stick to projects the Lord has given us to do pleasing to God? How do you know? Evidence?

2. Is God irritated or provoked if we continue in prayer, repeating the same petitions over a period of time? How do you know? How can we know when to stop praying?

3. Why are God's responses to our prayer petitions sometimes delayed?

4. How is praising God an aid to an effective prayer life?

5. Do trials and difficulties have a positive side? What must we do to attain the benefits?

6. Do biblical principles apply exclusively to believers? Do they apply in everyday life as well as in the spiritual realm? Can unbelievers benefit from following principles established in the Bible?

7. Even though certain personality traits are generally negative in character, can they be transformed to make them acceptable and advantageous?

8. Does human experience as recorded in history confirm the validity of the principle of diligence and perseverence? Examples?

9. Should Christians withdraw from the affairs of this world to maintain their purity? What does God expect of us?

10. Does the principle of diligence and perseverence apply to nations as well as to individuals?

PERTINENT SCRIPTURES

Exodus 32:9; Exodus 33:3; Deuteronomy 4:7-9; Deuteronomy 6:6-19; Deuteronomy 9:6 & 13-14; Deuteronomy 11:22-25; Deuteronomy 28:1-2; Proverbs 10:4; Proverbs 12:24; Proverbs 13:4; Proverbs 18:9; Proverbs 22:29; Matthew 7:7-11; Matthew 10:22; Matthew 24:13; Matthew 28:18-20; Mark 11:24; Luke 8:15; Luke 11:5-13; Luke 18:1-8; Luke 21:19; Acts 14:22; Romans 5:3-5; Romans 12:8; I Corinthians 15:58; II Corinthians 10:5; Ephesians 6:18; Galatians 6:9; Philippians 2:16; Philippians 4:6; II Timothy 2:15; II Timothy 4:5; Hebrews 3:14; Hebrews 6:11-15; Hebrews 10:35-39; Hebrews 11:6; Hebrews 12:1-7; James 1:2-4 & 12; James 5:7-11; I Peter 2:19-21; I Peter 5:6-10; and II Peter 1:5-11.

Chapter XXXII

SIGNS OF THE TIMES

In these tumultuous, uncertain years on the threshold of a new millennium, Christians must understand the times like the ancient men of Issachar (I Chronicles 12:32). The lessons gleaned from past history are important, but also we need to discern what is happening today beneath the veil of deception woven by the media elite, international power brokers, and government insiders. Surely the principle of intimate communion with our God through prayer, meditation, and listening to His "still, small voice" should be a matter of daily practice and constant awareness, for it is our very lifeline.

Scripture commands us to "pray without ceasing" (I Thessalonians 5:17; cf. Romans 12:12), to "pray *always* in the Spirit" (Ephesians 6:18), and to be on the alert when deception, wickedness, persecution of the righteous, and tidings of wars, famines, and natural disasters assail us (Matthew 24:4-11). In the "last days," we are told, "people will be lovers of themselves, lovers of money, boastful, proud, ungrateful, unholy, without love, unforgiving, slanderous, without self-control, brutal, not lovers of good, treacherous, rash, conceited, lovers of pleasure rather than lovers of God – having a form of godliness but denying its power" (II Timothy 3:2-5). "In fact, everyone who wants to live a godly life in Christ Jesus will be persecuted, while evil men and imposters [including false prophets and fake Messiahs] will go from bad to worse, deceiving and being deceived" (II Timothy 3:12-13). "Because of the increase of wickedness, the love of most will grow cold [witness the apathy within the contemporary church], but *he who stands firm to the end* will be saved" (Matthew 24:12-13). Like Jesus's inner circle of disciples, we are being called to "watch and pray" (so that we will not be overwhelmed by temptation) and to teach Scripture and scriptural principles to equip fellow believers to persist in righteousness and good works even in the most trying circumstances (cf. Matthew 26:41 and II Timothy 3:15-17).

God's judgment of the United States has already begun and will become apparent to anyone with a modicum of spiritual discernment before long.

Violence, crime, and drug and alcohol abuse are endemic in this country; the economy (notwithstanding several years of unprecedented prosperity) is shaky; corruption, deception, chicanery, and immorality are evident even in the highest offices of the land; political strife, lawlessness, idolatry in many forms, and disrespect for God and His Word are evident everywhere; divorce, abortion, adultery, homosexuality, pornography, vulgarity, and other attacks on the family are epidemic; media misinformation is rife; the judicial system is slow and increasingly subjective; the educational system is a disgrace; cultural expression is decadent and largely irreligious or anti-religious; our government – especially the Federal Government – is wasteful, bureaucratic in the worst sense of the word, and intrusive; and true science has been tainted or attenuated by bogus environmental aims and a Darwinistic ideology that will not tolerate free inquiry and contributes to a God-denying worldview. A number of astute observers are also concerned about the spread of deadly diseases that develop resistance to known antibiotics and the possibility of a computer crisis in the year 2000 that could conceivably adversely affect government finances and payments, the banking system, food distribution, public transportation, public utilities, telecommunications, and other vital or desired services. Similar misgivings are beginning to be heard concerning the January 1, 1999 conversion of the currencies of various European nations to the Eurodollar, not only because the new system allows for a maximum of 6 decimal places rather than 4 and must be made compatible to diverse currencies throughout the world, but because of the present scarcity of competent computer programers.

In his book *Wealth for All,* Christian economist R.E. McMaster presents further indicators of a civilization in decline, including governmental redistribution of wealth from productive to non-productive members of society; soft and luxurious living promoting sloth; concentration of land holdings in the hands of the civil government or relatively few private parties and the concomitant concentration of power and decision-making in the hands of a powerful minority of elitists; an "exploding knowledge and increased complexity that results in each subsequent generation [*sic*] knowing less of the country's total cultural heritage than the generation that went before it"; breeding of a disproportionate number of children by the "least capable members" of society; excessive attention to the "rights" of women and minorities; excessive regulatory laws that "strangle" productive persons and businesses; increased belief in the occult; rampant inflation; popular disenchantment with the political processes;

obsession with self-gratification and passive recreation – spectator sports, television games, and copious varieties of "illusionistic entertainment" – rather than with "the real world"; and the widespread rebelliousness of youth.[17]

Although McMaster sees civilizations rising and falling through 510-year cycles, other observers such as Sir John Glubb (the British military officer who forged and commanded Jordan's Arab Legion) set 250 years as the average period for the rise and collapse of an empire.[18] Of course, the length of the cycles in the case of either civilizations or empires is somewhat arbitrary, depending on the dates selected. For example, either 1607 or 1776 might be cited as the beginning of the United States of America – the former representing the year in which the first permanent English colony was established and the latter being the year when the colonies declared their independence from Great Britain.

In many cases, it is equally difficult to assign exact years for the culmination of civilizations or empires; yet interpreters of history are prone to try. Glubb suggests that the Assyrian Empire lasted from 859 to 612 B.C., a period of 247 years; the Persian Empire from 538 to 330 B.C., a total of 208 years; Greece (including Alexander the Great and his successors) from 331 to 100 B.C. or 231 years (one could argue, of course, that the dates in question should be approximately 490 to 146 B.C., a period of 344 years); the Roman Republic from 260 to 27 B.C. or 233 years; the Roman Empire from 27 B.C. to A.D. 180 or 207 years (it could be contended that the division between the Roman Republic and Empire is arbitrary and that the dates are debatable: Rome's rule lasted roughly from 272 B.C. to A.D. 395 or even 476, a period of 667 or 748 years); the Arab Empire from 634 to 880 or 246 years; the Mameluke Empire from 1250 to 1517 or 267 years; the Ottoman Empire from 1320 to 1570 or 250 years; the Spanish Empire from about 1500 to 1750 or 250 years; Romanov Russia from 1682 to 1916 or 234 years; and Britain from 1700 to 1950 or 250 years (could it just as well be from the ascension of the Tudors in 1485 to the present, a period of 514 years?). Other nations or empires also could have been mentioned: for example, ancient Israel (c. 1000 to 720 B.C. or 280 years); Judah (c.1000 to 586 B.C. or 414 years); the Mongol Empire (1206 to about 1500 or 294 years,

[17]R.C. McMaster, *Wealth for All* (Whitefish, Montana: A.N. Inc.,1982), 262f.

[18]John Glubb, *The Fate of Empires and Search for Survival* (Edinborough: Blackwood, 1976), pp. 1-28.

though it ended much earlier in China); Ming China (1368 to 1644 or 276 years); Ch'ing (Manchu) China (1644 to 1912 or 268 years); and the United States (1607 to the present or 392 years).

If we assume the validity of Glubb's estimate that nations may expect a life span of about 250 years (or even a period extending, as others may contend, to 400 or 500 years), does this circumstantial evidence indicate that cycles of ascendency and decline are more or less fixed and inevitable? It may be recalled that Oswald Spengler believed that they were, though Arnold Toynbee (who likewise saw recurring patterns in history and put forth generalizations concerning the reasons for the ascent and collapse of civilizations) did not, believing that, by returning to its spiritual roots, a political-cultural entity could evade disaster. However, because of the flawed nature of man, it is doubtful that a degenerating civilization or empire can avert descent into mediocrity, weakness, obscurity, and perhaps even extinction.

Although Glubb does not address the larger philosophical aspects of the rise and decomposition of empires, he does attempt to characterize the various stages though which all empires seem to pass. The initial stage is generally one of "outburst" and conquest typified by displays of prodigious energy and courage, confident optimism, hardihood, perseverence, disregard of traditions, contempt for weakness and decadence, aggressiveness and offensive-mindedness (in contrast to the defensive-mindedness of wealthy but decaying empires), and a disposition to improvise, experiment, and accept risks.

In most instances, a poor, hungry, aspiring, determined, dynamic, and often barbarian (Glubb's term) people establish a new empire by conquering an opulent, effete, degenerate civilization or empire, but not always. In the case of the United States, for example, civilized European settlers established themselves, dispossessed or overwhelmed disparate and mostly undeveloped natives, and conquered a vast continent during what may be termed its "pioneer stage." Nevertheless, according to Glubb, subsequent stages in our nation's history have coincided with the general pattern of commercial expansion and establishment of peace and security; and the acquisition of wealth has enabled well-to-do individuals and businesses or organizations to patronize the fine arts, construct magnificent buildings and municipalities, and invest in remunerative enterprises of all sorts, including modern transportation and communication facilities.

Collectively, these developments usher in an age of affluence in which the drive for money gradually begins to become more important than public service or duty to one's country. For a time, according to Glubb, "enough of the ancient virtues of courage, energy, and patriotism survive to enable the state successfully to defend its frontiers..."; but a defensive spirit and lack of resolve almost imperceptibly take root, honor and the quest for adventure are eroded by an overriding desire to acquire or retain wealth, militarism is decried, and potential enemies are "bought off" as citizens become less courageous and more disposed to settle disputes through compromise, appeasement, or interminable negotiations. Military readiness is denounced as "primitive and immoral," while pacifism and disarmament become acceptable and even viewed as morally superior means of fostering "peace." (I Thessalonians 5:3 states that "while people are saying 'peace and safety,' destruction will come upon them suddenly... and they will not escape": one of the most important duties of civil government is to protect its citizens.) Education ceases to emphasize patriotism; instead, it focuses on preparing students for lucrative vocations. (Self-seeking acquisition of money to the exclusion of concern for God or one's fellow men is spiritually dangerous: "For what will a man be profited if he gains the whole world and forfeits his soul?" [Matthew 16:26, NASB].) Glubb observes that the pursuit of money and the luxuries and pleasures money will buy is a sign of an empire's degeneration – an assertion consonant with the scriptural teaching that preoccupation with material things is a form of idolatry and that "he who sows to his flesh will of the flesh reap corruption..." (Galatians 6:8, NKJ). Materialism or love of pleasure can easily supplant love for God, even in the lives of Christian people, and vitiate their Christian testimony. Surely that to which we dedicate most of our time and efforts will come to command our supreme allegiance. God will not tolerate such "a god" in the believer's life. He will not share His glory with a man-made idol. "Where your treasure is," we are told in Luke 12:34, "there your heart will be also"; and Matthew 6:24 emphatically states: "You can not serve God and Money" (cf. Luke 16:13).

As materialism increases, Glubb notes, there is a concomitant laxity of sexual morals, corruption of public officials, and religious apathy. Internal dissension grows apace resulting in factionalism, disunity, and intensification of political hatred. No decisions can be rendered without seemingly endless captious discussions that retard or prevent effective action. Cosmopolitan elites exercise a disproportionate influence on government, and women become increasingly influential in public life while attending less to their traditional role as nurturers of the family. Foreign immigrants flood into the land, frequently forming communities of their own, especially in the large cities; and minority issues come to dominate the political agenda. Intellectual accomplishments are accorded greater encomiums than dedicated public service and heroic deeds, and one's character and the substance of one's knowledge may be valued less than mental agility, a quick wit, and an engaging personality. The public at large tends to avoid military service and heavy manual labor, considering it undignified or menial. Heroes are no longer men and women whose hard work, dedication to duty, self-sacrifice, and courageous acts were once eulogized; rather they are athletes, entertainers, erotic pop singers, actors, and those elevated to celebrity status by reason of their off-beat ideas or bizarre activities. Almost incongruously, frivolity and sensuality intermingle with pessimism and an affected pity for the underprivileged that is manifested in state assistance to the young and the poor – a welfare system undermining personal initiative and productivity and contributing to sloth and a spirit of dependence.

However, as citizens lose their self-reliance and community coherence disintegrates, and in the midst of sensual indulgence and purposeless activity, seeds of spiritual revival may be sown that may eventually inaugurate new beginnings. If Glubb's hypothesis, based on insightful observations, is correct, Christians should not be despondent but encouraged to be "salt and light" – a purgative, cleansing, hope-giving, redemptive force – even in the most corrupt and iniquitous society, and to look expectantly to the Lord Jesus Christ, knowing that His climactic return to earth to rule the nations is drawing near (cf. Luke 21:28).

Many observers will recall, of course, that Christ's second advent has been anticipated from the time of the apostles, and that generation after generation of Christians have held fast to their blessed hope without experiencing the Parousia promised in Acts 1:11. However, believers should not be dismayed. II Peter 3:3-4 tells us that there will be scoffers in the last days who will jeer, "Where is this 'coming' He [Christ] promised? Ever since the fathers died, everything goes on as it has since the beginning of creation." The same derisive attitude was manifested by those destined for destruction before the great flood obliterated most of mankind (Genesis 1 through 8), and Scripture specifically equates the last days with "the days of Noah" (Matthew 24:27).[19]

The Lord God will surely bring judgment upon this earth, not by a flood as in the time of Noah but by warfare, economic collapse, famine, plague, natural disasters of various types, and fire because of the sins of mankind (cf. II Peter 3:7 & 12 and Revelation chapters 6 through 9, 16, and 20). The descendants of Noah continued to scorn the Creator God, refusing to leave their place of abode to fill the earth, establishing instead a unified, humanistic society and government that proudly and rebelliously sought to build a great city and a monumental tower to exalt themselves (Genesis 11:1-9). This attempt to institute centralized, universal governance contrary to God's command was thwarted by Divine intervention, but man's attempts to bring everything under his dominion have never ceased. Assyria, Babylon, Greece, and Rome all attempted it, as have modern conquerors such as Napoleon Bonaparte and Adolf Hitler. Prompted by the god of this world (John 12:31, John 14:30, John 16:11, II Corinthians 4:4, Ephesians 2:2, I John 4:4, and I John 5:19), men have concocted numerous schemes and conspiracies to bring about a rational, secular world order. Psalm 2 mentions this:

> "Why do the nations *conspire* [the King James version says "rage"] and the peoples plot in vain? The kings of the earth take their stand and the rulers gather against His Anointed One [repeated by members of the early church: see Acts 4:25-26].
>
> "Let us break their chains, they say, and throw off their fetters." (In other words, "let us establish our freedom from God's laws.")

In the light of Scripture, therefore, and in the light of historical evidence, there have been many conspiracies to deny the Creator's authority and to establish man's absolute and universal sway over human events – all in vain. A detailed recapitulation of these plots is not necessary here; for others have related them with convincing documentation, but a general sketch may be in order.[20] It is

---

[19]See Appendix III.

[20]See Appendix IV for bibliographical information.

fairly apparent that their instigator is Satan himself; for all are characterized by deception, occult activity, and the exercise of arbitrary, often usurped and dictatorial power enforced by violence, murder, deceit, treachery, and every form of evil. Total control is the aim, through false religion and misinformation; management of political, educational, and financial institutions; and molding of cultural patterns and modes of thinking.

A mystical strain emanating from arcane religious beliefs and observances may be detected in the Priory of Zion, founded by crusading prince Godfrey of Bouillon (C.1158-1100), scion of Merovingian royalty, whose conquest of Jerusalem in 1099 earned him the title "Defender of the Holy Sepulcher." Upon Godfrey's death in the following year, his brother Baldwin (d.1118) assumed the title "King of Jerusalem" and soon became the first Grand Master of the Knights Templar, pledged to protect pilgrims. At first the Templars were closely affiliated with the Priory of Zion, which may have encouraged them to excavate the gold and silver treasure hidden beneath the temple by Jewish priests before the Romans destroyed it in 70 A.D., but the two orders eventually separated. By whatever means, the Templars amassed enormous wealth before being forced to retreat to Cyprus after the Saracen sack of Acre in 1291. Soon thereafter, they returned to Europe and lent vast sums of money to leading kings and princes, while pursuing the goal of establishing a world government under a Merovingian prince. Coveting their wealth, the French king induced the Pope at Avignon to charge the Templars with heresy. Under great pressure, the pontiff acceded. The Order was persecuted and officially dissolved, its leaders were executed, and its assets were confiscated. Whether members of the Order were guilty of all the charges of heresy, occult practices, idolatry, and immorality leveled against them is impossible to know, but their unwillingness to submit to pope or king, secrecy, and riches invited enmity and brought about their demise. Their influence has lived on, however, not only in the Scottish Rite founded in Scotland by dispersed French adherents but also in Masonic lore and in certain Rosicrusion and Mormon rites. Madam Helena Petrovna Blavatsky's (d.1891) *The Secret Doctrine* made reference to the Order's esoteric wisdom, as did the occult Thule Society that contributed to the gnostic Aryan credenda of Adolf Hitler. The Templars' parent organization, the Priory of Zion, is still alive and well and apparently is still dedicated to promoting a Merovingian descendent, perhaps a Habsburg, to head an international coalition capable of managing European and perhaps world affairs.

This quest for world-wide power has motivated and is motivating many diverse entities – some of them interrelated, others having common interests or coincidental aims. One that has had a nefarious and enduring impact is the Illuminati, founded on "May Day" 1776 by a Jesuit-educated Ingolstadt University law professor named Adam Weishaupt (1748-1830), whose intention was to build an organization of "illumined" men – symbolized by the all-seeing eye – imbued with clairvoyant knowledge to be enhanced by mind-expanding drugs. Code names were assigned to each member, and an elaborate network of spies was set up to make sure that no one revealed secrets or strayed from prescribed dogma. The Order's original instructions told how to stir up animosity and bloodshed between people of different religions, ethnicity, and gender and to foment hatred within families, social unrest, and insurrections. The ultimate aim, revealed only to members of the inner circle, was to effect, through revolution, the abolition of existing civil governments, patriotism, the family as the basic unit of society, private property, and established religion in order to create a world government.

With the assistance of Masonic leader Baron Adolf Knigge, Weishaupt succeeded in grafting Illuminism into Continental Freemasonry, thereby uniting 3 million members of these secret societies in a common cause only imperfectly understood by the vast majority. In France, the King's brother the Duke of Orléans, Grand Master of the Grand Orient Lodge in Paris and an avid Illuminist, turned the royal palace and its environs into a staging ground for revolution, recruiting and training violent agitators, trouble-makers, and subversives from the dregs of society. It was this rabble that precipitated the French Revolution.

Although officially outlawed and abolished after their agenda were discovered in 1785, The Illuminati continued their activities, subjecting the French Church to severe persecution and the nation to state-sanctioned terrorism. Long after the overthrow and execution of hapless Bourbon King Louis XVI (r.1774-1793) and even after the meteoric rise, conquests, and fall of Napoleon Bonaparte, the Illuminists continued to subvert and infiltrate governments, spawning in the process the League of the Just (later the Communist League) as well as "utopian socialist" movements; anarchism; syndicalism; Pan-Slavism; rabid revolutionary nationalism in Italy, the German territories, and Ireland; Fabian Socialism in Britain; and Vladimir Lenin's (d.1924) brand of Bolshevism in Russia. Indeed, from their inception, the Illuminati have sown discord, sedition, and subversion; stirred up class hatred; employed mob action; and used lies, scurrilous literature, pornography, vice, treachery, bribery, blackmail, intimidation, terrorism, famine, and economic ruin to topple governments from within. Such means have been used not only in the French Revolution, but in every subsequent Marxist-Leninist revolution whether in Russia, China, Eastern Europe, Cuba, or third-world nations.

Of course, the "science of revolution" has been expanded and refined over the years, especially in the light of present world conditions and in view of the power of the media to mobilize opinion throughout the world. Nevertheless, the methods employed by Western socialist elites to effect their global agenda are just as ruthless as those employed by Marxist-Leninists, if more discreet in the early stages. In the course of time, methodology began to become increasingly important for would-be revolutionaries of every stripe. Italian communist leader Antonio Gramsci believed it was stupid to make a frontal assault on capitalist nations. He insisted that it would be better first to undermine their morality, culture, and religious beliefs to make them ripe for takeover. Gramsci was a dedicated communist, but he realized the effectiveness of subtle methods of revolution.

Even in matters of substance, communism and socialism are compatible in many respects. Certainly the latter is just as God-denying and materialistic as Marxist-Leninism, and both are bound to an ideology of change adapted from the Hegelian dialectic. Based partly on Freemason (probably Illuminist) Johann Gottlieb Fichte's (d.1814) conception of an impersonal, process-oriented moral order, Hegel's dialectic stresses the conflict of ideologies (thesis vs. antithesis) leading to a temporary accommodation or synthesis that becomes the new thesis evoking a new antithesis, thereby setting in motion another struggle. The continuing and ever-changing dialectic welcomes the existence of opposing intellectual forces as the mechanism of progressive renewal and change. Subsequently, Marx subordinated the ideational dialectic to one postulated in the social sphere – the ongoing class struggle; and many Western intellectuals, sometimes unwittingly, have broadly incorporated both the ideational and social aspects of the dialectical process.

Although Hegelian thought is antithetical to biblical teachings concerning absolute truth and moral verities and is not consciously accepted by the vast majority of Americans, it has been infused almost imperceptibly into the American mind-set over the years, giving rise to relativistic assumptions that are contrary to God's Word. A major force in disseminating Hegelian thought with its statist disposition among America's intellectuals is the secret order established at Yale University in 1832 for students carefully screened and selected before their senior year.[21] The Order (as it is commonly called) was founded as the Skull and Bones Society by William Huntington Russell and Alphonso Taft. During a ten-year sojourn in Germany (1831-1832), Russell had imbibed Hegelian thought and perhaps some Illuminist influences observable in rituals of the Order, which in 1856 became the Russell Trust. The Order has given birth to similar societies at other universities, including Cornell and Johns Hopkins; and, in accord with its Hegelian philosophy, its membership comprises eminent persons from both the political right and left. Through these members, its influence permeates the nation's premier tax-exempt foundations, elite law firms, the communications and education establishments, industry, the Federal Reserve System and top-level financial operatives, and the highest echelons of government. Numbered among its members are the Whitneys, Harrimans, and Rockefellers as well as such noted personages as Daniel Coit (first President of the University of California and Johns Hopkins University, the Carnegie Institution, and several other foundations), Henry Luce (founding publisher of *Time* and *Life* magazines), William Buckley of the *National Review*, Henry Sloan Coffin and Henry Sloan Coffin, Jr. of Union Theological Seminary in New York, Archibald McLeish (poet, professor, first Director of the prestigeous Nieman Fellowship in journalism at Harvard University, Librarian of Congress, Undersecretary of State, and the brains behind the UNESCO Constitution), McGeorge Bundy (assistant to Presidents Kennedy and Johnson on matters involving national security and President of the Ford Foundation), and our recent President George Herbert Bush.

The British counterpart to the Order is the Group (influenced by the Illuminati) whose objective, consonant with the will of its founder Cecil Rhodes, was to produce a secret "Society of the Elect" that would forge an Anglo-American federation, financed by wealthy individuals and agencies, that would usher in world government. This grand design was to be fostered by a

---

[21]See pp.92-93. The Order believes that society should be controlled by the state but that it in turn, as the dialectic continues, will be merged with other nations into a new world order.

scholarship program that Rhodes established to recruit promising young intellectuals. He also collaborated with Fabian Socialists Sidney and Beatrice Webb to institute the London School of Economics and established in 1891 the Round Table, a secret society headed by his friend Lord Alfred Milner (who later served as paymaster for the Rothschilds to Bolshevik revolutionaries). A network of spin-off groups developed after World War I to discuss, formulate, and lobby for policies to promote and implement universal peace and security through global government. Today non-government organizations such as the Royal Institute of International Affairs, the Council on Foreign Relations (CFR, founded under the auspices of President Wilson's *eminence grise*, Colonel Edward Mandell House, and affiliated with the RIIA), the Bilderbergers (who under the patronage of the Netherlands' Prince Bernhard, an important figure in Shell Oil, help coordinate American and European elites), The Club of Rome (dedicated to zero population growth), the Trilateral Commission (founded in 1973 by David Rockefeller to form economic bonds between the United States, Europe, and Japan), the Dartmouth Conference, the Aspen Institute for Humanistic Studies, the Atlantic Institute, the Business Council, United World Federalists, and other groups with benign-sounding names are pressing toward the same end.

The highest echelons of our government are surfeited with CFR members. In fact, membership appears to be almost an unofficial qualification for appointment to key diplomatic posts, Chairman of the Joint Chiefs of Staff, Director of the CIA, and Chairman of the Federal Reserve Board. The CFR effectively promotes its adepts from the two major political parties to influential positions. For example, regardless of their party affiliation, candidates seeking the Presidency are usually CFR members and, once elected, they appoint CFR members to important cabinet posts. The CFR has virtually controlled the State Department from the administration of Franklin Delano Roosevelt to the present day, and has held the reins of authority in the Defense Department and lately in the Department of Health and Human Services. Indeed, not only cabinet appointees but many of the bureaucrats heading federal agencies are at least philosophically attuned to the humanistic, globalist goals of the CFR. Is it any wonder that regardless of which party wins an election, policies remain much the same? Let us be appreciative of those public servants who are trying to make a difference and give them our encouragement and support.

A sampling of a few of the CFR's most noted members might include Democrats Dean Acheson (prominent in the State Department under F.D.R and Harry Truman and Secretary of State from 1949 to 1952); Alger Hiss (who was with Franklin Roosevelt at the Yalta Conference, presided over the founding of the United Nations Organization, and headed the Carnegie Endowment for World Peace before being tried for espionage and convicted of perjury); Soviet agents Owen Lattimore (who influenced our post-World-War-II policy regarding China), Harry Dexter White and Virginius Frank Coe (who at the Bretton Woods Conference in July 1944 helped inaugurate [along with communist Lauchlin Currie and Hiss] the International Monetary Fund [IMF] and the World Bank); Adlai Stevenson (Governor of Illinois, Presidential candidate, and Ambassador to the United Nations); John F. Kennedy (Congressman, Senator, and President) and his brother Robert F. Kennedy (Attorney General); W. Averill Harriman (Ambassador to the Soviet Union from 1943 to 1946 and briefly to the United Kingdom, Secretary of Commerce, Governor of New York from 1955 to 1959, and in 1968 chief U.S. negotiator at the Paris Peace Conference on Vietnam); diplomat and Undersecretary of State George Ball; Treasury Secretary Henry H. Fowler; Secretaries of State Dean Rusk (earlier President of the Rockefeller Foundation), Cyrus R. Vance, and others; John Kenneth Galbraith (Keynesian economist, Ambassador to India [1961-1963], and participant in the 1963 clandestine "Iron Mountain conclave" in New York that planned to publicize a phony pollution-of-the-environment crisis as a pretense for moving toward global controls); Arthur Schlesinger, Jr. (historian, public official, and special assistant to President Kennedy); John McCloy (longtime Chairman of the CFR, U.S. High Commissioner in Germany in which capacity he used Marshall Plan funds to promote socialism and the movement to unify Europe, Chairman of the Ford Foundation and the Chase-Manhattan Bank, World Bank President from 1947-1948, member of the Bilderberger steering committee, and one of the architects for the European Community); U.S. Senator, Vice President, and Presidential candidate Hubert Humphrey; and Presidents Jimmy Carter and Bill Clinton.

On the Republican side, CFR members include President Dwight D. Eisenhower (r.1953-1961); Secretaries of State John Foster Dulles, Christian Herter, William P. Rogers, Henry Kissinger, Alexander Haig, and George Shultz; all Republican Secretaries of Defense from the Eisenhower administration (Neil McElroy and Thomas S. Gates, Jr.) to the administration of George H. Bush, himself an insider (Richard B. Cheney); C. Douglas Dillon who served as

Secretary of the Treasury under Democrats John F. Kennedy and Lyndon Baines Johnson, confirming that party affiliation means little or nothing to the globalists; Elliot Richardson, who served as Undersecretary of State and in two different cabinet posts under Richard M. Nixon, who was likewise a CFR member; all CIA Directors from Allen W. Dulles to Robert M. Gates; Thomas E. Dewey (Governor of New York from 1943 to 1952, "racket-busting" special prosecutor, and two-time Presidential candidate); Senator Jacob Javits; Paul Hoffman, who pushed for population control while managing a UN fund established for that purpose by Secretary General U Thant; Robert McNamara, who was Secretary of Defense in two Democrat administrations (party labels mean little); John Gardner, a member of Democrat Johnson's cabinet and later (1970) founder of the citizens' lobby Common Cause; Henry Cabot Lodge, Jr., U.S. Senator from 1937-1944 and 1947-1953, Ambassador to the United Nations (1953-1960), and Ambassador to South Vietnam (1963-1964) where he shamelessly helped orchestrate the overthrow of President Ngo Dinh Diem; Nelson Rockefeller, Governor of New York from 1959 to 1973, Vice President under Gerald Ford (fellow member of the CFR), and Presidential candidate and kingmaker; and George H. Bush (member of the CFR, the Russell Trust, and the Trilateral Commission who as President strengthened the hand of the Environmental Protection Agency [EPA], imposed unprecedented regulations on American industries and businesses, and during and after the Gulf War became the stalking horse for the "New World Order").

Hundreds of names could be added to the few mentioned above to reveal the nature of the CFR's influence. Still, the organization's membership (about 3,000) is very small compared to its widespread influence through official government agencies, non-government organizations, its flagship publication *Foreign Affairs*, and the media elite. For the sake of political expedience, prominent Democrats and Republicans alike have endorsed the majority of its goals, though most would deny any intent to abolish the Constitution as the CFR advocates. Be this as it may, public officials promoting a one-world agenda are in reality breaking their oaths to support, uphold, and defend the Constitution of the United States.

The CFR works principally behind the scenes through government departments and bureaus like those noted above, the Federal Reserve Board, the Export-Import Bank, and private, tax-exempt foundations that dispense copious sums through grants-in-aid and other indirect means to left-wing groups, academics, and media fellow travelers. Among the most noted (some would say "the most notorious") are the Rockefeller Foundation, the Ford Foundation, the Carnegie Endowment for International Peace, the Peabody Foundation, the Sloan Foundation, the Slater Foundation, and the Twentieth-Century Foundation – most of them directed by trustees or board members connected with the CFR, the Trilateral Commission, or other globalist organizations.

Similarly, internationalists dominate the banking system. Most of the large banks have worked hand in glove with globalists since World War I – among them the Guaranty Trust (J.P. Morgan); Kuhn, Loeb & Company (Jacob Schiff and Paul Warburg); Dillon, Read & Company; Brown Brothers, Harriman; and the Chase Manhattan Bank (Rockefeller). Money from the Schiff-Warburg, Morgan, and Rockefeller coffers bankrolled the Bolshevik Revolution in Russia and helped consolidate it. Apparently these banking houses wished to attain and maintain a trade monopoly there free from competition. Ideologically amoral, these banks were willing to finance communists or fascists to further their ends. Thomas Lamont, head of Guaranty Trust and the Morgan banking network, advised Italian dictator Benito Mussolini and secured monetary assistance for him; and Otto Kahn, Director of the American International Corporation and Kuhn, Loeb & Company, encouraged investments in El Duce's regime, as did Ivy Lee, spokesman for the Rockefeller interests. Wall Street money also flowed to Adolf Hitler through the Rockefeller-controlled Vacuum Oil Company, General Electric, the Baltimore & Ohio Railroad, Standard Oil of New Jersey, and other businesses. Support for the Nazi regime also flowed from the W.A. Harriman interests in New York, particularly the Union Banking Corporation of New York City whose board of directors included two German Nazis and four members of the Russell Trust, through German steel magnate Fritz Thyssen.

Of course, for the international bankers, wars present an opportunity to make enormous profits and quickly to gain additional influence, even control, over the governments involved, who must borrow from them to purchase arms and munitions and to maintain their armed forces. Inevitably, the borrower becomes the slave of the lender just as stated in Proverbs 22:7.

That economics determine the movement of history is not merely a Marxist axiom: it is the premise on which the financial moguls of our day operate.

347

Viewed in dialectical terms, why can not capitalism and socialism (even of the most radical variety) be brought into synthesis, particularly if money is dispensed to all sides to effect such an accommodation? Governments dominated by elitists subscribing to such thoughts will engage in every imaginable means of accommodation with dictators, even to the point of forcibly repatriating to the Soviet Union some 4 million anti-communist Soviet subjects who had fled to the West during World War II and turning over Treasury Department plates to the Soviets that would enable them to print U.S. currency. Both of these reprehensible actions were taken by our government at the end of the war. The insiders seem to believe that weakening the national sovereignty of the United States, fostering socialist programs, educating our citizens for a global economy, and promoting communist takeovers throughout the world will further the dialectical process toward a managed world economic system. International financiers generally prefer to deal with highly centralized governments that can be manipulated rather than with decentralized governments whose economies are grounded in a free-enterprise system.

The assault on American liberties started before World War I and was especially furthered by the creation of the Federal Reserve System and passage of a graduated federal income tax in 1913. Much of the planning for these revolutionary measures was carried on in secret, and they were presented under the guise of initiating "banking reform" that would restrain monopolies. President Wilson's adviser Colonel House worked closely behind the scenes with German immigrant Paul Warburg, brother of Kaiser Wilhelm's confidant Max Warburg (head of an important bank closely affiliated with the *Reichsbank*), to secure passage of this legislation in order to promote global socialism under a dictator assisted by an oligarchic council – a system outlined in House's novel *Phillip Dru, Aministrator: A Story of Tomorrow* (1912). Warburg, who became the guiding genius of the Federal Reserve Board, was son-in-law to Solomon Loeb and brother-in-law to Jacob Schiff's daughter Frieda, who married his brother Felix. Both Paul and Felix were partners in Kuhn, Loeb & Company, which had connections with the European Rothschilds and other international banking firms on both sides of the Atlantic. The Rockefeller and Morgan interests were also much involved in forming the Federal Reserve System, which placed the nation's monetary system in the hands of a few unelected managers, who have worked ever since to forge a global economy and dominate the governments of the world.

The IMF and the World Bank, brought into being by communist sympathizers in 1944, have in effect extended the Federal Reserve System internationally, President Nixon separated U.S. currency from any backing of intrinsic worth in 1973 so that it can float with the world economy, and in 1980 Congress enacted a new banking act that compelled 40,000 banks to join the Federal Reserve System. Electronic money recorded and traced by computers is already here, as is the technology for a cashless society – worldwide. A super computer in Brussels can handle approximately 2 billion accounts, and the computer in Luxemburg built to serve the Common Market is capable of assigning a bank account number to every living person. It seems only a matter of time before encoded computer chips will be implanted in human beings, which will control all of their financial transactions (cf. Revelation 13:16-17). Mayer Amschel Rothschild (1743-1812), founder of the famous banking dynasty, once said: "Permit me to issue and control the money of a nation, and I care not who makes its laws."[22] Today Mammon rules and its worship is rife. Can it be doubted that the end of the age is near?

On February 17, 1950, James Warburg, son of one of the founding fathers of the Federal Reserve System, proclaimed before the United States Senate: "We shall have world government, whether or not we like it. The question is only whether world government will be achieved by consent or conquest."[23]

Certainly many forces are pressing us in that direction. The attempts to remove the Judaic-Christian God from the public square, the elevation of multiculturalism or cultural pluralism, and the propagation of moral relativism and New Age philosophies are all conditioning us for merger with nations and peoples of diverse beliefs, and one can hardly help but ponder why we have a continuing, deepening, and apparently insoluable education crisis. Is all of this occurring purely by accident or do the globalist conspirators want to render our populace incapable of independent thought? As early as 1952, Rowan Gaither, then President of the Ford Foundation, admitted to Congressman Norman Dodd

---

[22]Quoted in J. R. Church, *Guardians of the Grail ... and the Men who Plan to Rule the World* (Oklahoma City: Prophecy Publications, 1991), pp. 203-204.

[23]Senate Report quoted in William F. Jasper, *Global Tyranny ... Step by Step: The United Nations and the Emerging New World Order* (Appleton, Wisconsin: Western Islands Publishers, 1992), p. 88.

that persons within the State Department and various federal agencies had been operating for years "under directives issued by the White House ... to the effect that we should make every effort to so alter life in the United States as to make possible a comfortable merger with the Soviet Union."[24]

Even during the Reagan administration (in October 1985), the State Department and National Security advisers permitted the Carnegie Corporation of New York to negotiate with Soviet educators to develop curricula and materials for teaching children in the elementary schools. About a month later, on November 21, Secretary of State George Shultz signed a 41-page general accord with the Soviets that would allow and encourage cooperative projects in educational, scientific, and cultural matters. Teacher exchanges were to be facilitated at both the primary and secondary levels of education, and exchange of textbooks was encouraged as well as the conduct of joint studies from them. These steps to begin melding American and Soviet education and the current fad of multiculturalism serve to undermine traditional American thought and values and to prepare us to be assimilated into a new world order.

Fed a steady diet of globalist propaganda and saddled with a government staffed with internationalists, we seem well on our way to a new world order through the United Nations that President Bush sought to implement. In all probability, the establishment planners considered him, as a Republican and *ersatz* Conservative, to be less likely than a Democrat leader to arouse the suspicions of the American people by the actions and pronouncements he made. Therefore, George Bush was the man selected by the insiders to take soundings concerning a new world order and to get things started, but they apparently thought a more aggressive, ruthless, less principled operative was needed. Therefore, they orchestrated Clinton's election. He was to fix the focus of the electorate on the economy with the slogan "it's the economy, stupid," while Bush bowed to his handlers by running a very inept campaign, failing to address hot social issues that may have carried him to victory.

From the moment of his inauguration, Bill Clinton has energetically, underhandedly, and persistently (if often tactlessly) pressed toward humanistic,

---

[24]Quoted in *ibid.*, xiv.

globalist goals, confident of the support of his internationalist directors and mafia operatives.

In recent years, the only President who tried to set the United States on a course contrary to that mandated by the one-worlders was Ronald Reagan, who wanted to bring down "the Evil Empire" in the Soviet Union and to turn back the onslaught of communism in the Western Hemisphere. He was partly successful. The demise of the Soviet Union, dismantling of the Berlin wall, and the rapid changes within the former "Iron Curtain countries" of Europe (cleverly engineered by Pope John Paul II) probably would not have occurred without his initiative; but a pusillanimous Congress accustomed to operating according to "conventional wisdom" – a Congress usually controlled by Reagan's political opponents and confronted with an intrenched bureaucracy, a State Department packed with insiders, an unsympathetic or hostile media, the powerful NEA lobby, the doctrinaire cynicism of much of academe, and the globalist establishment – frustrated many of his initiatives on both the foreign and domestic fronts.

The 1998 elections demonstrate once more that political action is not succeeding in arresting the nation's moral and intellectual free-fall. Our culture and institutions are so twisted and corrupted (no longer resting on God's truth) that no human effort can turn things around. Only repentance and spiritual regeneration can bring any significant change. We must return to the God of the Bible, for only He can save our beloved nation. In the meantime, we must wage spiritual warfare persistently and valiantly. Knowing the nature of our Enemy, we must avail ourselves of every opportunity and exercise all the weapons God has given us to snatch as many "brands from the fire" as possible (Zechariah 3:2).

In many respects, the situation is just as analogous to the society in which Abraham's nephew Lot lived as to that of Noah; and, interestingly enough, the Bible makes reference to this fact. Luke 17:28-30 records our Lord's statement:

> "It was the same in the days of Lot. People were eating and drinking, buying and selling, planting and building. But the day Lot left Sodom, fire and sulfur rained down from heaven and destroyed them all. It will be just like this on the day the Son of Man is revealed."

We know from the biblical account that the culture of Sodom was totally perverse. Perhaps Lot had tried to change it ; but, if so, he failed to make a significant impression. We do know that he was despised as an outsider and derided as a pious meddler (Genesis 19:9). Are not Christians in our contemporary society looked upon in much the same way? In a sense, this is as it should be, for it reveals that believers have not entirely lost their "saltiness," that their morals and cultural standards differ from the postmodern tenets of the world system, and that they are uncomfortable and non-compliant in a corrupt environment – aliens whose citizenship is in heaven. It also may be that depravity and sin have attained such a grip over our culture that Christians can not recapture it and reconstitute it on godly principles without God's direct intervention – as was true in ancient Sodom and previously in the civilization of Noah's time.

Are we then to cease striving to change our culture and reform our institutions? Not at all: our mandate is clear. We may, however, need to shift our focus from the national political arena and cultural milieu to evangelism and teaching that will win individuals to Christ, restore their moral compass, and equip them to act as redemptive agents in society. Without abandoning our efforts to retard evil in the political, social, and cultural milieu of our day, we need to attend to our God-given priority to carry out the "great commission" but only under the unction and power of the Holy Spirit.

Perhaps we have been primarily using fleshly weapons and following our own campaign strategies to engage in political and cultural combat, because Satan and his minions have lured us into the battle on their terms, causing us to believe we can prevail by such means. If this is the case, we can not win, for we will be waging war on the devil's ground and by unspiritual rules and methods. Let us remember that our Lord himself did not inaugurate His earthly ministry until He was baptized in the Holy Spirit, nor did the early apostles go forth to do His bidding until the Holy Spirit came upon them in power as recorded in Acts chapters 1 and 2. We do not need political acumen, intellectual prowess, or cultural creativity as much as we need godly character and spiritual power, discernment, and weaponry. Let us seek our Lord's face in fasting and prayer, listen to His voice, submit entirely to His lordship, receive the Holy Spirit in power, and under His anointing obediently and unequivocally proceed to carry out Christ's great commission and whatever additional specific orders He may issue. We can not conduct the battle in our own wisdom or by the pragmatic methods of the world. As we follow God's campaign plan and battle instructions, we will not merely be "beating the air," and we will be victorious solely in His strength and to His glory.

Only the Sovereign God can touch the hearts of His creatures and orchestrate events to effect His eternal purpose. Let us learn to know Him intimately so that we can hear His voice and engage in effective spiritual warfare. We struggle in vain if relying on our own puny resources and machinations, but as we are faithful in holding on to our confession and start implementing what He has commanded us to do, He will intervene in judgment of people, societies, and nations. Everything that can be shaken loose will be shaken loose. Persons who seemed impervious to the Gospel message will, in anguish and desperation, look for a way out (though, of course, many will remain obdurate), for some hope, for some means of deliverance. That will be the hour when consecrated and spiritually-equipped Christians will reap an unprecedented harvest of souls in preparation for Christ's second advent and the inauguration of His personal reign on the earth.

With full dependence on God and confident that His timing for every action is always right, let us not tire or be slack in doing what is right (II Thessalonians 3:13) but depend entirely on Him for the harvest. According to Ecclesiastes 3:1-8, there is an appropriate and effectual "time for everything and a season for every activity under heaven: a time to be born and a time to die, a time to plant and a time to uproot, a time to kill and a time to heal, a time to tear down and a time to build, a time to weep and a time to laugh, a time to mourn and a time to dance, a time to scatter stones and a time to gather them, a time to embrace and a time to refrain, a time to search and a time to give up, a time to keep and a time to throw away, a time to tear and a time to mend, a time to be silent and a time to speak, a time to love and a time to hate, a time for war and a time for peace."

For many years, Christians in the United States have been blessed with peace, security, and affluence, but the time is coming, in fact is already here, when we will suffer rejection and persecution. In the midst of hardship, may we persevere with patience, fortitude, humility, and gladness of heart, knowing that any "light and momentary troubles" we bear are achieving for us "an eternal glory that far outweighs them all" (cf. II Corinthians 4:17). At the same time, as soldiers of Christ, may we be ready for battle – trained for spiritual combat, attentive to the voice of the Supreme Commander, and clad in the full armor provided for our protection: the helmet of salvation, which protects our mind from the psychological, philosophical, and religious arrows of the Enemy; the breastplate of righteousness (the righteousness of Jesus Christ imputed to us) to protect our heart; the shield of faith that enables us to stand against seemingly insuperable odds; the belt of truth that holds all our protective armor in place; and supple boots enabling us to carry the good news of salvation through Jesus Christ into every situation. Above all, we must be adept at wielding our offensive weapons – "the sword of the Spirit, which is the Word of God," and our prayer language, praying in the Spirit "on *all* occasions" (Ephesians 6:13-18; cf. I Corinthians 14:14-15). Equipped and prepared in this manner and laying aside every weight that encumbers us (Hebrews 12:1) – including hatred of persons who wrong us and any fear that tries to grip us – we can go about the business at hand and rest in God's promises until called to do battle, knowing that "the battle is the Lord's" (I Samuel 17:47). He will issue orders for engagement at the proper time; and, as we obey His commands, we will experience total victory over our spiritual foes.

In the meantime, let us encourage one another with the promises found in Psalm 37:1-11:

"Do not fret because of evil men or be envious of those who do wrong; for like the grass they will soon wither, like green plants they will soon die away.

"Trust in the Lord and do good; dwell in the land and enjoy safe pasture.

"Delight yourself in the Lord and He will give you the desires of your heart.

"Commit your way to the Lord; trust in Him and He will do this: He will make your righteousness shine like the dawn, the justice of your cause like the noonday sun.

"Be still before the Lord and wait patiently for Him; do not fret when men succeed in their ways, when they carry out their wicked schemes.

"Refrain from anger and turn from wrath; do not fret – it leads only to evil. For evil men will be cut off, but those who hope in the Lord will inherit the land.

"A little while, and the wicked will be no more; though you look for them, they will not be found.

"But the meek will inherit the land and enjoy great peace."

Chapter XXXIII

THE END OF THE AGE: A LAST DAYS SCENARIO

As we approach the end of this millennium, more and more people are wondering what lies ahead. Although future events do not lie within the purview of the historian, it is possible – in the light of history, contemporary events, and God's Holy Word – to understand the general nature of what is to come. How do the "signs of the times" presented in the previous chapter compare with the prophesies concerning "the last days' set forth by Jesus in Matthew chapter 24 and by the Apostle Paul in II Timothy 3:1-7? In these passages, we are told that they will be "terrible times" when people will love themselves and money (humanism and idolatry) rather than God. These days will be marked by apostasy, social and political upheavals, natural disasters (including earthquakes, famines, and pestilence), and wars and rumors of wars. On every side, there will be greed, arrogance, impurity, thanklessness, prideful ambition, blasphemy, disobedience to parents, slander, lying, resistence to the truth of God, despising of good and godly principles (ridicule of those who speak or practice them), lack of love and even self-control, brutality, headstrongness, lawlessness, rebelliousness, haughtiness, feminism (gullible women will be "loaded down with sins and swayed by all kinds of evil desires"), and religiosity – many will profess godliness and observe religious forms but deny the power of the living God. False prophets will lead the unwary astray, hatred and persecution of Christians will become increasingly common, and many church members' love and fervor for the Lord will wane; yet the Gospel of the kingdom of God will be preached to all nations.

Many Christians believe that believers will be caught up to meet Jesus Christ in the air before the "great end-time tribulation" occurs, while others believe the "rapture" (the snatching away of the church) will take place when Jesus Christ returns to earth for the second time in power and great glory to conquer the nations and establish His thousand-year reign on earth. In fact, there are also other schools of thought that believers entertain, but there is no reason to become snarled in fruitless theological disputations over this matter. No one knows the exact date when our Lord will return, but we are told that "he who stands firm to the end will be saved" (Matthew 24:13). It should behoove us, therefore, to be ready to meet Him at any time while not looking for an easy, convenient departure, thereby possibly attenuating our fervor in proclaiming the Gospel. The vast majority of church members today appear to be complacent, content to worship God once a week but encumbered by the sins of the world. Have their minds and hearts been captured by the Enemy? Have they become discouraged and demoralized by demons? Or have they been comfortably anesthetized by the belief that no matter what terrible calamities may come upon their society or the world at large, they will be snatched away to safety "in the nick of time"?

As followers of Christ, we are to occupy to the end without wavering, knowing that the promise of His second coming in the same manner that He departed will certainly be fulfilled, whether or not we are able to agree on the exact sequence of events. In the event that the Antichrist is revealed before Christ takes us to be with Him, we need to be prepared to endure very severe persecution. Multitudes of Christians in Sudan, Ethiopia, Egypt, Saudi Arabia, Iran, India, Pakistan, Burma, Cambodia, Vietnam, North Korea, Indonesia, China, much of Moslem Africa and other areas of the world are already experiencing persecution, often in the most brutal ways imaginable. Why should we be exempted? As tribulation continues to spread and mount in intensity, there will be unusual and frightening signs in the heavens (Matthew 24:29-31); however believers have been given still another clue concerning when Jesus will return: the "parable of the fig tree," a symbol or "type" of Israel. In the "parable," Jesus said of the fig tree: "when its branch has already become tender and puts forth its leaves, you know that summer is near; even so you too, when you see all these things, recognize that He [the Messiah, or some versions substitute "it" for "He"] is near, right at the door. Truly I say to you, this generation will not pass away until all these things take place" (Matthew 24:32-34, NASB). In other words, the generation that observes the fig tree (Israel) emerging from its winter dormancy will be on hand when Jesus returns to earth.

The modern nation of Israel came into being in 1948 and recovered the ancient city of Jerusalem in 1967. Therefore, if a generation constitutes forty years, the period of time required for the generation that left Egypt to perish in the wilderness, this prophecy may be fulfilled before or in the year 2007. In view of the rapid acceleration of events, our Lord could very well return by 2007 (although neither the temple nor temple ceremonies have been restored to date),

357

but nobody can predict the day and the hour when this will occur. Nevertheless, signs concerning the season of Christ's second advent have been given to members of the "body of Christ," so that the church may not be taken unawares but be brought into a mode of readiness and joyful expectation. Consequently, as the time draws nearer, more details will doubtless be revealed, but Scripture clearly states that the period prior to Christ's return will be like the days of Noah (Matthew 24:37-38) and those of Lot (Luke 17:28-30) when people appear to have been concentrating principally on their own everyday affairs, largely oblivious of God, and devoid of interest in spiritual matters. They were "eating and drinking, marrying and giving in marriage" (couples today often do not bother to marry); and wickedness was so prevalent that people's thoughts and inclinations were continuously evil – a fairly apt description of conditions in the contemporary world.

How should Christians conduct themselves under such circumstances? Does the life of Noah give us any clues? In Genesis 6:8-22, we read that Noah was a just and righteous man who tried to maintain his purity and integrity in the midst of a corrupt and violent generation and that he walked in close communion with God. Not only did he hear the Lord's voice, but he obeyed His commands to construct a gigantic ark and provision it as a refuge for all living creatures. He had implicit faith in God's Word to him and acted upon it. He courageously persevered in the face of ridicule and discouragement when no one outside of his family was following God or even listening to Him. Moreover, Noah was a good father who led his family in serving the God of the universe.

It may be wondered how many present-day Christians are hearing from God and acting in obedience to Him as Noah did. From all appearances, the remnant who are doing so is greatly outnumbered by those who are essentially going their own way. Is that because they have been beguiled by the glitter, lusts, and thought patterns of this present world? I John 2:5-17 clearly warns us:

> "Do not love the world, nor anything in the world. If any one loves the world, the love of the Father is not in him. For all that is in the world, the lust of the flesh and the lust of the eyes and the boastful pride of life is not from the Father, but is from the world. And the world is passing away, and also its lusts; but the one who does the will of God abides forever" (NASB).

Scripture also teaches that no one can serve God and money (Matthew 6:24 and Luke 16:13); yet both the presidential and mid-term elections of this decade have focused on the economy, and the majority of people seems to be more concerned with the acquisition of wealth than with anything else. If this is true, our nation is on very dangerous ground, for the Bible says that "the love of money is a root of all sorts of evil, and some by longing for it have wandered away from the faith and pierced themselves with many a pang" (I Timothy 6:10, NASB).

Let us keep these truths in mind as we turn our attention to a scenario based on the writings of several Old Testament prophets and the book of Revelation that soon may take place. In the latter book, the Apostle John relates how "the Son of Man" appeared to him and told him to write down what is about to be revealed to him concerning his own day and what will take place in the future. John is then instructed concerning the churches of the time, whose characteristics correspond rather closely to those found in churches throughout the world today (Revelation 1:19 through 3:22). Without going into particulars, we will simply remark that the proper starting-point for assessing conditions in the nations of our world is a discerning study of what the churches in those lands are doing. What the people of God do or fail to do has a profound causative influence on what happens in society; for the Lord God is the Supreme Governor of all human affairs, and He will be active in a particular society only to the degree that He is accepted and honored.

John then is given a vision of what is transpiring in heaven, what will happen on the earth before the end of this present age, and what the new heaven and new earth will be like (chapters 4 through 22). He is temporarily deeply saddened that no one in heaven can open a scroll held by the Ruler of the universe until the Lamb slain from the foundation of the world (Jesus Christ) takes it from His hand and begins to open it, one seal at a time.

In Revelation 6:1-8, John describes the scene:

"I watched as the Lamb opened the first of the seven seals. Then I heard one of the four living creatures [surrounding the throne of God and praising Him day and night] say in a voice like thunder, 'Come!' I looked and there before me was a white horse! Its rider

359

held a bow, and he was given a crown, and he rode out as a conqueror bent on conquest.

"When the Lamb opened the second seal, I heard the second living creature say, 'Come!' Then another horse came out, a fiery red one. Its rider was given power to take peace from the earth and to make men slay each other. To him was given a large sword.

"When the Lamb opened the third seal, I heard the third living creature say, 'Come!' I looked and there before me was a black horse! Its rider was holding a pair of scales in his hand. Then I heard what sounded like a voice among the four living creatures, saying, A quart of wheat for a day's wages, and three quarts of barley for a day's wages, and do not damage the oil and the wine!

"When the Lamb opened the fourth seal, I heard the voice of the fourth living creature say, 'Come!' I looked and there before me was a pale horse! Its rider was named Death, and Hades was following close behind him. They were given power over a fourth of the earth to kill by sword, famine and plague, and by the wild beasts of the earth."

What do these fearsome four horses represent? Biblical scholars differ, but is it not probable that the first horse, the white steed, represents deception epitomized in the Antichrist? After all, in Revelation 19:11-16 there is a picture of Jesus Christ – "King of kings and Lord of lords" – riding on a white horse and leading a heavenly army, also mounted on white horses. But the figure mounted on the white horse in Revelation 6:1-2 is not our Lord Jesus – the picture is deceptive. Even today we see false images, deluding speech abounds, and deceitful illusions are viewed on television and absorbed from popular culture. This situation is not surprising if we recall that Satan is the arch-deceiver and conspirator of the ages, "a liar and the father of lies" (John 8:44). For this very reason, Christians should be wary of feeding on the empty, fallacious, licentious fare presented on television, the radio, the internet, and in tabloid newspapers and all sorts of salacious books and magazines. Inevitably our minds are deluded, poisoned, and warped when we take in junk food of this type. A young Eskimo girl whom a missionary had won to the Lord approached her beloved mentor one day and said, "M'am, there's terrible fighting going on inside me between a kind, loving, gentle dog that wants me to do good things and a dog that snarls and bites and wants me to do bad things." Recognizing that the girl was describing a battle between spirit and flesh, the missionary asked, "Well, Missy, which dog is stronger?" "Oh," came the immediate reply, "it's the one I feed the most."

Just so, Christians need to feed on God's Word and edifying cultural experiences rather than ingesting sewage from the cultural cesspool in which we are immersed. (May we remember that we are baptized in Christ and refuse to be baptized in the culture of the world.) The clever lies of the Enemy are to be exposed, not assimilated; for as a man "thinks in his heart, so is he" (Proverbs 23:7, NKJ).

The white horse of deception is already galloping throughout the earth, persuading people to believe lies that motivate their actions in ways that tend to create a false reality – one that will fall in the long-term but can do untold mischief in the meantime. Likewise, the red horse representing warfare has been evident, especially in the present century; and the black horse symbolizing inflation and famine has not been absent. Famines even have been fostered by totalitarian regimes for political purposes – in the Ukraine, for example, during the 1930s or in Ethiopia in the 1980s. About one-third of the world's people – many of them living in Third-World countries – are starving or under-nourished, not because there are too many people but because of poor farming methods in some countries or, more frequently, inadequate distribution of food owing to inept administration, profiteering, theft, or inhumane government policies calculated to attain or maintain political supremacy.

Pestilence as represented by the pale horse is also widespread. AIDS is ravishing much of Africa and is more serious domestically and internationally than our administration is willing to admit. World health organizations fear fresh outbreaks of the deadly Ebola virus, and a number of diseases once thought under control are reappearing or spreading. In sub-Saharan Africa, more than a million children die annually from malaria, cholera epidemics have broken out in the Western Hemisphere, typhoid fever keeps re-emerging, and tuberculosis, meningitis, and sexually-transmitted diseases are developing strains resistant to the antibiotics used so effectively in the past. In the light of these observations, is it not very possible that the "four horsemen of the apocalypse" are already ranging throughout he world, bringing economic distress, war, misery, disease, starvation, destruction, and death?

Where do we stand in the last-days' scenario? Perhaps we are so close to events predicted in the Bible (of which we have pre-conceived mental images) and so accustomed to hearing about them that we give them only passing thought. On the other hand, certain events such as the sun's turning black, the moon's turning blood red, and the stars' plummeting from the sky while it rolls up as a scroll (Revelation 6:12-14) obviously have not yet occurred; and since these events are mentioned prior to certain occurrences that may have taken place (at least in part), it is difficult to assess where we are on the Divine time-table. For example, chapter 12 relates certain matters such as the birth of the Messiah that have already happened and other events that may have occurred (depending on one's interpretation of them), but many of the occurrences mentioned await fulfillment in the future.

In the passage just mentioned, the pregnant "woman clothed with the sun, with the moon under her feet and a crown of twelve stars on her head" (Revelation 12:1) represents Israel. The red dragon described in verse 2 as having seven heads (crowned with seven crowns) and ten horns is Satan, who stands ready to devour the woman's infant child at the moment of birth. Only by Divine intervention does the boy to whom the woman gives birth (the Messiah who will rule over all the nations) avert being destroyed and is snatched up to the throne of God (Christ's ascension). Although the chronology becomes a little confusing at this point, a war ensues between Michael at the head of the heavenly hosts and the dragon and his fallen angels until Satan is cast down to the earth, henceforth excluded from heaven. Filled with rage, he does his utmost to destroy the woman (Israel), causing her great suffering but failing to eradicate her. (Is this a picture of the repeated attempts made throughout the centuries, including the holocaust, to eliminate the Jews?). In frustration, the dragon makes war against the offspring of the woman – "those who obey God's commandments and hold to the testimony of Jesus" (Revelation 12:2-17). (In these last days, Christians can expect to suffer persecution and demonic oppression.)

John the Revelator now sees (Revelation 13:1-2) a gruesome beast arising out of the sea (a literal body of water or a "sea" of people? See Revelation 17:15) that has ten horns (connoting great physical or political power) and seven

362

heads, representing universal knowledge (seven is the number of completion) but not absolute, infinite knowledge and wisdom, which belongs only to God. The description is reminiscent of the dragon presented in Revelation 12:3, except that dragon wore seven crowns on his heads, while the beast that is given the dragon's power, wears crowns on its ten horns, probably indicating nations of the earth over which it holds sway. The beast, we are told, resembled a leopard with the feet of a bear and "mouth like a lion."

A parallel may be drawn between this composite beast and the four great beasts mentioned in Daniel 7:3-8 – one like a lion (Is this the lion of the tribe of Judah?) whose eagle-like wings (those of the tribe of Dan) were plucked off before this lion-like beast stood up in the manner of a man and received a man's heart (Is this a somewhat opaque reference to the establishment of the present Israeli state?); one like a bear devouring three ribs (Could this be the Russian bear? The Soviet regime "devoured " Eastern Europe and much of East Asia and Africa.); the third like a leopard with four wings and four heads (Do the wings and heads represent Germany's four empires or *Reichs*, the last one yet to come as leader of the European Community?); and a terrifying fourth beast with ten horns representing the end-times dominion of the Antichrist.[25]

The beast seen coming out of the ocean in Revelation 13:1-2 is the same as the fourth beast seen by Daniel. It derives its power and authority, not from God but from Satan. One of its heads apparently sustained a "fatal wound" that is now healed, to the astonishment of the entire world whose people render homage to both Satan and the beast. Who is this beast that arises out of the sea?

---

[25]The inferences given above are not my own, though I have long been dissatisfied with interpretations positing the lion as Babylon, the bear as Medo-Persia, the leopard as Greece, and the dreadful fourth beast as Rome. In his article "The Beasts of Daniel 7: Daniel's Troubled Vision of the Twentieth Century," *Prophecy in the News* (November 1998), the magazine's editor, J.R. Church, provides a thought-provoking explanation of my capsulized conjectures. Of course, the depiction in Daniel chapter 8 of a ram (Medo-Persia) and a conquering male goat with a long horn (the Greeks under Alexander the Great) that was broken and replaced with four small horns (the Alexandrian successor states) remains quite clear and still stands. The same is true of Daniel's interpretation of Nebuchadnezzar's dream (chapter 2) in which the king saw a statue with a head of gold (Nebuchadnezzar's Babylon), chest and arms of silver (Medo-Persia or Persia), belly and thighs of bronze (Greece), legs of iron (Rome), and feet of iron and clay (end-time empire arising from that once ruled over by Rome). All of these empires aspired to rule the world, and the end-time Antichrist empire will be demolished by the rock "cut out not by hands" (Jesus Christ), who will rule universally forever and ever.

It is, we believe, end-time, Satanically-inspired-and-empowered civil government aspiring to establish universal rule over the earth.

Universal rule had been instituted at the tower of Babel (Genesis 11:1-9), but it had suffered a fatal wound (or so it seemed) by the confusion of languages and the consequent scattering of peoples throughout the world. Now world governance (not the entire world but mainly the Western World) under the aegis of Satan is being revived (for a period of three and a half years: see Revelation 13: 4-5 & cf. Daniel 7:23-25).

The head of this "world government" (more aptly, "world governance," comprised of a coalition of nations) is an arrogant, demon-possessed leader commonly called the Antichrist whose mouth utters lies and blasphemies. He is opposed by the people of God, who are resisting not only his evil deeds but his godless venture. Many of them are killed, either by warfare or martyrdom, as much of the world succumbs to the "new world order." Still, God promises to avenge the suffering and death of these end-time saints, who are called upon to stand firm and remain faithful until the end (Revelation 13:10).

It is evident that the opposition to the Antichrist is not essentially political or military: it is principally religious and cultural, for Revelation 13:11-12 tells of another beast "coming out of the earth" that has two horns (false religion and a culturally decadent, mendacious media?) "like a lamb" (a counterfeit image of the Lamb of God), who "speaks like a dragon." (Today apostate Christianity is collaborating with humanistic cults, occult religions, "liberation theology" [that merges tenets of communism and Christianity in the service of world revolution], and monistic New Age metaphysics to promote a "common fabric of values" and "planetary citizenship.") This second beast (often referred to as "the false prophet") deceives the earth's inhabitants with "great and miraculous signs," revives faith in global government ("the beast who was wounded by the sword and yet lived"), imposes thought-control to insure acceptance of universal civil governance and culture, and employs the latest computer technology to exercise dictatorial control over a world economy (cf. Revelation 13:13-18).

As we saw in the previous chapter, it has been a long-standing goal of the international bankers to institute global governance. How startling it is to read about this in Scriptures penned by the Apostle John more than nineteen hundred years ago! In Revelation chapter 17, he writes about the "great prostitute who sits on many waters" ("peoples, multitudes, nations, and languages" – Revelation 17:15). "With her" (the money interests), an angel informs John, "the kings of the earth committed adultery and the inhabitants of the earth were intoxicated with the wine of her adulteries" (verse 2). Then John relates,

> "...I saw a woman sitting on a scarlet beast that was covered with blasphemous names and had seven heads and ten horns. The woman was dressed in purple and scarlet, and was glittering with gold, precious stones and pearls. She held a golden cup in her hand, filled with abominable things and the filth of her adulteries. This title was written on her forehead: MYSTERY BABYLON THE GREAT, THE MOTHER OF PROSTITUTES AND OF THE ABOMINATIONS OF THE EARTH. I saw that the woman was drunk with the blood of the saints, the blood of those who bore testimony to Jesus. When I saw her, I was greatly astonished. Then the angel said to me: 'Why are you astonished? I will explain to you the mystery of the woman and of the beast she rides, which has the seven heads and ten horns. The beast, which you saw, once was, now is not, and will come up out of the abyss and go to his destruction. The inhabitants of the earth whose names have not been written in the book of life from the creation of the world will be astonished when they see the beast, because he once was, now is not, and yet will come'" (Revelation 17:3-8).

The beast that "once was, now is not, and will come" represents, we believe, a coalition of nations under the Antichrist that will exercise dominion over a significant portion of the world for a short period of time. The account continues (Revelation 17:9-13):

> "This calls for a mind with wisdom. The seven heads [of the global governance system – "the new world order"] are seven hills on which the woman sits. They are also seven kings [or kingdoms]. Five *have fallen* [Babel, Assyria, the Neo-Babylonian Empire under Nebuchadnezzar, the Medo-Persian Empire, and the Greek Empire], one *is* [the Roman Empire], the other *has yet to come*; but when he does come, he must remain for a little while [perhaps a reference to

the communist states of the world aiming at installing communism throughout the world]. The beast who once was [world governance], and now is not [after Babel there has been no true world government: even the Roman Empire was not global in extent], is an eighth king [the end-time united international coalition headed by the Antichrist]. He belongs to the seven [he has the same demonic inspiration and goals, and exercises similar means of domination] and is going to his destruction.

"The ten horns you saw are ten kings who have not yet received a kingdom, but who for one hour, will receive authority as kings along with the beast. They have one purpose and will give their power and authority to the beast."

Are these "ten kings" European nations who were once under the Roman Empire, or could they be the equivalents of the tribal nations of biblical times mentioned in Psalm 83? The exact identity of these nations remains obscure.

After a parenthetic statement in verse 14, the account continues (Revelation 17:15-18):

"Then the angel said to me [John], 'the waters you saw where the prostitute sits, are *peoples, multitudes, nations, and languages* [under civil governments controlled by international financiers]. The beast and the ten horns you saw [the Antichrist and his global coalition] will hate the prostitute [the international bankers who have helped them establish their hegemony but to whom they owe enormous sums]. They will bring her to ruin and leave her naked; they will eat her flesh and burn her with fire. [After the international bankers install "the new world order," they will discover to their dismay that it will turn on them. It will repudiate its debts, seize all the assets of the financiers, throw off their influence, and obliterate their secret network as well as their financial power.] For God has put it into their hearts to accomplish His purpose by agreeing to give the beast their power to rule, until God's words are fulfilled. The woman you saw is the great city that rules over the kings of the earth'" [New York City?].

The abrupt and astounding destruction of Mammon, used by insiders who have manipulated the nations for years until finally achieving their dream of installing a "new world order," is dramatically announced by another angel (Revelation 18:2-3):

"Fallen! Fallen is Babylon the Great! She has become a home for demons and a haunt for every evil spirit, a haunt for every unclean and detestable bird.

"For *all the nations* have drunk the maddening wine of her adulteries. The kings of the earth committed adultery with her, and merchants of the earth grew rich from her excessive luxuries."

Then John the Revelator heard another voice from heaven say:

"Come out of her, my people, so that you will not share in her sins, so that you will not receive any of her plagues; for her sins are piled up to heaven, and God has remembered her crimes. Give back to her as she has given; pay her back double for what she has done. Mix her a double portion from her own cup. Give her as much torture and grief as the glory and luxury she gave herself. In her heart she boasts, 'I sit as queen; I am not a widow, and I will never mourn.' Therefore in one day her plagues will overtake her: death, mourning and famine. She will be consumed by fire, for mighty is the Lord God who judges her.

"When the kings of the earth who committed adultery with her and shared her luxury see the smoke of her burning, they will weep and mourn over her. Terrified at her torment, they will stand afar off and cry: 'Woe! Woe!, O great city, O Babylon, city of power! In one hour your doom has come!'" (Revelation 18:2-10).

How ironic it is that the very ones who helped overthrow the power of the global bankers suddenly awake to the fact that they were to a large degree dependent upon the commerce and services that private financial resources had supplied. Commercial agents and industrialists, of course, can hardly help but experience almost immediately the affects of the drying up of private monies. The voice from heaven continues (Revelation 18:11-13):

> "The merchants of the earth will weep and mourn over her because no one buys their cargoes any more – cargoes of gold, silver, precious stones and pearls; fine linen, purple, silk and scarlet cloth; every sort of citron wood, and articles of every kind made of ivory, costly wood, bronze, iron and marble; cargoes of cinnamon and spice, of incense, myrrh and frankincense, of wine and olive oil, of fine flour and wheat; cattle and sheep; horses and carriages; and *bodies and souls of men.*"

In today's society, there are a number of things that destroy body and soul: involvement in the occult, for example, but also drugs, pornography, and all manner of vices supported by money. The fact that tradesmen are lamenting over their loss of profits indicates that "Mystery Babylon" was, indeed, an economic power. This fact is commensurate with our contention that the "Babylonian prostitute" that the Apostle John saw riding on the nations represents the international bankers who for generations have been advising, influencing, and managing national governments and world affairs from behind the scenes.

The voice from heaven continues to describe the distress of the mercantile interests (Revelation 18:14-20):

> "They [merchants] will say, 'The fruit you longed for is gone from you. All your riches and splendor have vanished, never to be recovered.' The merchants who sold these things and gained their wealth from her ["Mystery Babylon"] will stand afar off, terrified at her torment. They will weep and mourn and cry out: 'Woe! Woe, O great city, dressed in fine linen, purple and scarlet, and glittering with gold, precious stones and pearls! In one hour such great wealth has been brought to ruin!'

> "Every sea captain, and all who travel by ship, the sailors, and all who earn their living from the sea, will stand afar off. When they see the smoke of her burning, they will exclaim, 'Was there ever a city like this great city?' They will throw dust on their heads, and

with weeping and mourning cry out: 'Woe! Woe, O great city, where all who had ships on the sea became rich through her wealth! In one hour she has been brought to ruin!'

"Rejoice over her, O heaven! Rejoice, saints and apostles and prophets! God has judged her for the way she treated you."

Then a "mighty angel" (verses 20-23) casts a large boulder into the sea, proclaims that the power of Babylon has been broken forever, and condemns the activities in which it has been engaged for so long:

"By your magic spell all the nations were led astray [and often into bloody wars]. In her was found the blood of the prophets and the saints [persecuted and martyred], and all who have been killed on the earth."

What a serious charge! Yet who can gainsay it? To investigate it exhaustively is beyond the scope of this interpretive essay, but fragments of cogent corroborating evidence come immediately to mind. It can hardly be denied, for example, that the passion for money and power has been a significant factor in generating the slave trade, wars, abortion, and criminal activities. Moreover, the international bankers are connected with international crime syndicates, drug dealing such as that affiliated with the BCCI, underhanded operations involving the big oil interests, terrorism, extortion, and other malefic activities. How true that "the love of money is a root of all sorts of evil" and that one "can not serve God and money"!

As early as the 8th century B.C. during the reign of kings Jotham, Ahaz, Hezekiah, and Manasseh of Judah, the prophet Isaiah looked forward to the Neo-Babylonian Empire in terms analogous to the description of "Mystery Babylon" in the book of Revelation. The haughtiness of its ruling monarchs corresponds rather closely to the attitudes of the "Babylonian Whore": "I will continue forever – the eternal queen!" (Isaiah 47:7)

Hubris of this nature has been displayed by the international financiers who have confidently manipulated world affairs for many years and expect to continue their hegemony over the nations. Their conspiracies will ultimately be thwarted just as were those of Nebuchadnezzar's Babylon of whom Isaiah said, "You have trusted in your wickedness and have said, 'no one sees me'" (Isaiah 47:10). The prophet goes on to say: "Your wisdom and knowledge mislead you when you say to yourself, 'I am and there is none besides me.' Disaster will come upon you that you can not ward off with a ransom [in other words, Babylon can not buy its way out]; a catastrophe you can not foresee will suddenly come upon you..., there is no one that can save you" (Isaiah 47:10-11 & 15).

More than a century later, another prophet – Habakkuk – lamented about conditions in the Kingdom of Judah under King Jehoiakim (609-598 B.C.) and predicted its conquest by the Babylonians. His prophecy opens with a complaint:

> "How long, O Lord, must I call for help, but You do not listen? Or cry out to You, 'Violence!' but You do not save? Why do You make me look at injustice? Why do You tolerate wrong? Destruction and violence are before me; there is strife, and conflict abounds. Therefore the law is paralyzed, and justice never prevails. The wicked hem in the righteous, so that justice is perverted" (Habakkuk 1:2-4).

Do these wrongs and injustices sound strangely familiar? Do we find them in our own nation? Ungodly conditions of this sort open the way for a "Babylonian" takeover, which the Lord God informs the prophet will take place:

> "I am raising up the Babylonians, that ruthless and impetuous people, who sweep across the whole earth to seize dwelling places not their own" (Habakkuk 1:6).

The description of this "ruthless and impetuous" nation has specific reference to the armies of Nebuchadnezzar that were to conquer and subjugate apostate Judah within a few years, but it also seems to have symbolic application to "Mystery Babylon" depicted in Revelation chapters 17 & 18. Notice God's description in verses 7-10 of this invading Babylonian army:

> "They are a feared and dreaded people; they are a law to themselves and promote their own honor [a prideful, humanistic, self-reliant people who see no need to honor God or observe His

principles]. Their horses are swifter than leopards, fiercer than wolves at dusk. Their cavalry gallops headlong; their horsemen come from afar. They fly like a vulture swooping to devour; they all come bent on violence. Their hordes advance like a desert wind and gather prisoners like sand. They deride kings and scoff at rulers. They laugh at all fortified cities" (Habakkuk 1:8-10).

Likewise, the international bankers with their globalist agenda "gather prisoners" and will brook no obstruction, viewing anyone or any nation that might try to oppose them with contempt.

Habakkuk recognizes the validity of the Lord's description, but still wonders why the wicked Babylonians are allowed to "swallow up those more righteous than themselves" (verse 13). He complains about their jubilantly catching men in a "dragnet" [a net of economic control?] as if they were fish and making a god of the dragnet, because by it they are able to live in luxury and enjoy the choicest food, while exploiting nations and destroying them "without mercy" (Habakkuk 1:15-17).

In response, the Lord gives his prophet a revelation that will not be understood until "*an appointed time*: it speaks of the *end* and will not prove false. Though it linger, wait for it; it will certainly come and will not delay" (Habakkuk 2:2-3). Significantly, this very passage is quoted by the author of Hebrews in specific reference to Christ's second coming, as is also the statement in Habakkuk 2:14 that in the end-time being described "the righteous [or "righteous one"] will live by his faith" (Hebrews 10:37-38).

It would appear that in the time immediately preceding our Lord's return, the Babylonian system comprised of money managers who control the nations (designated by the pronoun "he") will have unrighteous desires ("his desires are not upright," verse 4). "Indeed, wine betrays him; he is arrogant and never at rest. Because he is greedy as the grave and like death is never satisfied, he ["Mystery Babylon"] gathers to himself all the nations and takes captive all the peoples" (cf. Revelation 17:15), instituting widespread dominion under the Antichrist.

At this point, however, the Antichrist coalition of nations will throw off the yoke of the international bankers, just as stated in Revelation 17:16-18. God gives the following description to the prophet Habakkuk:

"Will not all of them [the coalition nations] taunt him ["Mystery Babylon"] with ridicule and scorn, saying, 'Woe to him who piles up stolen goods and makes himself wealthy by extortion [or loans]! How long must this go on?' Will not your debtors suddenly arise? Will they not wake up and make you tremble? Then you will become their victim. Because you have plundered many nations, the peoples who are left will plunder you. For you have shed man's blood; you have destroyed lands and cities and everyone in them" (Habakkuk 2:6-9).

The Lord continues (verses 9-10 & 12):

"Woe to him ["Mystery Babylon"] who builds his realm by unjust gain to set his nest on high, to escape the clutches of ruin! [American oil companies have reaped great financial profits by upholding the Communist regime in Angola]. You have plotted the ruin of many peoples.... Woe to him who builds a city with bloodshed and establishes a town by crime!" (This woe is apropos to drug traffickers such as the Columbian drug lords, who have built cites and even hired their own private armies.)

God repeats the charge that Babylon has shed much blood (Habakkuk 2:17; cf. Revelation 18:24) and upbraids it for its idolatry and deceit (verse 18): "Of what value is an idol... or an image that teaches lies [TV and the media?]?" In a preceding verse (verse 13), He asks: "Has not the Lord Almighty determined that the people's labor is only fuel for the fire, that the nations exhaust themselves for nothing?" This question recalls the words of Psalm 2:

"Why do the nations conspire and the peoples plot in vain? The kings of the earth take their stand and the rulers gather together against the Lord and against His Anointed One. 'Let us break their chains,' they say, 'and throw off their fetters.'

"The One enthroned in heaven laughs; The Lord scoffs at them. Then He rebukes them in His anger and terrifies them in His wrath, saying, 'I have installed My King on Zion, My holy hill.'

"I will proclaim the decree of the Lord: He said to Me, 'You are My Son, today I have become Your Father. Ask of Me, and I will make the nations Your inheritance, the ends of the earth Your possession. You will rule them with an iron scepter; You will dash them to pieces like pottery.'

"Therefore, you kings be wise; be warned, you rulers of the earth. Serve the Lord with fear and rejoice with trembling. Kiss the Son, lest He be angry and you be destroyed in your way, for His wrath can flare up in a moment. Blessed are all who take refuge in Him."

Blessed, indeed, will be believers who witness the downfall of "Mystery Babylon" (see Revelation 19:1-8), for then the defeat of the Antichrist and his system of world governance is imminent. In all probability, the Antichrist or "man of sin" is not only alive today but in a position of power or influence from which he can quickly assume direction over a strong coalition of nations. He will be recognized as "the lawless one" because he will subvert the God-given basis of law and thereby weaken and eventually eliminate the effective rule of law, which has served as a restraint upon wrongdoing and criminal activity from the time of John the Revelator (Roman law) until the present day. The Apostle Paul spoke of this in II Thessalonians chapter 2. After admonishing the Thessalonian believers not to be deluded by reports that "the day of the Lord has already come" (II Thessalonians 2:2), Paul states:

"Don't let anyone deceive you in any way, for that day will not come until the rebellion occurs and the man of lawlessness is revealed, the man doomed to destruction. He will oppose and will exalt himself over everything that is called God or is worshiped, so that he sets himself in God's temple, proclaiming himself to be God.

"Don't you remember when I was with you I used to tell you these things? And now you know what is holding him back [the rule of law], so that he may be revealed at the proper time. For the secret power of lawlessness is already at work; but the one who now holds it back will continue to do so till he [or it] is taken out of the way. And then the lawless one will be revealed, whom the Lord Jesus will overthrow with the breath of His mouth and destroy by the splendor of His coming" (II Thessalonians 2:3-8. See also verses 9-12 and Daniel 7:25).

Although the "lawless one" has not yet been fully revealed, the rule of law has been seriously undermined in this nation in the past few years, and soon Satan will enter into "the lawless one" (who is already under demonic influence) just as he came fully into Judas Iscariot (Luke 22:3) at a critical moment, and the restraint of law (not that of the church or the Holy Spirit) will be practically removed. But not only will the Antichrist have little regard for law, he will be a propagator of the new world order to the detriment of his own country – a power-hungry deceiver who, like his master, will pose as a religious person of great humanity. He will be a consummate politician who will corrupt his associates and the processes of government, pander to all sorts of evil or dissatisfied factions, and cultivate public opinion with the help of the media. He will consider himself above the law though pretending respect for it. He will be a man of indifferent morals who will use falsehood, chicanery, bribery, intimidation, and even murder if necessary to attain his ends or conceal his deeds. He will speak much of peace and endeavor to bring peace in troubled areas of the world, especially in the Middle East, while exalting Mammon and enjoying the strong support of various crime syndicates and the international banking interests until he is able to consolidate his power. After sustaining what appears to be a fatal political wound (Revelation 13:3 may well pertain to the head of the system of world governance as well as to the coalition itself), he will recover to usher in a form of international governance (itself once thought to be dead), perhaps under the United Nations.

Acclaimed by world religious leaders and with strong support from the media, which will burnish his image, silence critics, and help promulgate a centralized economy (Revelation 13:14-18), the Antichrist will speak much of peace and, through force and diplomacy, will try to impose peace in troubled areas of the world. Could the Antichrist be Bill Clinton? Might he use the Y2K crisis (or some other real or imagined crisis) as a pretext to suspend constitutional government, incarcerate presumed opponents in concentration camps or prisons, eliminate all opposition, make himself a virtual dictator, and move us into a "new world order"? Or could he accomplish the same end by acquiring a position of power in a greatly strengthened United Nations? Is it possible that he is a scion of the lost Israelite tribe of Dan, which some biblical scholars, on the basis of Jacob's prophecy recorded in Genesis 49:16-17 and intriguing circumstantial evidence, believe will bring forth the Antichrist.[26]

For a time, the peace initiatives of the "man of sin" will meet with some success, especially in the Middle East where an unprecedented peace accord will be implemented (Daniel 9:27). Christian dissenters will be oppressed while the Antichrist rules almost unopposed for three and a half years (Daniel 7:25). But just when he seems to have attained unrivaled hegemony over a great coalition of nations, he will break his treaty with the Jewish nation and institute abominable religious practices (Daniel 9:27) that will bring Divine judgment (Revelation chapters 15 &16).

Notwithstanding the ferocity of the plagues poured out to punish evildoers, they will not repent of their sins but will curse "the God of heaven" (Revelation 16:8-11). At about this time, the nations under the Antichrist's sway will repudiate their debts to the international bankers, precipitating a world-wide economic crisis; and the Satanically-motivated "man of sin," supported by a God-denying culture and powerful news syndicates, will mobilize the nations to fight against Israel and other nations of the Middle East (Daniel 11:36-45; Revelation 16:13-16; and Revelation19:19). This demonically-inspired army will appear to be invincible. Two-thirds of Israel's inhabitants will perish (Zechariah 13:8) and Jerusalem will be captured, its houses ransacked, and half of its populace carried into exile. In the midst of this terrifying scenario, the Jewish people who remain will recognize Jesus as their Messiah (Zechariah 12:10; 13:8; and 14:1-5) as a tremendous earthquake splits the city into three parts and Jesus Christ returns as "King of kings and Lord of lords" to deliver His people, strike down His enemies, and establish His millennial kingdom on earth (Revelation 19 through 20:4). Then "the earth will be filled with the knowledge of the Lord as the waters cover the sea" (Habakkuk 2:14).

---

[26]See J. R. Church, *Guardians of the Grail...*, pp. 101-130.

At the end of one thousand years, Satan (who had been imprisoned after his defeat) will be released from the abyss for a time, and he will mobilize a massive army drawn from "the four corners of the earth," possibly consisting largely of multitudes from what are today Islamic nations extending from Syria through Iraq, Iran, former Soviet Central Asia, and Pakistan to Indonesia (see Revelation 20:7-10 and Ezekiel chapter 39). Why is Satan allowed the opportunity to gather his forces for one final attempt to overthrow Divine authority? Only God knows, but perhaps this is His way of compelling all the inhabitants of the globe to make a choice whether they will follow Him or the Evil One. In one climactic battle the Lord God will conquer His foes once and for all and cleanse the earth of them. Satan will be hurled into the "lake of fire" to suffer everlasting torment with his demonic cohorts ("fallen angels") and the rest of the "unholy trinity" (previously sent there) – the Antichrist and the "false prophet." After this, God will judge the unbelieving dead and commit them, along with Death and Hades, to the "lake of fire." He will then renew the universe and establish the Holy City, the New Jerusalem – an impeccably pure and unspeakably beautiful and blissful city where only the saints can dwell – as His earthly capital.

Resting on the sure promises of Scripture and recognizing Almighty God's controlling hand in the history of mankind, from start to finish, Christian historians can expectantly await the second advent of our Lord Jesus Christ, "the Alpha and Omega, the First and the Last, the Beginning and the End" (Revelation 22:13). With co-religionists from every era of God's great historical saga, let us praise and worship the Lamb of God slain from the foundation of the world (Revelation 13:8) and rejoice that His return is imminent. Even so, come, Lord Jesus!

APPENDICES

Appendix I

GOD-HONORING VS. MAN-WORSHIPING CYCLES IN HISTORY

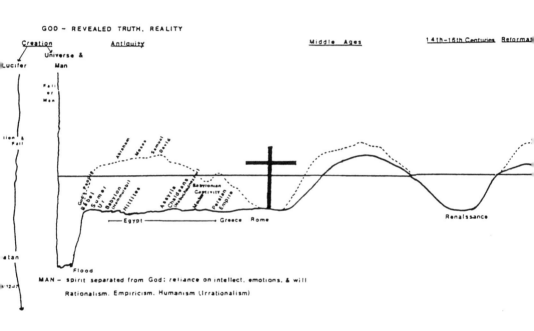

GOD – REVEALED TRUTH, REALITY

Creation   Antiquity   Middle Ages   14th–16th Centuries   Reformation

Lucifer   Universe & Man

Fall of Man

Abraham   Moses   Samuel   David

God's People   Babel   Sumer   Ur   Babylon (Hammurabi)   Hittites   Assyria   Chaldeans   Babylonian Captivity   Medes   Persian Empire

——— Egypt ———   Greece   Rome   Renaissance

Flood

MAN – spirit separated from God; reliance on intellect, emotions, & will

Rationalism. Empiricism. Humanism (Irrationalism)

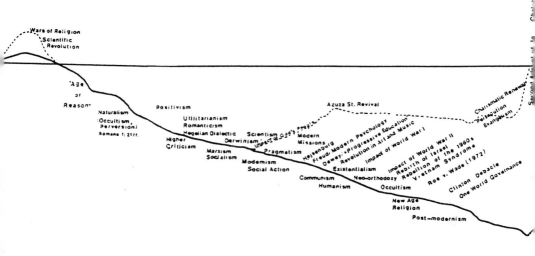

Appendix II

IDEOLOGICAL POLITICAL SPECTRUM

"Moderates"

Middle

Communism Fascism	Socialism	Liberalism	Conservatism	Libertarianism	Anarchy
Man-made attempts to institute utopia.	Government controls the economy to redistribute wealth.	Benevolence flows down from centralized government. A strong government with broad scope is needed - similar to authoritarian, benevolent governments envisioned by the 18th - century "enlighteners."	Private enterprise, market determines conditions for exchange of goods, Constitutional limitations on government. (Heritage of 19th - century liberalism.) Contrast with European & Latin American conservatism which correspond more closely with present day American "liberalism."	*Laissez faire* in economics and society and politics.	

No schema to portray the political spectrum can convey an infallible representation of reality; yet the schema depicted above comes closer to doing so from an ideological vantage point than those placing communism on the far left and fascism on the far right. Fascism is not the logical ultimate expression of conservative thought.

On the other hand, it must be admitted that the characteristics of American conservatism (depicted here) are not generally the same as those of European or Latin American "conservatism." The latter forms of "authoritarian conservatism" are more closely akin to 18th-century "enlightened despotism," the ideological forerunner of present-day American "liberalism."

Present-day liberalism is an outgrowth of the utilitarian views of the 18th-century "enlighteners" rather than those of the parliamentarian liberals of the 19th century (forerunners of modern conservatism: the "government that governs best is the government that governs least"). Eighteenth-century liberal thought asserted that the monarch did not rule by Divine right but by reason of being the "first servant of the people" – a slogan adopted by the so-called "enlightened despots." Rulers such as Holy Roman Emperor Joseph II, Prussian King Frederick II, Czarina Catherine II of Russia, Spanish monarch Carlos III, and others assumed an authoritarian stance (counterbalanced, nevertheless, to some degree by traditional institutions, a hidebound class structure, customary usages, and bureaucracies that were less pervasive than those of today, and means of communication that were slower and less efficient than in our contemporary world) for the sake, as they said, of the public welfare. Joseph II informed the Brabant estates in 1789: "I do not need your consent to do good and I regard [it] as my chief duty to save you, even in spite of yourselves, from the danger to which you would perhaps be exposed should I await your consent." This "big brother" attitude is the spirit of modern liberalism in the United States and probably the spirit of some conservatism – that of an authoritarian nature – in Europe (where the class structure, tradition, and the concept of *noblesse oblige* are stronger) and in Latin America. This should not be surprising; for without a distinctively biblical base (such as that on which the United States was originally founded), both "liberals" and "conservatives" tend to operate upon humanistic premises – including "humanitarianism," pragmatism, or an eclectic mixture – all of them man-centered. In the United States, however, contemporary conservatism is inclined more toward constitutionally limited government while liberalism moves in the direction of making government – especially that in Washington, D.C. – the source of all blessings, the solver of all problems.

To the ideological right of the conservatives (including some members of the Christian "New Right") are the libertarians, who worship at the shrines of Adam Smith and perhaps Ludwig Von Mises without regard for any biblical principles. Although they may favor some of the same things that conservatives generally stand for (for example, free enterprise and free trade), libertarians do so from different premises, characteristically assuming a completely *laissez faire* attitude on both economic and social issues (for example, marijuana should be legalized, pornography need not be curbed, and women should have full control over their own bodies – a rationale for abortion).[27] For this reason, it is important that Christians do not make formal alliance with libertarians lest believers be "unequally yoked." If libertarians wish to support certain conservative initiatives or positions, let them; but Christian conservatives should not become entangled with any group in a manner that might require their supporting part of an unbiblical agenda.

The logical extension of libertarianism, with its emphasis upon unrestrained individual "rights" and freedom from all government regulation, is the virtual elimination of government control (contrary to Romans 13:1-7 and I Peter 2:13-17), so that everyone may "do what is right in his own eyes." The obvious result is ineffectual government or even anarchy. If the latter should occur, reaction would doubtless set in; for citizens would probably be willing to trade liberty, perverted into license, for security, stability, and order by ushering in a strong man or a dictatorial regime. Philosophically, however, totalitarian governments would not result from the extension of American conservatism (with its desire for constitutionally limited government) through libertarianism to its logical conclusion of anarchy. Rather, totalitarian regimes result when a sufficient number of powerful groups on the right react against anarchy and perhaps form a coalition with elements of the left (already disposed toward authoritarian solutions to bring in a government that can impose its will upon all of society.

Ideologically, it is the left – not the right – that is moving toward totalitarianism of some form. Liberals, who tend to look to the central government to solve all manner of problems, think that society can be improved through social legislation and schemes to redistribute wealth. Logically, this mind-set leads to socialism, which requires central planning.

Redistribution of wealth can be achieved by government either through state regulation of private capitalistic enterprise by calling the tune for both management and labor (as was done in pre-World-War-II fascist regimes), or it can be achieved by governmental takeover of the means of production in behalf of the "proletariat," as has been done in the Soviet Union. "Communism," as it existed in the former Soviet Union, and fascism are merely different forms of totalitarianism – different approaches to rid society of its "bad apples" for the sake of ushering in a man-made utopia. (Rousseau's concept of the "general will" – not necessarily majority opinion, but an ideal will, what ought to be – was effected in the French Revolution by Robespierre, by Lenin in the name of the Russian working class, and by Mao Tse-tung in the name of the Chinese people. In each case, a small group of gangsters seized control in the

---

[27]Christian libertarians view pornography and abortion somewhat differently.

name of the people and with the enunciated purpose of eliminating the evils and inequalities of the past.) Therefore, communism of the Soviet variety and fascism are merely two different forms of totalitarianism, which itself is rooted in 18th-century thought (not in 19th-century liberalism) and is a further logical extension of "big-brother government" and socialism (*El Duce* was a socialist for a time, and Hitler was the head of the National Socialist Party). Despite their differences, communist totalitarianism and fascist totalitarianism have much in common. In either case, the state becomes god and individual rights are trampled upon or destroyed. To be sure, Hitler sought alliance with the church in his early years in power, but he ultimately subordinated it to his will – in a manner not totally unlike that of the Soviet Union. Moreover, though Hitler and Mussolini stressed a form of ultra-nationalism, neither was adverse to expanding national territories and for a time did so just as effectively as the Soviet Union, notwithstanding all the latter's emphasis upon extending Marxism-Leninism throughout the world. Franco of Spain, of course, did cooperate with the church because it served his purpose to do so, given the religious temperament of the Spanish people, But Franco was perhaps as much a traditional autocrat as a fascist though historians generally categorize him as the latter. (This may be the case with many governments categorized as "friendly" or "benevolent" fascist regimes.) In any event, extreme forms of fascism and communism are both totalitarian in nature. Both are evil, for they are not based upon biblical covenantal principles of government. Indeed, they do not recognize God as the source of all authority but rather hold sway by exercising raw power and intimidation (Satanic techniques). That they are illegitimate, outlaw regimes may perhaps be most readily observed in the manner in which they conduct foreign affairs. Struggles between regimes that rule by power rather than God-given authority may be likened to the bloody gang fights or "warfare" between various elements of the Mafia. It must be remembered that unity and harmony can exist only in Jesus Christ (Colossians 1:16-17); Satan is the author of treachery, chicanery, dissembling, deceit, lying, enmity, hatred, disharmony, dissension, strife, fear, intimidation, extortion, terrorism, and every form of evil device. Therefore, even were he to win a victory, it would be transient, because the forces mobilized by him are only held together temporarily by their common hatred for God, God's people, and God-sanctioned authorities. That is why every apparent victory of Satanic forces is quickly nullified. Satan's minions are as rebellious in nature as he, having accepted his spirit of rejecting God, the Source of all unity. They always seek to advance themselves at the expense of everyone else – even co-religionists with whom they may have allied for a season.

Appendix III

"THE DAYS OF NOAH": A MODERN ANALOGY

"Repent for the kingdom of heaven is at hand" (John the Baptist in Matthew 3:2; Jesus the Messiah in Matthew 4:17). **"Prepare the way of the Lord; Make straight paths for Him"** (John the Baptist in Matthew 3:3).

We are living in perilous times. Evil forces are at work to corrupt God's intended order for the world, undermine constitutional government in this land, and destroy our bases of ethics and morals. Biblical standards are constantly called into question, ridiculed, or eroded by salacious literature, unbalanced or biased news reporting, self-serving political action, ill-conceived legislation, pragmatic executive policies, relativistic judicial decisions, socialistic and humanistic schooling, behavioristic psychology, and demonically-inspired entertainment, music, art, and pornography. Our society is being flooded with images and thoughts promoting sexual perversion, violence, dishonesty, sharp practice, and irreverence as the Devil attempts to eradicate from the minds and hearts of men, women, and children knowledge of God's ways, His proper order, and His ordained patterns of authority.

In other words, Satan is trying to invert the natural order of creation, erase the law of God from the human heart, and eliminate God-given standards revealed in Holy Writ. The Adversary wants to efface the Divine image in man – upon whom God originally conferred regency over the earth. He wants to supplant the knowledge and fear of God in man's heart by denying the reality of a Creator and by conditioning mankind to view the universe, human society, government, the economy, and culture from a relativistic, evolutionary perspective. The Scripture says that "as it was in the days of Noah, so it will be at the coming of the Son of Man" (Matthew 24:37): as in the days of Noah, so it is today – a time when evil is prevalent, even normative; a time when social norms and man-made laws are increasingly not in harmony with God's eternal law; and when "law" is used by those in power to subvert righteousness.

Satan's strategy has always been to usurp God's authority by subverting His regents. He succeeded in the garden of Eden, and he has tried ever since to work in and through man's prideful, fallen nature to thwart God's loving and benevolent plan for all creation. Because of sin, man's spirit – through which he communicated directly with God – became inactive and dormant as the Enemy endeavored to destroy the image of the Creator in him. Separated from God, man was unable to perceive His Creator, truth, or reality in the created order, and instead relied almost solely on his intellect for guidance. No longer responsive to the spiritual truths of God, man became susceptible to Satan's falsehoods and willing to confine himself to a search for truth through purely rational and empirical means. The "Father of Lies" was, of course, jubilant over his conquest of God's regents. He believed he had ruined the image of God in man and had reduced him permanently to reliance solely upon his intellect and senses, which Satan intended to influence and manipulate to rule the earth.

Satan wanted to bring man's will – which God created free – into subservience, and for a time he seemed to be succeeding. In Genesis chapters 4 through 6, we read of the hatred, pride, and evil deeds of men no longer in communion with their Creator. They had become so vile that God determined to wipe them off the face of the earth. Yet, the image of God had not been entirely eradicated in man; for one man called Noah sensed in his spirit that there was something beyond what he comprehended through his natural senses. He was able to incline his heart toward God and to receive from Him spiritual renewal. Therefore, he perceived a reality that his contemporaries – consumed with the pursuit of power, intellectual accomplishment, material well-being, and pleasure – did not know existed. Their atrophied spirits were inoperative, and they pursued their lusts and material gain – just as we see people doing today.

The Bible states that "everyone who wants to live a godly life in Christ Jesus will be persecuted" (II Timothy 3:12), and doubtless this was true of Noah. Just imagine what a laughingstock he must have been! He was probably dubbed a "neanderthal man" out of touch with reality. Can't you just hear his neighbors calling his belief in God "absurd" and "obsolescent," "pre-scientific" and "irrational"? "No doubt about it," they would opine, "Noah is a lunatic (though a relatively harmless one); otherwise he would not be spending most of his time building a gigantic boat far from any large body of water. He doesn't even have a truck or trailer to haul it to a boat ramp for launching. If anyone was ever out of his gourd, it is Noah. In fact, he has led his whole family astray – they are all 'touched in the head' because they are helping 'old looney bird' who claims that 'the true God' – 'the Creator of all things' – has told him to build a boat big enough to hold a select menagerie of all living things. Who can swallow that fairy tale? If Noah's dry-land shipyard does not conclusively prove him to be crazy, his hallucinations about a God who speaks to him certainly do. There are gods all over the place, and perhaps a majority of folks worship them in one fashion or another; but intellectuals know that 'gods' are merely figments of the human imagination. By every empirical test, it has been demonstrated that no actual 'God' exists. Oh sure, some people still refer to natural catastrophes as acts of God, but it is just a figure of speech. There are scientifically verified forces in nature that man admittedly does not yet fully understand, and there are those who believe in some sort of cosmic energy, but polls reveal that virtually no one believes in a Creator-God such as Noah speaks of – especially one with whom a sane person can carry on a conversation. Oh yes, there is old Methuselah who repeats primitive legends about a Creator – saying that Adam told him all about it; but modern men have *evolved* to a stage where they are no longer fooled by the words of ancient theologians, metaphysicians, or other myth-makers. In the new modern age, the universities, most of the public schools, the media, the psychologists, philosophers, lawyers and judges, artists, entertainers, and all 'the beautiful people' who amount to anything at all discount the primitive folklore. Man can now solve his own problems: he has long ago outgrown any need to believe in a God!

"Thankfully, we have eliminated pre-scientific attitudes from the community schools, and some four-year olds are now being enrolled in tax-supported pre-schools where trained professionals can watch over what they learn and disabuse them of superstitions that oddballs like Noah or (perish the thought!) their own parents may have instilled in them. For all too many years, parents imposed their own rigid values on their children, making them feel guilty by telling them to obey the precepts of an alleged 'Creator,' – a sort of super father figure whose so-called laws inhibit free expression and self-improvement. Although most modern parents seem to have discarded such foolish, old-fashioned notions, it is comforting to know that the public schools are trying to make sure that no child retains these superstitions. Fortunately – now that more mothers are working outside the home and pre-schools and government day-care centers are becoming popular – even the very young are learning how to make their own decisions and develop their own values.

"Noah and his wife, of course, do not approve of this and apparently they have persuaded their sons and daughters-in-law that the old ways are best. They keep talking about fearing 'the God of their fathers' and rearing their children to obey Him. Noah does not realize that he and his so-called 'traditional family' are completely out of step with the times. There are all sorts of 'families' and live-in arrangements in modern society; and one is just as good as another. I say if a man gets tired of his wife, he should not be bound to continue in a loveless marriage. Let the mother head the family alone – there's nothing wrong with that. A liberated woman can often get another man (whether she actually marries him or not). Or she can get a job or welfare assistance from the community. Let her live her own life. Let her choose whatever male friends she wishes to entertain or live with, or even female friends if she finds them attractive – what's the difference? The same goes for men. They should have full freedom to work out mutually satisfying living arrangements with other men, women, or children as they wish. One lifestyle is as good as another!

"Old mossbacks like Noah and Methuselah should not be permitted to make people feel uncomfortable by spouting their judgmental, legalistic nonsense. They are certainly not 'socially correct,' and their talk about a Creator-God and His 'revealed laws' can be very hurtful and upsetting. But what person in his right mind can believe their tales or even consider them? Everyone who knows Methuselah thinks he is either a liar or out of his mind. Oh, he's kindly enough, but he says the strangest things – even claiming on one occasion that his father Enoch never died but simply disappeared after mentioning that he yearned to be alone with 'God' and to 'commune' intimately with Him – whatever that is supposed to mean. It's true that nobody ever saw Enoch after that day, and no grave was ever discovered; but some accident probably overtook him which his family has tried to cover up. Certainly, the whole brood is out of step with society. Nobody gives credence to Methuselah's senile ramblings about the words he attributes to his father, to Adam, or to 'God'; however, his fantasies have infected Noah and his family. They talk about 'righteous living,' and they adhere to quaint and ludicrous moral concepts long since discredited, refusing to participate in all the fun everyone else is having. They discountenance alcoholic beverages, sexual activities outside of marriage, risque jokes, pornography, rock music, smoking pot, snorting coke, or doing anything else that is groovy, and their denunciations of abortion and infanticide tend to cast a pall over the good times of the sexually liberated.

"Noah's talk about marital fidelity and sexual abstinence before marriage is incredibly naive. Our young people are going to engage in sex anyway – didn't many former 'God-believers' do so before they came around to our way of thinking? We must be realistic. We can not afford to be like ostriches, 'keeping our heads in the sand.' We must deal with the situation as it is. Certainly, we must continue to permit abortion on demand. Unfortunate girls with unwanted pregnancies should have the right of choice. Indeed, all women must have the right of privacy and anonymity lest they be ostracized if they do not carry a pregnancy to term. Besides, beneficial uses are already being discovered for the fetal tissues!

"Speaking of benefit to society, would it not be well to think about relieving our oldsters of the misery of loneliness and poor health while at the same time relieving their children and society of the burden of caring for unproductive persons?

"Noah and his family, with their outmoded moralistic attitudes, have no compassion. As a matter of fact, their reference to sexually-active singles as 'fornicators' is crude and insensitive, and their prayers for persons they call 'adulterers' and 'homosexuals' make even some adults who are discreetly conducting sexual liaisons in private by mutual consent feel guilty. Yes, the narrow-minded, intolerant, judgmental attitudes of these 'holy Joes' are well-known, and all that jive about keeping 'God's laws' is simply *intolerable*! They should be compelled to be *tolerant*! After all, doesn't everyone have the right to do whatever he pleases so long as he does not actually injure someone else? Surely as long a person believes his conduct is O.K., it is O.K.; and the same principle must be *tolerantly* applied to everyone else. What right does a fundamentalist bigot such as Noah have to speak publicly about a Creator-God and His laws? Such talk is socially disturbing –destroying people's self-esteem and laying guilt trips on them. Soon, it may be hoped, such *hate language* will be squelched – either by legislation or, if necessary by more direct and painful means. It can not be *tolerated* any longer!

"It may be, of course, that drastic measures against these *intolerant* hate mongers will not be necessary. Noah and his weird family are giving more and more attention to completing their 'ark,' and nobody pays much attention to them anyway. Even the in-laws have as little as possible to do with their daughters who married Noah's sons. Everyone knows they have been brainwashed, but attempts to take them away from their husbands to de-program them have failed.

"As for doddering old Methuselah, he can't last much longer. It is said that he is more than 960 years of age, though no one can be sure when he was born. His name is very peculiar if not downright bizarre: 'When he dies, then it will occur.' What kind of parents could possibly have named him that? Only superstitious believers in a Creator-God would inflict a handle like that on a child. Curious name though. If anything of note should happen after 'old Methusy's' death, there are always a few irrational lamebrains who may try to attach some special significance to it. Oh well, it will not be long before, not only Methuselah but that stupid jerk Noah and his wife will pass away, and perhaps then someone can reason with his deluded family. Not that it really matters: they are already socially ostracized and isolated. Little wonder what with their strange behavior, stubbornness, and sanctimonious attitudes . A person could develop a guilt complex just by being around them. All their talk about a Creator and man's duty to live according to His laws – what nonsense!

"Would you believe that at one time Noah disturbed a lot of people – especially the local children – with all his asinine ideas? But that was before he was ordered to stop teaching without a certificate because of a 'compelling popular interest.' For several years, he protested that his God-given rights of freedom of speech were being violated – crazy old coot: there are no rights except those granted by the civil order! Actually he has been treated very leniently. He can believe whatever he wants to as long as he does not proselytize, and he can always say anything he pleases within his family circle. The authorities have been very patient with him, and he should be grateful.

"If you want my opinion, the authorities have been far too lenient. Noah really should be put away somewhere – perhaps in an asylum where he can be helped. He is constantly causing trouble of one sort or another. His latest gambit was to invite neighbors into his tent for home meetings, which thankfully were closed down as a violation of zoning regulations. He was also told to stop preaching to tourists and curious onlookers who came to see what he was doing, because he was making a public nuisance of himself. All that spiel about faith in a Creator-God was just too much to put up with, even if the tourist trade has slackened a bit since the injunction.

"For that very reason, it may be just as well that the authorities have been indulgent in not forbidding Noah to sing what he calls 'praises to the God of the universe' while he is building that monstrosity of a boat. After all, if he wants to continue to make a fool of himself, let him. Everyone knows he is crazy anyhow, and his singing does amuse onlookers who come from other areas and spend their cash here. What can it matter now that he is prohibited from upsetting people with that 'doom and gloom' nonsense he used to preach!

"Fortunately, the most respectable and religious members of Arkland – as we call our country for the sake of the tourist trade – did not protest the decisions forbidding Noah's 'doom and gloom' prophecies. In fact, they immediately saw through his negativism and pointed out that if he were a true prophet, he would be proclaiming positive and uplifting messages. Whether his singing about faith in a Creator-God and praises to his 'Maker' will prove troublesome remains to be seen. If it does, the authorities will doubtless take action, but so far the fact that Noah is a cultural oddity seems to have attracted big bucks to this area with few discernible ill affects.

"Eventually, of course, they will find a way to take over that monstrous boat and turn it into a cassino, but the time is not right. So long as outlanders keep crowding into the present gaming facilities, bars, brothels, strip shows, and local lodging and eating establishments, it may be best to leave well enough alone. After all, profits are soaring and the stock market is booming. Why risk a change that may have unforeseen affects. If the financial situation begins to decline, then the government can always intervene – as it should – to stimulate the economy. That's the bottom line. Everything else is of little consequence, regardless of all Noah's talk about honoring God, preserving family values, and rearing children by so-called godly principles. All of this is irrelevant; and his protests that women should not be free to terminate unwanted pregnancies are chauvinistic and sexist. Fortunately, the opinion-makers in our community are clever enough to make him appear ridiculous and retain a virtual monopoly on all news disseminated beyond this immediate area. They are in touch with the evolving mores and are doing a good job of making them the accepted modes of thought.

"One traveler told us today that Methuselah is about to die. Now we'll lay to rest once and for all Noah's dire predictions that water will cover the earth as a judgment of God; for he has implied that this would occur when Methuselah passes away. What fantasies! We have learned enough about our earth to know that such a calamity could never happen. If there were a god or gods, *he, she, or they or it* would act in accord with natural forces. Some say we ourselves are gods, and certainly we have the knowledge to control anything that might happen. Several years ago when thousands suddenly died after engaging in what some gay blades term 'kinky sex,' there were a few nitwits who speculated upon the deaths being a judgment of some sort, but common sense prevailed. Many people are still dying from some mysterious disease, but we are now teaching how to have safe sex according to one's personal choice. A solution is surely in sight. What fools were our primitive forefathers to have believed in a Creator-God! What illusions misguided emotional cripples such as Noah still entertain! There is no reality beyond what we experience and no God except what we may create in our imaginations!"

"As it was in the days of Noah, so it will be at the coming of the Son of Man," says God's Word. The Psalmist David states: "The fool has said in his heart: 'There is no God'" (Psalm 14:1). Scripture also tells us that "the just [or righteous] shall live by faith" (Hebrews 10:38) and that "without faith it is impossible to please God, because anyone who comes to Him must believe that He exists and that He rewards those who earnestly seek Him" (Hebrews 11:6). Then, immediately thereafter, the author of Hebrews states: "By faith Noah, when warned about things not yet seen, in holy fear built an ark to save his family. By his faith he condemned the world (if Noah was capable of exercising faith, so were his contemporaries) and became heir of the righteousness that comes by faith" (Hebrews 11:7).

What is our attitude today – in a time like that preceding the great flood? Do we, like Noah, believe in God and impending judgment? Are we fervent in warning the lost, trying to bring them to Jesus Christ – the only Savior, the only Salvation for mankind – and teaching the ways of the Lord to all who will listen? Are we doing everything we can to retard evil in our society? Are we doing the works of our Lord and boldly speaking His Word to our generation, preparing for the day of His return when "the earth will be full of the knowledge of the Lord as the waters cover the sea" (Isaiah 11:9)? Let us be about our Father's business!

Appendix IV

"CONSPIRACY": AN ABBREVIATED BIBLIOGRAPHY

Abraham, Larry, *Call It Conspiracy*. Seattle, Washington: Double A Publications, 1971, 1983 & 1985.

Allen, Gary, *The Rockefeller File*. Seal Beach, CA: '76 Press, 1976.

Angebert, Jean-Michel, *The Occult and the Third Reich*. New York: Macmillan, 1974.

Barruel, Abbé Augustin, *Memoirs illustrating the History of Jacobism*. 4 vols., London: T. Burton, 1797-1798.

Bennis, Phyllis, and Michel Moushabeck (eds.), *Altered States: A Reader in the New World Order*. New York: Olive Branch Press, 1993.

Billington, James H., *Fire in the Minds of Men: The Origins of the Revolutionary Faith*. New York: Basic Books, 1980.

Bowen, William, Jr., *Globalism: America's Demise*. Schreveport, LA: Huntington House, 1984.

Church, J.R., *Guardians of the Grail ... and the Men who Plan to Rule the World*. Revised ed., Oklahoma City, OK: Prophecy Publications, 1991.

Epperson, Ralph, *The Unseen Hand: An Introduction to the Conspiratorial View of History*. Tucson, AZ: Publius Press, 1985.

Freedom from War: The United States Program for General and Complete Disarmament in a Peaceful World. Department of State Publication 7277. Washington, D.C.: U.S. Government Printing Office, 1961.

Gill, Stephen, *American Hegemony and the Trilateral Commission*. Cambridge: Cambridge University Press, 1990.

Golitsyn, Anatoly, *New Lies for Old.* New York: Dodd Mead, 1984.

Golitsyn, Anatoly, *The Perestroika Deception.* London & New York: Edward Harke, Ltd., 1995.

Griffen, Des, *Fourth Reich of the Rich.* Pasadena, CA: Emissary Publications, 1978.

Griffin, G. Edward, *The Creature from Jekyll Island, a Second Look at the Federal Reserve.* Westlake, CA: American Media, 1994.

Griffin, G. Edward, *The Fearful Master: A Second Look at the United Nations.* Boston, Western Islands, 1964.

Hodde, Lucien de la, *The Cradle of Rebellions: A History of the Secret Societies of France.* New York: John Bradburn, 1864.

House, Edward Mandell, *Philip Drew, Administrator: A Story of Tomorrow, 1920-1935.* Published anonymously, New York: B. W. Huebsch, 1912.

Irving, David, *Churchill's War.* New York: Avon Books, 1991.

Isaacson, Walter, and Evan Thomas, *The Wise Men: Six friends and the World They Made.* New York: Simon & Schuster, 1986.

King, Alexander, and Bertrand Schneider, *The First Global Revolution.* A Report by the Council of the Club of Rome. New York: Pantheon Books,1991.

King, Francis, *Satan and the Swastika: The Occult and the Nazi Party.* St. Albans, Herts: Mayflower, 1976.

Lee, Robert W., *The United Nations Conspiracy.* Appleton, Wisconsin: Western Islands, 1981.

McIlhany, William H. II, *The Tax-Exempt Foundations* New Rochelle, New York: Arlington House, 1980.

McIlvany, Donald S., *Toward a New World Order: the Countdown to Armageddon*. 2nd ed.; Phoenix, AZ: Western Pacific Publishing Company,1992.

McManus, John F., *The Insiders: Architects of the New World Order*. 3rd ed., Appleton, Wisconsin: The John Birch Society, 1992.

Martin, Malachi, *The Keys of This Blood: Pope John II verses Russia and the West for Control of the New World Order*. New York, London: Touchstone, 1990.

Mullins, Eustace, *Secrets of the Federal Reserve*. Staunton, VA: Bankers Research Institute, 1983.

Nimock, *Milner's young Men: The "Kindergarten" in Edwardian Imperial Affairs*. Durham, NC: Duke University Press, 1968.

Our Global Neighborhood: The Report of the Commission on Global Governance. Oxford University Press, 1995.

Perloff, James, *The Shadows of Power: The Council on Foreign Relations and the American Decline*. Appleton, Wisconsin: Western Islands, 1988.

Quigley, Carroll, *The Anglo-American Establishment: From Rhodes to Clivedon*. New York: Books in Focus, 1981.

Quigley, Carroll, *Tragedy and Hope: A History of the World in our Time*. New York: Macmillan, 1966.

Report from Iron Mountain on the Possibility and Desirability of Peace. New York: Dial Press, 1967.

Robertson, Pat, *The new World Order*. Dallas, TX: Word Publishing, 1991.

Robison, John, *Proofs of a Conspiracy*. 1798. Boston: Western Islands, 1967.

Schulzinger, Robert D., *The Wise Men of Foreign Affairs: The History of the Council on Foreign Relations*. New York: Columbia University Press, 1984.

Schwartzchild, Leopold, *Karl Marx: The Red Prussian*. New York: Grosset & Dunlap, 1947.

Seymour, Charles (ed.), *Intimate Papers of Colonel House*. 4 vols., New York: Houghton Mifflin, 1928.

Sherry, George L., *The United Nations reborn: Conflict Control in the Post-Cold-War World*. Council on Foreign Relations Critical Issues series. New York, 1990.

Shoup, Lawrence H., and William Minter, *Imperial Brain Trust: The Council on Foreign Relations and United States Foreign Policy*. New York : Monthly Review Press, 1977.

Sitarz, Daniel (ed.), *Agenda 21: The Earth Summit Strategy to Save Our Planet*. Boulder, CO: Earthpress, 1993.

Sklar, Holly (ed.), *Trilateralism: the Trilateral Commission and Elite Planning for World Management*. Boston: South End Press, 1980.

Still, William, *New World Order: The Ancient Plan of Secret Societies*. Lafayette, La: Huntington House, 1990.

Sturdza, Prince Michael, *Betrayal by Rulers*. Belmont, MA: Western Islands, 1976.

Sutton, Anthony C., *The Best Enemy Money Can Buy*. Billings, Montana: Liberty House, 1986.

Sutton, Anthony C., *National Suicide: Military Aid to the Soviet Union*. New Rochelle New York: Arlington House, 1974.

Sutton, Anthony C. *Wall Street and the Bolshevik Revolution*. New Rochelle, New York: Arlington House, 1974.

Sutton, Anthony C., *Wall Street and F.D.R.* New Rochelle, New York, 1975.

Sutton, Anthony C., *Wall Street and the Rise of Hitler*. Seal Beach, CA: '76 Press, 1976.

Sutton, Anthony C., *Western Technology and Soviet Economy Development, 1917-1965*. 3 vols., Stanford: The Hoover Institution, 1968-1973.

Tansill, Charles Callan, *America Goes to War*. Boston: Little Brown, 1938.

Tansill, Charles Callan, *Back Door to War: The Roosevelt Foreign Policy, 1933-1941*. Chicago: Henry Regnery, 1952.

Tinbergen, Jan; Anthony J. Dolman; and Jan van Ettinger (eds.), *Reshaping the International Order: A Report of the Club of Rome*. New York: E. P. Dutton, 1976.

United Nations, *Global Outlook 2000: an Economic, Social, and Environmental Perspective*.

Webster, Nesta H. *Secret Societies and Subversive Movements*. London: Boswell, 1924.

Webster, Nesta, *World Revolution*. 1921, revised ed., Devon, England: Britons, 1971.

Wittke, Carl, *The Utopian Communist: A Biography of Wilhelm Weitling, Nineteenth-Century Reformer*. Baton Rouge, Louisiana: State University Press, 1950.

INDEX

Apostles' Creed 25
Arab 29, 32, 45, 178, 219-221, 223-
    226, 258, 279, 335
Arab Legion 335
Arabian 32
Arabic 29
Arafat, Yasser 224
Aragon 54
Archbishop of Canterbury 82
Arian 19, 22-24, 213
Arius 19, 125
Aristotle 33, 148
Armagh 213
Arnauld, Antoine 77, 78, 129
art, arts 36, 46, 48-52, 91, 97, 100, 116,
    117, 129, 141, 173, 336
Asa 281
Ashcroft, John 193
Asia Minor 321
Asia 69, 70, 111, 363
Aspen Institute for Humanistic Studies
    344
Assyria 11, 181, 283, 284, 335, 339,
    365
Aswan 223
Athanasius 19, 125, 325
Athens 12
Atlantic 14, 214n., 282, 348
Atlantic Charter 282
Atlantic Institute 344
Auca Indians 307
Augsburg Confession 60
Augustine 22, 55, 56, 60, 77, 125, 126,
    152, 325
Augustine of Canterbury 23
Augustinius 77
Augustus 13-15
authority 23, 25, 27, 28, 30, 31, 38, 41,
    42, 44, 53, 55, 58-61, 63,
    70, 89, 99, 100, 116, 120,
    136, 140, 141, 143, 149,

    151, 174, 190n., 191,
    199, 202, 220 236, 249,
    259, 262, 269, 283, 287-
    307, 310-312, 327, 339,
    344, 363, 366, 376
Averroës, Averroëism 32, 33, 50
Avicenna 32
Avignon 40-43, 56, 61, 340
Axis 220, 282
Baal 282, 304
Babel 171n., 174, 364, 365
Babylon, Babylonian 11, 59, 174, 181,
    211, 245, 246, 269, 283,
    284, 339, 363n., 365,
    367, 368-373
Baldwin of Bouillon 340
Balfour Declaration 219
Ball, George 345
Baltic Sea 217
Baltimore & Ohio Railroad 347
Bancroft, George 137, 138
Baptists 79
Baronius, Caesar 128
Barth, Karl 100
BCCI 369
Beard, Charles 136, 138
Beatrice 34
Bede 126
behaviorism 96, 100, 101, 158-161,
    298, 299, 383
Belgium, Belgian 68, 218
Bell, Nelson 325
Ben-Gurion, David 221, 223
Ben-Yehuda, Eliezer 222
Benedictine 23, 126
benefit of clergy 42
Benjamin 211, 232, 270
Bergson, Henri 118, 119
Berkowitz, David 163
Bevin, Ernest 220
Bible College of Wales 218

Guaranty Trust 347
Guicciardini, Francesco 127
Gulf of Aqaba 223, 224
Gulf War 346
Gulf-Chevron 257
Guyon, Madam 77
Habakkuk 370-372
Habsburg 63, 215
Haganah 220
Hagar 279
Haggai 11
Haig, Alexander 345
Haiti 206, 207
Hall, G. Stanley 101
Hampton Roads 256
Hanani 281
Hancock, John 276
Harriman, W. Averill 345, 347
Harrimans 343, 347
Hartshorne, Charles 118
Harvard 118, 143, 150, 343
Hasmonean Kingdom 14, 211, 226
Hebrew 53, 227, 230
Hebrews 98, 123, 149, 181, 184, 211, 269, 311
hedonism 103, 116, 121, 219, 230
Hegel, Georg Friedrich 12, 92, 93, 100, 103, 135, 138, 139, 297, 342, 343
Heisenberg, Werner 103, 133
Hellenism 13, 14, 15, 18, 32, 159, 211, 212
Helvétius, Claude Adrien 84
Hemingway, Ernest 98-99
Henry III 27
Henry IV 27, 67, 76
Henry VI 28
Henry VII 62
Henry VIII 62, 67
Hercules 13
Herder, Johann Gottfried 131

Herod the Great 14
Herodotus 123
Herter, Christian 345
Hezekiah 304, 369
Higher Criticism 91, 297
Hindu 117, 207
Hippo 22, 125
Hispanic 111, 115
Hispaniola 206, 215
Hiss, Alger 345
historicism 91, 135, 136
History of Charles XII 129
History of Florence 127
History of the Popes 134
Hitler, Adolf 100, 139, 140, 142, 217-219, 269, 339, 340, 347, 382
Hoffman, Paul 346
Hogarth, William 81
Hohenstaufen 28, 32
Holbach, Paul Henri Thiry d' 84, 85
Holmes, Oliver Wendell Jr. 150
holocaust 142, 262
Holy Roman Emperor 27, 28, 42, 45, 56, 62, 63, 67, 71-72, 215
Holy Spirit 16, 19, 87, 115, 122, 149, 152, 153, 159, 161, 163, 165, 172, 176, 193, 194, 202, 207, 228, 236, 237, 239, 240, 260, 261, 274, 311, 326, 352, 374
Homeric 12, 123
homosexuality 12, 107, 113, 114, 116, 132, 192, 214, 230, 231, 232, 235, 289, 334, 387
hospitals 25, 215, 295
House, Edward Mandell 344, 348
Howells, Rees 218
Huguenots 67, 76-77, 313
humanism , humanistic 10, 12, 13, 35, 45, 54, 61, 63, 64, 66, 67,

Pharisees 14, 141, 266
Philip II 73
Philip IV 39, 40
Philippi 320
Philistine 270, 280, 306, 307
Phillip Dru, Aministrator: A Story of Tomorrow 348
philosophes 85-87, 88, 129, 131
Philosophiae Naturalis Principia Mathematica 83, 128
philosophy 1, 7, 22, 29, 32, 33, 45, 47, 50, 54, 94, 97, 98, 99, 129, 140, 145, 162
Phineas 304
phonics 107
Pico della Mirandola 50
pietism 80, 130
Pike, Nelson 118
Pilate 172
Pinnock, Clark 118
Pittinger, Norman 118
Pius X 100
Plan for Reforming the Church 71
Planned Parenthood 298
Plato, Platonism, Platonic 22, 33, 49, 50
Platonic Academy 49
Platonic realists 33
Plotinus 49, 148
pluralism, pluralistic 117, 298, 349
Poland 74, 215-217
Pole, Reginald 71
politics 2, 12, 13, 16, 27, 28, 30, 31, 36, 38, 39, 41, 45, 46, 47, 50, 51, 61, 62, 65, 67, 70, 71, 75, 79, 87, 93, 94, 100, 103, 105-107, 109, 110-112, 114, 115, 117, 127, 129, 138, 140, 154, 172, 185, 204, 212, 215, 220, 221, 241,

256, 282, 284, 285, 287, 301, 310, 330, 334, 336, 338, 340, 343, 344, 346, 351, 352, 356, 361, 362, 364, 374
Pollock, Jackson 97
Pompey 14
Poor Clares 34
pope , papacy, papal 19, 23, 24, 27-32, 34, 36, 39-46, 49-52, 54, 55, 57-59, 61-65, 68, 69, 70-74, 76, 78, 89, 100, 128, 134, 214, 215, 325, 340, 351
Pope, Alexander 83
Popular Movement for the Liberation of Angola (MPLA) 257
pornography 116, 117, 164, 192, 284, 334, 342, 368, 380, 381n., 383, 386
Port Royale 77, 78
Portugal 257
positivism 85, 90, 91, 93, 100, 118, 135, 156, 297
postmodern, postmodernism 12, 17, 116, 117, 123, 145, 151, 352
Pound, Roscoe 150
Pragmatic Sanction of Bourges 61
pragmatism 97, 98, 100, 203, 219, 297, 299, 353
Prague 43
Praise of Folly 54
predestination 9, 23, 67, 77, 226, 247, 248, 250, 330
Presbyterian 67, 79, 82, 201, 325
Prince Bernhard 344
Priory of Zion 340
process theology 118
Progressive School 138
progressive education 102, 104
proletariat 94

Protectorate 76
Protestant, Protestants 67, 68, 72-75, 79, 80, 82, 99, 100, 128, 149, 215
Provincial Letters 78
Prussia, Prussian 77, 130, 137, 173
psychoanalysis 157, 158
psychology 9, 91, 96, 99-101, 103, 116, 119, 138, 141, 156, 160-162, 170, 289, 298, 354
Puritans 79, 80, 82, 310
purgatory 34, 56-58
Quesnel, Pasquier 18, 79
Quietism, Quietists 77
quotas 107, 110, 244
racism 96, 111, 115, 117, 133
Ranke , Leopold von 134
Raphael 51, 272
rationalism 90-92, 128, 130, 139
Reagan, Ronald 288, 315, 350, 351
recapitulation theory 101
Reconquista 32, 54, 55
Red Sea 223
reductionism 92, 99
Reformation 53-74, 86, 100
Regensburg 72, 73
Rehoboam 211, 269
Reichsbank 348
relativism 85, 103, 104, 109, 151, 205, 298, 343, 349
Renaissance 45, 47, 49, 62, 66, 85-86, 126, 129, 138-139, 145, 272
Republic of Virtue 89
Republicans 345, 346, 350
Reuchlin, Johann 53
Reuther, Walter 105
revolutionary calendar 185
Rhenish 24, 34, 64
Rhine 34, 35, 64, 67
Rhodes, Cecil 343

Ribbentrop-Molotov pact 217,
Richardson, Elliot 346
Richelieu 76
Robert of Naples 45
Robespierre, Maximilien 88
Robinson, James Harvey 5
Rockefellers 112, 343-348
Rockefeller Foundation 112, 345, 347
Rockefeller, David 344
Rockefeller, Nelson 346
Rogers, Carl 161
Rogers, William P. 345
Roman 2, 13, 16, 17, 18, 20, 21, 23, 28, 34, 55, 83, 124, 213, 221, 232, 340, 365, 366, 373
Roman Empire 2, 14, 213, 215, 335, 365, 366
Romanov Russia 335
romanticism 90, 91, 130, 131, 134, 139, 140, 142
Rome 14, 18, 20-25, 27, 30, 31, 40, 42, 43, 47, 49, 50, 54, 55, 57, 59, 61, 62, 65, 68, 69, 70, 74, 75, 78, 124, 125, 129, 212, 213, 266, 335, 339, 363n.
Roosevelt, Franklin Delano 104, 220, 282, 344, 345
Rosicrusion 340
Rothschild, Mayer Amschel 349
Rothschilds 344, 348, 349
Round Table 344
Rousseau, Jean Jacques 88
Royal Institute of International Affairs 344
Runstedt, Gerd von 218
Rusk, Dean 345
Ruskin, John 272
Russell , William Huntington 343
Russell Trust 343, 346, 347

Slater Foundation 347
slavery, slave trade 10, 81, 88, 114, 138, 139, 164, 175, 205, 206, 213, 214, 227, 253, 256, 262, 263, 294, 321, 325, 329, 369
Sloan Foundation 343
Smith, Adam 177
Sobieski, John 215, 216
Social and Cultural Dynamics 143
social compact 87, 311
social correctness 117
social engineering 158
socialism 102, 104, 220, 221, 258, 298, 302, 303, 341, 342, 344, 345 348
Society of Jesus (Jesuit Order) 69, 70, 74, 75, 77-79, 86
Society of the Elect 343
sociology 4, 85, 91, 96, 100, 119, 132, 136, 137, 143, 151, 156, 234, 292, 298
Sodom 231, 279, 351, 352
sodomy 231
Sojourners magazine 303
Solomon 11, 211, 281
Sorokin, Pitirim 143
South America 214
Soviet Union 94, 103-105, 108, 142, 217, 220-226, 257, 258, 269, 282, 296, 345, 348, 350, 351, 362, 376
Spain, Spanish 24, 32, 38, 43, 51, 54, 58, 61, 62, 68, 73, 74, 111, 115, 214, 215, 335
Spanish-Americans 111. See also Hispanics.
Spencer, Herbert 96
Spengler, Oswald 143, 144, 46
Spiritual Exercises 69
Spiritual Franciscans 41

Sputnik 105, 108
St. Columba 213
St. Columbanus 23, 213
Stalinism 108
Standard Oil of New Jersey 347
Standonck, John 61
Starhemberg, Rudiger von 216
State Department 257, 344, 345, 350, 351
Stephen 207, 325
Stephensdom 216
Stevenson , Adlai 345
stimulus-response 101, 159
Strait of Tiran 224
Strasbourg 67
Suadi Arabia 221, 357
Sudan 357
Suez Canal 223, 225, 226
Summa contra Gentiles 33
Summa Theologica 33, 149, 234
superego 157, 163
Supreme Court 113, 301, 314
surrealism 97
Suso, Heinrich 34
Sweden, Swedes 129, 218
Swiss 37, 67, 77, 100, 218
Switzerland 67
Symonds, John Addington 138
syncretism 10, 11, 49, 50, 120, 123, 162, 282, 285
syndicalism 133, 341
Synod of Dordrecht 68
Synod of Whitby 23
Syria 220, 221, 224-227
Taft, Alphonso 343
Talmud 15, 18
Taoism 151
Tara 213
Tata, Joni Erikson 325
Tauler, Johann 34